CORNELL STUDIES IN CLASSICAL PHILOLOGY

EDITED BY

FREDERICK M. AHL * KEVIN C. CLINTON
JOHN E. COLEMAN * G. M. KIRKWOOD
GORDON M. MESSING * PIETRO PUCCI

VOLUME XLII

## Epicurus' Scientific Method
*by Elizabeth Asmis*

From Myth to Icon:
Reflections of Greek Ethical Doctrine
in Literature and Art
*by Helen F. North*

Lucan: An Introduction
*by Frederick M. Ahl*

The Violence of Pity
in Euripides' *Medea*
*by Pietro Pucci*

# EPICURUS' SCIENTIFIC METHOD

*Elizabeth Asmis*

CORNELL UNIVERSITY PRESS

ITHACA AND LONDON

CORNELL UNIVERSITY PRESS GRATEFULLY ACKNOWLEDGES GRANTS FROM
THE ANDREW W. MELLON FOUNDATION AND CORNELL STUDIES IN CLASSICAL
PHILOLOGY WHICH AIDED IN BRINGING THIS BOOK TO PUBLICATION.

First published 1984 by Cornell University Press.
Published in the United Kingdom by Cornell University Press, Ltd.,
London.

International Standard Book Number 0-8014-1465-2
Library of Congress Catalog Number 83-45133

Printed in the United States of America

*Librarians: Library of Congress cataloging information
appears on the last page of the book.*

*The paper in this book is acid-free and meets the guidelines
for permanence and durability of the Committee on Production
Guidelines for Book Longevity of the Council on Library Resources.*

# Contents

## III

## SIGNS

## IV

## EPICURUS' SCIENTIFIC DOCTRINES: FUNDAMENTAL THEORIES

# Preface

EPICURUS is widely known as an empiricist. Kant viewed him as a representative of "dogmatic" empiricism, and Hegel suggested that he was "the discoverer of empirical natural science."[1] Yet very little is clear about Epicurus' scientific method. Indeed, it is generally believed that Epicurus did not have a coherent method of scientific inference.[2] This book aims to show, first, that Epicurus did propose a unified method of scientific investigation, and, second, that he attempted to apply this method consistently throughout the development of his physical doctrines, from the fundamentals of his atomic theory to the explanation of remote astronomical events.

1. *Immanuel Kant's Critique of Pure Reason*, translated by Norman Kemp Smith, 2d ed. (London, 1933), A 471/B 499; and G. W. F. Hegel, *Vorlesungen über die Geschichte der Philosophie*, edited by K. L. Michelet, vol. 14 of *Georg Wilhelm Friedrich Hegels Werke* (Berlin, 1833), 497 ("Man kann so sagen, Epikur ist der Erfinder der empirischen Naturwissenschaft, empirischen Psychologie").

2. F. M. Cornford takes the extreme view that Epicurus had no scientific method at all (*Principium Sapientiae*, 12–30, esp. 16). Eduard Zeller sums up the view of many in criticizing Epicurus' attempt at an empirical epistemology as "too superficial" (*Die Philosophie der Griechen*, vol. 3, pt. 1, 406). An outspoken admirer of Epicurus, Cyril Bailey commends Epicurus for attempting to unify the atomic theory under the "central principle of the infallibility of sense-perception" (*The Greek Atomists and Epicurus*, 275; cf. 232), but fails to show how Epicurus proposed to submit all scientific claims to the test of observation. It is perhaps a reflection of Epicurus' poor reputation as a scientist that few studies have dealt with his method of investigation as a whole. Apart from the chapters in Bailey's *Greek Atomists* and John M. Rist's *Epicurus*, the most important are Theodor Tohte, *Epikurs Kriterien der Wahrheit* (1874); Fridericus Merbach, *De Epicuri Canonica* (1909); D. K. Glidden, "The Epicurean Theory of Knowledge" (1971); and Gisela Striker, Κριτήριον τῆς ἀληθείας (1974). The first three of these studies focus on problems of epistemology

Epicurus wrote a book titled Κανών, or *Rule*, in which he set out his method of scientific investigation. Unfortunately this book is lost, and we now rely on a wide range of evidence, dating from Epicurus' own lifetime, 341–271 B.C., to the time of Sextus Empiricus, about A.D. 200, and even later. Epicurus' extant works provide important evidence concerning his method; next in importance are the writings of two of his followers in the first century B.C., Philodemus and Lucretius; valuable additional help is supplied by the summaries of Epicurus' scientific method provided by Diogenes Laertius and Sextus Empiricus some two or three centuries later; and of the remaining sources, the essays on Epicurean doctrine by Cicero (first century B.C.) and Plutarch (first century of the Christian era) contain many useful details.

Although these sources furnish ample information, their wide chronological range poses a serious problem. There was a great deal of interest and innovation in scientific method in the centuries after Epicurus. Accordingly, Epicurus' own method of inquiry came to be viewed in the light of current theories, with the result that his original position is often difficult to ascertain. A primary aim of this book, therefore, is to sort out Epicurus' position by placing the various reports of his method in their proper historical context. This procedure will, I think, show that Epicurus' empiricism is much more coherent than has been thought.

The general plan of this work is first to examine Epicurus' rules of investigation and then to show how they apply in his own practice. The first two parts of the book are an analysis of Epicurus' two rules of investigation: the requirement for initial concepts and the requirement for observations. The third part continues the discussion of Epicurus' second rule by examining how observations serve as signs of what is unobserved. The fourth and fifth parts examine Epicurus' own scientific inferences in an attempt to show how consistent his practice is with his theory. The last part of the book aims to show how Epicurus' method of inquiry is related to that of the early atomists.

My discussion focuses on several key problems of Epicurean methodology. The first is the basic problem: did Epicurus in fact

_____

rather than on scientific method; and none includes a comprehensive examination of how Epicurus' own scientific inferences are related to his methodology. Rist's, Glidden's, and Striker's studies all mark an important advance on previous work; and I have learned much from them despite frequent disagreements with their interpretations. Numerous more specialized studies deal with individual aspects of Epicurean epistemology or scientific method; they will be cited in their appropriate places.

formulate precise rules of scientific inquiry, and if so, what are they? Scholars have generally held, on the authority of Diogenes Laertius, that Epicurus proposed three criteria of truth: sense perceptions, initial concepts, and feelings. Yet it is not clear how these standards are related to each other or how they apply to Epicurus' scientific theories. I take Epicurus' own procedural note in his *Letter to Herodotus*, a summary of his physics, as a starting point. Here Epicurus sets out two rules of investigation: first, he demands that we have concepts, corresponding to our utterances, as a means of judging the problem under investigation; second, he demands that we have observations in accordance with our perceptions and feelings as a means of inferring what is unobserved. The first rule is a requirement for concepts acquired prior to the investigation; the second is a requirement for empirical evidence. In my discussion of these two rules, I examine how the initial concepts of investigation are related to empirical observations as well as to scientific concepts. I conclude that Epicurus' two rules are compatible with Diogenes Laertius' later analysis, and that they make up a single, comprehensive method of scientific inquiry.

A second problem concerns the requirement for observations, and it is by far the most widely discussed problem of Epicurean methodology. Epicurus was notorious in antiquity for holding that "all perceptions are true." What is the meaning of this claim? The answer to this question determines what facts Epicurus admitted as evidence of his scientific theories. Scholars have generally held that Epicurus did distinguish between sense perceptions that are truthful (in the sense of showing what exists in the world) and those that are not, or, in other words, between sense perceptions that provide a reliable basis for scientific inference and those that do not. I argue that Epicurus made it an initial assumption of his method of investigation that everything that is perceived directly, without the addition of opinion, is a real feature of the world, and that he accordingly admitted everything shown directly by the senses as evidence of his scientific theories.

A third main problem is how observed facts serve to show what is unobserved. To what extent, and by what methods of argument, did Epicurus rely on observations to furnish evidence of scientific theories? The prevailing view is that he used a variety of methods to support his theories, including a priori assumptions, inductive reasoning, and the deductive reduction of a hypothesis to an incompatibility with observed facts. It is held that these methods are related only loosely to each other, and indeed conflict with one another. I try to show that Epicurus himself proposed a unified system of verification, according to which those scientific theories are true that are shown by the use of reason to follow from observed facts. This method of verification, which encompasses both inductive inferences and the reduction of a hypothesis to an incompatibility with the phenomena, may be called "deduction from the phenomena."

Fourth, it has generally been held that there is a wide disparity between the way in which Epicurus proves the fundamental theories of his physics and the way in which he subsequently develops his more detailed explanations. Is Epicurus' own practice, then, not in agreement with his theory? I attempt to answer this question by testing Epicurus' two rules of investigation against his own development of his physics, with special emphasis on the fundamental theories.

This examination leads directly to the last key problem, the relationship of Epicurus to his atomist predecessors. Epicurus took over most of his fundamental physical theories from the early atomists Leucippus and Democritus. Did he also take over their method of proving these theories? The traditional view is that the early atomists were predominantly rationalists who attempted to explain the physical world by adopting hypotheses that are strongly indebted to the Eleatics, and that Epicurus' empiricism is incompatible with this approach. I propose that Epicurus' method of inference originated with the early atomists, and that it belongs to an important empirical tradition of inquiry that once rivaled the systems of Plato and Aristotle but has been largely lost from view in the history of scientific method.

Epicurus has generally been regarded as an unscientific thinker. Ever since ancient times, he has had a reputation for caring little about scientific investigation, and in particular for using physical doctrines only as a means to the ethical goal of liberating humankind from fear. Certainly, Epicurus did believe that the doctrines he proposed about the physical world are necessary for happiness; and he did set a limit to the amount of scientific knowledge that one must have in order to be happy. But this emphasis does not imply that he did not consider his physical doctrines or his method of inference to be valid in their own right. It is, I think, fair to say that Epicurus was not interested in exploiting his method of inquiry to its full potential; and clearly his more specialized doctrines, particularly in the field of astronomy, lag far behind contemporary scientific advances. This conservatism indicates, it seems to me, that Epicurus embraced a method of explanation that originated in an earlier period. It does not show that he did not have a unified method of scientific investigation, or that he was not strongly committed to the results that he did obtain by it. If Epicurus lacked the early atomists' enthusiasm for discovery, his devotion to human happiness made him the more enthusiastic about the method that he did adopt and the theories that he owed to it.

I have received much help in the preparation of this book, for which I am profoundly grateful. I extend very warm thanks to John Rist and Michael Stokes, who read the manuscript at an early stage and made numerous valuable suggestions. I am also grateful to Michael Boylan, Ralph Johnson, Gordon Kirkwood, Joan Kung, Pietro Pucci, Stanley Szuba, and the anonymous readers for Cornell University Press for their very helpful comments. The deficiencies that remain would have been much greater were it not for the generous help of these friends and colleagues. Special thanks go, too, to Ann Hawthorne for her expert editorial advice, and to Diane Baldwin, Florence Halprin, and the entire staff at the Computer-Aided Design group for their devoted technical assistance in the preparation of the manuscript. I first began work on this book as a recipient of the Mary Isabel Fellowship during a sabbatical leave from Cornell University in 1973–74; since then, I have received research grants from Cornell University and from the University of Chicago. I thank those who were responsible for granting these awards.

Finally, my greatest debt of gratitude is to my husband, William Mitchell, for his unfailing encouragement and assistance.

Elizabeth Asmis

*Chicago, Illinois*

# Abbreviations

Arr.     Graziano Arrighetti, ed. and trans. *Epicuro: Opere.* 2d ed. With commentary. Turin: Einaudi, 1973.

D     Karl Deichgräber. *Die griechische Empirikerschule.* 1930. Reprint Berlin and Zurich: Weidmann, 1965.

DK     Hermann Diels and Walther Kranz, eds. *Die Fragmente der Vorsokratiker.* 3 vols. 6th rev. ed. Berlin: Weidmann, 1951–52.

DL     Diogenes Laertius.

*Dox.*     Hermannus Diels, ed. *Doxographi Graeci.* Berlin: Reimer, 1879.

*Her.*     Epicurus. *Letter to Herodotus.*

KD     Epicurus. Κύριαι δόξαι [Authoritative opinions].

*Men.*     Epicurus. *Letter to Menoeceus.*

OP     Sextus Empiricus. *Outlines of Pyrrhonism.*

*Pyth.*     Epicurus. *Letter to Pythocles.*

SVF     Ioannes von Arnim, ed. *Stoicorum Veterum Fragmenta.* 4 vols. Leipzig: Teubner, 1905 (vols. 1–3), 1924 (vol. 4). (The number cited is the volume number followed by the fragment number.)

U     Hermannus Usener, ed. *Epicurea.* Leipzig: Teubner, 1887. (The number cited is the fragment number.)

# PART I

*Initial Concepts*

# [ 1 ]

# Epicurus' First Rule
# of Inquiry

## EPICURUS' STATEMENT OF THE RULE

EPICURUS held that the study of physics begins with the adoption of a method of inquiry. He set out his method in detail in a book titled Κανών, which is not extant.[1] As indicated by the term κανών, which denotes a straight rod or ruler and, metaphorically, any type of measure or standard, the book deals with the standards by which investigations are guided.[2] The entire subject was called "canonic" (κανονικόν).

Epicurean canonic takes the place of logic as a branch of philosophical inquiry. Epicurus held that logic, as practiced by other philosophers, is of no use to the scientist, and that the guidelines proposed in his canonic are sufficient to guide the scientific investigator to the truth.[3] As a result, some ancient critics accused Epicurus of rejecting logic altogether and recognizing only two of the requisite three branches of philosophy, physics and ethics.[4] It

1. Diogenes Laertius cites the title of Epicurus' book as Περὶ κριτηρίου ἤ Κανών at 10.27, and simply as Κανών at 10.14, 10.30, and 10.31. See U 34 for additional references to the book.
2. Gisela Striker has a brief discussion of the historical development of these meanings in Κριτήριον, 61–63.
3. See DL 10.31 and U 242, 243.
4. Sextus Empiricus *Adv. math.* 7.15 (U 242). Sextus adds that according to others, Epicurus rejected only Stoic logic, so that in effect he recognized all three branches of logic (ibid. 7.22). According to Seneca (*Epistulae morales* 89.11, U 242), the Epicureans divided philosophy into two parts, physics and ethics, classifying canonic as an adjunct to physics. Diogenes Laertius (10.29) attributes to the Epicureans a threefold division of philosophy into canonic, physics, and ethics. In

would be more accurate to say, however, that in substituting canonic for logic Epicurus subordinated logic to physics. As the Epicurean spokesman Torquatus claims in Cicero's *On Ends*, Epicurus held that the science of physics ultimately provides the answers sought by the logician: "It is by this science [that is, physics] that the meaning of words, the nature of discourse, and the relationship of consequence or conflict can be understood."[5] Canonic guides the scientist to these goals by making certain preliminary distinctions, which are subsequently refined by physical inquiry into complete explanations.

Although Epicurus' detailed work on his method is lost, his own extant summary of his physics, the *Letter to Herodotus*, contains, appropriately, a summary of his canonic immediately preceding the summary of physical doctrines. This outline of canonic is divided into two parts, each stating a rule of inquiry. In the first rule, Epicurus demands that at the very beginning of an inquiry the investigator have concepts corresponding to the words that are used. In the second rule, he demands that the inquirer use empirical observations as evidence of what is unobserved. Following is Epicurus' statement of the first rule, which I translate very literally:

> First, Herodotus, it is necessary to have grasped what is subordinate to the utterances [τὰ ὑποτεταγμένα τοῖς φθόγγοις . . . δεῖ εἰληφέναι], so that we may have the means to judge what is believed or sought or perplexing by referring to this, and so that it may not be the case that everything be unjudged by us as we demonstrate to infinity, or that we have empty utterances. For it is necessary that the first concept in accordance with each utterance be seen and not require demonstration, if we are to have [a standard] to which we shall refer what is sought or perplexing and believed.[6]

This very compressed statement is clumsy even in the original Greek, but the general intent of the rule is clear. Epicurus de-

---

addition to rejecting Stoic logic, the Epicureans clearly rejected Peripatetic logic, as exemplified by Polystratos' disparaging reference to "syllogisms" and "inductions" in his treatise *De contemptu*. Polystratos claims that it is not "by completing syllogisms or inductions [συλλογισμοὺς ἢ ἐπαγωγάς] or by word chopping" but by the investigation of nature (φυσιολογοῦντας) that we learn the truth (cols. 4b8–5b12 Wilke; cols. 13.25–14.25 Indelli).

5. Cicero *De finibus* 1.63: ea scientia et verborum vis et natura orationis et consequentium repugnantiumve ratio potest perspici.

6. *Her.* 37–38: πρῶτον μὲν οὖν τὰ ὑποτεταγμένα τοῖς φθόγγοις, ὦ Ἡρόδοτε, δεῖ εἰληφέναι ὅπως ἂν τὰ δοξαζόμενα ἢ ζητούμενα ἢ ἀπορούμενα ἔχωμεν εἰς ταῦτα

mands that before we investigate a problem, we must have acquired concepts corresponding to the words used to state the problem, in order to have standards by which to judge the problem. In Epicurus' terminology, we must have "grasped" (εἰληφέναι) what is "subordinate to the utterances" (ὑποτεταγμένα τοῖς φθόγγοις) before we undertake the investigation. This prior understanding furnishes the standards to which we refer what we believe (that is, "an object of opinion," δοξαζόμενον), or doubt, or seek, in order to make a decision about it. Epicurus justifies the requirement by saying that otherwise we would be involved in an infinite regress of demonstration or we would use empty words. Epicurus concludes his explanation by stating that there can be no standard unless the first concept corresponding to each utterance is "seen" (βλέπεσθαι) without requiring demonstration.

An important supplement to Epicurus' statement is Diogenes Laertius' explanation of προλήψεις, "presumptions" or "preconceptions," in his summary of Epicurus' canonic. Diogenes prefaces this summary by saying that in his Κανών Epicurus acknowledges three "criteria of truth" (κριτήρια τῆς ἀληθείας): "perceptions" (αἰσθήσεις), "presumptions" (προλήψεις), and "affections" or "feelings" (πάθη).[7] Diogenes then gives an explanation of each criterion in turn. His explanation of presumptions is as follows:

> Presumption [πρόληψις], they [the Epicureans] say, is something like apprehension or right opinion or a concept or a stored universal thought, that is, a memory of that which has often appeared from outside, for example, that man is this sort of thing. For at the same time that "man" is spoken, immediately by presumption the outline of man also is thought of, as a result of preceding perceptions. In the case of every name, then, that which is first subordinate [τὸ πρώτως ὑποτεταγμένον] is evident [ἐναργές]. And we would not have sought what we seek, unless we had previously learned it. For example, is the thing standing in the distance a horse or a cow? We must have learned at some time by presumption the form of a horse and a cow. Nor would we have named anything if we had not previously learned its outline by presumption. Presumptions,

---

ἀναγαγόντες ἐπικρίνειν, καὶ μὴ ἄκριτα πάντα ἡμῖν ἢ εἰς ἄπειρον ἀποδεικνύουσιν ἢ κενοὺς φθόγγους ἔχωμεν. ἀνάγκη γὰρ τὸ πρῶτον ἐννόημα καθ' ἕκαστον φθόγγον βλέπεσθαι καὶ μηθὲν ἀποδείξεως προσδεῖσθαι, εἴπερ ἕξομεν τὸ ζητούμενον ἢ ἀπορούμενον καὶ δοξαζόμενον ἐφ' ὃ ἀνάξομεν.

This is H. S. Long's text; there are no serious problems in the manuscripts, although the use of καὶ instead of ἢ before δοξαζόμενον seems careless.

7. DL 10.31.

then, are evident. Further, an object of belief [τὸ δοξαστόν] depends on something prior that is evident, by reference to which we state [the belief]; for example, how do we know whether this is a man?[8]

In this very sketchy explanation, Diogenes uses the technical term πρόληψις to designate the initial concepts demanded by Epicurus in his first rule. Literally, a πρόληψις is a "grasp" that has been obtained "before" an inquiry. In his own statement, Epicurus avoids the use of the technical term, but prepares and explains it in ordinary language by using the perfect infinitive εἰληφέναι, "to have grasped."[9] This procedure is in harmony with the rule

8. DL 10.33: τὴν δὲ πρόληψιν λέγουσιν οἱονεὶ κατάληψιν ἢ δόξαν ὀρθὴν ἢ ἔννοιαν ἢ καθολικὴν νόησιν ἐναποκειμένην, τουτέστι μνήμην τοῦ πολλάκις ἔξωθεν φανέντος, οἷον τὸ Τοιοῦτόν ἐστιν ἄνθρωπος· ἅμα γὰρ τῷ ῥηθῆναι ἄνθρωπος εὐθὺς κατὰ πρόληψιν καὶ ὁ τύπος αὐτοῦ νοεῖται προηγουμένων τῶν αἰσθήσεων. παντὶ οὖν ὀνόματι τὸ πρώτως ὑποτεταγμένον ἐναργές ἐστι. καὶ οὐκ ἂν ἐζητήσαμεν τὸ ζητούμενον, εἰ μὴ πρότερον ἐγνωκείμεν αὐτό· οἷον Τὸ πόρρω ἑστὼς ἵππος ἐστὶν ἢ βοῦς· δεῖ γὰρ κατὰ πρόληψιν ἐγνωκέναι ποτὲ ἵππου καὶ βοὸς μορφήν. οὐδ' ἂν ὠνομάσαμέν τι μὴ πρότερον αὐτοῦ κατὰ πρόληψιν τὸν τύπον μαθόντες. ἐναργεῖς οὖν εἰσιν αἱ προλήψεις· καὶ τὸ δοξαστὸν ἀπὸ προτέρου τινὸς ἐναργοῦς ἤρτηται, ἐφ' ὃ ἀναφέροντες λέγομεν, οἷον Πόθεν ἴσμεν εἰ τοῦτό ἐστιν ἄνθρωπος;

This is again H. S. Long's text. Most editors make a paragraph break after ἐναργεῖς οὖν εἰσιν αἱ προλήψεις (so Usener, Bailey, Arrighetti). No break should be made, since, as Bailey himself remarks in his note on the example "man," the evident standards on which opinions depend are presumptions (*Epicurus*, 416). Strictly speaking, no break should be made after ἄνθρωπος either, for Diogenes continues with a discussion of opinions; however, since we gain no further information here about presumptions, I have omitted this part. The text is unproblematic except for mss. ἐπιτεταγμένον after πρώτως, which I have replaced, along with most editors, by ὑποτεταγμένον; ἐπιτεταγμένον is not used elsewhere to designate the correlate of a word.

9. The etymological connection between εἰληφέναι and πρόληψις was previously pointed out by Merbach, *Canonica*, 48. Cicero mentions that πρόληψις is Epicurus' own technical coinage (*De natura deorum* 1.44). That the type of concept required by Epicurus in his first rule is technically a πρόληψις is maintained by Bailey (*Epicurus*, 176), as well as by Knut Kleve (*Gnosis Theon*, 81 n. 3), A. A. Long ("*Aisthesis, Prolepsis,* and Linguistic Theory in Epicurus," 124), and Striker (Κρίτηριον, 68–69). David Sedley disputes this, on the ground that a comparison between the *Letter to Herodotus* and Epicurus' larger work, *On Nature*, indicates that Epicurus had not developed the notion of πρόληψις at the time of writing the *Letter* ("Epicurus, *On Nature* Book XXVIII," 14–15). The textual evidence cited by Sedley seems to me too slender to support this view. In addition, the suggestion seems to me to conflict with *Her.* 72–73, where Epicurus uses the term πρόληψις; Sedley regards this as a later addition. D. K. Glidden also denies that Epicurus is referring to προλήψεις at *Her.* 37–38, though on different grounds. He argues that all of the procedural note from πρῶτον to σημειωσόμεθα states a single requirement, the requirement for empirical evidence, and that τὰ ὑποτεταγμένα in the first sentence is subsequently explained in the last sentence as the evidence provided by the senses ("The Epicurean Theory of Knowledge," 163–78); and he maintains that προλήψεις are fallible, since they are opinions, and so do not qualify

itself, which is precisely a demand for an initial, ordinary understanding of terms prior to any technical elaboration. Epicurus does
use the technical term later in the *Letter to Herodotus* when he explains that time is not investigated like other things by being referred to "presumptions [προλήψεις] that are seen in ourselves."[10]

Diogenes' account begins with alternative explanations of Epicurean πρόληψις. Diogenes here goes beyond Epicurus' statement
of his first rule by showing that presumptions are empirically
acquired. He goes on to claim, like Epicurus, that presumptions
are a prerequisite of investigation and of belief (or "opinion");
and he adds that they are a prerequisite even of naming. To illustrate the function of a presumption in an investigation, Diogenes
proposes the problem of identifying an object seen at a distance,
such as a horse or a cow. The use of concepts in formulating
opinions is illustrated by the claim "this is a man." In place of
Epicurus' demand that presumptions must be seen without requiring demonstration, Diogenes states repeatedly that presumptions are "evident" (ἐναργεῖς).

The basic difference between Diogenes' and Epicurus' statements is that Diogenes does not present a rule of inquiry as such,
but instead offers an explanation of Epicurus' rule. Accordingly,
Diogenes makes an important departure from Epicurus' own order of exposition: he includes an explanation of how presumptions
are acquired. Epicurus himself does not indicate how presumptions are acquired until his second rule of inquiry. This departure
from Epicurus' order is accompanied by a complete reversal of
Epicurus' two rules of inquiry: before offering an explanation
of presumptions, Diogenes has already explained perception, the
subject of Epicurus' second rule of inquiry. In Diogenes' exposition, the explanation of perception thus leads directly to the explanation of presumptions; Epicurus, by contrast, sets out the
requirement for presumptions first, and then adds a second requirement, the demand for empirical evidence.

In past discussions of Epicurus' canonic, Diogenes' summary
has been relied upon as the basic text, to the neglect of Epicurus'

---

as standards of truth (168–94). Although I agree that the second part of the
procedural note explains what we are to think of in connection with utterances,
and that these are empirical facts, I take it that Epicurus is proposing two separate
requirements, one for thoughts corresponding to our words, the other for empirical evidence, and that προλήψεις are reliable for the very reason that they consist of empirical observations.

10. *Her.* 72.

own statement of his rules in the *Letter to Herodotus*. As a result, Epicurus' canonic has generally been viewed as an epistemology, which proposes sense perceptions and concepts as criteria for testing the truth of beliefs, rather than as a methodology, which proposes two rules that govern the conduct of an inquiry from the beginning. This interpretation has tended to obscure the fact that Epicurus has a method of inquiry that is fixed prior to any investigation and must be followed throughout an investigation independently of any epistemological conclusions that may result from its use. Diogenes' summary is not, in my opinion, inaccurate; and it will be used extensively in the following examination of Epicurus' canonic. As an exegesis and reformulation of Epicurus' rules, however, it cannot take the place of Epicurus' own statement of his rules, but has secondary importance as an aid to understanding these rules.

The main problem raised by Epicurus' statement of his first rule is: what things are "subordinate to the utterances?" The remainder of this chapter is an attempt to sketch a general answer to this question. The next three chapters then deal with three aspects of Epicurus' rule: the demand that the initial concepts of investigation be seen and not require demonstration; the use of initial concepts as standards of investigation; and the origin of initial concepts. The entire examination draws, like Diogenes' account, on material that is properly no part of Epicurus' own statement of his rule.

## UTTERANCE AND CONCEPT

Epicurus' basic demand in his first rule of investigation is that the investigator must have learned what is "subordinate to the utterances" (ὑποτεταγμένα τοῖς φϑόγγοις). Epicurus describes these subordinate entities as standards by reference to which we make judgments; and he argues that they are self-evident, requiring no demonstration. He also indicates that they are something primary that we think of in connection with our utterances. These details furnish an outline of a theory of meaning, but they are not sufficient to show what, if anything, is distinctive about this theory in the history of Greek philosophy. There is, however, a hint of uniqueness in the expression "subordinate to the utterances." The terms ὑποτεταγμένον and φϑόγγος were not used by Plato, Aristotle, or any rival Hellenistic philosophical school (as far as our sources indicate) to state their theories of meaning. Epicurus evidently intended the words to be understood by the beginning student in the most general sense, without any technical connotations; but their joint use also serves as a label for a special theory of meaning. A brief discussion of this theory now will provide a framework for the subsequent discussion of Epicurus' first rule, as well as throw further light on Epicurus' repudiation of logic.

There is little to be said about the grammar of "utterances" in Epicureanism; for Epicurus did not think it worthwhile to make a grammatical analysis of language.[11] Although Epicurus seems to have accepted the commonplace division of words into nouns and verbs, he made no use of these distinctions to frame a theory of meaning or truth.[12] This refusal to peg ontological distinctions to grammatical distinctions is reflected in our sources by the variety of expressions standing for presumptions (προλήψεις). The expressions are for the most part single words, but they also include combinations of individually meaningful words. Examples are "man," "cow," "philosopher," "creating," "good businessman," "goodness of a poem," "pleasure is to be sought in and for itself, and pain is to be avoided in and for itself."[13]

Evidence concerning what is "subordinate" to utterances is scattered and presents serious difficulties. First, in his statement of the first rule Epicurus rephrases the demand that we "have grasped what is subordinate to the utterances" by saying that "the first concept [ἐννόημα] in accordance with each utterance" must be seen.[14] Does this explanation imply that what is subordinate to an utterance is some type of thought? This suggestion is supported by a number of Epicurean texts, in which what is subordinate to a linguistic expression is identified as a belief or intention.[15] On the

11. Sextus Empiricus notes Epicurus' rejection of the technical study of grammar at *Adv. math.* 1.49 and 1.272.

12. The words ὄνομα and ῥῆμα seem to occur in Epicurus *On Nature* 28 fr. 12 col. 4 (Arr. 31.5.13). Also, Diogenes of Oenoanda divides utterances into nouns and verbs in fr. 10 col. 2.13–14 Chilton.

13. "Man": DL 10.33 and Philodemus *De signis* col. 34.10–11 De Lacy; "cow": DL 10.33; "philosopher": Philodemus *Rhetorica* 4 col. 10a1–4 Sudhaus (1:191); "creating": Lucretius 5.186; "good businessman": Philodemus *Oeconomicus* col. 20.9–32 Jensen; "goodness of a poem": Philodemus *De poematis* 5 col. 30.34–36 Jensen; and "pleasure . . .": Cicero *De finibus* 1.31.

14. My translation of ἐννόημα as "concept" is not intended to imply any particular degree of abstraction from sensory experience. I use the translation "concept" rather than "thought" to render the force of the prefix ἐν-; the prefix suggests that the thought is a general notion that has become fixed in the mind (see chap. 4).

15. Examples are: the thought (διάνοια) subordinate to poetic expressions, at Philodemus *De poematis* 5 cols. 19.15–16, 19.22–23, 27.9–10, and 27.34–28.1 Jensen; and the false opinion (δόξα) subordinate to articulate sounds (λέξεσιν), in Epicurus *On Nature* 28 fr. 18 col. 2 (Arr. 31.16.4).

other hand, there is also clear evidence that Epicurus and his followers correlated words directly with physical reality; and this
points to a theory of meaning in which the initial thoughts that
correspond to utterances present things as they exist in the physical world.

The most explicit evidence that we have about the correlation
of words with physical things consists in two late Hellenistic reports, one by Sextus Empiricus and the other by Plutarch, both
contrasting the Epicurean theory of meaning with that of the
Stoics. According to Sextus, the Stoics correlated three entities
with one another: "the significant" (τὸ σημαῖνον), which is the
voice (φωνή); "the significate" (τὸ σημαινόμενον, also called τὸ
λεκτόν, "what is said" or "what is meant"), which is the object
of thought; and the underlying external thing (τὸ τυγχάνον, literally "what happens"). The significate is incorporeal, whereas the
other two entities are corporeal.[16] In modern thought, the distinction between the significate and the external underlying thing
has been compared to the distinction between sense and reference.[17] Both Plutarch and Sextus Empiricus point out that Epicurus did not recognize the intermediate category of the significate, but held that there are only two entities directly related to one
another, the voice and the externally underlying thing.[18] Plutarch
adds the criticism that in this way Epicurus eliminated the means
by which "teaching, learning, presumptions (προλήψεις), thoughts,
impulses, and assent" come to be.

Cicero appears to attribute the same general position to the
Epicureans. In arguing against Epicurus' claim that pleasure is the
supreme good, he protests that Epicurus did not know at times
"what this word 'pleasure' sounds [or "is the sound of," *sonet*], that
is, what thing underlies this word."[19] Cicero's use of "sounds" instead of "signifies" or "means" at first seems very odd. But this
usage is entirely in agreement with the view that there are sounds
and external referents but no intermediate meanings: because
there is no intermediate reality to be signified, sounds are not
regarded as signifiers, but are correlated directly with external

16. Sextus Empiricus *Adv. math.* 8.11–12 ( = *SVF* 2.166; cf. 167). See further
Benson Mates, *Stoic Logic*, 11–26; and William and Martha Kneale, *The Development
of Logic*, 139–58.

17. See Mates's comparison of the Stoic theory with the positions of Frege and
Carnap; *Stoic Logic*, 19–26.

18. Sextus Empiricus *Adv. math.* 8.13 (cf. 8.258) and Plutarch *Adv. Colotem* 1119f–
1120a (all cited at U 259).

19. Cicero *De finibus* 2.6: . . . quid sonet haec vox voluptatis, id est quae res
huic voci subiciatur.

reality as sounds "of" it and so have only the function of "sounding" their correlate.[20]

Cicero's strained usage, moreover, seems to mirror the Epicureans' own usage. As Diogenes Laertius reports, the Epicureans claimed that logic is useless, since "it is sufficient for physicists to proceed in accordance with the utterances for [strictly, "of"] things [κατὰ τοὺς τῶν πραγμάτων φθόγγους]."[21] Although the use of the noun φθόγγος with a dependent genitive is even more awkward than Cicero's use of *sonare* followed by the accusative, the intent is the same.[22] The Epicureans are contending that it is sufficient for scientists to use words referring directly to external reality, without having any need of such logical refinements as propositions or other types of intermediate meaning.

It appears, therefore, that whereas Sextus and Plutarch used Stoic distinctions and vocabulary to explain the Epicureans' twofold distinction between sounds and reality, the Epicureans' own terms for this distinction are "utterances," φθόγγοι, and "things," πράγματα. This terminology is in agreement with Epicurus' consistent use of πράγματα to refer to occurrences in the physical world.[23]

Granted that Epicurus correlated utterances directly with physical things, it is reasonable to suppose that he called the latter "subordinate" to the former. But where does this leave the primary concepts, or thoughts, that correspond to sounds? They do not form a separate semantic category, I suggest, because they present physical reality just as it is. Epicurus held an analogous position concerning perception: what is presented in perception, he main-

20. Cicero uses *sonare* in the same way in a Stoic context at *De officiis* 3.83: honestate igitur dirigenda utilitas est, et quidem sic, ut haec duo verbo inter se discrepare, re unum sonare videantur ("Therefore, utility must be measured by the standard of morality, and in such a way that these two seem to differ in word, but to sound a single thing in fact"). *Honestas* and *utilitas* are here presented as having a single reference (that which they "sound"), even though they not only are two distinct words but also, in accordance with Stoic theory, have two distinct "meanings" (λεκτά). Cf. ibid., 3.11.

21. DL 10.31: ἀρκεῖν γὰρ τοὺς φυσικοὺς χωρεῖν κατὰ τοὺς τῶν πραγμάτων φθόγγους. Bailey, following Bignone (*Epicuro*, 207), translates "in accordance with the voices of things" (*Epicurus*, 414) and "it is sufficient for physicists to be guided by what things say of themselves" (161). The view that things issue utterances seems to me implausible.

22. The use of φθέγγεσθαι with an accusative, where the accusative stands for the reference just as in Cicero's construction, is found in Aristotle, *Posterior Analytics* 77a1–3. Aristotle points out that the geometer does not argue about the particular line that "he has uttered" (ἔφθεγκται), but about "what is shown" (δηλούμενα) by particular lines. Aristotle seems to allude here to the very type of semantic theory later embraced by Epicurus, while indicating its inadequacy.

23. For Epicurus' use of the term πρᾶγμα see esp. *Her.* 75 and *KD* 37 and 38.

tained, is in reality just as it appears, without there being any possibility of distortion or misrepresentation. Since the initial concepts of investigation are memories of what has appeared from outside, it follows that they too do not admit of any distinction between inner object of awareness and outer reality. It makes no difference, therefore, whether we view the thought of the physical thing or the physical thing itself as subordinate to the utterance: in either case what is associated with the utterance is the physical thing as it really is.[24]

An obvious objection to such a direct correlation of words with physical things is that words do not always designate something that exists. The Epicureans attempted to meet this objection by making a distinction between presumptions, which are thoughts of what exists, and opinions formed with the aid of presumptions, which are not necessarily thoughts of what exists. Sextus Empiricus shows in a discussion of "demonstration" (ἀπόδειξις) that the Epicureans were committed to the view that whatever a person thinks of by presumption exists. In keeping with his normal procedure, Sextus explains the concept of demonstration before going on to investigate whether there is demonstration as thus conceived. As he turns to the problem of existence, he notes that the Epicureans consider this part of the discussion idle:

> Some persons, especially the followers of Epicurus, are accustomed to object to us rather crudely: "Either you conceive, or you do not conceive, what demonstration is. But if you conceive of it and have a concept [ἔννοια] of it, there is demonstration; and if you do not

24. Epicurus' theory includes all three divisions of Aristotle's well-known analysis at *De interpretatione* 16a3–8: sounds (φωναί), affections of the soul (παθήματα τῆς ψυχῆς), and external things (πράγματα), as noted by A. A. Long ("*Aisthesis*," 121). Long also suggests that Epicurean προλήψεις "mediate between words and things in a manner which is analogous to the function of λεκτά in Stoic linguistic theory" (ibid.). Long's main argument, however, that otherwise there can be no false beliefs, is met by the Epicurean distinction between presumptions and added opinions. It may be noted, too, that the Stoics viewed λεκτά as distinct from the psychological process by which they are understood. Victor Goldschmidt suggests, similarly to Long, that Epicurus regarded the τύποι, "forms," of which the concepts are said to consist, as equivalent to Stoic λεκτά ("Remarques sur l'origine épicurienne de la prénotion," in *Les stoïciens et leur logique*, 163–64). Fritz Jürss likewise suggests that images intervene between sounds and external objects, although he takes the images to be representations of external reality ("Epikur und das Problem des Begriffes (Prolepse)," 214; cf. 217). I agree with Estelle and Phillip De Lacy, who mention briefly that in Epicureanism there is no mental entity to which words refer, and that the meaning of words is "purely extensional" (*Philodemus: On Methods of Inference*, 1st ed. pp. 141 and 139; cf. rev. ed. p. 184).

conceive of it, how do you search for what is not conceived of by you to begin with?"[25]

Epicurus' followers are here adapting Meno's well-known paradox to their own purposes. They contend that the preinvestigative concept of demonstration implies the existence of demonstration, so that there is no point in going on to investigate whether demonstration exists. What invites Sextus' charge of crudity is that, in his view, the Epicureans refuse to distinguish between an "apprehension" (κατάληψις), which implies the reality of what is thought of, and a "presumption" (πρόληψις), which is a "mere movement of the mind" and does not imply reality. To illustrate his view, Sextus points out that Epicurus surely has a presumption of the four elements even though he does not assent that there are four elements that make up the physical world.[26]

Sextus does not offer an Epicurean reply to his criticism; but a defense was available to the Epicureans. Presumptions, they might have pointed out, are thoughts of entities that exist either by themselves or as properties of self-existing entities. This does not imply, however, that whatever one thinks of exists. For in addition to presumptions, there are thoughts that are formed by the combination of a presumption with some other concept or with an object of perception; and the combinations formed in this way do not necessarily exist.[27] Thus there is nothing to prevent Epicurus from having a presumption of each of the four substances earth, water, air, and fire without being committed to the view that the physical world is made up of these four substances as elements. If pressed, the Epicureans might even admit that there is a presumption of the claim that the universe is made up of four elements; and they might point out that since this presumption exists as a philosophical claim, it does not commit them to the belief that the universe is made up of four elements. Similarly, to take the standard example of a centaur, the Epicureans might argue that we have preconceptions of the various parts of a centaur, and that all these parts exist, but that these preconceptions do not

25. Sextus Empiricus *Adv. math.* 8.337: καίτοι τινὲς εἰώθασιν ἡμῖν, καὶ μάλιστα οἱ ἀπὸ τῆς Ἐπικούρου αἱρέσεως, ἀγροικότερον ἐνίστασθαι, λέγοντες "ἤτοι νοεῖτε τί ἐστιν ἡ ἀπόδειξις, ἢ οὐ νοεῖτε. καὶ εἰ μὲν νοεῖτε καὶ ἔχετε ἔννοιαν αὐτῆς, ἔστιν ἀπόδειξις· εἰ δὲ οὐ νοεῖτε, πῶς ζητεῖτε τὸ μηδ' ἀρχὴν νοούμενον ὑμῖν;"

26. Ibid., 8.334a–336a. At *OP* 2.1–9 Sextus also addresses the charge (this time without naming any opponents) that the skeptics must already have "apprehended" the very thing they doubt.

27. See further chap. 8.

commit us to the belief that there is a living creature composed of these parts; or else they might argue that we have a preconception of a centaur, and that this object exists as a poet's or painter's creation, not as a living creature.

Epicurus' physical theory provides confirmation that he did not admit meanings intermediate between sounds and physical reality. He argued that only body and void exist by themselves, and that for the rest there are only properties of body and void.[28] Epicurus divided these properties into permanent and temporary properties, and claimed that neither kind can exist apart from physical reality. With respect to the permanent properties of bodies, Epicurus denies specifically that they are independently existing entities, and he also denies that they are incorporeal entities accompanying a body; instead he proposes that the permanent nature of a body is wholly constituted of them.[29] As for temporary properties, Epicurus points out that these, too, do not exist by themselves; and he notes that they exist just as they are perceived.[30] It is clear that throughout his analysis of properties Epicurus repudiates the view that there are correlates of words that are not part of physical reality. Epicurus' primary target appears to be Plato's theory of self-existent Forms. At the same time, Epicurus sweeps from his ontology Stoic meanings along with all other abstractions that are intended to mediate between language and physical reality.

Although we may suppose, then, that what is subordinate to an utterance is physical reality, Epicurus does not point out this correlation in his statement of his first rule. What he demands here is that the investigator have the type of awareness which, by not requiring demonstration, may serve as a standard of judgment. That this is an awareness of physical reality is implied subsequently by Epicurus' second rule of investigation, where he demands that the concepts that the investigator has prior to an investigation consist of empirical observations.

28. *Her.* 39–40 and 68–73 and Lucretius 1.418–82. In addition, Sextus Empiricus offers a brief summary of Epicurean ontology at *Adv. math.* 10.219–27.

29. *Her.* 68–69. Epicurus rejects two other positions in addition to those I have mentioned: one is that permanent properties "wholly are not"; the other is that they are "parts" (μόρια) of a body. Bailey attributes to Plato the view that permanent properties are independently existing entities, and to Aristotle the view that permanent properties are incorporeal accompaniments of a body (*Epicurus*, 236–37; *Greek Atomists*, 301). The first identification seems to me correct, the second wrong. I suggest that in the second case Epicurus has in mind the Stoic position that predicates are incorporeal meanings. (See *SVF* 2.183 and 184).

30. *Her.* 71.

Scholars have generally looked to Epicurus' expression "first concept in accordance with each utterance" as a key to understanding what he means by "subordinate to the utterances." The notion of "first concept," however, is itself problematic. In the past, "first concept" has been interpreted roughly in three ways: as the primary or basic meaning of a word; as the obvious or commonly used meaning; and as the first meaning associated with a word in the history of mankind. Accordingly, Epicurus' first rule has been interpreted as a demand for a proper, or ordinary, or conservative use of language.[31]

These interpretations assign a meaning to "first concept" which is extraneous to Epicurus' argument in the statement of his first rule. Epicurus shows what he means by "first concept" when he explains that "the first concept in accordance with each utterance must be seen and not require demonstration" since otherwise there would not be a basis for judgment. What makes the concept "first" is precisely that it is first in the order of investigation: it serves as the starting point of investigation, from which all other concepts follow. It is as a starting point, or ultimate basis of investigation, that it must not require demonstration; for otherwise there would be an infinite regress of starting points.[32] Implicit in

31. For the first interpretation see Bignone (*Epicuro*, 73) and Arrighetti (*Epicuro: Opere*, 36); for the second, Carlo Guissani (*T. Lucreti Cari De rerum natura libri sex*, 1:12), Bailey (*Greek Atomists*, 269–71; *Epicurus*, 176–77), and Jürss ("Prolepse," 218); for the third, J. H. Dahlmann (*De philosophorum Graecorum sententiis ad loquellae originem pertinentibus capita duo*, Diss. Leipzig 1928, 13–14), Robert Philippson ("Neues über Epikur und seine Schule" [1929], 134–35), and Kurt von Fritz in a review of Achilles Vogliano's *Epicuri et Epicureorum scripta in Herculanensibus papyris servata*, *Gnomon* 8 (1932): 68–69. These positions overlap to some extent. The last view is distinguished from the rest in that the "first concept" is regarded as the first concept associated with an expression in the history of mankind (see *Her.* 75–76). There are in addition several divergent views. A. A. Long identifies first concepts with Locke's "obvious sensible ideas" and proposes that they are the ideas first associated with a word in a person's experience ("*Aisthesis*," 124–25). Merbach takes the first concept to be historically first, although he suggests at the same time that Epicurus combined this view with an acceptance of ordinary usage; and he explains that the original meaning of an expression is passed on from one generation to the next through the education of children (*Canonica*, 52–53 and 48). Last, Manuwald agrees with Merbach that meanings are passed on from one generation to another but suggests that the first concept is more accurately described as the "proper meaning" rather than as the historically original concept (*Prolepsislehre Epikurs*, 112–13 and 97).

32. Striker has rightly pointed out that here, as elsewhere, Epicurus uses the term ἀπόδειξις (and ἀποδεικνύειν) in the sense of "demonstration," that is, of showing by argument what is not self-evident (Κριτήριον, 70–73). Further examples of the use of ἀπόδειξις (ἀποδεικνύειν) are at *Her.* 45 and 73 and in *On Nature* 2 fr. 18 col. 1 and fr. 20 col. 2 (Arr. 24.42.11–12 and 24.50.17–18). Bignone blunts the force of Epicurus' argument by proposing that ἀποδεικνύειν in the pro-

Epicurus' use of "first concept" is a distinction between primary concepts corresponding to utterances, which do not require investigation, and secondary concepts corresponding to utterances, which are obtained by reference to primary concepts. The former must be present to the investigator from the start so that the latter may be judged by reference to them.[33]

This is not to deny that the initial concepts used by the investigator may also be concepts that constitute the basic meaning of a word, or are ordinarily associated with a word, or have generally been associated with a word throughout its history. They are certainly basic in the sense that they serve as standards by reference to which other concepts are developed. As it turns out, they are also commonly held concepts, and they tend to be historically primitive. But this is a consequence of a certain view of concept acquisition and of language development that is no part of Epicurus' first rule of investigation.

Epicurus underscores the difference between first, undemonstrated concepts and secondary concepts by a terminological distinction. At *Letter to Menoeceus* 123–24 Epicurus claims that the beliefs that are widely promulgated about the gods are not προλή-ψεις, "presumptions," but ὑπολήψεις ψευδεῖς, "false assumptions." His explanation is that many people assign to the gods attributes, such as harming or helping men, that are incompatible with the primary concept, or presumption, of god as an indestructible and blessed living being. In this case, the beliefs that have been formed by reference to the initial concept are incompatible with it. The corresponding true belief, which is by implication a true ὑπόληψις, is set out by Epicurus as *Authoritative Opinion* 1, and consists in attaching to the presumption of god the claim that god "does not have trouble himself or make trouble for another, with the consequence that he is subject neither to anger nor to favor." Epicurus' terminological distinction incidentally shows that he was not averse

---

cedural note means *dichiarare* and not *dimostrare* (*Epicuro*, 73 n. 2). Bignone is followed by Bailey, who claims that the meaning is to "explain" rather than "prove" (*Epicurus*, 176). I agree with Striker that Epicurus is using an infinite regress argument of the same general type as that used by Aristotle at *Posterior Analytics* 72b20–22 to show that the first premises of demonstration must be undemonstrated (Κριτήριον, 71). This does not, of course, imply that Epicurus' notion of primary concepts or of demonstration is the same as Aristotle's.

33. If the emendation "first subordinate" in Diogenes' text is correct (see n. 8 above), then what is grasped as subordinate to an utterance prior to any investigation is also said to be "first subordinate." What is secondarily subordinate to an utterance may then be viewed as a physical feature discovered by scientific investigation.

to straining ordinary language in order to express technical distinctions. Epicurus clearly held, however, that technical language, like technical concepts, belongs to the outcome of an investigation and not to its beginning.

In demanding, therefore, in his first rule of investigation that we have grasped what is "subordinate to the utterances," Epicurus is making the formal requirement that prior to any investigation we have concepts, corersponding to the words used, that do not require demonstration. In his second rule of investigation, Epicurus supplies a content for these concepts by specifying that they must be an awareness of physical reality exactly as perceived by the organs of perception. The ultimate standards of investigation are thus furnished directly by observed physical reality, not by language or any abstract correlates of language.

An excellent illustration of this view of language is provided by Epicurus' discussion of time in the *Letter to Herodotus.* As a sequel to his examination of permanent and temporary properties, Epicurus points out that time is not to be investigated like other properties of bodies by being referred to a presumption.[34] Instead we must compare the evident occurrence (ἐνάργημα), by reference to which we use the expressions "short time" and "long time," with other evident occurrences of the same type. The evident occurrence, as I interpet it, is a property that is perceived to last for a short or long time. Epicurus later sums up these properties as nights and days, motions and rests, and feelings or absences of feeling. It is understood that we have presumptions of these properties. These concepts permit us to investigate time, even though we do not have a presumption of time itself; for time is nothing but the relative duration of properties.[35]

---

34. *Her.* 72.

35. My interpretation differs from that of others in that I take ἐνάργημα to refer to the self-evident temporary properties that are said to last for a long time or a short time, and do not take it to refer to time itself. In contrast, Giussani understands ἐνάργημα as the "intuition of time" (*De rerum natura,* 1:30–31); he is followed by Bailey (*Epicurus,* 241–42) and Manuwald (*Prolepsislehre,* 76–78). As I interpret Epicurus' position, there is nothing evident about time as such (otherwise we would have a presumption of it), but time can be understood by reference to certain evident properties. Whereas Bailey explicitly distinguishes ἐνάργημα from πρόληψις and attributes to Epicurus the view that there is no presumption of time, others suppose that Epicurus does recognize a presumption of time (for example, Jürss, "Prolepse," 221). In addition, I understand συγγενικῶς to mean "within the same general type" and I keep mss. περιφέροντες, so that συγγενικῶς τοῦτο περιφέροντες designates the process of comparing the durations of different events of the same general type (for example, the durations of different acts of running). Additional testimony about Epicurus' theory of time is in Sextus Empiricus *Adv.*

From this analysis of time Epicurus draws the lesson that "neither must we change to other expressions as being better but we must use the existing expressions concerning it [that is, time], nor must we predicate anything else of it as having the same being as this unique entity."[36] Epicurus is warning that we should neither change our language to suit reality nor change reality to suit our language. There is no initial concept corresponding to the utterance "time"; but this is no reason to discard the term (for it does have reference in conjunction with other utterances) or to invent an addition to our ontology (for time does have a reality of its own). Every investigation begins with the use of conventional language, even though conventional language does not mirror reality. Nor is there any harm in this, for language draws the attention of the investigator not to itself or to any underlying abstraction but directly to physical reality.[37]

---

*math.* 10.181–88 and 219–27 (cf. *OP* 3.137), as well as in a very fragmentary book of Epicurus' *On Nature*, PHerc. 1413 (Arr. 37, esp. 37.17, 37.25, and 37.31); this last text is discussed by Adelmo Barigazzi in "Il concetto del tempo nella fisica atomistica."

36. *Her.* 72: καὶ οὔτε διαλέκτους ὡς βελτίους μεταληπτέον, ἀλλ᾽ αὐταῖς ταῖς ὑπαρχούσαις κατ᾽ αὐτοῦ χρηστέον, οὔτε ἄλλο τι κατ᾽ αὐτοῦ κατηγορητέον ὡς τὴν αὐτὴν οὐσίαν ἔχοντος τῷ ἰδιώματι τούτῳ·

37. The same conventionalist adherence to language is stated by Epicurus in book 28 of *On Nature* fr. 17 col. 4 (Arr. 31.14.8–12): ". . . our usage is not outside customary expressions, nor do we transpose words in the case of evident things" (. . . οὐκ ἔξω τῶν [ε]ἰθισμένων λέξεων ἡμῶν χρ[ω]μένων οὐδὲ μετατιθέντων ὀνόματα ἐπὶ τῶμ φανε[ρ]ῶν). This seems to imply that Epicurus used ordinary language except in the case of things that cannot be observed. Thus Epicurus seems to have restricted innovations in language to the use of technical terms. At fr. 12 col. 4 (Arr. 31.5) Epicurus allows a name change in those few cases in which a thing that has not been observed is shown by investigation to be other than previously conjectured. On the basis of these and other fragments of book 28, Sedley suggests that early in his career Epicurus tried to improve upon ordinary language but later turned to a conventionalist view ("Epicurus, *On Nature* Book XXVIII", 22–23). The texts cited by Sedley seem to me too fragmented to show a historical development of this sort.

# [ 2 ]

# Rejection of Demonstration
# and Definition

## DEMONSTRATION

EPICURUS demands in his first rule of investigation that the
first concepts of investigation "be seen" (βλέπεσθαι) and not
require "demonstration" (ἀπόδειξις). Otherwise, he points out,
either we would be engaged in an infinite process of demonstration with the result that nothing could be judged, or else we
would use empty sounds; in either case, there would be no standard by reference to which a judgment could be made. Epicurus'
argument is clear in general. The first alternative is that we attempt, without ever succeeding, to establish precise meanings;
the second is that we use meaningless sounds. To illustrate the
former case, supposing that we were to demonstrate the concept
corresponding to the utterance "god," we could do so only by
reference to some other concept of god, and this concept would
need to be demonstrated in turn, so that the demonstration would
go on to infinity.[1]

In using the term βλέπεσθαι, "to be seen," to describe the cognitive attitude of having presumptions, Epicurus appears to be
indebted to Plato.[2] Plato uses the verb βλέπειν or the compound

---

1. See chap. 1, n. 32, on Epicurus' use of the infinite regress argument. For
Epicurus' text, see chap. 1, n. 6.

2. Epicurus also uses βλέπειν at *Her.* 72 with reference to presumptions; see
also Philodemus *Rhetorica* PHerc. 1669 col. 21.13, Sudhaus 1:255. As for Plato,
he uses ἀποβλέπειν and βλέπειν in the *Phaedrus* at 237d and 238d, respectively,
to signify "looking" toward definitions. Ἀποβλέπειν occurs also at *Euthyphro* 6e,
with εἶδος and ἰδέα as the object of contemplation; similarly at *Meno* 72c, with
εἶδος as the object; and at *Republic* 484c, with a paradigmatic Form as the object.

form ἀποβλέπειν to describe the awareness of universals and of Forms. Neither Plato's nor Epicurus' usage implies that the object of apprehension has the appearance of a visual object although Epicurean presumptions occur as visual outlines. The term βλέπειν suggests an immediate acquaintance with the object, of the sort that occurs in sense perception.

In Diogenes Laertius' account of Epicurean presumption, the term ἐναργής, "evident," takes the place of the phrase "to be seen and not require demonstration." Ἐναργής is used in Epicureanism and in Hellenistic philosophy in general to mean "self-evident," that is, "not requiring demonstration." Epicurus himself applies the term to the presumption of god in the *Letter to Menoeceus* when he claims that the knowledge of the existence of the gods is ἐναργής.[3]

Epicurus' followers did not alter his position that the initial concepts of investigation do not require demonstration. We have evidence, however, that some, at least, were prepared to offer arguments in support of initial concepts. These arguments were not intended to serve as demonstrations of the concept, since they are themselves dependent on the concept as undemonstrated, but were designed to strengthen one's commitment to the concept.

An example is the discussion of the shape of the gods in Cicero's *On the Nature of the Gods*.[4] The Epicurean spokesman Velleius claims that we know immediately from our initial concept of the gods that they have human shape. But Velleius then adds two syllogisms showing that the gods have human shape: his reason is that he does not want "everything to be referred to first concepts." As he explains, "partly nature [*natura*] reminds" us of the shape of the gods by means of initial concepts, and "partly reason [*ratio*] teaches" us the shape.[5] The two syllogisms are carefully cast in the mold of contemporary logic: they are "not in your manner but in that of the logicians, of which your tribe is wholly ignorant," as Velleius' critic Cotta sneers.[6] It is clear that Velleius is engaged in

---

3. *Men.* 123. In addition, we have Clement's explanation of Epicurean presumption as "an application to something evident and to the evident concept of the thing" (ἐπιβολὴν ἐπί τι ἐναργὲς καὶ ἐπὶ τὴν ἐναργῆ τοῦ πράγματος ἐπίνοιαν, U 255). There is some confusion in Clement's use of ἐπιβολή; in Epicureanism what one "applies" (that is, "attends") to is the external object; the thought is the "application" (see chaps. 7 and 8).

4. The Epicurean position is set out at *De natura deorum* 1.46–49 and criticized in detail at 1.71–102.

5. Ibid., 1.46: ac de forma quidem partim natura nos admonet, partim ratio docet.

6. Ibid., 1.89: non vestro more sed dialecticorum, quae funditus gens vestra non novit.

a debate with other philosophers as he adopts their techniques to defend the Epicurean concept of god.

The basic format of this debate can, moreover, be made out with some precision. Velleius' two syllogisms belong to an inquiry, which he has just announced, concerning the form, life, and thought of the gods. The entire inquiry, Velleius says, is intended "to strengthen the opinion" (*ad . . . confirmandam opinionem*) that god is everlasting and blessed, and consequently is free from anger and favoritism and does not pose any threat to humans.[7] This "opinion," as already noted, is the first of Epicurus' *Authoritative Opinions* and comprises both the initial concept of god and an inference derived by reference to this concept. Velleius undertakes to strengthen the opinion by further inquiry, even though, as he says, the opinion by itself is sufficient for a pious worship of the gods and for freedom from superstition. Velleius' motive seems inspired directly by Plato's contention in the *Meno* that "true opinions" are a sufficient guide for life, but that they are not firmly fixed unless they are secured by a detailed dialectical examination, or "calculation of the cause." Plato held in addition that "opinion" (δόξα) is in this way converted to "knowledge" (ἐπιστήμη).[8] After Plato, the distinction between opinion and knowledge was elaborated by the Stoics, who held that opinion is "weak assent" and that knowledge, in contrast, is "secure apprehension that cannot be overthrown by reason [λόγος]."[9] Accordingly, the distinction between opinion and knowledge or reason (λόγος, *ratio*) came to be adopted as a standard framework of philosophical discussion in the Hellenistic period.[10] To judge from Velleius' distinction between opinion and argument, the Epicureans too used this framework in an attempt to defend their doctrines against their opponents. At the same time, the Epicureans dissented in one important respect. Velleius concedes to Plato and the Stoics that

7. Ibid., 1.45.

8. Plato *Meno* 85c–d and 98a (αἰτίας λογισμῷ).

9. See, for example, *SVF* 1.60, 69 on "opinion," 1.68 on "knowledge."

10. Cicero uses the distinction also to structure his discussion of Stoic theology in *De natura deorum* 2; see esp. 2.5 (where Cicero calls the belief in the existence of god an "opinion," *opinio*) and 2.44–45 (where, after discussing the self-evident existence of god, Cicero proposes to show by argument "what sort" (*qualis*) god is). Cf. *Tusculanae Disputationes* 1.36, where Cicero claims: ut deos esse natura opinamur, quales sint ratione cognoscimus, sic permanere animos arbitramur consensu nationum omnium, qua in sede maneant qualesque sint ratione discendum est ("Just as we hold the opinion by nature that there are gods and know by reason what sort they are, so we believe by the unanimous agreement of all nations that souls persist [after death], but we must learn by reason where they abide and of what sort they are").

an opinion may be secured by argument; but, significantly, he refrains from calling the result of this process "knowledge." This position is in keeping with the fundamental tenet of Epicurean science that there is no level of cognition superior to true opinion. The reason, which will be explored throughout this study, is that the Epicureans did not recognize any truths that are not verified either directly or indirectly by empirical observation.

Velleius' procedure may be compared with that of another Epicurean spokesman, Torquatus, in the first book of Cicero's *On Ends.* Torquatus here defends Epicurus' claim that pleasure is the supreme good and pain the supreme evil. He notes at the beginning of his discussion that Epicurus held that this is known by sense perception, as a judgment of nature (*natura*), and that there is no need to prove it by the use of reason (*ratio*).[11] Torquatus agrees, but adds that he and other Epicureans think "that since very many things are said by many philosophers as to why pleasure should not be counted among goods and pain among evils, we should not trust too much in our case but should offer proof and precise discussion, and should debate about pleasure and pain by constructing arguments."[12] Torquatus is here undertaking to support by argument a fact that is apprehended directly by sense perception. Just like a presumption, this apprehension is a judgment made by nature, without the use of any argument; and as such it is self-evident. Torquatus' purpose in using argument to corroborate what is self-evident is to counter opposing arguments. In other words, he is proposing to satisfy precisely the requirement by which the Stoics distinguished knowledge from opinion: he is proposing to make a belief incontrovertible by argument. At the same time, Torquatus is not abandoning Epicurus' position that there is nothing more certain than the evidence of sense perception itself.

In using argument to defend self-evident facts, Velleius and Torquatus are adopting a position similar to that of a group of philosophers mentioned by Cicero. These philosophers, whom Cicero does not identify by name, "maintained that they would not say anything first in support of what is self-evident, but thought that they should respond to what is said in opposition, lest they be

11. Cicero *De finibus* 1.30.
12. Ibid., 1.31 (with Torquatus as speaker): alii autem, quibus ego assentior, cum a philosophis compluribus permulta dicantur cur nec voluptas in bonis sit numeranda nec in malis dolor, non existimant oportere nimium nos causae confidere, sed et argumentandum et accurate disserendum et rationibus conquisitis de voluptate et dolore disputandum putant.

deceived in some way."[13] The reason these philosophers will not argue on their own initiative for what is self-evident is that this is precisely what does not need to be inferred from something else. However, since there are those who are adept at overthrowing what is self-evident by argument, argument is needed to make these attacks ineffectual.

## DEFINITION

Epicurus also denied that the initial concepts of investigation require definition. He does not say so explicitly in the procedural note of the *Letter to Herodotus* or elsewhere in his extant writings, but Cicero and others attribute the position to him. It may be taken as implied by Epicurus' requirement that the first concepts of investigation not require demonstration; for if there were a need to define the concept that corresponds to an utterance, then the correctness of the definition would need to be demonstrated by reference to another definition, and so on without end, so that there would be an infinite regress of demonstration.

There are two late testimonies concerning Epicurus' rejection of definition, and both are disappointingly brief. One is the comment that Epicurus held that words are clearer than definitions.[14] The other is that according to Epicurus the intrinsic clarity of a term is destroyed by definition.[15] The most we can extract from these reports is that the ordinary use of words is clearer than the use of definitions in place of the words.

13. Cicero *Academica* 2.17: alii autem negabant se pro hac evidentia quidquam priores fuisse dicturos, sed ad ea quae contra dicerentur dici oportere putabant, ne qui fallerentur. Cicero has just pointed out that *evidentia* translates ἐνάργεια. The other group mentioned by Cicero consists of those who hold that there is no need whatsoever to defend what is self-evident.

14. Pap. 9782 col. 22.39–42 (*Anonymer Kommentar zu Platons Theaetet*, edited by H. Diels and W. Schubart, p. 16): Ἐπίκου[ϱ]ος τὰ ὀνόματά φησ[ι]ν σαφέστερα εἶναι τῶν ὅϱων. The commentator adds immediately that it would indeed be ridiculous to greet another by using a definition instead of a name (so as to say, "Hail, mortal rational animal" instead of "Hail, Socrates"), but defends the use of definitions by explaining that they are not intended as greetings or as more concise expressions than words but that they serve to unfold (ἀναπλῶσαι) common concepts (cols. 22.42–23.8). The commentator is here answering a standard objection to the use of definitions; see Sextus Empiricus *OP* 2.211.

15. Erotian (U 258). The text is corrupt just before the introduction of Epicurus' name, and it is not exactly clear where Epicurus' view begins and ends. I take it that the general position expressed by αἱ δὲ συνήθεις . . . φαϱμάκου (U 258.16–20) is Epicurus', although the phrasing may not be his. Erotian's argument against definition appears to be a variant of the standard argument that definition is impossible if all terms require definition and unnecessary if only some terms require definition (cf. Sextus Empiricus *OP* 2.207–8).

More revealing is Epicurus' own statement in the *Letter to Pyth-ocles* that "one must investigate nature not according to empty axioms and stipulations [κατὰ ἀξιώματα κενὰ καὶ νομοθεσίας] but as the phenomena demand."[16] Since definitions are among the "axioms and stipulations" used by other scientists, Epicurus is here rejecting definitions along with any other a priori assumptions made by other scientists. In the same spirit, Torquatus in Cicero's *On Ends* denounces the Platonic disciplines of music, geometry, arithmetic, and astronomy on the ground that "starting from false principles" (*a falsis initiis profecta*) they cannot but have false conclusions.[17] This position accords with Proclus' remark that the Epicureans proposed to "overthrow the principles of geometry."[18]

Last, there is an excellent source for Epicurus' rejection of definition, and it deserves some detailed examination. This is Cicero's presentation of Epicurean ethics in the first two books of *On Ends*. Cicero himself takes on the role of critic of the Epicureans in this discussion, and he prepares the ground at the beginning of his presentation by including the elimination of definition in a detailed list of transgressions allegedly committed by Epicurus against logic.[19] Later, when the Epicurean spokesman Torquatus has finished his defense of Epicurean ethics, Cicero asks him to define pleasure. Torquatus thereupon exclaims: "Who is there who does not know what pleasure is or who requires a definition in order to know it better?"[20] Cicero has already anticipated this refusal in the way in which he puts his request to Torquatus. For he points out that whereas Epicurus agreed with Plato's demand, as stated in the *Phaedrus*, that the subject of an investigation be determined at the very beginning of the investigation, Epicurus did not understand the logical consequence that sometimes the subject must be defined if the participants are to be agreed on

16. *Pyth.* 86: οὐ γὰρ κατὰ ἀξιώματα κενὰ καὶ νομοθεσίας φυσιολογητέον ἀλλ' ὡς τὰ φαινόμενα ἐκκαλεῖται.

17. Cicero *De finibus* 1.72.

18. Proclus *In primum Euclidis Elementorum librum,* edited by G. Friedlein, Leipzig: Teubner 1873, pp. 199–200 and 214–15 (with τὰς γεωμετρικὰς . . . ἀρχὰς ἀνατρέπειν at 199.9–10). The Epicurean Zeno should be included among those who rejected the principles of geometry; for, although he does not attack any of these directly, as Proclus notes, he attacks them all indirectly by showing that they are insufficient. (This is contrary to the view of Gregory Vlastos that Zeno did accept the principles of geometry; "Zeno of Sidon as a Critic of Euclid," in *The Classical Tradition: Literary and Historical Studies in Honor of Harry Caplan,* edited by L. Wallach, Ithaca: Cornell University Press, 1966, 148–59.)

19. Cicero *De finibus* 1.22.

20. Ibid., 2.6: quis . . . est qui quid sit voluptas nesciat aut qui quo magis id intellegat definitionem aliquam desideret?

what it is.[21] Cicero also remarks that Torquatus did occasionally make an "unwitting" use of definition in his preceding exposition; in particular, he accuses Torquatus of defining the supreme good as "that to which all correct acts are referred, whereas it itself is not referred anywhere." Torquatus had explained at the beginning of his exposition that in the opinion of all philosophers the supreme good is "such that all things must be referred to it, whereas it itself [is referred] nowhere."[22] It appears, therefore, that Epicurus and his followers refused in principle to give definitions, on the ground that they are unnecessary. This policy does not, however, exclude such explanations as Torquatus' explanation of the supreme good.

As Cicero's reference to Plato's *Phaedrus* indicates, the dispute between Cicero and Torquatus on the need for definitions is conducted along Platonic guidelines. In requesting a definition of pleasure, Cicero is appealing to Plato's distinction in the *Phaedrus* between terms such as "iron" and "silver," which do not require definition, and other terms, such as "justice," "goodness," and "love," which do. In the latter case, Plato explains, a definition is needed to assure agreement on the subject of investigation. By "looking at [ἀποβλέποντες] and referring to [ἀναφέροντες]" the definition, Plato claims, the investigators are able to conduct an inquiry that has clarity and coherence.[23] Cicero goes Plato one step further by defining definition itself as a "disclosure of things that are covered up as it were, when it is revealed what each thing is."[24]

Torquatus too indicates that Epicurus agreed with Plato that the subject of an investigation must be clear from the very beginning; for he introduces his entire presentation by saying: "I will proceed in the manner approved by the author of this doctrine; I shall set out what and of what sort the subject of investigation is." But this agreement clearly does not carry with it a commitment to give a definition of the subject under investigation. Torquatus

21. Ibid., 2.4. Plato's demand in the *Phaedrus* is at 237b–d (cf. 265d and 277b).

22. Cicero's accusation is at *De finibus* 2.5. The definition, as worded by Cicero, is: id . . . quo omnia quae recte fierent referrentur neque id ipsum usquam referretur. Torquatus' original explanation is at 1.29: tale debet esse ut ad id omnia referri oporteat, ipsum autem nusquam. There are two significant differences between the two statements: Cicero uses a Stoic expression, *recte fierent* (standing for κατορθώματα), and he has replaced *tale* by *id* in order to make his definition formally correct.

23. Plato *Phaedrus* 263a–d (on the distinction between terms) and 237d and 265d (on the use of a definition).

24. Cicero *De finibus* 2.5: haec patefactio quasi rerum opertarum, cum quid quidque sit aperitur, definitio est.

immediately qualifies his statement by explaining, "not because I think that you do not know, but in order that the discussion may proceed in a rational and methodical way."[25] This explanation is modeled on Plato's reason for giving definitions. Torquatus' explanation, however, differs from Plato's in the very important respect that Torquatus does not think there is any need to define the subject of investigation; for, as he says, all the participants already know it. Torquatus subsequently describes what the supreme good is agreed to be, as cited above; and he fails to give any definition of pleasure.

In his response to the Platonic demand for definition, Torquatus makes clear that Epicurus understood the requirement for an initial determination of the subject of investigation very differently from Plato in the *Phaedrus*. The requirement to which Epicurus agrees is in fact his first rule of investigation, as stated in the *Letter to Herodotus*. Epicurus demands that the investigator already have clear concepts corresponding to the words used. These concepts do not, in addition, require definition; if they did, they could not serve as a standard of reference for the investigation. For Epicurus, the definitions that Plato proposes as standards of investigation in the *Phaedrus* can be nothing but "empty axioms and stipulations." This rejection of definition does not imply, however, that the initial concepts of investigation cannot be explained. As Torquatus illustrates, it is sometimes useful to set out what everyone is agreed upon. But such explanations are not regarded by Epicurus or his followers as definitions at all; rather they are intended as summary descriptions of the initial concept, technically known as ὑπογραφαί or ὑποτυπώσεις ("outlines," "sketches") in the Hellenistic period. The ultimate standard of reference is, therefore, still the initial undefined and undemonstrated concept.

Summary descriptions or "sketches" (ὑπογραφαί, ὑποτυπώσεις) were well recognized in the Hellenistic period as a category of explanation quite distinct from definition. The technical term for a definition was ὅρος; and, as Cicero indicates in the debate with

---

25. Ibid., 1.29: . . . sic agam ut ipsi auctori huius disciplinae placet: constituam quid et quale sit id de quo quaerimus, non quo ignorare vos arbitrer, sed ut ratione et via procedat oratio. The term *constituam* may render Greek ὁρίζω. In that case, ὁρίζω is used not in the strict technical sense of "define," but in the sense "determine," "demarcate"; in this wider sense, ὁρίζω embraces short descriptions (see following note). This wide use of ὁρίζω occurs at PHerc. 1056 fr. 7 col. 1 (Arr. 34.20.2–6): πρὸς τὸ ὡρισμένον καὶ τὰ πάντα ἐξελέγχον τῆς ἀναφορᾶς γινομένης, καὶ οὐ πρὸς ἀόριστα καὶ κρίσεως προσδεόμενα.

Torquatus, a definition was thought to "unfold" or "explicate" what a thing is, or, in other words, to display what is implicit in the ordinary concept of a thing. In contrast, an "outline" or "sketch" was said to be a description that brings to mind the ordinary, empirically acquired concept of a thing by stating certain prominent features that are obvious to everyone.[26] Accordingly, whereas a definition was designed to replace an ordinary concept as a standard of investigation, an outline description was used to remind the investigator of the ordinary concept so that the ordinary concept might serve as a standard of investigation.

Although it is not at all clear that in the *Phaedrus* Plato is proposing definitions of the type recognized in the Hellenistic period, it is clear, I think, that Epicurus and his followers did repudiate all preinvestigative explanations of terms that do not serve merely to bring to mind the concept that the investigator already has. Accordingly, the Epicureans rejected all definitions as standards of investigation, although they did resort quite frequently to outline descriptions. The best example in Epicurus' extant writings is his description of god in the *Letter to Menoeceus* as an "indestructible and blessed living being."[27] The purpose of this description

---

26. In addition to the definition of "definition" at *De finibus* 2.5 (see n. 24, above), Cicero explains definition at *Topica* 26 as *oratio quae id quod definitur explicat quid sit* ("speech that unfolds what the defined thing is"); cf. *Topica* 9, where the term *evolvit*, "unfolds," is used. See also *Orator* 116, *Tusculanae Disputationes* 4.53, and above, n. 14. As for outline descriptions (ὑπογραφαί, ὑποτυπώσεις), Galen notes that they are "definitions pertaining to our concepts" (ἐννοηματικοὶ ὅροι) that "do not express more than all men know," and adds that those who are strict in the use of terms do not consider them definitions (ὅροι) (*SVF* 2.229; see also Galen's distinction between definition and outline description at *SVF* 2.227). Sextus Empiricus is one writer who included outlines under the general heading of definition (ὅρος). At *OP* 2.212, he cites the following two views of what a definition is: a definition is "an account that by a short reminder leads us to the concept of the things that are subordinate to the sounds [τῶν ὑποτεταγμένων ταῖς φωναῖς πραγμάτων]"; and a definition is "an account that shows the essence [τὸ τί ἦν εἶναι]." The use of the term ὑποτεταγμένα indicates that the first view is Epicurean; at any rate the type of definition that is proposed is strictly an outline. In *Subfiguratio empirica* 7 (p. 63.4–10 D), Galen mentions that an outline, in contrast to a proper definition, consists of the "evident attributes" (ἐκ τῶν ἐναργῶς ὑπαρχόντων) of a thing, that is, of "evident phenomena" (ἐκ τῶν ἐναργῶς φαινομένων). See also Ammonius *In Porphyrii isagogen* 2.15 (*Commentaria in Aristotelem graeca*, vol. 4 pt. 3, edited by A. Busse, Berlin: G. Reimer 1891, pp. 54–55), where a definition is said to be constructed from "essential" attributes (ἐκ τῶν κατὰ οὐσίαν ὑπαρχόντων), and an outline (likened to a σκιαγραφία) from "concomitant" attributes (ἐκ τῶν συμβεβηκότων).

27. *Men.* 123. Epicurus adds to his description that this is ὡς ἡ κοινὴ τοῦ θεοῦ νόησις ὑπεγράφη (ὑπεγράφει F). Here Epicurus appears to be using ὑπογράφειν

is quite clearly to remind others of their own initial concept of god, as it exists without the accretion of any opinions that have been formed secondarily. Torquatus' purpose in describing the supreme good is somewhat different. Although he also sets out a generally agreed concept, he observes in addition the standard contemporary procedure, which seems to be inspired by Plato's *Phaedrus*, of first explaining a concept and then showing in detail what corresponds in reality to this concept.

In addition to charging Epicurus with the elimination of definitions, Cicero accuses him of neglecting the problem of ambiguity.[28] There is, however, good evidence that Epicurus and his followers concerned themselves with the problem, and that they proposed outline descriptions as the solution. As just noted, Epicurus used an outline to segregate the initial concept of god, which everyone possesses, from secondary interpretations. In this way he ensures that all are using the term "god" in the same way. Epicurus' follower Philodemus makes a similar use of an outline to clarify the notion of art or skill (τέχνη). According to Philodemus, everyone has a presumption of art as something methodical, and consequently the extension of the term to skills that rely on conjecture is a misuse.[29] Here Philodemus is relying on a summary description to remind his readers of the difference between the initial and the extended concept. Philodemus also recognizes cases in which the same expression may have two different presumptions corresponding to it. Examples are the expressions "good businessman" and "spirit" (θῦμος), each of which may evoke different primary concepts.[30] In these cases, a verbal outline serves to make clear what primary concept is to be associated with the expression.

A further indication that Epicurus concerned himself with the problem of ambiguity is the fact that he wrote a book titled Περὶ ἀμφιβολίας, which is not extant.[31] More tangibly, it is clear that

---

in the technical sense, although the verb form is strange. Perhaps the verb should be emended to ὑπογράφει. Manuwald summarizes other interpretations of the term in *Prolepsislehre*, 57–60. Sextus Empiricus uses ὑπογράφειν in the technical sense when he reports that Epicurus, "in outlining [ὑπογράφων] 'true' and 'false,'" claimed that "the true is that which is as it is said to be" and "the false is that which is not as it is said to be" (*Adv. math.* 8.9).

28. Cicero *De finibus* 1.22.

29. Philodemus *Rhetorica* 2 cols. 26–42, Sudhaus 1:53–76 (esp. cols. 41–42, Sudhaus 1:74–75).

30. Philodemus *Oeconomicus* col. 20.16–32 Jensen (cf. col. 12.12–15) on ἀγαθὸς χρηματιστής, and *De ira* cols. 44–45 Wilke (esp. 45.1–5) on θῦμος.

31. The work is mentioned by Epicurus in *On Nature* 28 fr. 17 col. 4 (Arr. 31.14.26–27 [ = U 92a]).

Epicurus recognized ambiguity as a problem in the historical development of language. Distinguishing between two stages of language development, a natural and a conventional stage, Epicurus held that in the conventional stage an attempt is made to remove ambiguity.[32] Last, there is a tantalizing papyrus fragment in which Epicurus associates error with the multiple uses of words: ". . . every error of men has no other form than that which happens in the case of presumptions, and of phenomena because of the varied usages of expressions. . . ."[33] Unfortunately, the context is too fragmentary to shed any light on this obscure claim. On the surface, the claim needs to be modified, for, as other evidence amply shows, Epicurus proposed that error and falsehood belong to opinions that fail to be verified by the phenomena. However, it is entirely plausible that Epicurus also recognized that error can arise when one person uses a word in one sense and another understands it in a different sense. We may suppose that Epicurus' solution to this problem is the use of outline descriptions, although critics such as Cicero were unlikely to be satisfied by any solution short of a definition.

The claim that investigation begins with ordinary, undefined concepts earned Epicurus the reputation of making philosophy depend on the speech habits of uneducated villagers.[34] This has encouraged a view of Epicurus as the ordinary man's philosopher.[35] Although there are grounds for regarding Epicurus as the champion of the ordinary person, Epicurus' view of initial concepts and language is an epistemological position that is only incidentally related to his humanitarianism. Epicurus' avowed reason for relying on concepts expressed by ordinary language is that this alone assures a proper basis for investigation.

A brief survey of the Epicurean concept of a human being illustrates the distinctiveness of the Epicurean view of definition. Sextus Empiricus reports that Epicurus gave an ostensive explana-

---

32. *Her.* 76.
33. Epicurus *On Nature* 28 fr. 16 col. 3, Arr. 31.10.6–12: ὅτι πᾶσα ἡ ἁμ[α]ρτία [ἐ]στὶν τῶν ἀνθρώπων οὐδὲν ἕτερον ἔχουσα σχῆμα ἢ τ[ὸ] ἐπὶ τῶμ προ[ο]λήψεων γιγν[ό]μενον, καὶ τῶμ φαιν[ομ]έν[ων] διὰ τοὺς πολυτρόπου[ς ἐθι]σμοὺς τῶν λέξεων. . . . This is a much discussed passage; see esp. Manuwald, *Prolepsislehre*, 87–102; and Long, "*Aisthesis*," 123–24. Both Manuwald and Long refer to the πρῶτον ἐννόημα of *Her.* 38 as Epicurus' solution to the problem, taking this as the preferred usage (see chap. 1, n. 31).
34. Cicero *De finibus* 2.12, 50.
35. This view is promoted especially by Bailey, who attributes Epicurus' rejection of logic to his predominant desire "to be the teacher of the 'plain man'" (*Greek Atomists*, 233).

tion of man as "this sort of form with soul in it [μετ' ἐμψυχίας]."[36] Epicurus is here revising Democritus' claim that man is what we all know to have a certain shape; and he does so in order to meet Aristotle's objection that since, according to Democritus, man is known by shape and color, a man could be a corpse.[37] However, in adding "with soul in it" to Democritus' explanation, Epicurus is not abandoning anything of Democritus' empiricism. Rather, he is making explicit what is implicit in Democritus' explanation by adding another observed feature, that of being animated. This additional component has nothing in common with Aristotle's claim that man is, in essence, soul. Both Democritus and Epicurus held that man is something that we all know directly by sensory experience.

The debate on the concept of man continued through the succeeding centuries. The standard definition of man came to be "rational, mortal living being."[38] In the first century B.C., the Epicurean Philodemus proposed that the presumption, or initial concept, of man is "rational living being" (ζῷον λογικόν), and that the property "mortal" is inferred by reference to this concept by an empirical investigation of human beings.[39] The explanation "rational living being" at first seems far removed from Epicurus' own explanation of man as a certain shape having soul. However, since in Epicurus' explanation "having soul" designates a certain kind of observed behavior, and this behavior is that of a rational being, Philodemus' explanation is close enough, given his polemical purposes, to that of Epicurus. As Philodemus sets out the presumption, it is clearly inadequate as a definition of man, since as a definition it would apply equally to men and to gods. It qualifies as a brief description, ὑπογραφή, of man, because the two components "rational" and "living being" immediately evoke a notion of man. By insisting that the property "mortal" is not part of

36. Sextus Empiricus *OP* 2.25 (τὸ τοιουτοῒ μόρφωμα μετὰ ἐμψυχίας) and *Adv. math.* 7.267, both at U 310.

37. Aristotle *De partibus animalium* 640b29–35. Similarly, Sextus Empiricus writes that, according to Democritus, "man is that which we all know" (*Adv. math.* 7.265). That Epicurus is responding to Aristotle's criticism has been suggested by Harold Cherniss, *Aristotle's Criticism of Presocratic Philosophy*, 259 n. 168.

38. See above, n. 14. Sextus Empiricus attacks this definition as augmented by the phrase "receptive of understanding [νοῦ] and knowledge" at *Adv. math.* 7.269–80 (cf. *OP* 2.211).

39. Philodemus *De signis* cols. 34.10–35.32 De Lacy (cf. cols. 16–17, 22–23). Philodemus calls the presumption a "proper [that is, unique] account" (λόγος ἴδιος) at col. 34.5–6; this expression was used to designate not only definitions in the strict sense but also outlines (Galen *Subfiguratio empirica* 7; p. 63.6 D).

our ordinary concept but is inferred by reference to the ordinary concept, Philodemus shows that the standard definition does not qualify as a starting point of scientific inquiry, but must itself be proved by reference to an ordinary concept.

# [ 3 ]

# Reference in an Inquiry

INITIAL concepts are required, Epicurus states in his first rule of investigation, to serve as standards to which we may refer what is believed (or "opined," δοξαζόμενον), or sought (ζητουμέ-νον), or perplexing (ἀπορούμενον), in order to make a judgment. Diogenes gives an example of how what is "sought" is referred to an initial concept: a thing appears in the distance, and the viewer seeks to know whether it is a horse or a cow. Along with the example, Diogenes points out that we could not seek what we seek unless we had already learned it. Here, what was previously learned is what a horse or a cow is; and the inquiry gets under way as soon as the viewer applies the previously learned concept of horse or cow to the present situation. Previously learned concepts thus serve to demarcate a problem by supplying a possible answer. Similarly, when we form any belief at all, as Diogenes illustrates by the belief "this is a man," we use a previously learned concept to serve as an answer to a problem.[1]

The use of initial concepts as standards of investigation was a prominent theme of Plato's epistemology long before Epicurus. The preceding chapter contained one example, Plato's demand in the *Phaedrus* that in any investigation the participants must refer to a single agreed concept throughout the investigation if the inquiry is to have coherence. As we saw, Epicurus proposed presumptions to satisfy the same need to demarcate a topic of investigation. Plato in addition developed the view that the concepts

1. For Epicurus' and Diogenes' texts, see chap. 1, notes 6 and 8.

with which an investigation begins already contain the answer to the problem under investigation. He presented this view in the *Meno*, in response to Meno's famous paradox: "How will you seek, Socrates, that of which you do not know at all what it is? For what sort of thing, of those that you do not know, will you propose as the object of your search? Or if you should ever so much hit upon it, how will you know that this is what you did not know?"[2] Socrates' answer is, in brief, that we have innate concepts that we aim to recollect throughout the investigation, so that we already have the answer at the very beginning of our inquiry even though we do not realize this. According to Plutarch, the Epicureans proposed presumptions as the solution to Meno's puzzle.[3]

How are we to understand Plutarch's claim? Diogenes' example of identifying an object at a distance illustrates one way in which the investigator may already, in a sense, know the answer to the problem under investigation. In this case, one has previously come to know the type of object that the particular object under investigation is subsequently observed to exemplify. But this is not the sort of problem that Plato has in mind in the *Meno*, nor does Diogenes' example show how presumptions function in a scientific inquiry as understood by Epicurus. According to Epicurus, a scientific inquiry concerns physical objects that cannot be observed. How can presumptions demarcate the problem and set out a possible answer in such an investigation?

First, it is important to note a basic difference between Plato's and Epicurus' views of the function of initial concepts in nonscientific, empirical investigations. In the *Phaedo* Plato argues that unless we have previously come to know the general types that perceptible instances approximate, we cannot perceive at all. For example, we must have acquired (εἰληφότας) a knowledge of what equality is before (πρό) we ever perceive equal things, in order to be able to refer (ἀνοίσειν) the things of perception to that standard.[4] The language used by Plato here is so close to that of Epicurus' first rule of investigation that it is very tempting to sup-

---

2. Plato *Meno* 80d: καὶ τίνα τρόπον ζητήσεις, ὦ Σώκρατες, τοῦτο ὃ μὴ οἶσθα τὸ παράπαν ὅτι ἐστίν; ποῖον γὰρ ὧν οὐκ οἶσθα προθέμενος ζητήσεις; ἢ εἰ καὶ ὅτι μάλιστα ἐντύχοις αὐτῷ, πῶς εἴσῃ ὅτι τοῦτό ἐστιν ὃ σὺ οὐκ ᾔδησθα;
3. Plutarch *apud Olympiodorum in Platonis Phaedonem*, p. 125.10 Finckh (partly at U 255; the missing context is at *SVF* 2.104). Plutarch adds to this the standard objection that if the presumptions are already precisely articulated (διηρθρωμένας), the investigation is superfluous, and if they are not, we do not already have a concept of what is sought.
4. Plato *Phaedo* 75b, and in general 74e–75e.

pose that Epicurus' coinage of the word πρόληψις was inspired
by Plato. But whatever Epicurus' debt to Plato's terminology, it
clearly does not extend to Plato's theory. Plato demands concepts
as a precondition of sense perception, and thus concludes that
we had concepts even before birth. Epicurus rejects the view that
presumptions are a precondition of sense perception, and holds
instead that they are derived from sense perception. Although
Epicurus does not say this in his first rule of investigation, he provides a clue to his position by omitting sense perception from his
list of things that need to be referred to initial concepts. Nor
is sense perception included by any other authors among the
functions of Epicurean presumptions: apart from opinion, search,
and perplexity, presumptions are said to be necessary for refutation, debate, naming, and understanding.[5] Diogenes' example of a
search, it should be noted, is not an illustration of how we come
to perceive. Rather, it illustrates how we add an opinion to what
we are already perceiving. Plato uses the same type of example
in the *Theaetetus* to illustrate the function of empirically acquired
concepts.[6]

Although Epicurean presumptions are not a prerequisite of
sense perception, they are a prerequisite for forming expectations about what may be perceived. Epicurus calls such objects of
expectation προσμένοντα, literally, things that are "waiting" or
"expected" to be perceived; and he contrasts them with ἄδηλα,
things that are "nonapparent" or imperceptible.[7] The latter are
the subject of scientific inquiry, φυσιολογία. In the case of προσμένοντα, there is an expectation that is not based on scientific
argument, and confirmation consists in a subsequent, present perception. As Diogenes illustrates, the expectation may be that a
perceived distant object will turn out to be of a certain sort. But,
as other examples show, the expectation need not consist in an
attempt to identify an object; it may be any kind of conjectural
anticipation of a future perceptible state of affairs, and it may
involve not only a mental operation but also the production of
what is anticipated.

Epicurus provides one example of how presumptions are used
to form expectations that have nothing to do with the identification of a distant object. In *Authoritative Opinions* 37 and 38 he

5. U 255 (including DL 10.33 on naming).
6. Plato *Theaetetus* 193c. Plato's example is that of mistakenly assigning the
distantly viewed Theaetetus and Theodorus each to the other's mental image,
which was acquired previously by sense perception.
7. *Her.* 38; see chap. 10 for a detailed discussion of these two categories.

explains that a law is just if it turns out to be advantageous for the community, and is not just if it turns out not to "fit the presumption" of justice; the presumption is the notion that what is just is communally advantageous. The lawgiver, we may suppose, initially frames a law by reference to the presumption of justice in the expectation that the law will be just; but whether the law really is just depends on whether events subsequently show that the law matches the presumption. The search, in this case, is for a particular occurrence of justice; and what makes the search possible is that there is a concept of justice to begin with.

Lucretius hypothesizes a very similar search when he argues that language could not have been imposed by a namegiver, since such a namegiver would have required a concept of language, and this could not have been acquired except from the actual use of language.[8] Lucretius uses the same type of argument to show that the world could not have been divinely created. God would have required a concept of the world to begin with, he points out, and this could not have been provided except by the created world itself.[9] Lucretius is here opposing Plato's claim, as stated in the *Timaeus*, that god created the world by looking to an unchanging model. He agrees with Plato that purposeful activity requires previous acquaintance with a model, but denies that this can be acquired except empirically.

In sum, a nonscientific inquiry or quest—one that concerns προσμένοντα—begins with a general notion of a particular event that is expected to occur and is successfully concluded when the particular event that was expected turns out in actuality to match the general concept. As both Diogenes Laertius and Lucretius indicate, moreover, the initial general concept has been empirically acquired. A scientific investigation, by contrast, clearly cannot be concluded by matching the initial concept with a presently observed state of affairs. Does scientific investigation, then, begin nonetheless with empirical concepts? Or do we somehow already have scientific concepts, for example of atoms, or of the void in which the atoms move, prior to the investigation? None of our sources gives any hint of such prior scientific concepts. What place is there, then, for initial concepts in scientific inquiry? Modern scholars have offered some very tentative answers to this question. Cyril Bailey suggests very briefly that presumptions have a role "in those combinations of ideas which constitute abstract thought";

8. Lucretius 5.1046–49.
9. Lucretius 5.181–86.

and David Furley also notes briefly that since the propositions of
science cannot be tested directly against perceptions, they must
be tested against presumptions.[10] At the same time, scholars have
tended to reduce the role of presumptions in scientific investigations by arguing either that because presumptions are derived
from perceptions, they do not properly constitute a distinct standard of investigation; or that presumptions and perceptions form
two mutually exclusive standards of investigation.[11]

Against the attempt to diminish the role of initial concepts in
an investigation, it may be pointed out that both Epicurus and
Diogenes Laertius state plainly that initial concepts, corresponding
to our words, are required for *every* investigation. Let us, then,
take a problem from Epicurean science and try to determine how
initial concepts function as a means of judging the problem. To
simplify a little, early in his sequence of arguments about the physical world, Epicurus attempts to answer the problem "Is there void
[κενόν]?" To solve this problem, it seems that we need a concept
corresponding to the utterance "void" ("empty"), as well as a concept corresponding to the utterance "there is." These concepts,
I suggest, have been empirically acquired and are refined into
scientific concepts in the course of the investigation. We come
to the investigation with the ordinary concept of "empty" as something incorporeal, and by reference to this concept we develop
the scientific concept of subperceptible empty spaces. Similarly,
we start with the ordinary concept of "being" as something that
applies to bodies, and we end with the scientific concept of being as something that applies also to subperceptible empty spaces.
The investigation begins as soon as we extend the empirically
acquired concepts to situations to which they can no longer be
observed to apply; and the investigation ends when the initial

10. For Bailey's suggestion, see *Greek Atomists*, 248; for Furley's suggestion, see
*Two Studies in the Greek Atomists*, 209 n. 6. Furley is followed by Rist, *Epicurus*,
29–30. Furley also suggests that since presumptions are "derivatives of sense perception," it is probable that "the elevation of πρόληψις to the position of a third
criterion along with sensation and feeling is the work of doxographers" (206).

11. Among those who argue for the first alternative are Tohte (*Kriterien*, 2),
Bailey (*Greek Atomists*, 238), Furley (see preceding note), and Rist (*Epicurus*, 28–29).
Among proponents of the second position, Norman Wentworth DeWitt holds that
προλήψεις form a criterion that is entirely independent of sense perception; his
reason is that presumptions are innate, and that they are restricted to such concepts as those of justice and the gods (*Epicurus and His Philosophy*, 142–50). The
other main representative of the second interpretation is Striker, who, though
admitting that presumptions are based on perceptions, maintains that they are not
reducible to them (Κριτήριον, 59–61, esp. 59 n. 3). Striker offers a detailed analysis
of the use of presumptions, as distinct from perceptions, as standards of investigation (80–82).

concepts have been shown to apply, or not to apply, at this imperceptible level.

Even though neither Diogenes Laertius nor any other ancient source gives an explanation of how initial concepts are used in a scientific investigation, Lucretius' poem contains two very helpful examples, which have been overlooked in the past. First, as part of a discussion showing that the atoms move continuously with frequent collisions among themselves, Lucretius asks the reader to contemplate, as an "image and picture" (*simulacrum et imago*) of atomic movement, the swirling of dust particles in a beam of sunlight, "in order that you may gather from this what it is like for the atoms to be always tossing in the great void, so long as a small thing can provide a model [*exemplare*] of great things and the traces of a concept [*vestigia notitiai*]."[12] The "small thing" described by Lucretius is the observed movement of dust particles; and this provides, according to Lucretius, the "traces," or outline, of a concept of continuous, colliding motion. Ordinary experience, then, furnishes a concept that is subsequently transformed into the scientific concept of atoms moving continuously, with frequent collisions, in the void. Although Lucretius is here concerned to teach an already discovered scientific concept to the student, the investigator is initially in the same position as the student: both must have an empirical concept to begin with in order to recognize the problem and learn the answer.

Immediately after showing that the observation of dust particles in the sunlight furnishes a concept of continuous, colliding motion, Lucretius cites the same observation of dust particles as proof that there is a continuous, colliding motion of atoms. He writes: "For this reason, too, it is the more appropriate for you to pay attention to these bodies which are seen to jostle in the sun's rays: for such disturbances signify that there are hidden and invisible bodily motions below."[13] Lucretius goes on to explain that many of the dust particles change direction as a result of invisible collisions; and he

12. Lucretius 2.112–24 (including at 112 *simulacrum et imago*). Lines 121–24 are:

conicere ut possis ex hoc, primordia rerum
quale sit in magno iactari semper inani.
dumtaxat rerum magnarum parva potest res
exemplare dare et vestigia notitiai.

13. Lucretius 2.125–28:

hoc etiam magis haec animum te advertere par est
corpora quae in solis radiis turbare videntur,
quod tales turbae motus quoque materiai
significant clandestinos caecosque subesse.

argues that these collisions are due ultimately to the movements of individual atoms. This section of proof is clearly distinguished from the preceding explanation of the concept. As it happens, the same observations that furnish the initial concept also furnish proof that the initial concept applies to unobserved bodies; however, the acquisition of the concept is entirely distinct both in time and in method from the construction of the proof.

In dividing his discussion into an explanation of the concept and a subsequent section of proof, Lucretius follows the order of Epicurus' two rules of investigation, as laid down in the *Letter to Herodotus*. Epicurus requires, first, that we have concepts by which to judge a problem, and second, that we have observations to serve as evidence of what is unobserved. Lucretius' distinction also conforms to the standard philosophical procedure, exemplified earlier in our discussion of the concept of the supreme good, of first setting out a concept and then showing in full what there is in reality that corresponds to the concept.

Lucretius' other example of a concept used in scientific investigation is the concept of colorless bodies. Lucretius proceeds in the same order as in his discussion of atomic motion: he first sets out the concept of colorless bodies, then goes on to prove that the atoms are colorless. In this discussion, however, Lucretius has a special purpose in setting out the concept. This is to answer the objection that "colorless body" is something inconceivable. Lucretius argues as follows:

> If by chance you think that the mind cannot conceive of these bodies [that is, colorless matter], you are far wrong. For since the blind, who have never seen the light of the sun, nonetheless know by the sense of touch, from the beginning of their lives, bodies accompanied by no color, you may know that bodies not tinted by any color may be turned into a concept in our minds too. Moreover, what we ourselves touch in the blind darkness is perceived by us without being stained by any color.[14]

14. Lucretius 2.739–47:
  in quae corpora si nullus tibi forte videtur
  posse animi iniectus fieri, procul avius erras.
  nam cum caecigeni, solis qui lumina numquam
  dispexere, tamen cognoscant corpora tactu
  ex ineunte aevo nullo coniuncta colore,
  scire licet nostrae quoque menti corpora posse
  verti in notitiam nullo circumlita fuco.
  denique nos ipsi caecis quaecumque tenebris
  tangimus, haud ullo sentimus tincta colore.

Lucretius' contemporary Philodemus shows the general polemical context of this argument in his treatise *On Significations*. Among other objections to the Epicurean method of inference, Philodemus cites the following: since all bodies in our experience are colored, and since, according to the Epicureans, all scientific theories are inductive inferences, the Epicureans must admit that colorless bodies are inconceivable. Philodemus answers this objection by noting, like Lucretius, that the sense of touch presents to the observer bodies that have no color.[15] Lucretius himself appears to be addressing a version of this criticism that is typical of the Pyrrhonist Skeptics. As illustrated by Sextus Empiricus, one strategy used by these philosophers to throw doubt on the existence of a thing is to show that it cannot even be conceived of.[16] Lucretius counters this type of strategy by showing that there can be a concept of colorless bodies; he is then ready to adduce a series of proofs showing that there are colorless bodies. In setting out the concept of colorless bodies, he shows incidentally how ordinary concepts are used in scientific investigation to yield scientific concepts. The sense of touch provides the investigator with a concept of colorless bodies, and the investigator then tests whether this concept applies also to bodies that cannot be perceived at all.

Nonscientific and scientific inquiry are similar, therefore, in that both begin with the proposed extension of an empirically acquired concept to a situation to which it does not self-evidently belong, and both continue with the attempt to verify or falsify this extension. The basic difference between the two types of inquiry consists in the manner of verification or falsification. In the nonscientific type of inquiry an answer is verified or falsified directly by observation; in a scientific investigation an answer is verified or falsified by means of an argument that relates what is observed to what is unobserved. Consequently, whereas a nonscientific investigation may be carried through by reference to a single concept, a scientific investigation depends on a series of concepts connected by argument. To return to our previous example, one way in which Epicurus attempted to solve the problem "Is there void?" was to argue that if there were no void, bodies would not move as they are seen to move. The investigation therefore

---

*Animi iniectus* (l. 740) is literally "an application [ἐπιβολή] of the mind"; see chap. 2, n. 3.

15. Philodemus *De signis* cols. 5.1–4 and 18.3–10 De Lacy.

16. See Sextus Empiricus' discussion of man at *Adv. math.* 7.263–82, and his discussion of body at *Adv. math.* 9.366–440.

56    *Initial Concepts*

involves at least the concepts of being, void, motion, and bodies.
All these concepts were empirically acquired. It may also happen
that the solution to a particular problem rests on previously developed scientific concepts; since scientific concepts rest ultimately
on empirical concepts, however, all scientific investigation begins
with empirical concepts.[17]

To what extent, then, do empirical concepts already contain the
answers sought by the scientist? An answer to this question demands a detailed examination of Epicurus' theory of verification
and falsification; and this examination belongs to a discussion of
Epirucus' second rule of investigation. One important aspect of
the use of presumptions, however, can be explored further now.
Epicurus' account of the history of mankind provides a remarkable illustration of how previously learned concepts have been
used through the ages to make one discovery after another. As
Lucretius shows in lavish detail, the method by which humankind
raised itself from its beastlike beginnings to the present high stage
of technological and scientific advancement was that of extending
previously acquired, empirical concepts to ever-new situations and
thereby making ever-new discoveries. A brief look at this progress shows how, according to Epicurus and his followers, empirically acquired concepts guided the development of one skill after
another, until finally they resulted in the most important skill of
all, the scientific exploration of nature.

In the *Letter to Herodotus* Epicurus offers a general analysis of
human progress as an introduction to his analysis of linguistic
development. According to Epicurus, discoveries occur in two successive stages: a stage of nature (φύσις), and a stage of calculation
(λογισμός). In the first stage, human nature "is taught and compelled by things themselves"; in the second, "calculation gives precision and adds discoveries to what is handed on by it [that is, by
nature]."[18] Epicurus then illustrates this sequence by describing the

17. Jürss has a very different interpretation of the development of scientific concepts. Using, among other examples, the Epicurean theory of the void, Jürss proposes that the scientific concept of "empty" is itself a presumption (πρόληψις), and
that it is not acquired by reference to any nontechnical presumption of "empty,"
but by reference to the presumption of movement ("Prolepse," 218–19). Although
I agree that the concept of movement is used to develop the scientific concept of
"empty," it is still necessary to have a nonscientific concept of "empty" to begin
with. In addition, although scientific concepts may themselves be used to formulate
further scientific problems, the term "presumption" is restricted to nonscientific,
empirical concepts, as Diogenes Laertius' summary shows.

18. *Her.* 75: ἀλλὰ μὴν ὑποληπτέον καὶ τὴν φύσιν πολλὰ καὶ παντοῖα ὑπὸ αὐτῶν
τῶν πραγμάτων διδαχθῆναί τε καὶ ἀναγκασθῆναι. τὸν δὲ λογισμὸν τὰ ὑπὸ ταύτης

two stages of linguistic development. At first, Epicurus claims, humans uttered words in response to their feelings and images, and these utterances varied with the location of each tribe. Later, words were imposed in common over the entire community in an effort to reduce ambiguity and to make the expressions more concise, and new words were added as a result of new discoveries.

In the first stage of development, then, humans respond directly to the environment without any critical reflection upon their responses; in the second they use calculation to take control of their responses to the environment. Because the second stage results in the imposition of policies on others, it may also be called a stage of νόμος, "convention"; accordingly, the two stages exemplify the traditional contrast between φύσις, "nature," and νόμος, "convention." An important feature of Epicurus' analysis is the claim that calculation takes over what has previously been fashioned by nature. Progress, then, begins with natural compulsion. Although Epicurus does not mention the formation of concepts specifically, his analysis implies that concepts are formed initially by natural compulsion and are subsequently refined through calculation.[19]

In his comprehensive, step-by-step account of human progress, Lucretius supplies numerous examples of the natural formation of concepts, and he indicates, moreover, that the natural stage of concept formation encompasses considerable experimentation. Concerning agriculture, Lucretius points out that "nature itself, the creator of things, was first the model of sowing and the origin of grafting."[20] Lucretius here uses "nature" to refer to the environment rather than to human nature, contrary to Epicurus' usage; but the point is the same. Agriculture, Lucretius indicates, began

παρεγγυηθέντα ὕστερον ἐπακριβοῦν καὶ προσεξευρίσκειν. . . . (The text is corrupt at the end of the sentence.)

19. At *Laws* 10, 889a, Plato summarizes one view of how nature precedes convention: ". . . the greatest and most beautiful things are accomplished by nature and chance, and the smaller things by art, which by taking from nature the creation of these great first products fashions and builds all the smaller products, which we all call 'technical'" (τὰ μὲν μέγιστα αὐτῶν καὶ κάλλιστα ἀπεργάζεσθαι φύσιν καὶ τύχην, τὰ δὲ σμικρότερα τέχνην, ἣν δὴ παρὰ φύσεως λαμβάνουσαν τὴν τῶν μεγάλων καὶ πρώτων γένεσιν ἔργων, πλάττειν καὶ τεκταίνεσθαι πάντα τὰ σμικρότερα, ἃ δὴ τεχνικὰ πάντες προσαγορεύομεν). This description (along with the following detailed analysis) looks very much like a critical interpretation of atomist cosmology; and Epicurus' view of human development fits well into this general framework of explanation, although it is doubtful whether he would call the products of nature greater than the products of calculation.

20. Lucretius 5.1361–62: at specimen sationis et insitionis origo / ipsa fuit rerum primum natura creatrix.

with the observation of spontaneous natural growths, resulting in the concepts of sowing and grafting; these concepts, which were imposed on human nature by the environment, were then used by humans to guide the discovery of cultivation. Cooking provides another good example of natural concept formation. As Lucretius points out, the sun "taught" humans how to cook, when they observed the softening effect of solar heat on the fruits of the field.[21] Likewise, metalcraft began with the observation of naturally shaped lumps of metal.[22] Music, in turn, began with the observation of birds singing, which encouraged humans to sing, and with the observation of winds whistling through the reeds, which led first to the practice of breathing through hemlock stalks and then to playing on pipes.[23] In all these cases, the environment may be said to have "taught and compelled" humans by implanting concepts that were then extended by humans to new situations; and this extension was the beginning of each craft. Each craft, moreover, advances through new applications of concepts. Lucretius illustrates this progression particularly clearly with reference to warfare: cavalry fighting gave way to fighting from two-horse chariots, and this strategy was succeeded by the use of four-horse chariots and scythed chariots, which was succeeded in turn by the use of elephants, bulls, lions, and other animals as combatants.[24] In this prolific succession of military strategies, each new discovery grew out of a previous one by the application of empirically formed concepts. As in all other crafts, the adaptation of a concept to a new situation results in new observations, which may then inspire further experimentation.

In detailing the history of each craft, Lucretius does not draw any explicit distinction between a natural and a calculative stage of development. He alludes to it, however, in his general summary of the development of the crafts:

> Shipbuilding, agriculture, walls, laws, arms, roads, clothes, and other things of this kind, as well as absolutely all the rewards and pleasures of life, songs, pictures, and the polishing of elaborate statues, were taught little by little, to persons progressing step by step, by practice [*usus*] together with the trials [*experientia*] made by a lively mind. Thus time brings forth each thing little by little and

21. Lucretius 5.1102–04.
22. Lucretius 5.1257–68.
23. Lucretius 5.1379–87.
24. Lucretius 5.1297–1340.

reason [*ratio*] raises it into the shores of light. For they saw in their mind one thing become clear after another, until they came to the uppermost summit of the arts.[25]

The terms "practice" or "habit" (*usus*, Greek τριβή) and "trial" or "experience" (*experientia*, Greek πεῖρα or ἐμπειρία) were regularly used to denote the stage of inquiry that precedes the technical elaboration of a skill by the use of argument or reason (*ratio*, λόγος). Lucretius appears to apply this standard distinction to Epicurus' own contrast between a stage of nature and a stage of calculation: thus, we may suppose, there is a gradual evolution of a skill through a natural stage of development, as concepts that are "taught" by the environment keep on being tried out; subsequently the discoveries that have been made in this way by continual experimentation and practice are refined technically by the use of reason.[26]

Apart from Epicurus' discussion of linguistic progress, the extant Epicurean accounts of the development of political life provide some evidence of a division into a natural and a calculative stage. Lucretius traces the beginning of social organization to the notion that "it is fair for all to pity the weak."[27] This rudimentary concept of justice led to covenants among neighbors; subsequently kingships were established, to be succeeded by mob rule and fierce competition for power, until rampant violence led to the development of laws. Although Lucretius does not identify any particular stage in this progress as a stage of calculation, the Epicurean

---

25. Lucretius 5.1448–57:

> navigia atque agri culturas moenia leges
> arma vias vestis ⟨et⟩ cetera de genere horum
> praemia, delicias quoque vitae funditus omnis,
> carmina picturas, et daedala signa polire,
> usus et impigrae simul experientia mentis
> paulatim docuit pedetemptim progredientis.
> sic unumquicquid paulatim protrahit aetas
> in medium ratioque in luminis erigit oras.
> namque alid ex alio clarescere corde videbant,
> artibus ad summum donec venere cacumen.

26. Τριβή and ἐμπειρία are the hallmarks of an empirical, nonrational skill in Plato (see especially *Gorgias* 463b). The distinction between a pretechnical and a technical stage of medicine is already prominent in the Hippocratic treatise *On Ancient Medicine* 3–5. The general distinction between a pretechnical and a technical stage is commonplace in Hellenistic accounts; see especially Maximus Tyrius, a second-century Platonist, *Philosophumena* 6.2, 39a (pp. 66–67 Hobein) on the development of shipbuilding, medicine, and other crafts.

27. Lucretius 5.1023: imbecillorum esse aequum misererier omnis.

Hermarchus indicates that this stage begins with the establishment of laws. According to Porphyry's report of Hermarchus' social theory, Hermarchus held that humans at first perceived in a forgetful and uncalculating way what was useful, and so for the most part refrained from killing one another; they did not have any laws imposed upon them at this stage. Subsequently, certain individuals made a "calculation" (ἐπιλογισμός) of what was useful and prevailed upon others to do the same, and tried to restrain the rest from killing one another by imposing penalties fixed by law.[28] The general Epicurean view of political development, it appears from these two analyses, was that humans tried out a succession of social organizations as a direct response to their environment, until reflection upon what they were doing caused them to impose laws for their greater advantage.

Like all the other skills, the science of physics evolved from concepts taught directly by the environment. Lucretius depicts the beginnings of physical science as follows: "The sun and moon, watchfully revolving with their light about the great turning expanse of the world, taught humans that the seasons rotate and that events occur with a definite explanation and order."[29] Humans were taught by the movements of the sun and moon that there is regularity in nature. This general concept of regularity may be regarded as the initial concept of all scientific inquiry. To adapt Epicurus' words, nature furnishes a concept of regularity, then calculation takes over this concept in order to discover the underlying causes of observed regularities. In physical inquiry too, therefore, a pretechnical, natural stage of concept formation is succeeded by a technical stage in which ordinary concepts are refined and augmented.

28. Porphyry *De abstinentia* 1.7–11 (fr. 24 Krohn).
29. Lucretius 5.1436–39:

> at vigiles mundi magnum versatile templum
> sol et luna suo lustrantes lumine circum
> perdocuere homines annorum tempora verti
> et certa ratione geri rem atque ordine certo.

Lucretius recognizes the science of physics as a recent discovery (5.335–37). We may suppose that he credited Epicurus with perfecting this branch of knowledge; at 5.1–21 he argues that Epicurus' discoveries are immeasurably superior to the mythical discovery of wheat by Ceres and of wine by Liber, on the ground that Epicurus' discoveries are essential to a good life, whereas the others' are not.

# [ 4 ]

# Formation of Initial Concepts

THE preceding chapters have indicated that the initial concepts of scientific investigation are empirically formed. As has been noted, this claim is no part of Epicurus' own first rule of investigation. Epicurus' statement of this rule contains nothing that a philosopher who proposes to rely wholly on a priori concepts might not accept. Epicurus demands that we have self-evident concepts prior to an investigation to use as standards for the investigation; and to this both empiricist and rationalist philosophers might assent. Not until his second rule of investigation does Epicurus announce what differentiates his method of investigation from that of other philosophers, by demanding that the initial concepts of investigation be given by perception.

This chapter offers a preliminary examination of the origin of initial concepts by turning from Epicurus' procedural note to Diogenes Laertius' explanation of presumptions. I quote again the part of Diogenes' explanation that deals with the formation of presumptions; the Epicureans, he reports, held that πρόληψις is

> something like apprehension [κατάληψιν] or right opinion [δόξαν ὀρθὴν) or a concept [ἔννοιαν] or a stored universal thought [καθολικὴν νόησιν ἐναποκειμένην], that is, a memory of that which has often appeared from outside, for example, that man is this sort of thing. For at the same time that "man" is spoken . . . the outline [τύπος] of man also is thought of, as a result of preceding perceptions [προηγουμένων τῶν αἰσθήσεων].[1]

1. See chap. 1, n. 8 for the Greek text.

Diogenes' list of alternative explanations reflects an attempt by Epicurus' followers to explain Epicurean πρόληψις by using concepts that were current in other philosophical schools. In keeping with the trend toward a standard conceptual framework, the Epicureans point out various correspondences between their notion of presumption and notions used by other philosophers. At the same time, the Epicureans show the distinctiveness of their position by pointing out that presumptions are memories of appearances obtained from outside.

Diogenes' first term, "apprehension," κατάληψις, is a Stoic term signifying an "assent to an apprehensive presentation"; an "apprehensive" presentation is a presentation that necessarily displays its cause exactly as it is, or, to put it loosely, is a presentation that cannot be false.[2] Although κατάληψις is not a technical term of Epicurean epistemology, it came to be adopted as a standard term by all the philosophical schools.[3] We have already noted its use to describe the presumption of demonstration.[4] As an explanation of presumption, the term indicates that what one conceives of is necessarily real.

The next expression used by Diogenes, "right opinion," δόξα ὀρθή, has also been touched upon previously.[5] As the term κατάληψις relates Epicurean presumption to Stoic epistemology, so this term relates Epicurean presumption first to Platonic epistemology, and secondarily also to Stoic epistemology. It is not clear whether Epicurus himself described a presumption as an opinion.[6] If so, he must have held (as the Epicureans later held) that not every opinion needs to be verified by reference to some prior concept; for presumptions are self-evidently true. What makes the description of a presumption as a right opinion appropriate in the general context of Greek philosophy is that a presumption is a belief that

2. See *SVF* 2.91, 97; and 2.65, 1.59.
3. There are numerous examples of the Epicureans' use of καταλαμβάνειν and κατάληψις. A prominent use of the terms is made in the anonymous treatise dealing with perception (PHerc. 19/698 Scott); by stating that what is perceived is "apprehended," the author states the distinctively Epicurean view that whatever is perceived is real. Epicurus himself uses καταλαμβάνειν repeatedly to signify a cognitive grasp (*Her.* 78; *Pyth.* 88, 89; *Men.* 125); but these uses appear to be instances of the nontechnical usage that is the source of Stoic usage, rather than being indebted to Stoic usage.
4. Sextus Empiricus *Adv. math.* 8.334a; see chap. 1 (Utterance and Concept).
5. See chap. 2 (Demonstration).
6. Epicurus' use of δοξαζόμενον in his statement of his first rule tells somewhat against this possibility. Also, in *KD* 24 Epicurus speaks of "opinionative concepts," δοξαστικαὶ ἔννοιαι, as still requiring confirmation.

is verified by empirical observation and is not an insight into some general truth that transcends the evidence of perception.

Next, ἔννοια, "concept," is glossed by the phrase "stored universal thought," καθολικὴ νόησις ἐναποκειμένη. A "concept," ἔννοια, is a thought that is stored, or established, "in" the mind; and for the same reason that it is stored, it is also "universal" (or "general").[7] "Universal," καθολική, as used here, implies the gathering of a number of impressions into an overall view. As the subsequent description of the concept as "a memory of that which has often appeared from outside" shows, the term καθολική does not imply an Aristotelian type of essence, or indeed any type of universal entity that is not an accumulation of individual perceptual impressions. The concept may therefore be of a single individual, such as Socrates, or of a type of being exemplified by a number of individuals, such as mankind. The expression "stored" implies that the thought is a fixed element in a pattern of thinking; it does not imply that the thought is always present to the mind, as though cooped up in it. According to Epicurus, what makes concepts "stored" is the ability of the mind to select images at will from an ever-changing stream of images.[8] The feminine ending of the terms ἔννοια and νόησις, as of πρόληψις, appears to connote a mental attitude or act, as distinct from an effect produced in the mind; the latter seems to be rendered by the neuter ἐννόημα (the form used by Epicurus in his procedural note). However, since the attitude and the effect are coextensive, this distinction is unimportant, and indeed often seems to be ignored by the Epicureans.

Diogenes' list of explanations culminates in the description of a presumption as "a memory of that which has often appeared from outside." This explanation has rightly been a focus of scholarly attention in the past. Clearly it marks Epicurus as an empiricist, and this has provoked much controversy about whether Diogenes'

7. The explanation of ἔννοια as something "stored" (ἐναποκειμένη) appears to be Stoic. It is found in Plutarch's *De sollertia animalium* 961c–d (νοήσεις ἃς ἐναποκειμένας μὲν ἐννοίας καλοῦσι, κινουμένας δὲ διανοήσεις, "thoughts that they [the Stoics] call 'concepts' when stored, and 'discursive thoughts' when moving") and in *De communibus notitiis* 1085a (as emended by Pohlenz; see *Moralia*, trans. Cherniss, 863 n. e). Galen divides memories of perceptible objects into "thought," νόησις, which is in motion, and "concepts," ἔννοιαι, which "are at rest" (ἡσυχάζουσαι τύχωσιν); but he adds that the Greeks often call a "concept" a "thought" (*Institutio logica* 3.2).

8. See below, chap. 7; Carlo Diano points this out in "La psicologia d'Epicuro e la teoria delle passioni," pt. 1, 138–39.

report is accurate. The description also marks Epicurus as a special
kind of empiricist; and this needs to be emphasized more than
it has been. The explanation of the concept as a memory of appearances implies that there is no universal entity distinct from
the many particulars that have appeared. The general features
that one thinks of by presumption are features that have appeared
the same from one observed instance to another. Epicurus therefore opposed not only Plato's theory of Forms, but also Aristotle's
and the Stoics' view of concept formation. Aristotle and the Stoics
held the same general position: that "experience," ἐμπειρία, consisting in an accumulation of memories, precedes the formation of
concepts as a separate stage of development, and that the transition from the one to the other is a transition from an unscientific
awareness of particulars to the recognition of necessary universal
truths; the latter, they held, forms the beginning of scientific inquiry.[9] Epicurus, in contrast, held that the initial assumptions of
scientific inquiry are given directly by experience. Accordingly,
Epicurus recognized only a single stage of cognition, where Aristotle and the Stoics recognized two stages.

Epicurus' empirical view of concept formation is in partial agreement with the position of the Empiricist physicians, whose school
dates from the third century B.C. The Empiricists held that experience (ἐμπειρία) furnishes the theorems of medical science, and
that these theorems are "a memory of that which has often been
seen in the same way."[10] Epicurus and the Empiricists are agreed
that the conceptual foundation of science consists in empirical observation; but there is this important difference, that the Empiricists admitted no scientific truths apart from memories, whereas
Epicurus viewed memories as a starting point toward discovering
what is unobserved. The Empiricist position has a close affinity
with the empiricism that Plato attacks so vigorously in the *Gorgias*.
Against the claim that experience "makes a science [τέχνην]," Plato
argues that an endeavor that "preserves only a memory of what is
accustomed to occur" and does not investigate the "nature and

9. For Aristotle, see *Posterior Analytics* 100a3–9 and *Metaphysics* 980b25–982a3;
for the Stoics, see *SVF* 2.83. In the Stoic text, ἐμπειρία is defined as a "multitude
of presentations of like kind"; it is therefore to be distinguished from "concept,"
ἔννοια, which must be taken as a single entity (*contra* Manuwald, *Prolepsislehre*, 9–
10).
10. Galen *De sectis ad eos qui introducuntur* 2 (Mueller, 3:3.8–17; p. 95.12–18 D).
Cf. Galen 18 B p. 645 Kühn ( = fr. 92, pp. 144–45 D.) See further chap. 5
(Observation) and chap. 10 (Other Hellenistic Theories of Signs).

cause" cannot be scientific.[11] Epicurus takes the position that the nature and causes of appearances can be discovered only by reliance on concepts that are memories of appearances.

Cyril Bailey has likened the Epicurean process of concept formation to the production of a "composite photograph."[12] This much-cited comparison is appropriate so long as we do not take it to mean that individual traits lose their individual distinctiveness as they merge into a single general presentation. Rather, we must suppose that there are similarities that remain the same from one individual appearance to another, and that in forming a general concept one focuses on these similarities while disregarding the dissimilarities.

What "has often appeared from outside" includes not only things that appear to the five senses but also things that appear directly to the mind. As we shall see in detail later, Epicurus proposed a unique theory of mind, according to which the mind engages in acts of perception just like those of the five senses. Whenever the mind has a thought, an appearance has been produced by particles that have entered the mind from outside. Accordingly, presumptions include memories of objects that have appeared directly to the mind without ever appearing to the senses, among them gods and such imaginary creatures as centaurs.

Diogenes follows up his description of a presumption as a memory by calling it an "outline," τύπος, formed as a result of "preceding perceptions." The term τύπος was also used by Epicurus to designate the arrangement of atoms that enter the eyes to produce a visual presentation; and it seems to have been used generally by philosophers to signify an impression produced in a person's awareness from outside.[13] The addition of the phrase "preceding perceptions" makes it clear that the τύπος is not only a general outline, but also an impression obtained in response to external influences. The phrase is a very abbreviated way of making the general claim, as put by the Epicurean Torquatus in Cicero's *On Ends*, that "whatever we discern by the mind arises, all of it, from the perceptions [or "senses," *sensibus*]."[14] Diogenes elaborates this claim in his summary of Epicurus' canonic under

11. Plato *Gorgias* 462c (cf. 448c) and 501a (cf. 463a–b).
12. Bailey, *Greek Atomists*, 245.
13. See *Her.* 49 and *SVF* 2.58–59.
14. Cicero *De finibus* 1.64: quidquid porro animo cernimus, id omne oritur a sensibus.

the heading of perceptions by stating that "all thoughts come to be from the perceptions by incidence [περίπτωσιν], analogy, similarity, and combination, with some contribution by calculation."[15]

Neither the general claim about the perceptions nor the fourfold division of thoughts was unique to the Epicureans; indeed, the Epicureans seem to have borrowed their analysis from other philosophers. Sextus Empiricus presents the claim that "incidence through sense perception [τὴν διὰ τῆς αἰσθήσεως περίπτωσιν] must precede [προηγεῖσθαι] every thought" as a common philosophical belief; and he explains the belief by the same fourfold division of thoughts as Diogenes. Unlike Diogenes, Sextus supplements his classification with examples: as the result of a direct sensory contact (or "incidence"), we think of black, white, and so on; by analogy with perceptible objects, we think of a Cyclops (by mentally increasing the ordinary human being) or a pygmy (by a corresponding decrease); by similarity with perceptible objects, we think of the absent Socrates (as a result of seeing a likeness of him); and by a combination of perceptible objects, we think of a centaur (by mentally combining a horse and a man).[16] We have no explicit information about how the Epicureans related the fourfold division of thoughts to presumptions. But since they held that presumptions are memories of appearances that have occurred not only to the five senses but also to the mind, and since appearances of the latter kind admit of all three stated relationships to sense perception, it seems that the Epicureans held that presumptions are formed in all four ways. In adapting the common scheme to their own epistemology, however, they maintained the distinctive view that all four types of presumption are formed by a direct contact with the external world: although not all are memories of appearances obtained by the senses, all are memories of appearances presented directly from outside.

In addition to Diogenes' explanation of the formation of presumptions, Cicero's *On the Nature of the Gods* contains two highly controversial passages dealing in particular with the formation of the presumption of god. The first of these texts presents an argument based on the claim that the concept of god is formed by

15. DL 10.32: καὶ γὰρ καὶ ἐπίνοιαι πᾶσαι ἀπὸ τῶν αἰσθήσεων γεγόνασι κατά τε περίπτωσιν καὶ ἀναλογίαν καὶ ὁμοιότητα καὶ σύνθεσιν, συμβαλλομένου τι καὶ τοῦ λογισμοῦ.

16. Sextus Empiricus *Adv. math.* 8.58–60 and 9.393–95; at 8.60 Sextus asserts: πάσης οὖν ἐπινοίας προηγεῖσθαι δεῖ τὴν διὰ τῆς αἰσθήσεως περίπτωσιν. Diogenes attributes the four types of thought, with additions, to the Stoics at 7.52 (*SVF* 2.87).

nature. In the words of the Epicurean spokesman Velleius, Epicurus alone recognized that "there are gods, since nature itself has imprinted [*impressisset*] a concept of them on the minds of all; for what nation or race of men is there that does not have a certain presumption [*anticipationem*] of the gods without any teaching [*sine doctrina*]?"[17] After noting that Epicurus called this concept a πρόληψις, Velleius explains further that this concept makes a firm foundation for his inquiry:

> For since the opinion has not been established by some convention or custom or law, and there abides a firm and unanimous agreement, it must be understood that there are gods; for we have implanted or rather inborn concepts of them [*quoniam insitas eorum vel potius innatas cognitiones habemus*]. But that on which the nature of all agrees must be true; hence it must be admitted that there are gods.[18]

Although Cicero has not delineated the argument with precision, the basic structure is clear: since all men believe by nature that there are gods, and what all believe by nature is true, it follows that there are gods. Velleius subsequently adds that the same nature that gave us an outline of the gods "engraved" (*insculpsit*) in our minds that we should consider them everlasting and blessed.[19]

Velleius' argument is based on a distinction between nature and teaching; the latter embraces convention, custom, and law. Velleius claims that presumptions, and the presumption of god in particular, are naturally formed and not imposed by an authority of any kind. Plato makes a similar distinction in the *Laws* when he argues against the view that the gods are by art (τέχνῃ), or certain conventions (νόμοις), and not by nature (φύσει).[20] Velleius' distinction is also in close agreement with the Stoic division of concepts into presumptions (called προλήψεις, by a borrowing of Epicurus' term), which are formed "naturally" (φυσικῶς) and "nontechnically" (ἀνεπιτεχνήτως), and concepts acquired "by teaching and ef-

17. Cicero *De natura deorum* 1.43: esse deos, quod in omnium animis eorum notionem impressisset ipsa natura. quae est enim gens aut quod genus hominum, quod non habeat sine doctrina anticipationem quandam deorum?

18. Ibid., 1.44: cum enim non instituto aliquo aut more aut lege sit opinio constituta maneatque ad unum omnium firma consensio, intellegi necesse est esse deos, quoniam insitas eorum vel potius innatas cognitiones habemus; de quo autem omnium natura consentit, id verum esse necesse est; esse igitur deos confitendum est.

19. Ibid., 1.45.

20. Plato *Laws* 889e.

fort" (διὰ . . . διδασκαλίας καὶ ἐπιμελείας). The Stoics agreed
with Plato and the Epicureans that the concept of the gods is
formed by nature.[21]

A little later in his discussion, Velleius also contrasts nature with
reason (ratio), as was previously discussed.[22] This detail, along with
the others, suggests that Velleius is modeling his distinction on
Epicurus' overall division of human development into a natural
stage, in which human nature responds directly to the environment, and a subsequent stage of calculation, in which the products
of nature are refined technically and conventions are introduced.
We may expect, therefore, that what makes the concept of god
natural is that it is imposed on human nature from outside, and
that it is not the product of calculation. But how is this to be
reconciled with Velleius' claim that the presumptions of god are
"implanted or rather inborn" (insitas . . . vel potius innatas)? Also,
how does Velleius' claim agree with Diogenes' description of a
presumption as a "memory of that which has often appeared
from outside"? According to some scholars, Velleius' explanation
is evidence that Diogenes' account of presumptions is incomplete.
Norman DeWitt proposed that innatas means "innate," and that
Epicurus regarded presumptions as a special category of concepts,
differing from the concepts described by Diogenes in that they
are innate, and including, for example, the concepts of god and
of justice.[23] An alternative suggestion is that of Knut Kleve, who
conjectures that insitas and innatas may refer respectively to two
distinct components in concept formation, insitas to the impression made from outside, and innatas to the contribution of human
reason from within.[24] Although both of these views have been criticized in detail in the past, some further discussion of the terms
insitas and innatas will, I think, help to explain Velleius' meaning.

As others have pointed out, innatas must be understood as a
term that adds a qualification, or precision, to insitas.[25] Insitus is a

21. For the distinction of concepts, see SVF 2.83. See also DL 7.54 for the Stoic
description of a presumption as a "natural concept of what is universal" (ἔννοια
φυσικὴ τῶν καθόλου); cf. SVF 2.104. For the Stoic concept of god, see esp. Cicero
De natura deorum 2.5. The claim that the gods are by nature, not by convention,
is also made by Cicero in Tusculanae Disputationes 1.30; Cicero adds here that the
unanimity of all peoples must be considered a "law of nature" (lex naturae).

22. Cicero De natura deorum 1.46; see chap. 2 (Demonstration).

23. DeWitt, Epicurus, 142–50. DeWitt's theory has been criticized in detail by
Kleve (Gnosis Theon, 30–34); Rist (Epicurus, 165–67); Manuwald (Prolepsislehre, 11–
14); and others.

24. Kleve, Gnosis Theon, 33–34. Kleve adds a detailed analysis of the contribution of human reasoning at pp. 80–96.

25. This is pointed out against Kleve's interpretation by Günter Gawlick in his

term used by Lucretius to describe the acquisition of empirical concepts.[26] If we look elsewhere in Cicero's writings, we find that Cicero uses *insitus* along with *naturalis* to describe the Epicurean presumption of pleasure as the supreme good.[27] As for the joint use of *insitus* and *innatus*, in one place Cicero contrasts "received" (*recepta*) with "inborn" (*innata*), and then elaborates this contrast by opposing "brought to me [from outside]" (*delata*) to "deeply fixed and implanted [*insita*] in my heart and feelings."[28] These usages indicate, it seems to me, that in Velleius' explanation Cicero uses *innatas* not to mean "innate," but to reinforce *insitas* so as to make it clear that the concept has developed naturally within a person, and has not been imposed by some external authority. Throughout the argument, Velleius has been stressing that the concept has not been adopted on anyone else's authority—as a result of a law, convention, or some other form of teaching; what he now emphasizes again is that the concept inheres naturally within a person. This is entirely compatible with the claim that the concept is a response to the environment; what matters is that the concept is a response of human nature, developed from within an individual. Instead of making a contrast with *insitas*, *innatas* adds rhetorical force and precision to it by making clear that what is "implanted" has not been grafted on from the outside but has inhered within an individual from the start.

We shall return to Cicero's use of *innatus* later. Let us now note that Velleius claims not only that the concept of god is formed naturally, but also that it is held by all men. Velleius uses this joint claim as proof that the gods exist. But why does Velleius appeal to the universality of the concept of god if, as was concluded earlier, any presumption at all implies the existence of what is thought of? One way of solving the difficulty might be to suppose that *all* presumptions are held by all, or, to use Epicurus' own term, that all presumptions are "common" (κοιναί).[29] But this is

---

review of Kleve's *Gnosis Theon*, in *Gnomon* 37 (1965): 467; see also Dietrich Lemke, *Die Theologie Epikurs*, 48 n. 36, and Manuwald, *Prolepsislehre*, 18.

26. Lucretius 5.182 and 1047.

27. Cicero *De finibus* 1.31.

28. Cicero *In C. Verrem* 2.5.139: reliqua est ea causa, iudices, quae iam non recepta sed innata, neque delata ad me sed in animo sensuque meo penitus adfixa atque insita est. Cicero also joins the two terms at *De finibus* 4.4: insitam quandam vel potius innatam cupiditatem scientiae.

29. At *Men.* 123 Epicurus mentions that the presumption of god is "common" (κοινή), that is, held by all. There is some confusion about the meaning of the term κοινή as applied to concepts. Some have taken it to mean "universal" or "general" in the sense of presenting certain general features of a thing (so Rist, *Epicurus*, 26). This interpretation seems to me contrary to the attested usages.

not permissible. Since presumptions are formed by a direct response of human nature to the environment, and the environment is not the same for all, presumptions must vary from one group of people to another. For example, some groups will have naturally formed concepts of tigers and elephants, while others will not. Epicurus himself indicates that presumptions need not be held by all when he points out that at a certain stage of human development there were some groups of humans who were without a concept of justice.[30]

If, then, there are presumptions that are not universally held, and all presumptions are of things that exist, why does Velleius use the claim of universality to prove god's existence? Part of the answer, it seems to me, is that Velleius is here defending Epicurean theology against criticism by other philosophers. Accordingly, he is using an argument for the existence of god that was used also by other dogmatic philosophers. This argument conforms to a standard type, in which the major premise is that what all agree upon by nature is true. The skeptical philosophers opposed this type of argument by claiming that there is no unanimity on the particular issue and hence that the conclusion is false. At the end of Velleius' presentation, the Academic Cotta reveals Velleius' strategy by pointing out that his argument is used by other philosophers as well, and he tries out the standard skeptical response, by claiming that as a matter of fact not all people are agreed that god exists.[31]

At the same time, Velleius needs the claim of universality in order to secure a foundation, as he puts it, for his inquiry. If the presumption of god were not universally held, then some persons would lack immediate evidence of the gods' nature and existence, and so would lack the standard by which all of Velleius' remaining inquiry must be judged. It is conceivable that these persons would be able to infer the nature and existence of the gods from other evidence; but they would have no reason to assent to Velleius', or Epicurus', sequence of arguments about the gods.

Although our sources contain no explicit distinction between presumptions that are universally held and those that are not, the distinction is clearly attested for the perceptions and feelings; and here the importance of common experiences in scientific investi-

---

30. *KD* 32 (cf. 33).
31. Cicero *De natura deorum* 1.62–64. In the same treatise Cicero also adduces the claim that all human believe in the existence of god as a Stoic proof of the existence of god (2.12; 3.11).

gation becomes clear. Epicurus claims, with respect to both perceptions and feelings, that we must pay attention "to those that are common [κοιναῖς] in accordance with what is common, and to those that are individual [ἰδίαις] in accordance with what is individual."[32] In the development of his scientific doctrines, we hear no more about individual perceptions and feelings. Instead, Epicurus appeals explicitly to the universally experienced perception of bodies as evidence for his fundamental physical claim that there are bodies. Epicurus also appeals to the universal feelings of pleasure and pain as evidence for his fundamental ethical claim that pleasure is the supreme good and pain the supreme evil.[33] As I shall argue later, Epicurus held that all perceptions and feelings show what is the case; hence individual perceptions and feelings are just as valid as those that are common. The reason that only the latter are admitted as evidence of certain basic claims of Epicurean science is that Epicurus' theory of verification demands that the evidence be self-evidently present to each investigator if a claim is to be judged true by the investigator. Although some relaxation of this rule was admitted by Epicurus' followers, Epicurus and his followers seem to have been agreed that the most fundamental doctrines should admit of personal verification by each adherent.[34] Since the evidence used by the scientist occurs in the form of presumptions, it follows that the basic presumptions of Epicurean science must be common to all. The presumption of god is clearly among these.

The occurrence of *innatas* in an argument used also by other philosophers suggests that the term has a special function in addition to that of stressing the fact that the concept of god inheres in a person by nature. *Innatus* corresponds closely in meaning and form to Greek ἔμφυτος, a term that the Stoics are known to have used in connection with certain concepts, such as the concepts of good and bad.[35] Cicero uses the term *innatus* again later in *On the*

32. *Her.* 82.
33. See *Her.* 39 (and chap. 14, The Existence of Bodies and Void) on the perception of bodies; and Cicero *De finibus* 1.30 on pleasure and pain.
34. See chap. 11, pp. 203–4.
35. See *SVF* 3.69 for the Stoic use; cf. Plutarch *De communibus notitiis* 1085b. There has been no agreement about the meaning of the term in Stoicism. F. H. Sandbach argues that the term ἔμφυτος may signify what is "part of one's nature," although he also suggests that the later Stoics used the term in the sense of "innate" ("Ennoia and Prolēpsis in the Stoic Theory of Knowledge," in *Problems in Stoicism*, 28–29). Werner Liebich suggests that the later Epicureans introduced ἔμφυτοι προλήψεις from Stoicism, and that in Stoicism these are concepts dependent on the inner perception of oneself (συναίσθησις), as opposed to concepts derived

*Nature of the Gods* to apply to the Stoic concept of god: the belief in
the existence of god, the Stoics claimed, is "inborn in all."[36] Although it is not clear precisely what the Stoics meant by describing
certain concepts as ἔμφυτος, the well-attested Stoic distinction between natural concepts and technical concepts indicates that the
Stoics either identified ἔμφυτοι concepts with natural concepts, or
at any rate subsumed them under natural concepts. Galen later
distinguished between concepts formed by a memory of sense
perceptions and concepts that are "inborn in all" (ἔμφυτοι πᾶσιν);
the latter, Galen notes, were called "axioms" (ἀξιώματα) by the
ancients.[37] Since Epicurean presumptions are memories of appearances, they are clearly excluded from the second of Galen's
divisions. It is clear from Velleius' argument, however, that the
Epicureans claimed that universally held presumptions have the
authority attributed by Galen and the Stoics to concepts that are
"inborn in all." It seems plausible, then, that the Epicureans identified universally held presumptions with the category of concepts
commonly known as ἔμφυτοι πᾶσιν, and that Cicero translates
this Epicurean use of ἔμφυτος by *innatus*. Velleius' use of *innatus*
thus suggests not only that the concept inheres in a person by
nature—a meaning that attaches to ἔμφυτος no less than to *innatus*—but also that the concept belongs to that privileged class
of concepts that other philosophers regarded as axiomatic. Even
though—and indeed, because—universal presumptions are memories of appearances, the Epicureans insisted, they qualify as primary truths that none can doubt.

Cicero's description of the Epicurean presumption of god as
*innatus* thus illustrates the same tendency of the Epicureans to appropriate terminology from other philosophers as does Diogenes
Laertius' general account of presumptions. Another example of
this tendency is Velleius' use of *impressisset*, "imprinted," and *insculpsit*, "engraved," to describe the natural formation of presump-

---

from the perception of external things ("Ein Philodem-Zeugnis bei Ambrosius,"
125, 129). I agree that the Epicureans may well have borrowed the term ἔμφυτος
from the Stoics; but there seems to me no evidence that the term was used by
either Stoics or Epicureans to single out concepts that are dependent on inner
perception. Liebich also suggests that at *De finibus* 1.31 Cicero uses *insitus* to translate Epicurean ἔμφυτος, and that at *De natura deorum* 1.44 he misunderstands an
original ἔμφυτος so as to translate it not only by *insitus* but also by *innatus* (meaning
"innate") (ibid., 127–28). Since *innatus* need not mean "innate," no such misunderstanding need be imputed to Cicero.

36. *De natura deorum* 2.12.

37. Galen *Institutio logica* 3.2 (p. 8.3–6 Kalbfleisch).

tions. *Insculptum* occurs along with *innatum* in Cicero's account of the Stoic concept of god; and both verbs are very close in meaning to Greek ἐναπομάττειν and ἐναποσφραγίζειν, used by the Stoics to define "apprehensive" presentations.[38] Velleius' use of these terms identifies a presumption as an "apprehension," κατάληψις, just as Diogenes claims.

The other section of text in Cicero's *On the Nature of the Gods* that has a bearing on the formation of presumptions comes shortly after the argument just discussed. Velleius now adds the following details about the presumption of god:

> Epicurus, who not only sees in his mind things that are concealed and deeply hidden but also grasps them as though by the hand, teaches that this is the power and nature of the gods that, first, it is discerned not by sense perception but by the mind, and not with any solidity or individuality like the things that he calls στερέμνια because of their firmness; but by means of images apprehended by similarity and transition [*imaginibus similitudine et transitione perceptis*], when an unending appearance of very similar images is formed out of innumerable atoms and flows to us [*ad nos*; mss. *ad deos*], the mind, focusing and fixing upon these images with the greatest pleasure, obtains an understanding of what is both a happy and an eternal nature.[39]

This is probably the single most debated text in Epicureanism. An immediate difficulty is the manuscript reading "to the gods" (*ad deos*). This reading has led some interpreters to suggest that images, or atoms that go to make up images, flow to the gods and in this way make up the physical nature of the gods.[40] It is

38. Cicero *De natura deorum* 2.12; and *SVF* 1.59. At *Academica* 2.18 Cicero uses the expression *impressum effictumque* to translate the two Greek verbs.

39. Cicero *De natura deorum* 1.49: Epicurus autem, qui res occultas et penitus abditas non modo videat animo sed etiam sic tractet ut manu, docet eam esse vim et naturam deorum ut primum non sensu sed mente cernatur, nec soliditate quadam nec ad numerum, ut ea quae ille propter firmitatem στερέμνια appellat, sed imaginibus similitudine et transitione perceptis, cum infinita simillumarum imaginum series ex innumerabilibus individuis existat et ad nos [mss.: deos] adfluat, cum maximis voluptatibus in eas imagines mentem intentam infixamque nostram intellegentiam capere quae sit et beata natura et aeterna.

40. This is the view developed by J. Lachelier ("Les Dieux d'Epicure") and Walter Scott ("The Physical Constitution of the Epicurean Gods") and followed by Bailey (*Greek Atomists*, 445–51) and others. For a detailed survey of the problems raised by the passage see A. S. Pease's edition of Cicero's *De natura deorum* (1:312–24), also Günther Freymuth (*Zur Lehre von den Götterbildern in der epikureischen Philosophie*, 25–39, and "Methodisches zur Epikureischen Götterlehre"); Kleve (*Gnosis Theon*, esp. 82–96); and Lemke (*Theologie*, esp. 23–41).

quite implausible, however, that the gods should exist as the products of images, and even if they did, this would not explain how images produce in us a concept of gods. What is needed is the claim that images flow to the minds of humans from the gods; and we know both from Cicero later on in the same treatise and from other sources that this does in fact happen.[41] Thus the text should very likely be emended to *a deis* or *ad nos*, as many editors have done.[42]

Granted that Cicero is referring to an unending series of similar images flowing from the gods to men, the most serious difficulty about the text is: what does the expression *similitudine et transitione* mean? The phrase occurs again in Cotta's summary of Velleius' statement:

> For this is what you said, that the appearance of god is apprehended by thought and not by sense perception, and that there is in it no solidity nor does it persist as the same individual, and that it is viewed in such a way that it is discerned by similarity and transition [*ut similitudine et transitione cernatur*] and that the addition of similar [images] from infinite bodies never fails; and that as a result our mind, intent upon these things, considers this nature to be happy and eternal.[43]

In both Velleius' original statement and Cotta's summary, a distinction is made between the sensory perception of a solid individual entity and the thought of a general "nature." The nature that is being considered is the nature of god as a perfectly happy and indestructible being; accordingly, what is in question is the presumption of god as a perfectly happy and indestructible living being. This type of being is said to be known "by similarity and transition" by means of a never-ending succession of similar images.[44]

41. Cicero *De natura deorum* 1.114; cf. Lucretius 5.1169–82.

42. Mayor, for example, emends to *a deis*, Lambinus to *ad nos*, and Heindorf to *a diis ad nos*.

43. Cicero *De natura deorum* 1.105: sic enim dicebas, speciem dei percipi cogitatione non sensu, nec esse in ea ullam soliditatem, neque eandem ad numerum permanere, eamque esse eius visionem ut similitudine et transitione cernatur neque deficiat umquam ex infinitis corporibus similium accessio, ex eoque fieri ut in haec intenta mens nostra beatam illam naturam et sempiternam putet.

44. Cicero's testimony on how one apprehends the nature of god seems to me quite compatible with the much discussed scholion on *KD* 1 ( = U 355), which divides the gods into (a) individuals and (b) a single anthropomorphic type. As Philippson has argued, a contrast is made here between the cognition of individual gods and the cognition of the species of god ("Zur epikureischen Götterlehre,"

There have been two main interpretations of the expression *similitudine et transitione*. One is that it describes the physical process by which similar images pass either through space or through one's consciousness.[45] The other interpretation is that the expression renders Greek καθ' ὁμοιότητα μετάβασις, "inference by similarity," a method of inference discussed at length by Philodemus in his treatise *On Significations*. Proponents of the latter interpretation have understood an "inference by similarity" to be an argument by analogy, and they have proposed specifically that the perfect happiness and indestructibility of the gods are inferred by analogy with the imperfect happiness and endurance of human life.[46]

There is, it seems to me, very good evidence for taking *similitudine et transitione* as a translation of καθ' ὁμοιότητα μετάβασις; at the same time, I suggest, the "similarity" to which Cicero refers consists in a similarity among individual gods and not in an analogy between human beings and gods. In his treatise, Philodemus lists the formation of presumptions as one of four ways in which the method of "inference by similarity" operates.[47] This method is understood by Philodemus as the inductive method of inferring an unobserved similarity on the basis of observed similarities. Among the rules that Philodemus outlines for using the method is that

---

579–83). In *De natura deorum*, Cicero is concerned only with the latter type of cognition, since he is explaining the presumption of god. Both Cicero and the scholion explain the cognition of the species as due to a continuous flow of similar images.

45. Scott suggests a passage through space to the gods ("The Physical Constitution," 219); and Bailey proposes that the expression may signify either a passage through space to the human mind or a succession of images within the human mind (*Greek Atomists*, 447–49).

46. This view was proposed about the same time by Philippson (*De Philodemi libro qui est περὶ σημείων καὶ σημειώσεων*, 76–77; cf. "Zur epikureischen Götterlehre," 601–06) and by Paul Schwenke ("Zu Cicero *De natura deorum*," 623–24). Whereas Schwenke suggests only briefly that the similarity consists in an analogy between the gods and human beings, Philippson develops in detail the view that there is an analogy between the bliss and indestructibility of the gods on the one hand and human happiness and endurance on the other. Kleve argues in favor of Philippson's interpretation (*Gnosis Theon*, 80–96); although he accepts the view that the concept of god depends on an analogy with humans, he adds the proposal that the indestructibility of the gods is inferred on the basis of the everlasting flow of material to the gods. Among the many criticisms of Philippson's interpretation, Claudio Moreschini's "Due fonti sulla teologia epicurea" provides a good overview (362–67). It should be noted that *percipere*, which has been the subject of much discussion, is a term used by Cicero to signify "apprehend," and does not in itself either imply or exclude a reasoning process (see also Kleve, *Gnosis Theon*, 93).

47. Philodemus *De signis* col. 34.5–12 De Lacy; see also chap. 11, below.

we must observe a large number of very similar instances in order to be able to generalize about all instances anywhere. With reference to the initial concept of the gods, this implies that we must have many images of happy and enduring gods before we may generalize that the nature of the gods is happy and everlasting. Cicero indicates this process of inference when he mentions that there is a never-ending succession of very similar images. It is because we see an endless succession of similar, ever-happy and ever-vigorous individuals that we infer that they belong to a type of being that is happy and everlasting.

The expression "inference by similarity" was also used by non-Epicurean philosophers in the Hellenistic period to designate various types of inductive inference. The general use of the expression in the sense of inductive inference had already been anticipated by Aristotle. He writes in the *Posterior Analytics* that in order to find definitions one must collect groups of instances that are "similar and without differences" (ὅμοια καὶ ἀδιάφορα) and "pass" (μεταβαίνειν) in this way from the particular to the universal.[48] Later, apart from Epicureanism, the method of inference by similarity is attested especially prominently for Empiricist medicine. In cases in which an illness called for a previously untried treatment, the Empiricists sought to infer an appropriate treatment by making detailed comparisons with treatments used for similar illnesses in the past.[49] Other thinkers agreed with the Epicureans in recognizing inference by similarity as the general method by which the initial concepts of investigation are acquired.[50] A narrower use of the method is implied by the standard fourfold

48. Aristotle *Posterior Analytics* 97b7–39 (esp. ll. 7–8 and 29). Another related use of the term μεταβαίνειν occurs at 75a38, where Aristotle claims that it is not possible to demonstrate a thing by passing (μεταβάντα) to a different genus, for example, by passing from arithmetic to geometry; cf. Plato *Phaedrus* 262a.

49. For the use of inference by similarity by the Empiricists, see chap. 10 (Other Hellenistic Theories of Signs).

50. As Cicero reports (though without using any term corresponding to μετάβασις), the Stoicizing philosopher Antiochus explained the formation of initial concepts as a construction from similars (Cicero *Academica* 2.30). A later example is Alexander's claim in *In Aristotelis Metaphysica commentaria*, on 980b25 (p. 5.5–6 Hayduck), that τέχνη is distinguished from ἐμπειρία by ἡ τοῦ ὁμοίου μετάβασις. This claim may be compared with Alexander's explanation in *De anima*, p. 85.21–22 Bruns, that the mind first forms a concept (νόημα, ἔννοια) when "by transition from a continual activity concerning perceptible things it obtains from them a certain contemplation of the universal" (κατὰ μετάβασιν ἀπὸ τῆς περὶ τὰ αἰσθητὰ συνεχοῦς ἐνεργείας ὥσπερ ὄψιν τινὰ ἀπ' αὐτῶν λαμβάνοντος τοῦ καθόλου θεωρητικήν). This description bears a close resemblance to Cicero's description at *De natura deorum* 1.49 and 105 as well as to the scholion on *KD* 1.

division of concepts into concepts derived from sense perception by incidence, analogy, similarity, and combination. Sextus Empiricus describes the latter three types of concepts as obtained by "inference" (μετάβασις) from what is evident.[51] Cicero uses *transire* joined with *similitudine*, corresponding to καθ' ὁμοιότητα μετάβασις, to explain that we acquire the concept of temperance by recognizing the "similarity" between the beauty of physical shapes and that of words and deeds, and by "passing" from the former to the latter.[52] Cicero's example appears to fit a category that embraces both similarity and analogy as distinguished in the fourfold division of concepts.

Cicero's expression *similitudine et transitione* thus corresponds to a very prominent philosophical concept; and the details of his own exposition, together with Philodemus' view of καθ' ὁμοιότητα μετάβασις, indicate that he is referring to the general method of forming a concept by an examination of numerous similar instances. This interpretation gains support from the fact that, about Cicero's time and a little earlier, inference by similarity was the subject of a lively debate between the Epicureans and other philosophers. Philodemus' treatise *On Significations* was an attempt to defend the Epicurean use of inference by similarity. Philodemus was, moreover, an acquaintance of Cicero; and either Philodemus himself or one of his sources was the source of Cicero's presentation of Epicurean theology in *On the Nature of the Gods*. It is not at all surprising, then, that the Epicurean use of inference by similarity should receive mention in Cicero's discussion.

As for the suggestion that the images pass successively through space or through one's consciousness, either type of passage applies not only to the formation of presumptions, but also to the formation of any visual impression at all, whether by the sight or by the mind. Hence the phrase *similitudine et transitione perceptis* would not distinguish concept formation from sensory perception, although Cicero's text implies such a distinction.

Supposing, then, that by *similitudine et transitione* Cicero means "inference by similarity," the next problem is: precisely how does this type of inference function in the formation of the concept of god? Granted that the succession of very similar images in Cicero's description is that of individual gods, is it nonetheless necessary to make a comparison with other beings of a similar sort, in par-

51. Sextus Empiricus *Adv. math.* 9.393–94.
52. Cicero *De finibus* 2.47.

ticular human beings, in order to derive from the images the general notion of a happy and everlasting being? According to the fourfold division of concepts, as previously analyzed, the concept of god belongs to the category of similarity or of analogy; in either case, some process of reasoning is required by which the gods are related to objects perceived by the senses. Moreover, in his analysis of presumptions as inferences by similarity, Philodemus makes clear that reasoning is used to distinguish similarities from differences. But does this requirement for a process of reasoning agree with Diogenes' contention that a presumption is a "memory of that which has often appeared from outside"? Thus the question arises anew whether Diogenes' explanation of presumptions is complete.[53]

Two important additional texts on the presumption of god provide evidence on this question. One is Lucretius' explanation of how the concept of god was first formed in the history of mankind. As Lucretius describes this development, some process of reasoning was clearly involved. Taking each of the three features that Epicurus assigns to the presumption of god—animate existence, indestructibility, and happiness—Lucretius explains that humans attributed sense perception to the gods because they saw them moving and uttering sounds, that they attributed eternity to the gods because their appearance did not change and they exhibited great strength, and that they attributed happiness to the gods because they saw them suffering no fear of death or any toil. To these three inferences Lucretius immediately adds a fourth: the false belief that the gods are responsible for the events in the heavens.[54] The other text is a report by Sextus Empiricus that some thinkers, whom Sextus does not identify by name, hold that although the concept of the gods begins with the reception of images during sleep or with the contemplation of the universe, the perfect happiness and indestructibility of the gods are inferred by

---

53. Kleve has argued in detail for a special contribution by human reasoning; see nn. 24 and 46 above. Jürss also maintains that although the concept of god is empirically acquired, it is not simply a memory ("Prolepse," 224). Jürss's general view is that there is a range of presumptions, from those that are a memory of sense impressions to scientific concepts (see chap. 3, n. 17). Goldschmidt recognizes three kinds of presumption: memories of sense impressions; concepts formed on the basis of sense impressions by analogy, similarity, and combination; and philosophical concepts, due to λογισμός, which alone may serve as the starting point of a philosophical investigation ("Remarques sur l'origine épicurienne de la prénotion," 161–62).

54. Lucretius 5.1171–93.

analogy with humans.[55] Since the first of the two stated alternatives clearly applies to Epicurean theology, it may well be that the
thinkers in question include certain Epicureans, and that accordingly some Epicureans held that the concept of divine bliss and
indestructibility implies a comparison with human happiness and
endurance.

Although both of these texts indicate that the initial concept of
god involves some process of reasoning, they do not, it seems to
me, undermine Diogenes' claim that a presumption is a memory
of that which has often appeared from outside. For it is open
to the Epicureans to maintain that the process of reasoning that
occurs in the formation of a presumption is reducible to the re-
tention of appearances from outside. Admittedly, the mind must
be able to collect similarities and distinguish differences; and this
may be viewed as a process of inference. But this type of inference
is a special, immediate type: it does not consist in the use of concepts to judge the appearances from outside, but is the result
of a mechanical sorting process that occurs without the use of
concepts. Thus, to take the presumption of god, the mind sorts
and retains numerous appearances of individual gods, all having a
very high degree of similarity with one another. In order to accom-
plish this sorting, the mind sorts numerous other appearances having various degrees of similarity with the appearances of the gods,
including appearances of human beings. Thus the mind acquires
a general concept of god by comparing numerous instances of life,
happiness, and endurance among all types of beings, including
human beings. This process of comparison, intricate though it is,
does not depend on the use of concepts to interpret the facts
presented from outside; the final result is a judgment about appearances and the whole process may be called a reasoning process, but every step of this process consists in an immediate, irrational response to similarities and differences presented from
outside.

In summary, the initial concepts of investigation, or presumptions, are concepts whose truth does not need to be demonstrated
and that serve as standards by reference to which an investigation
is made. Presumptions are empirically formed as a record of perceptual impressions; and scientific investigation begins when one
attempts to extend these concepts beyond the range of perception
to what cannot be observed. In his first rule of investigation, Epi-

55. Sextus Empiricus *Adv. math.* 9.45.

curus makes no mention of the empirical formation of initial concepts, but demands only that there be initial concepts by reference
to which problems are proposed and answered. In his second rule
of investigation, which will be considered next, Epicurus demands
that the facts that serve as the means of answering problems be
empirical facts.

# PART II

*Observations*

# [ 5 ]

# Epicurus' Second Rule
# of Inquiry

## EPICURUS' STATEMENT OF THE RULE

E PICURUS' second rule of inquiry, as stated in the procedural note of the *Letter to Herodotus* immediately after the first rule (quoted on p. 20), is as follows. Again I translate very literally.

> Next, it is necessary to observe all things in accordance with the perceptions [κατὰ τὰς αἰσθήσεις δεῖ πάντα τηρεῖν] and simply the present applications [ἐπιβολὰς], whether of the mind or of any of the criteria [κριτηρίων], and similarly [in accordance with] the affections [πάθη] that obtain, so that we may have the means to infer both what is expected [to appear] [τὸ προσμένον] and what is nonapparent [τὸ ἄδηλον].[1]

The text is more difficult than that of the first rule, partly because the structure of the sentence is not clearly articulated, and partly because the text is full of terms that need elucidation—however clear Epicurus may have supposed them to be to his own students.

1. *Her.* 38: εἶτα κατὰ τὰς αἰσθήσεις δεῖ πάντα τηρεῖν καὶ ἁπλῶς τὰς παρούσας ἐπιβολὰς εἴτε διανοίας εἴθ᾽ ὅτου δήποτε τῶν κριτηρίων, ὁμοίως δὲ κατὰ τὰ ὑπάρχοντα πάθη, ὅπως ἂν καὶ τὸ προσμένον καὶ τὸ ἄδηλον ἔχωμεν οἷς σημειωσόμεθα. This text is faithful to the manuscripts except that εἶτα (after Gassendi) takes the place of mss. εἴτε; προσμενόμενον of some of the manuscripts is rejected in favor of προσμένον of the rest; and mss. καὶ (before τὰ ὑπάρχοντα) has been emended to κατὰ (so Giussani and Bailey). Editors have attempted to clarify the relationship of αἰσθήσεις to ἐπιβολὰς and πάθη by (a) inserting κατὰ after ἁπλῶς (Gassendi, followed by Bailey) and altering καὶ before τὰ ὑπάρχοντα to κατὰ (Giussani, Bailey) or inserting κατὰ after καὶ to read καὶ κατὰ τὰ ὑπάρχοντα (Gassendi); or (b) omitting κατὰ before τὰς αἰσθήσεις and changing πάντα to πάντων (Bignone) or

It can be seen at first glance, however, that the new rule is phrased in such a way as to balance the first. In each case, the statement of the rule is followed by an explanation: first, Epicurus claims, we need initial concepts corresponding to our words in order to be able to make judgments about problems, and, second, we need observations based directly on our perceptions and affections (or "feelings") in order to be able to infer what is not observed.

Before we examine Epicurus' statement of the rule, it is again useful, as in the case of the first rule, to take note of Diogenes Laertius' corresponding explanation in his summary of Epicurus' canonic. Diogenes deals with the perceptions in the first main part of his summary; he follows this with an explanation of presumptions, as examined in the preceding chapters; and he concludes with a short discussion of the affections. In his discussion of the perceptions, Diogenes presents a number of arguments intended to demonstrate the truthfulness of all sense perception; and he concludes that "one must infer what is nonapparent from the phenomena." He also adds that all thoughts are derived from the perceptions, and he ends by explaining that the hallucinations of madmen, as well as the visions seen in one's dreams, are "true" (ἀληθῆ).[2] Diogenes' explanation supplies a justification for Epicurus' rule: it is because all perceptions are "true" that they serve as an appropriate basis of inference concerning things that are not observed.

In his much briefer discussion of the affections, Diogenes explains that they are two, pleasure and pain, and that they serve as a criterion of choice and avoidance.[3] Diogenes therefore regards the affections as a guide to action. This view poses a problem for Epicurus' second rule of inquiry, for here Epicurus seems to regard the affections not as determinants of action, but as a means of inference.

In his statement, Epicurus demands that we "observe" (τηρεῖν)

---

changing κατά to καί and πάντα to πάντως (von der Muehll); or (c) omitting πάντα altogether (Jürgen Mau, *Studien zur erkenntnistheoretischen Grundlage der Atomlehre im Altertum*, 13). Bailey's and Gassendi's modifications are slight and yield a text that makes good sense. It is possible, however, to obtain the same sense by leaving καί ἁπλῶς τάς as it is (so Arrighetti); and it may even be possible to obtain this sense without adding κατά before τά ὑπάρχοντα (so Arrighetti, who translates "in base alle sensazioni . . . , e in generale in base agli atti apprensivi . . . , egualmente in base alle affezioni"). Readings (b) and (c) assign, it seems to me, an inappropriate meaning to τηρεῖν (as discussed later in this chapter).

2. DL 10.31–32, including the claim περὶ τῶν ἀδήλων ἀπὸ τῶν φαινομένων χρὴ σημειοῦσθαι.

3. DL 10.34.

in accordance with the perceptions and affections in order to have the means of inferring, or to have "signs" of (implied by the verb σημειωσόμεθα), both what is yet to be observed (τὸ προσμένον) and what cannot be observed (τὸ ἄδηλον). There are two main problems concerning this statement. The first is: what sort of observations does Epicurus demand? The second is: how are these observations used to infer what is unobserved? Accordingly, the following examination of Epicurus' second rule is divided into two main parts, a discussion of "observations" and a discussion of "signs."

Concerning observations, Epicurus' statement immediately raises three questions, which I shall attempt to answer in a preliminary fashion in this chapter before going on to a detailed analysis in subsequent chapters. The first is: how is the phrase "and simply the present applications [as I have translated ἐπιβολὰς], whether of the mind or of any of the criteria" related to the immediately preceding word, "perceptions" (αἰσθήσεις)? Cyril Bailey suggests that the expression "applications of the mind" is here used in the special sense of a direct insight into scientific truths, so that the applications of the mind constitute a different type of cognition from the perceptions. Bailey takes the "applications" of the other "criteria" to consist in "acts of attention" by the five senses; and since, according to Bailey, these are acts of perception that are free from error or distortion, he takes the reference to the applications of the senses to restrict the scope of the preceding term "perceptions" to just those perceptions that are truthful.[4] Bailey is opposed by those who hold that all acts of sense perception are applications (or "contacts" or "views") by which the senses direct themselves to some object, and that the mind engages in acts of perception—applications—just like those of the senses.[5] According to this interpretation, the applications of the senses, and possibly also the applications of the mind, are coextensive with the "perceptions." My view is that Epicurus is using the entire phrase "and simply the present applications, whether of the mind or of any of the criteria" as coextensive with "perceptions", and hence that the perceptions are coordinate with the affections. I also propose that Epicurus considered that all perceptions alike show what is real, or, in other words, are truthful.

The second question concerns Epicurus' use of the word "cri-

---

4. For Bailey's interpretation, see further pp. 124–25 and 151.
5. See pp. 125 and 151–52.

terion" (κριτήριον). In his statement of the second rule, Epicurus uses the term to denote the five senses and the mind. But there seems to be a discrepancy between this use and Diogenes' claim that Epicurus recognized three "criteria of truth" (κριτήρια τῆς ἀληθείας): perceptions, presumptions, and affections. Scholars have generally held that the two uses are quite distinct. Unless this apparent discrepancy is resolved, it is hard to understand how Epicurus' second rule is related to his first, or what Epicurus' method of inquiry is at all. I argue, with the help of Sextus Empiricus' discussion of Epicurus' criterion of truth, that Diogenes' first criterion, the perceptions, corresponds to Epicurus' own view of κριτήριον.

The third problem is the meaning of the term τηρεῖν. I have translated this as "observe," although others take it in the much more general sense of "check" or "scrutinize." My translation goes along with the view that Epicurus held that all perceptions, since they are all equally applications to what is real, equally provide signs of what is unobserved. Accordingly I propose that in his second rule of investigation Epicurus is neither making a general demand for a control of our theories by sense perception nor demanding a scrutiny of the perceptions as such, but rather that he is demanding that we take whatever we perceive, exactly as we perceive it, as evidence of what is unobserved.

## SENSE PERCEPTION AND MENTAL PERCEPTION

Let us first consider the scope of the phrase "and simply the present applications, whether of the mind or of any of the criteria." Epicurus' text leaves the grammatical relationship of the phrase unclear; my translation attempts to resolve the ambiguity by making the phrase parenthetical to "in accordance with the perceptions" and making "in accordance with the perceptions" parallel to "in accordance with the affections."

One argument in favor of conjoining the perceptions in this way with the affections is that both are mentioned four times subsequently in the *Letter to Herodotus* as joint standards of investigation, each time, it seems, by reference to the procedural note. Epicurus mentions the perceptions and the affections together at both the beginning and the conclusion of his discussion of the soul. He states at the beginning of this discussion that one must "refer to the perceptions and the affections" in order to have the "firmest" assurance; and he reiterates at the end that one must "refer all these calculations about the soul to the affections and perceptions, remembering what was said in the beginning."[6] Of the other two occurrences, one serves to close the entire discussion of physical theory in the *Letter to Herodotus*,[7] and the other comes in the discussion of atomic size.[8] In none of these places are the "applications of the mind" mentioned. Although there is one place in the *Letter to Herodotus*[9] where perception is cited by itself as a basis for inferring what is nonapparent, the four joint occurrences show that the affections too serve as a basis of inference.

Further evidence concerning the relationship of the perceptions, mental applications, and affections to each other is provided by Diogenes Laertius. In his summary of Epicurean canonic, Diogenes reports that although in the Κανών Epicurus posited three criteria of truth—perceptions, presumptions, and affections—Epicurus' followers added "the presentational applications of the mind" (τὰς φανταστικὰς ἐπιβολὰς τῆς διανοίας) as a fourth criterion. Diogenes also points out that Epicurus mentions this additional criterion in the *Letter to Herodotus* and in his *Authoritative Opinions*.[10] Diogenes himself does not refer to the applications of the mind again in his own summary, although he mentions at the end of his section on perceptions that the visions of madmen, along with those seen in dreams, are true; these, as we shall see, are one type of presentational application of the mind. Cicero ascribes the same three criteria to Epicurus as does Diogenes, listing these in the same order as perceptions, presumptions, and (in lieu of the generic "affections") pleasure.[11] Diogenes' testimony about Epicurus' followers is confirmed by a fragment in Philodemus' *On Significations* in which all four criteria appear.[12]

Applications of the mind are mentioned in two places in the *Letter to Herodotus* apart from the procedural note. In sections 50–51, Epicurus argues that whatever is grasped by an application of the mind or the senses is without falsehood; and section 62 contains the aphoristic statement, which appears to be a sum-

6. *Her.* 63 and 68.
7. *Her.* 82.
8. *Her.* 55.
9. *Her.* 39.
10. DL 10.31.
11. Cicero *Academica* 2.142: omne iudicium in sensibus et in rerum notitiis et in voluptate constituit. Cicero translates κριτήριον by *iudicium*.
12. Philodemus *De signis* fr. 1 De Lacy.

mary of what is argued at 50–51, that "everything that is viewed [θεωρούμενον], or obtained by application by the mind, is true."[13] In sections 50–51, Epicurus offers a single, covering explanation for the applications of the mind and of the senses; he argues that even in those cases in which the mind and senses "apply to" things that are ordinarily thought of as false or nonexistent, such as dream appearances, there is no falsehood in the applications themselves. In *Authoritative Opinion* 24 Epicurus speaks of "that which is present in accordance with the perception and the affections and every presentational application of the mind." In agreement with the fourfold division of Epicurus' followers, the "presentational application of the mind" is here distinguished from the perceptions and affections.

Since the followers of Epicurus were generally scrupulous not to make any revisions in Epicurus' own doctrine except insofar as they regarded these as clarifications of his own position, there is some initial reason to suppose that their addition of the "presentational applications of the mind" as a fourth criterion was not intended to exceed Epicurus' own three criteria, but rather to make explicit what was already implicit in them. It seems plausible, therefore, that Epicurus included the applications of the mind among the perceptions. This has in fact been proposed by a number of scholars, most recently by John Rist, on the ground that since the mind engages in applications just like those of the senses, mental applications may be regarded as a type of perception.[14]

A possible objection to extending the meaning of "perception" (αἴσθησις) in this way is that it is contrary to the philosophical use of the term as it had evolved by the time of Epicurus. Aristotle consistently uses αἴσθησις to signify perception by the five senses, to the exclusion of such activities of the mind as dreams and hal-

13. *Her.* 62; the authenticity of this sentence seems to me suspect (see chap. 8, n. 6).

14. Rist, *Epicurus*, 32–37. Zeller previously suggested that Epicurus included the "presentational applications of the mind" among the perceptions (*Philosophie der Griechen*, vol. 3, pt. 1, 398, n. 7). Philippson elaborates this view thus: in the Κανών, Epicurus used the term αἰσθήσεις to embrace mental applications and sense perceptions, whereas later, in the *Letter to Herodotus* and the *Authoritative Opinions*, he substituted for αἰσθήσεις the phrase αἱ τῆς διανοίας φαντασίαι, which covers both αἰσθήσεις (now used in a restricted sense) and φανταστικαὶ ἐπιβολαὶ τῆς διανοίας; at this later stage, Philippson suggests, Epicurus himself recognized the four criteria subsequently adopted by his followers (*De Philodemi libro*, 11–19). There is not, it seems to me, sufficient evidence for such a historical development; and it is fundamental to Epicurus' theory of perception that sense perceptions are entirely free from any activity by the mind.

lucinations; and this usage was standard in the Hellenistic period.
The occurrences of αἴσθησις and its cognates in Epicurus' extant
writings do not make clear the scope of the term, but some of the
uses by Epicurus' followers are clearly in compliance with contemporary philosophical usage.[15] Although Lucretius uses *sensus* together with *animi* to signify "perception of the mind," this use
does not infringe standard usage; for the explicit addition of *animi*
indicates that Lucretius is here extending the meaning of *sensus*
in a way that was admitted by other philosophers.[16] Plutarch, for
example, describes the mind (νοῦς) as the "proper sense organ
[αἰσθητήριον] of the soul."[17]

Against the argument from standard usage, however, it may be
pointed out that Epicurus held a distinctive theory of perception
according to which perception consists in a direct response by the
perceptual organ to influences from the outside. Since this process
is exactly the same for the sense organs as for the mind, it would
seem appropriate for Epicurus to use the term αἴσθησις in a distinctive way to apply to both the sense organs and the mind. It
would also seem appropriate that in the procedural note Epicurus
should immediately explain the peculiarity of his usage by adding
the parenthetical phrase "and simply the present applications,
whether of the mind or of any of the criteria" after his mention
of the perceptions.

Moreover, there is evidence in Plato's *Theaetetus* of a similar
wide use of the term αἴσθησις. In this dialogue, when Theaetetus
suggests that knowledge is "perception," αἴσθησις, Socrates interprets this to mean that whatever "appears" (φαίνεται) to a person
is the case, and he subsequently points out that these "appearances" include dreams, the experiences of madmen and other
sick persons, and other cases of which one would ordinarily say

15. Apart from the distinction between αἴσθησις and "the presentational application of the mind" made by Epicurus' followers, the clearest evidence of later
Epicurean usage is provided by Lucretius. He speaks, for example, of the "five
senses" (*quinque . . . sensibus*) at 3.626 (cf. the examples at 4.486–88); and he distinguishes the senses (*sensibus*) from the mind (viewed as an organ of perception)
at 5.149. See also Torquatus' use of *sensibus* (cited in chap. 4, n. 14); and Diogenes'
corresponding use of αἰσθήσεων (cited in chap. 4, n. 15). As for Epicurus' own
usage, according to the traditionally accepted reading at *Her.* 50 Epicurus makes
a distinction between the mind and the "sense organs" (αἰσθητήρια). This reading,
however, is very doubtful (see below, chap. 7, n. 17).

16. Lucretius 4.731; at 3.98 and 104 the same phrase appears to be used more
widely to include both perception and feeling by the mind. At 4.763 Lucretius distinguishes sense perception from the mind's own type of perceptual activity by
exceptionally adding the modifier *corporis* to *sensus* to describe the former.

17. Plutarch *Non posse suaviter vivi* 1096e.

that one misperceives.[18] Plato's use of the term "perception" here includes the perceptual type of activity that Epicurus assigns to the mind. As I shall argue later, Epicurus agreed with the position that all appearances that occur directly to a person from outside show what is real. Hence there is good reason to suppose that Epicurus too included dreams, hallucinations, and all other cases of alleged misperception, among "perceptions." This is not to say that in including mental applications among perceptions Epicurus is thinking primarily of allegedly deceptive appearances. Mental applications also include memories of sense perceptions; and without these no investigation can proceed. In his procedural note, Epicurus appears to stress the importance of memories by mentioning the applications of the mind before those of the senses.

It is likely, therefore, that Epicurus included the applications of the mind among the perceptions, and that his followers later set apart the perceptual applications of the mind as a fourth criterion of truth in recognition of the standard contemporary philosophical usage that restricted αἴσθησις to perception by the five senses. The descriptive term "presentational" (φανταστική) identifies the applications of the mind as perceptual acts. By restricting the applications of the mind to those that consist in presentations (φαντασίαι), like the applications of the senses, the term excludes those mental applications, among them scientific theories, that are not simply a response to external influences. This limitation is understood in the procedural note from the use of the qualifying word "present" (παρούσας) together with the preceding use of αἰσθήσεις.[19]

In *Authoritative Opinion* 24, Epicurus himself seems to have made a concession to contemporary usage, without, however, intending the "presentational application of the mind" to count as a separate criterion. As Diogenes Laertius indicates, this concession, along with the explanation of "perceptions" in the procedural note of the *Letter to Herodotus*, may well have provided the impetus for the Epicureans' later reformulation of Epicurus' criteria. This reformulation was the more important as other philosophers drew a clear distinction between the senses and the mind in their theories of the criterion of truth.

From this preliminary discussion of perceptions, it appears that in his second rule of investigation Epicurus does not include a de-

18. Plato *Theaetetus* 151e–52a and 157e–60c.
19. On the different types of application, see further chap. 8 (Perception, Interpretation, and Reason).

mand for a special kind of scientific intuition among the prerequi-
sites of investigation, nor does he single out a special type of perception from the general category of perceptions. Rather, Epicurus' statement seems to imply that all perceptions alike, including perceptions ordinarily thought of as deceptive, qualify as a
basis of inference for what is unobserved.

## CRITERIA

In ascribing to Epicurus three "criteria of truth" (κριτήρια τῆς
ἀληθείας), Diogenes Laertius is using the term "criterion" in a different sense from that in which Epicurus uses it in the procedural
note in the *Letter to Herodotus*. Whereas Diogenes Laertius applies
the term to three different types of awareness, Epicurus uses it to
designate the five senses and the mind. This difference in usage is
accompanied by a difference in the classification of the standards
of investigation. Whereas Diogenes recognizes three distinct standards, in his procedural note Epicurus joins the perceptions with
the affections to form a single overriding category—that of observations—and thus recognizes in effect two categories of investiga-
tive standards: presumptions, and observations in accordance with
the perceptions and affections.

The fact that Cicero agrees with Diogenes in attributing the
same three "criteria" to Epicurus suggests that Diogenes' classification was the accepted account of Epicurean methodology in the
Hellenistic period.[20] But, given the difference in usage, how accurately does this account represent Epicurus' own methodology?
An answer to this question demands a brief analysis of how the
notion of "criterion" evolved from the time of Epicurus to a much
later period.

First, modern scholars have thought that Epicurus does at times
use "criterion" in the same way as Diogenes, and that accordingly
Epicurus does recognize three criteria of truth, just as Diogenes
claims.[21] However, an examination of Epicurus' usage elsewhere in

20. For Cicero, see above, n. 11.
21. Bailey, for example, claims that although κριτήριον means "instrument of
judgment" at *Her.* 38 and 51, elsewhere Epicurus uses κριτήριον in the "full technical sense of the 'standards of judgment,' which are αἴσθησις, πάθος, and πρόληψις" (*Epicurus*, 178; see also 256, where Bailey notes that the criteria mentioned
at *Her.* 82 include "the senses and feelings, the πρόληψις or general concept, and
possibly also the ἐπιβολὴ τῆς διανοίας"). Elaborating on Bailey's view, Striker argues in detail that Epicurus distinguished between κριτήριον as "Erkenntnisver-
mögen" (at *Her.* 38 and 51) and κριτήριον as "Urteilsmittel," that is, as perceptions,
presumptions, and affections (Κριτήριον, 52–63, esp. 59–63).

his extant writings indicates that Epicurus' usage is quite consistent throughout his writings.

Apart from the procedural note, the word κριτήριον occurs three times in the *Letter to Herodotus*. Two of these uses occur in a single sequence of argument at sections 51–52. Epicurus here denies that there is any falsehood in any of the "applications of the mind or the remaining criteria"; and he ends with the warning that unless a distinction is made between what is immediately presented to the mind or the senses from outside and what is added as an opinion from within, either "the criteria in accordance with the evidence" (τὰ κριτήρια . . . τὰ κατὰ τὰς ἐναργείας) will be eliminated, or else the admission of error will confuse everything. In the first of these occurrences, "criteria" is clearly used in the same way as in the procedural note, to designate the mind and the five senses. We may thus expect this usage to carry over into the phrase "the criteria in accordance with the evidence" in the conclusion of the argument. Furthermore, Epicurus' argument shows that "evidence" (ἐνάργεια) consists in an impression made directly on the mind or the senses. What makes the five senses and the mind "criteria," therefore, is that they have impressions imposed directly from outside: they are tribunals, as it were, that judge what is the case (by an extension of the basic sense of κριτήρια) by having "evidence" before them in the form of presentations that are produced from the outside without the addition of any opinion.

The third occurrence of the term κριτήριον in the *Letter to Herodotus* is in the final methodological note at section 82. Here Epicurus states that we must pay attention to the affections and perceptions, both common and individual, and to "all the evidence that is present in accordance with each of the criteria" (πάσῃ τῇ παρούσῃ καθ᾽ ἕκαστον τῶν κριτηρίων ἐναργείᾳ). As suggested earlier, this note appears to be a final reminder of the second rule of investigation. Since there is also a close verbal similarity with the expression "the criteria in accordance with the evidence" of section 52, it appears that here too the term "criteria" is used to designate the mind and the senses.

One more important use of κριτήριον by Epicurus occurs in *Authoritative Opinion* 24. In claiming that one will "throw out every criterion" if one does not distinguish between what is expected and what is "present in accordance with the perception and the affections and every presentational application of the mind," Epicurus is drawing the same conclusion as in *Letter to Herodotus* 51–52. Accordingly, we may suppose that Epicurus is here including the senses and the mind among the criteria that would be thrown out, although his warning applies also to any other criterion that anyone might propose.

There are several other occurrences of the term "criterion" in Epicurus' writings, but their context is too sparse to shed any light on the meaning.[22] It appears, therefore, that what Epicurus understands by a criterion is the faculty or instrument that judges what is real by having it present as evidence (ἐνάργεια), and that accordingly Epicurus uses the term consistently to designate the mind and the senses.[23] Epicurus' usage thus seems remote from that of Diogenes.

There is, however, another text that shows considerable agreement with Epicurus' own view and at the same time indicates how Diogenes' and Epicurus' analyses may be reconciled. This is a detailed account of Epicurean methodology by Sextus Empiricus. It belongs to a comprehensive criticism of the notion of criterion of truth, as proposed by various dogmatic philosophers. Sextus begins this entire discussion with a careful preliminary analysis of the notion of criterion of truth. First he distinguishes between a "criterion of truth" (κριτήριον τῆς ἀληθείας), also called "criterion of reality" (κριτήριον τῆς ὑπάρξεως), and a "criterion of choice and avoidance" (κριτήριον αἱρέσεως . . . καὶ φυγῆς). The former is used to determine what there is, the latter to determine what is to be done; and the dogmatists use both, whereas the Pyrrhonist Skeptics accept only the latter.[24] Sextus then analyzes the criterion of truth as having three increasingly narrow senses. In the widest sense, a criterion of truth is "every measure of apprehension" (πᾶν μέτρον καταλήψεως) and includes natural measures such as sight, taste, and hearing. Second, in a narrower sense, a criterion of truth is "every technical [τεχνικόν] measure of apprehension"; this includes such measures as the rule and compass, and excludes natural measures. Third and narrowest, a criterion of truth

22. Epicurus mentions "criteria and affections" at *Pyth.* 116; he also uses the term joined with ἀρχὴν and κανόνα in *On Nature* (PHerc. 1056, 697, 1191) fr. 7 col. 13, Arr. 34.32 (with very doubtful occurrences at Arr. 34.23, 30–31).

23. This use of κριτήριον agrees with that of Aristotle at *Metaphysics* 1063a2–3, where the sense organ of taste is described as αἰσθητήριον καὶ κριτήριον of flavors. Cf. Plato *Theaetetus* 178b, where Socrates explains the view that sense perception is knowledge by saying that the subject has "the criterion within himself" (τὸ κριτήριον ἐν αὑτῷ).

24. Sextus Empiricus *OP* 1.21 and 2.14 and *Adv. math.* 7.29–30. In making this classification, which is intended to apply in general to all philosophical systems, Sextus does not distinguish between the meanings of ἀλήθεια, "truth," and ὕπαρξις, "reality."

is "every technical measure of apprehension of a nonapparent thing [ἀδήλου πράγματος]." Sextus calls this the "logical" (λογικόν) criterion; and he explains that this no longer includes the criteria that have to do with life, but is used by dogmatic philosophers for the discovery of the truth.[25] After announcing that his examination will focus on the logical criterion, Sextus subdivides the logical criterion into three types: "by which" (ὑφ' οὗ), for example, "man"; "through which" (δι' οὗ), for example, "perception" (αἴσθησις) or "mind" (διάνοια); and "according to which" (καθ' ὅ), for example, the "impact of the presentation" (προσβολὴ τῆς φαντασίας).[26]

In the widest sense, then, according to Sextus, a criterion of truth is a measure that is used to apprehend what is the case. As implied by the use of the Stoic term "apprehension," this judgment cannot be mistaken. Sextus divides the criterion of truth into three kinds, natural faculties as exemplified by the senses, technical aids as used by craftsmen, and the "logical" criterion used by the philosopher. The last is called "logical," I suggest, because it is used for the apprehension of what is not self-evident, which must be inferred by the use of reason, λόγος, on the basis of what is self-evident.[27]

25. Sextus Empiricus *OP* 2.15 and *Adv. math.* 7.31–33.

26. Sextus Empiricus *OP* 2.16 and *Adv. math.* 7.34–37. A. A. Long discusses the origin of this threefold division in "Sextus Empiricus on the Criterion of Truth," 36.

27. Sextus' analysis appears to be indebted, probably by way of Stoic theory, to Plato's analysis of the arts (τέχναι) at *Philebus* 55d–58e. Plato begins by distinguishing two main categories: the less exact arts, such as music, which rely on the experience gained through sense perception and do not use measurement; and the more exact arts, such as building, which use such measures as the rule and compass. In this latter group the most exact arts are arithmetic, measuring, and weighing, and these are in turn divided into a less exact type, used by nonphilosophers, and a more exact type, used by philosophers. Last there is the most exact art of all, dialectic, which is not practiced like the rest for its usefulness but for the sake of the truth (57e–58e). Sextus' analysis agrees in broad outline with Plato's hierarchy: both thinkers recognize a progressive increase in exactness from sense perception to technical measures and finally to the use of reason ("dialectic" according to Plato, and the use of the "logical" criterion according to Sextus); and of these, the last division aims at truth instead of usefulness. Cicero refers to this last division by the expression *iudicia ista dialecticae* at *Academica* 2.141.

Striker has suggested that in his definition of "logical criterion" Sextus is using the term ἄδηλον in the special skeptical sense in which everything except one's own subjective impressions are nonapparent (Κριτήριον, 106). Striker's reason is that the Stoic and Epicurean "logical" criteria, as identified by Sextus, are both used to apprehend what is self-evident. Neither the Stoic nor the Epicurean criterion, however, is used to apprehend only what is self-evident. By showing, in the first place, what is self-evident, they show in addition what is nonapparent; and it is with this latter function that Sextus is concerned. Furthermore, Sextus is purporting to present a classification used by the dogmatists and for the rest uses

Turning to Epicurus' criterion of truth, Sextus reports that this consists in "presentation" (φαντασία); and he adds that Epicurus also used the term ἐνάργεια, "evidence," for φαντασία.[28] Sextus then explains in detail Epicurus' distinction between presentation and opinion. A presentation, he points out, is an affection that, just like the affection of pleasure or pain, is produced by something that really is just as it appears. Sextus illustrates this claim by reference to sight and hearing; a color or shape, he explains, is in reality just as it is seen to be, and a sound is in reality just as it is heard to be. Any mistake, Sextus writes, is due to the addition of opinion; for the opinion adds something to the presentation or takes something away from it. Further, Sextus divides all opinions into conjectures about what is yet to appear (such as the conjecture that the distant indistinct figure is Plato), and opinions about what is nonapparent (such as the opinion that there is void). Both types of opinion, Sextus explains, are verified or falsified by reference to presentations, which thus turn out to be the foundation of all inference.

We will examine Sextus' exposition of Epicurean methodology in detail later. What appears from this survey is that there is a close correspondence between what Sextus says about Epicurus' criterion and Epicurus' own notion of criterion. Whereas Sextus uses the term "criterion" to refer to the impression obtained by the organ of perception from outside, Epicurus uses it to refer to the organ of perception itself insofar as it obtains an impression from outside. In both cases, the criterion consists in having a presentation directly from outside, without the addition of any opinion. In both cases, too, this impression is viewed as a means of inferring what is nonapparent. The difference between the two views may be summed up by saying that whereas Sextus places Epicurus' criterion in his third subdivision—"according to which"—Epicurus himself places it in what Sextus would recognize as the second subdivision—"through which."

Sextus' own classification, moreover, suggests an explanation for this shift in the meaning of "criterion." Increasing precision and standardization in the Hellenistic debate on the criterion of truth led philosophers to distinguish three aspects of the logical criterion, of which the second adds precision to the first, and the

---

terms in the sense in which that group used them. Finally, if ἄδηλον were used in the skeptical sense, it would not serve to distinguish Sextus' third division from the other two.

28. Sextus Empiricus *Adv. math.* 7.203; the discussion continues to 7.216.

third to the second; these categories were then pressed as closely as possible upon theories obtained quite independently of them. For Epicurean canonic, the third category, "according to which," was readily supplied by evidence (ἐνάργεια) or presentation (φαντασία), even though Epicurus' own notion of a criterion fits the second category better than the third. Sextus omits this second category because he can give a more exact account by focusing on the third.

Diogenes Laertius' analysis of Epicurus' criteria agrees with Sextus' report in that it identifies the phenomena, as obtained directly through perception, as the means of inferring what is non-apparent.[29] Diogenes in effect identifies the impression obtained directly through perception, called φαντασία and ἐνάργεια in Sextus' report, as Epicurus' logical criterion. Both Diogenes' and Sextus' analyses are thus in agreement with Epicurus' view that the criteria are the mind and the senses, having the evidence present to them by a direct perceptual response to external influences.

The first of Diogenes' three criteria, the perceptions, thus seems to be coextensive with the criterion attributed to Epicurus by Sextus, as well as with the criteria proposed by Epicurus himself. But how do Diogenes' other two criteria, the presumptions and the affections, fit this view? To consider, first, the affections, Epicurus recognizes them as a basis of inference jointly with the perceptions throughout the *Letter to Herodotus*. He therefore seems to view the affections as a criterion of truth in the sense of Sextus' logical criterion. Sextus, on the other hand, explicitly distinguishes what he calls the "primary affections" (πρῶτα πάθη), pleasure and pain, from presentations.[30] Sextus thus appears to exclude the affections from Epicurus' logical criterion. It appears, moreover, that Sextus has good reason to exclude the affections. For our sources indicate that Epicurus' affections were generally regarded in the Hellenistic period as a criterion of action and not of truth. Although Diogenes initially lists the affections as one of Epicurus' three criteria of truth, he describes them in his subsequent analysis as a criterion of "choice and avoidance," that is, of action.[31] Similarly, Cicero describes pleasure and pain as standards of choice and avoidance and names the perceptions (*sensus*) as the "criterion of truth and falsehood."[32]

29. DL 10.32.
30. Sextus Empiricus *Adv. math.* 7.203.
31. DL 10.34.
32. Cicero *De finibus* 1.22–23; cf. 1.71 on the function of the perceptions. Lucretius discusses the perceptions as a criterion of truth at 4.507–21.

Although the later testimonies on the affections appear to be in conflict with Epicurus' own methodological remarks in the *Letter to Herodotus*, they are also clearly based on Epicurus' own doctrine about the affections. For Epicurus clearly assigns to them the function of determining choice and avoidance. The best example is his remark about pleasure in the *Letter to Menoeceus*: "from it [pleasure] we begin every choice and avoidance and to it we revert, judging every good by the affection [πάθει] as though by a rule [κανόνι]."[33] The later authorities therefore seem to differ from Epicurus in assigning just one function to the affections, whereas Epicurus recognized two.

Can the later testimonies be reconciled with Epicurus' own remarks? Although most scholars, relying closely on the later sources, hold that Epicurus distinguished between the perceptions as a standard of truth and the affections as a standard of action, some have suggested briefly that Epicurus may have subsumed the affections under the perceptions as a standard of truth.[34] The most plausible view, it seems to me, is that Epicurus himself assigned a double function to the affections and did not subsume them under the perceptions, but that his followers later reclassified the affections as a criterion of action alone, while subsuming their epistemological role under that of the perceptions. This reclassification may readily be explained as an attempt by the Epicureans to bring their analysis of criteria into line with the standard accepted analysis, in particular with the division of criteria into a criterion of truth and a criterion of action. The Epicurean reformulation involves no change in doctrine, because, in conformity with standard usage, the Epicureans extended the term "perceptions" to include what Epicurus meant by "affections."

Why, then, did Epicurus distinguish the affections from the perceptions as a separate standard of truth? In common with other philosophers, Epicurus held not only that all sensory awareness is the result of an affection (πάθος, used in the most general sense) of the perceptual organ, but also that sensory awareness is of two kinds, an awareness of things as external to ourselves and an awareness of inner conditions. Epicurus called the former αἴσθησις,

---

33. *Men.* 129: . . . ἀπὸ ταύτης καταρχόμεθα πάσης αἱρέσεως καὶ φυγῆς καὶ ἐπὶ ταύτην καταντῶμεν ὡς κανόνι τῷ πάθει πᾶν ἀγαθὸν κρίνοντες.

34. Among the majority are Tohte (*Kriterien*, 19), Bailey (*Greek Atomists*, 249–50), and Rist (*Epicurus*, 31). Striker, though assenting to the majority view, considers the function of the affections unclear in the *Letter to Herodotus* and suggests that possibly in the Κανών the affections were subsumed under the perceptions (Κριτήριον, 60). Manuwald also suggests briefly that the affections may have been subsumed under the perceptions (*Prolepsislehre*, 52).

"perception," and the latter πάθος, "affection"; and he identified the "affections," understood in the restricted sense in which they are a type of awareness, or "feeling," as pleasure and pain. Accordingly, perceptions and affections complement each other by showing two distinct kinds of reality, external objects and inner conditions. In recognition of this complementarity, I suggest, Epicurus assigned equal functions to the perceptions and the affections in his second rule of inquiry.[35]

Cicero provides confirmation that Epicurus' followers later abandoned Epicurus' terminological distinction between the perceptions and the affections by subsuming the latter under the former. In Cicero's discussion of Epicurean ethics in *On Ends*, the Epicurean spokesman Torquatus claims that it is judged by "perception" (*sensu*) that pleasure is the supreme good and pain the supreme evil; and he explains that this is "perceived" (*sentiri*) just as it is perceived that fire is hot, snow is white, and honey is sweet.[36] This is in contrast to Epicurus' own use of πάθος in the *Letter to Menoeceus* (129). In addition, there is reason to suppose that Sextus included Epicurean affections, insofar as they are a criterion of truth, in the category of φαντασία, "presentation." For the term ἐνάργεια, "evidence," which Sextus cites as Epicurus' synonym for φαντασία, appears to have been used by Epicurus in the *Letter to Herodotus* (82) to refer to the conditions of pleasure and pain as well as to the perceptions proper; and it was certainly used to refer to the affections later in an anonymous Epicurean papyrus in which the "innate goals, by which measurements of what is to be chosen and avoided are made," are said to "present the most conspicuous evidence [τὴν ἐγδηλοτάτην ἐνάργειαν]."[37]

I conclude that the later sources sum up the whole of Epicurus' second rule of investigation by identifying the perceptions, or φαντασία, or ἐνάργεια, as Epicurus' criterion of truth. Since Epicurus' affections are functions of his "criteria"—the senses and the

35. On the type of affection that occurs in an act of perception, see chap. 6 (The Perceptual Stream and the External Source); and on the objects of perception, see chap. 7 (Compacting and Remaining). Glidden has argued in detail that Epicurus distinguished the affections (πάθη) from the perceptions by assigning to the former the function of self-awareness ("Epicurus on Self-Perception"). Glidden draws the inference, which I do not share, that Epicurus recognized the affections as a foundation for ethics only, not for knowledge.

36. Cicero *De finibus* 1.30–31.

37. PHerc. 1251 col. 13.8–12 Schmid: κ]αὶ δῆλον ὅτι καὶ τὰ συγγενικὰ τέλη π[ϱ]οσφεϱόμενα τὴν ἐγδηλοτάτην ἐνάϱ[γ]ειαν, οἷς αἱ παϱαμετϱή[σ]εις γίνονται τῶν αἱϱετῶν καὶ φευκτῶν.

mind—no less than the perceptions are, Epicurus' own use of "criterion" and the later use of the term in the sense of "logical criterion" coincide. Diogenes' initial classification of the affections (which he analyzes as a criterion of action) as a "criterion of truth" appears to reflect Epicurus' own view of the affections. Even as a criterion of action, however, the affections qualify as a criterion of truth in a wide sense; for the Epicureans held that pleasure and pain determine action by showing what is truly pleasant and good, and truly painful and bad.

We are left with the "presumptions," προλήψεις, which Diogenes lists as a third criterion of truth. How are they related to Epicurus' criteria and to Sextus' logical criterion of truth? Important help is provided by Sextus, who shows that the same three criteria ascribed by Diogenes to Epicurus were also attributed to Democritus. Sextus reports that, according to a certain Diotimus, Democritus proposed three "criteria" (κριτήρια): the "phenomena" (φαινόμενα) as a criterion of "the apprehension of what is nonapparent (τῆς . . . τῶν ἀδήλων καταλήψεως); the "concept" (ἔννοιαν) as a criterion of "investigation" (ζητήσεως); and "the affections" as a criterion of "choice and avoidance" (αἱρέσεως . . . καὶ φυγῆς).[38] Under the first category Sextus mentions Anaxagoras' dictum that "the phenomena are the sight of what is nonapparent"; and under the second he refers to the requirement, stated by Plato in the *Phaedrus*, that one must know the subject of an investigation from the very beginning. However faithful this account is to Democritus' own thought, it agrees very well with what is reported about Epicurus' criteria by Sextus, Diogenes, and Cicero. Diogenes' summary of Epicurean canonic is an expanded version of the same threefold division of criteria, in the same order in which Sextus lists them. Cicero, moreover, explicitly links Epicurus' presumptions with Plato's requirement for initial concepts in the *Phaedrus*; and Sextus, Diogenes, and Cicero all agree in identifying the perceptions—or what appears in perception—as the means of judging what is nonapparent. There is also clearly a close correspondence between the first two criteria and Epicurus' two rules of investigation as set out in the *Letter to Herodotus*: Epicurus demands concepts as a means of investigation in his first rule; and he demands phenomena as a means of inference in his second rule.

It becomes clear, then, that not only Epicurus but also his fol-

---

38. Sextus Empiricus *Adv. math.* 7.140.

lowers recognized precisely two standards of investigation: (*a*) presumptions, and (*b*) "perceptions" and "affections" (as Epicurus used the terms), or "perceptions" simply (as Epicurus' followers used this term). In this twofold division, the second category alone constitutes a criterion of truth in the strict sense. Presumptions, or initial concepts corresponding to our words, are not in themselves criteria of truth: they form standards by reference to which we make any judgment at all in the investigation of a problem. But since Epicurean presumptions are memories of perceptions and affections, they also show what is real and hence serve secondarily as a criterion of truth. Diogenes, therefore, is justified in calling the presumptions a criterion of truth, even though this is a derived function.

To summarize, Epicurus proposed two standards to be used in an investigation: initial concepts corresponding to our words as a means of making judgments about problems, and observations made in accordance with our perceptions and feelings as a means of inferring what is unobserved. In Epicurus' terminology, the perceptions and feelings are activities of the "criteria," the senses and the mind, which judge, by an immediate act of apprehension, what is real. In later terminology, the perceptions (now viewed as including the feelings of pleasure and pain) constitute Epicurus' "criterion of truth." Epicurus' twofold division was later reformulated as a threefold division, consisting of the perceptions as a criterion of truth (in the strict sense), of presumptions as a criterion for making judgments in an investigation, and of affections (feelings) as a criterion of action. Epicurus' followers added a fourth category to the threefold distinction, the "presentational applications of the mind," which Epicurus had included in the category of perceptions. Epicurus' followers also changed the order of his classification in recognition of the fact that perceptions precede the formation of presumptions. This whole restructuring of Epicurus' original distinction between two rules of investigation does not involve a distortion of his doctrine, but was designed to bring it into conformity with a conceptual framework that was used also by other Hellenistic philosophers.

## OBSERVATION

A key term in Epicurus' second rule of investigation is τηρεῖν, which I have translated as "observe." The primary meaning of this term in ordinary Greek is to "keep" or "watch"; the narrower meaning of "observe" had evolved by the time of Epicurus.[39] Epicurus indicates by the addition of "in accordance with the perceptions . . . and affections" that he is using the term in this narrower sense. Empirical observations, therefore, furnish the investigator with the means of inferring what is yet to be observed and what cannot be observed at all.

A close parallel to this use of τηρεῖν is found in Empiricist medicine. The Empiricists explained "experience" (ἐμπειρία) as the "observation" (τήρησις) of what has often appeared in the same way. In commenting on this explanation, Galen points out that τήρησις is here used in the sense of memory rather than, as is customary, to designate the act of observation that is subsequently retained as a memory; and he suggests as alternative formulations that experience is "observation [τήρησις] and memory" or simply that it is a "memory" of what has often appeared in the same way.[40]

Two uses of τηρεῖν by Epicurus apart from the procedural note suggest that, like the Empiricists, he understood the term in the sense of keeping observations in one's memory, rather than of making individual acts of observation. First, Epicurus states at *Letter to Pythocles* 88 that "one must observe" (τηρητέον) the appearance of each thing in the heavens and distinguish this from features attributed to it by inference from the phenomena that occur on earth. The intent of this precept is to warn the student against ignoring anything of the appearances in the heavens (even though these appearances are admittedly imprecise) when offering interpretations of them. Here τηρεῖν has a strong connotation of preserving: the observation is viewed as something that must be kept safe in one's awareness.

The connotation of preserving is even stronger at *Letter to Herodotus* 77, where Epicurus requires that we "observe" (τηρεῖν) the sanctity of the gods in all the names that we assign to them, so

39. Before Epicurus, the extant uses of τηρεῖν in the sense of "observe" are rare. There are several occurrences in Aristotle: at *De caelo* 292a7–8, Aristotle uses οἱ παλαὶ τετηρηκότες to refer to observers of the stars; other examples are at *De generatione animalium* 756a33 and *Topica* 129a26 (where τηρεῖν is a ms. variant for παρατηρεῖν; cf. 129a23).

40. Galen *Subfiguratio empirica* 3–4, esp. pp. 48.12–19 and 50.9–51.9 D; cf. frr. 50, 51, 53, 54 D. A similar peculiarity is the Empiricists' use of the term αὐτοψία "seeing for oneself." Galen explains that the earlier Empiricists used this term to designate not only the activity of seeing for oneself, but also the knowledge resulting from it, and that accordingly they also explained experience as αὐτοψία (*Subfiguratio empirica* 3, p. 47.10–24 D). On the Empiricists see further chap. 10 (Other Hellenistic Theories of Signs).

as not to form opinions that are contrary to their sanctity. The same meaning is rendered by the compound verb διατηρεῖν in *Letter to Pythocles* 97, where Epicurus states that the divine nature must be preserved (διατηρεῖσθω) as something that is free from all duties and wholly blessed. In these two examples, the particular awareness is the initial concept of god as an indestructible and perfectly happy being; and Epicurus demands that this concept be preserved as one speculates about the nature of god. The notion of preserving is so strong in these instances that it seems quite remote from the notion of empirical observation. Since, however, according to Epicurus, the concept of god is reducible to the empirical observation of individual gods in one's dreams or waking imagination, the nature of god is both an empirically observed fact and a concept that is preserved in one's awareness. The word τηρεῖν embraces both notions.[41]

In the past, τηρεῖν has been taken in the general sense of "keep" or "watch" rather than "observe," and there have been two main lines of interpretation. Keeping πάντα ("all things") as the direct object of τηρεῖν, Bailey and others take Epicurus' meaning to be (at least in part) that we must keep all our investigations under the control of our perceptions, or in other words that we must check all our beliefs by the use of the senses.[42] Others emend πάντα so as to make τὰς αἰσθήσεις the direct object of τηρεῖν, and accordingly take the sense to be that we must "watch" or "scrutinize" the perceptions themselves.[43]

The second interpretation assigns an otherwise unattested meaning to τηρεῖν, and one that makes dubious sense. Whereas

---

41. Epicurus also uses τηρεῖν at *KD* 24; the term may be understood here in the most general sense of "preserve," although it does not seem implausible to me that Epicurus is using the term to imply that the opponent's alleged "observations" will be subject to controversy; see the discussion of *KD* 24 in chap. 8 (Truth, Falsehood, and Evidence). Epicurus' only other uses of the term are in *Vatican Saying* 80 (to mean "watch over") and (apparently) in *On Nature* 28 fr. 17 col. 1 (Arr. 31.11.19).

42. Bailey translates "we must keep all our investigations in accord with our sensations" (*Greek Atomists*, 266) and "we must keep everything under the control of the senses" (in his essay on ἐπιβολή in *Greek Atomists*, 564, and in *Epicurus*, 263). Rist follows Bailey in taking the meaning to be "we must check everything by the use of the senses" (*Epicurus*, 36); similarly Arrighetti rénders "e in base alle sensazioni che bisogna tener conto di tutto" (*Epicuro*, 36).

43. For the textual emendations see above, n. 1. Bignone, taking αἰσθήσεις as the direct object of τηρεῖν and emending to πάντων, translates "bisogna scrutare sempre le sensazioni che riceviamo d'ogni cosa" (*Epicuro*, 73). Similarly, DeWitt translates "under all circumstances to watch the sensations" (*Epicurus*, 139); and Mau adopts the meaning *befolgen, beachten* for τηρεῖν (*Studien*, 13).

it is normal usage to "watch" (τηρεῖν) the things that one perceives, it seems very strained to speak of a person as "watching"
the acts of perception themselves. This meaning seems especially
inappropriate for Epicureanism, since, according to Epicurus, it is
not the acts of perception as such that require scrutiny, but the
opinions that are added to them. The first suggestion, on the other
hand, is contrary to the stated goal that τηρεῖν should provide
us with the means of inferring what is unobserved. What Epicurus demands is not that we "watch" the investigation itself or
the theories developed in the course of the investigation; rather
he demands that we watch all things by empirical observation in
order to have evidence for our theories. This is not to deny that
Epicurus agrees with the general demand that we control our
theories by our perceptions and feelings. But this is not the demand that he states in his second rule of investigation: he makes
the much more specific demand that we use our observations, as
given directly by perception, as a basis of inference. Τηρεῖν is thus
a keyword of Epicurean methodology. It signals the view that
scientific investigation consists in relying on empirical observations
to discover what is unobserved.

It follows from Epicurus' second rule that the concepts required
in the first rule are empirical observations that are retained in the
mind. This is new information for the newly initiated student who
is reading Epicurus' rules of investigation for the first time. The
beginning investigator who has read only the first rule might take
Epicurus as a follower of Plato or Aristotle. It is in the second
rule that Epicurus proclaims his opposition to these predecessors
by stipulating that the knowledge we have at the outset of an investigation consists of empirical observations, and that the extension of knowledge consists in using these observations as a basis
of inference for what is unobserved.

The following detailed examination of the perceptions and affections attempts to show how Epicurus proposed to distinguish
between uninterpreted empirical facts and added opinions, in
such a way as to obtain a secure basis of inference.

# [ 6 ]

# Perceptions: Impact
# from Outside

## PRELIMINARY SURVEY:
## THE FIVE SENSES AND THE MIND

THE following chapters on perception draw on Epicurus' own
scientific theory of perception to show what evidence the investigator must have in order to make a scientific discovery. Since
the theory is itself based on the rule that it is to explain, this may
seem a perverse procedure. Epicurus, however, also uses his theory
of perception in the *Letter to Herodotus* to explain and justify his
initial demand for a reliance on the perceptions; and this procedure has the explicit approval of the Epicurean Torquatus in
Cicero's *On Ends*. In pointing out that "unless the nature of things
is recognized, we shall not be able in any way to defend the judgments of the senses," Torquatus is claiming that the use of the
senses as criteria cannot be justified except by the theory that explains sense perception.[1] Clearly, if the theory is able to provide an
explanation that justifies the initial reliance on the senses, then
the internal consistency of the system helps to justify the adoption
of the rule. At the same time, it is important to keep in mind that
the investigator must be able to apply the rule without taking into
account anything of the theory that is subsequently developed by
its use.

The order followed in the next three chapters is basically the
order in which Epicurus explains the perception of sight, and
along with it thought, in the *Letter to Herodotus*. These two types

1. Cicero *De finibus* 1.64: nisi autem rerum natura perspecta erit, nullo modo
poterimus sensuum iudicia defendere.

of perception are explained by Epicurus in a single detailed analysis that culminates in a defense of the sight and mind as criteria of investigation. The other senses will be included within this general framework as the evidence warrants. This emphasis on sight and thought reflects the overall emphasis of our sources.

Briefly, according to Epicurus there are six types of perception, the five types associated with the five senses—sight, hearing, smell, taste, and touch—and mental perception or "thought" (διάνοια). In all cases, the perceptual organ obtains an impression through the impact of particles from outside. Sight and thought are produced in the eyes and chest respectively by the impact of atomic complexes called "eidola" or "images" (εἴδωλα). These images are thin networks of atoms arranged in such a way as to show color and shape; and they are emitted from the surface of external solid objects, or combined out of various atoms or other eidola in midair. Hearing is produced in the ear by atoms that have spread in a fanlike formation from the sounding object; smell is produced in the nose by atoms that have been dispersed in the air from the interior of an object; and taste is produced by the immediate contact of the palate and tongue with atoms squeezed from an object. The sense of touch obtains an impression of an external body through an immediate contact of the percipient's body with atoms from the surface of the external body.[2]

The explanation of thought, διάνοια, as a process like sight deserves special notice. The term διάνοια, generally translated as "mind," refers to the activity or faculty of thinking (διανοεῖσθαι) just as the term ὄψις, "sight," refers to the activity or faculty of seeing (ὁρᾶν). In both cases, the activity consists in having images.

---

2. Epicurus gives explanations of sight and thought, of hearing, and of smell in *Her.* 49–53. Lucretius gives detailed explanations of sight, hearing, smell, taste, and thought in bk. 4 (239–521 on sight, preceded by a section on the eidola at 46–238; 524–614 on hearing; 615–72 on taste; 673–721 on smell; and 722–822 on thought). Neither provides a separate discussion of the sense of touch, although Lucretius gives some details about touch at 4.259–68 and 2.431–43. In the latter passage, Lucretius divides touch into the perception of external objects (2.435–36) and the perception of inner corporeal changes (2.436–41). The latter type of touch was commonly called "inner touch" (*interiorem [tactum]* at Cicero *Academica* 2.20 [cf. *tactu intumo* 2.70] and ἐντὸς ἁφήν at *SVF* 2.852) and was distinguished from the perception of external things as a faculty of self-awareness. In dividing touch into an awareness of external objects and an awareness of inner conditions, Lucretius appears to be subsuming Epicurean self-awareness—the affections of pleasure and pain—under the general category of perception, in conformity with standard Hellenistic distinctions. Additional information about the Epicurean theory of perception, including the sense of touch, is provided by PHerc. 19/698 (Scott); other testimonies are at U 317–28.

Διάνοια, therefore, does not imply the use of reason.[3] The images that occur in thought may be rationally organized by λογισμός, "calculation," but thought includes also such irrational processes as dreaming, daydreaming, and hallucinating. What is strikingly peculiar about the Epicurean position is that all thought consists of images produced by particles entering from outside a person.

The objects of sight and thought are variously identified by Epicurus as shape, or color and shape, or shape and its concomitants.[4] An anonymous Epicurean author of a treatise on perception shows more precisely what the object of sight or thought is by demarcating the object of sight from the object of touch.[5] He argues that just as sight is the perception of color, together with the perception of shape and size at a distance, so touch is the perception of body, together with (it is implied) the perception of bodily shape and size. The anonymous author also explains visible shape as the "outermost placement of colors," and visible size as "the outer placement of several colors." Accordingly, shape and size are not objects common to the senses of sight and touch, but are entirely different objects of perception: as perceived by sight, shape and size are entities situated at a distance; as perceived by touch, they are corporeal entities situated immediately next to the observer. This analysis is in agreement with the general Epicurean position that each sense has its own proper object of perception, without having any objects in common; the consequence is that no sense can pass judgment on the objects of any other sense.

It is generally held that Epicurus, like Democritus, reduced all sense perception to the sense of touch.[6] So stated, this interpreta-

---

3. According to Aetius (U 312) and a scholion on *Her.* 66 (U 311), Epicurus divided the soul into an irrational part, which is spread throughout the body, and a rational part, which is situated in the chest. This information is misleading, since rationality is only one of the functions performed by the concentration of soul atoms in the chest. Philippson takes the extreme position that διάνοια is never rational, but is a *Vorstellungskraft* separate from λόγος, *Vernunft* ("Zur epikureischen Götterlehre," 571–77, and his review of Bailey's *Greek Atomists*, 470–72).

4. *Her.* 49–50; cf. Sextus Empiricus *Adv. math.* 7.206–10.

5. See PHerc. 19/698 cols. 17, 18 (where visible shape and size are explained), 22, 25, and fr. 21 Scott. At col. 26.11–12, -ληρων should be completed as σκληρῶν rather than πληρῶν, as Scott proposed, for the term is conjoined with μαλακῶν.

6. This view goes back to Aristotle, who criticizes Democritus along with others for reducing all objects of perception to objects of the sense of touch (*De sensu* 442a29–b12). Aristotle also charges that the same thinkers regard common objects of perception—that is, size and shape, roughness and smoothness, sharpness and bluntness—as proper objects of perception. As the anonymous Epicurean writer on perception illustrates, the Epicureans later defended the position attacked by Aristotle.

tion is inaccurate. Certainly all sense activity consists in a contact between the sense organ and the particles that impinge on the sense organ. However, a distinction needs to be made between the sense of touch itself and the imperceptible contact that occurs in all types of perceptual activity: the sense of touch has no part in the activity of the other senses.

## FORMATION AND SPEED
## OF THE VISUAL STREAM

The type of atomic stream that results in sight and thought consists of eidola or images. These are "outlines," τύποι, that are much finer than anything that can be seen. Eidola are released in quick succession from the surface of a solid object and either preserve for a long time the arrangement that the atoms had on the surface of the solid or at times become disarrayed. Eidola may also be composed spontaneously in midair, like clouds gathering in the sky, without coming from a solid. A third possibility is that eidola from solids may combine in midair to form a compound eidolon; for example, a horse eidolon and a man eidolon may combine in midair to produce the eidolon of a centaur. This third type of eidolon is especially delicate; accordingly it enters the mind rather than the eyes, because the mind is of finer composition than the eyes.[7]

The eidola are generated very rapidly and travel very rapidly.[8] Because of this rapid flow, an object is perceived instantaneously, that is, without there being a perceptible interval of time between the formation of the eidolon and the perception of the object. Epicurus explains this in a very obscurely worded passage in the *Letter to Herodotus*. Just after introducing the topic of the eidola, he continues:

7. *Her.* 46–48; and Lucretius 4.26–142 and 722–48. At *Her.* 48 Epicurus distinguishes among eidola coming from solids, spontaneous combinations in the environment, and "other methods" of formation, which are not specified. Lucretius discusses eidola coming from solids at 4.26–109 and adds at 4.129–42 that there are also eidola formed spontaneously in midair. At 4.735–38 he distinguishes between thought eidola formed by a combination of eidola emitted from solids and thought eidola formed spontaneously in the air.

8. *Her.* 46–47 (on the movement of the eidola through space) and 48 (on the formation of the eidola); and Lucretius 4.143–75 (on the formation of eidola) and 176–215 (on the movement of the eidola). Bk. 2 of Epicurus' *On Nature* also contains a very fragmentary discussion of the speed of the eidola, with a summary at PHerc. 1010 fr. 20 cols. 2–3, Arr. 24.50.17–51.8.

A movement through the void, provided [the moving body] does
not meet any colliding [bodies], accomplishes every comprehended
[περιληπτόν] length in an incomprehensible [ἀπερινοήτῳ] time. For
collision [ἀντικοπή] and lack of collision take on a likeness of slowness and quickness. Nor with respect to [its] moving body does it
[the eidolon] arrive at several places at once by reference to the
times viewed by reason [κατὰ τοὺς διὰ λόγου θεωρητοὺς χρόνους];
for this is unthinkable. But arriving all at once in a perceptible time
from anywhere at all in the infinite, it will not be separate from the
place from which we comprehend the motion. For it [the quickness
of the motion] will have a similarity to collision even if we leave the
quickness of the motion without collision up to this point.[9]

Epicurus argues next that because the eidola are exceedingly fine
they are exceedingly fast. His explanation, stated in a doubtful
text, seems to be that the eidola have a path along which the
atoms meet with little or no collision, although in many cases there
is immediate collision.[10]

Because much is very puzzling in the cited text, a very tentative explanation must suffice. Since the cited passage is embedded
in a discussion of eidola and deals in part with the perception of
time, the subject of the third and fourth sentences is best understood as "eidolon." Accordingly, in the passage as a whole the first
two sentences present a general theory of motion, which is then
applied to the movement of the eidola in the remainder of the
passage. The general theory is that a body moving over a known
distance without any collision moves incomprehensibly fast, and
that slowness and quickness are determined by the number of col-

9. *Her.* 46–47: καὶ μὴν καὶ ἡ διὰ τοῦ κενοῦ φορὰ κατὰ μηδεμίαν ἀπάντησιν
τῶν ἀντικοψάντων γινομένη πᾶν μῆκος περιληπτὸν ἐν ἀπερινοήτῳ χρόνῳ συντελεῖ.
βράδους γὰρ καὶ τάχους ἀντικοπὴ καὶ οὐκ ἀντικοπὴ ὁμοίωμα λαμβάνει. οὐ μὴν
οὐδὲ ἅμα κατὰ τοὺς διὰ λόγου θεωρητοὺς χρόνους κατὰ τὸ φερόμενον σῶμα ἐπὶ
τοὺς πλείους τόπους ἀφικνεῖται (ἀδιανόητον γὰρ καὶ τοῦτο)· συναφικνούμενον δ'
ἐν αἰσθητῷ χρόνῳ ὅθεν δήποθεν τοῦ ἀπείρου οὐκ ἐξ οὗ ἂν περιλάβωμεν τὴν φορὰν
τόπου ἔσται ἀφιστάμενον. ἀντικοπὴ γὰρ ὅμοιον ἔσται κἂν μέχρι τοσούτου τὸ τάχος
τῆς φορᾶς μὴ ἀντικόπτον καταλίπωμεν.
   I have retained the text of the manuscripts except to write ἀντικόπτον (following
Usener) for mss. ἀντικοπεον, ἀντικοπτέον, and to add δ' after συναφικνούμενον.
κατὰ τὸ φερόμενον is awkward; and κατὰ should perhaps be emended to καὶ
(Usener) or αὐτὸ (von der Muehll). In any case, the reference, as I understand it,
is to the body of the eidolon. συναφικνούμενον should not be emended. The prefix συν- indicates that there is a simultaneous arrival, and this is, I suggest, the
simultaneous arrival of the eidolon in all the places of its journey in a single perceptible time.
   10. *Her.* 47. The manuscript readings ἀπείρῳ and ἀπείροις are very doubtful.
That eidola are infinite in number (which must be the sense in both cases) is
irrelevant to Epicurus' claim. Moreover, this would be a different kind of infinity
from the one just discussed. Bailey emends ἀπείρῳ to ἀπορρῷ and leaves ἀπείροις.

lisions suffered during the movement from one place to another. Subsequently, when Epicurus comes to apply this theory to the movement of the eidola, he makes a distinction between perceptible time and time that is too small to be perceived and hence is recognized only by reason. As I interpret this part of the text, Epicurus now points out that although an eidolon travels over any perceived distance in an instant of perceptible time, we must not suppose that an eidolon is at several places at once. For although with respect to perceptible time the eidolon is simultaneously at the place at which it started and at its goal, time is further subdivided by reason in such a way that with respect to these subdivisions the eidolon occupies different places at different times.[11]

This interpretation of eidolic speed is partially confirmed by Lucretius, who makes the general claim that eidola can pass over an immense distance "at a point of time" (*temporis in puncto*) and illustrates this with the example of star eidola traveling from the heavens to the earth at a point of time.[12] This "point of time" appears to be an instant of perceptible time, that is, a time too short to be perceived as an interval. Lucretius also draws a distinction between perceptible time and periods of time that are recognized by reason to underlie any single perceptible time.[13]

In asserting that there is imperceptibly fast motion, Epicurus adopts a position previously rejected by Aristotle. Aristotle denies the existence of imperceptible time in general, and rejects in particular the theory, which he attributes to Empedocles, that the passage of light occurs in spatiotemporal stages (like all locomotion) but is simply too fast to be noticed.[14] In a comparison of the speed of sunlight with the speed of eidola, Lucretius maintains, similarly

11. The difficulties of the cited passage have prompted Bailey (following Giussani) to transfer the first two sentences to the end of *Her.* 61 and the remainder to the end of *Her.* 62. Bailey's explanation is that the first two sentences deal with the movement of the atoms—not of the eidola—and that the rest deals with the movement of compound bodies in general (*Epicurus*, 190 and 216–25). Bailey's interpretation seems to me unconvincing; for the first two sentences state a general law that applies not only to atoms but also to compounds such as eidola. Also, the last sentence is incomprehensible except as a follow-up to the first two sentences. Last, Bailey mistakes the sense of the fourth sentence by understanding ἔσται ἀφιστάμενον as "it would be taking its departure" instead of as "it will be distant (separate)." Mau assigns the same sense as Bailey in translating "würde dann . . . seine Bewegung nicht an jenem Ort beginnen, wo wir sie beginnen sahen" and substituting ἀφικνούμενον for mss. ἀφιστάμενον (*Zum Problem*, 44). On Epicurus' theory of motion, see further chap. 16.

12. Lucretius 4.192–93 (on the eidola in general) and 4.214–15 (on the starry heavens).

13. Lucretius 4.794–96.

14. Aristotle *De anima* 418b20–26 and *De sensu* 446a25–28.

to Empedocles, that sunlight travels imperceptibly fast; and he points out in addition that since the eidola are much finer than sunlight and come from the surface of bodies, they travel much faster than sunlight.[15] Epicurus provides a justification for these claims in the cited passage of the *Letter to Herodotus*. By dividing perceptible time into smaller periods of time, which, though imperceptible, may be recognized by reason, Epicurus attempts to show that it is not absurd to suppose that a body travels to us by successive stages "from anywhere at all in the infinite" in a time that is too short to be noticed.

What still remains obscure is exactly how the occurrence or absence of collisions is related to the speed of the eidola. The general principle seems clear: the greater fineness of the eidolic complexes causes them to collide less with other atoms and so to travel faster than any other atomic complexes. Lucretius adds some precision to this principle when he explains that the fineness of the eidola allows them to slip through intervals of air.[16] There are, however, two complications. First, as a complex of atoms, an eidolon is subject to internal collisions; second, an eidolon is subject to collisions from the outside, particularly from the air. Even though Lucretius points out that the eidola slip through the network of air particles, he also claims that the distance of an object is known by the amount of air that the successively arriving eidola push ahead of themselves.[17] Thus, it seems that although eidola collide less with air particles than does any other type of atomic complex, it would be rare for an eidolon to enter the eye without having suffered any external collisions at all. This, together with the likelihood of internal collisions, suggests that the imperceptibly fast speed of the eidola is due not to an absolute lack of collision, but to a relative freedom from collisions, compared with other atomic complexes.

15. Lucretius 4.183–208.
16. Lucretius 4.198.
17. For the collision of eidola with particles of air, see Lucretius 4.244–55. The effect of either type of collision on the speed of the eidola may be inferred from what Lucretius says about the movement of the sun's heat and light, to which he compares eidolic movement at 4.161–65 and 185–208. At 2.150–64 Lucretius explains that the sun's light and heat, even though they travel very quickly, nevertheless move much more slowly than single atoms, for two reasons: the sun's light and heat are obstructed from the outside, because they do not travel through empty space but "as it were lash apart the waves of the air" (2.152); and as combinations of atoms, the sun's light and heat are "drawn back among themselves" (2.155), that is, are restrained within the complex by internal collisions. We must suppose that for the same two reasons the eidola move much more slowly than individual atoms, even though they move much faster than the sun's light and heat.

There seems, then, to be a range of eidolic speeds, from the highest, in which the eidolon suffers few or no collisions, to very low speeds, in which the eidolon suffers frequent collisions; but because the eidola are so fine that they suffer far fewer collisions, either internal or external, than other atomic complexes, their movement is imperceptibly fast. The first two sentences of the cited passage thus offer a general explanation for the eidola's imperceptibly fast movement: it is very largely free from collision. Although each atom within an eidolon is likely to meet with some colliding bodies (from either within or without), each atom within the complex travels a long distance without any collision and hence all atoms collectively move very fast from the source of the eidolon to the goal. In the final sentence of the passage, Epicurus seems to refer to movements that are entirely without collision; and he appears to be asserting the principle that there is a ratio between the speed of a movement that occurs without any collision and the speed of a movement that includes collisions. Although it would be rare for an eidolon to arrive at its goal without any collision, this principle has an application to the movement of the eidola in general. For no matter how often an eidolon suffers collisions, whether from within or from without, the movement of the eidolon as a whole consists in a network of individual movements without any collision.

Epicurus does not offer a comparable explanation of the movement of particles that produce smelling and hearing. These perceptions differ from sight in that there is clearly at times a perceptible interval; and this interval, we may infer, is due to the lesser fineness of these particles. The problem of a perceptible interval does not arise at all for taste or touch, for in these cases there is no space intervening between the source and the percipient. As for thought, Epicurus' theory of eidolic speed applies to it no less than to vision. Indeed, since the eidola that produce thought are finer than those that produce vision, thought must occur even faster than vision.

## THE PERCEPTUAL STREAM
## AND THE EXTERNAL SOURCE

After explaining the formation and speed of the eidola, Epicurus undertakes to show that it is by means of eidola that we see and think of external solids. He points out that eidola enter the sight or mind from external objects, of like color and shape with

them, and produce a "presentation," φαντασία. Epicurus describes
the formation of this presentation in the following very compressed clause:

> . . . the single and continuous [stream] produces the presentation
> [φαντασίαν] and preserves a sympathy with the underlying thing in
> accordance with the support derived commensurably from there, as
> a result of the vibration of the atoms deep in the solid.[18]

This description shows that Epicurus is answering the problem of
how we can see or think of an object that is at a distance from
ourselves. The solution that he proposes is that there is a continuum ("the single and continuous") between the observer and
the external solid. This is a flow of eidola that has its base in
the solid from which it comes and its termination in the perceptual organ. Because the flow of eidola is supported by movements
deep within the solid, there is a "sympathy" that extends from the
underlying solid to the presentation.[19]

Epicurus has previously mentioned at *Letter to Herodotus* 48 that
the eidola "preserve the position and arrangement of the atoms
on the solid" for a long time, although there is sometimes a disturbance. It is not clear whether the cited description of the eidolic
flow applies only to cases in which the position and arrangement
of atoms remain unaltered, or whether it applies also to cases in
which there has been a disturbance. In his corresponding description of the acoustic stream, however, Epicurus draws a clear distinction between two types of perception, one of which is the
result of a disturbance. An acoustic affection (πάθος), Epicurus
explains, is produced by a stream of particles flowing from the
sounding object; this stream preserves a "unity of a distinctive
kind":

---

18. *Her.* 49: τοῦ ἑνὸς καὶ συνεχοῦς τὴν φαντασίαν ἀποδιδόντος καὶ τὴν συμπά-
θειαν ἀπὸ τοῦ ὑποκειμένου σῴζοντος κατὰ τὸν ἐκεῖθεν σύμμετρον ἐπερεισμὸν ἐκ
τῆς κατὰ βάθος ἐν τῷ στερεμνίῳ τῶν ἀτόμων πάλσεως. Most editors change the singular participles ἀποδιδόντος and σῴζοντος to plurals to modify τύπων in the preceding clause, but this change is unnecessary. I take the participles to modify τοῦ
ἑνὸς καὶ συνεχοῦς, which is the continuum formed by the stream of eidola. Epicurus similarly speaks of the single acoustic stream (described as ἑνότητα) producing hearing (*Her.* 52; the manuscript readings ποιοῦσαν and παρασκευάζουσαν
should be kept).

19. Epicurus' notion of a continuum between the percipient and the external
source is similar to Aristotle's claims that a continuum of air produces sight (*De
anima* 419a14) and that a "single and continuous" air produces hearing (ibid.,
419b34–20a4).

[The particles preserve] a unity of a distinctive kind [ἑνότητα ἰδιό-
τροπον] extending to the source and producing a perception directly
on it [τὴν ἐπαίσθησιν τὴν ἐπ' ἐκείνου] for the most part, but otherwise making clear only what is outside. For without a certain sympathy that is relayed from there a direct perception [ἐπαίσθησις] of
this sort cannot occur.[20]

In hearing as in sight, a continuum of particles flows from the external object to the observer. This continuum produces an audi-
tory impression in one of two ways: for the most part, it preserves
a certain sympathy with the external source, causing the percipient
to have a perception directly "on" the source; for the rest, the
stream of particles makes clear only what is "outside" the source.[21]

In his account of Epicurus' methodology, Sextus Empiricus
throws light on the distinction between perception "on" the source
and perception of what is "outside." Using the term "presentation," φαντασία, to designate all sensory impressions produced in
an organ from outside, Sextus reports that the Epicureans defended the claim that all presentations are true by a detailed
analysis of sight.[22] What is seen, the Epicureans claimed, is not the
whole solid but the color of the solid, and the color is of two
kinds: color that is on (ἐπί) the solid itself, and color that is outside (ἐκτός) the solid and in the spaces next to it. The former
type is seen from nearby, the latter from afar. In the former case,
the color remains unaltered in the interval between the source and
the percipient, whereas in the latter the color is altered. For example, when a tower is seen from nearby, it appears large and square
because the eidola have traveled undisturbed from the tower to
the eyes. In this case the color, through which size and shape are

---

20. *Her.* 52–53: . . . ἑνότητα ἰδιότροπον διατείνουσαν πρὸς τὸ ἀποστεῖλαν, καὶ
τὴν ἐπαίσθησιν τὴν ἐπ' ἐκείνου ὡς τὰ πολλὰ ποιοῦσαν, εἰ δὲ μή γε, τὸ ἔξωθεν
μόνον ἔνδηλον παρασκευάζουσαν· ἄνευ γὰρ ἀναφερομένης τινὸς ἐκεῖθεν συμπα-
θείας οὐκ ἂν γένοιτο ἡ τοιαύτη ἐπαίσθησις. (See n. 18 above on the text.) For a
further analysis of the acoustic stream, see Edward N. Lee, "The Sense of an
Object: Epicurus on Seeing and Hearing," 31–34.
21. Bailey takes τὴν ἐπαίσθησιν τὴν ἐπ' ἐκείνου as "comprehension in the recipient," that is, as an understanding by the percipient of what another person
means by the words he utters; and he takes τὸ ἔξωθεν as "the external object,"
so that the contrast is between understanding words and simply hearing the sounds
without understanding them (*Epicurus*, 31 and 200). This interpretation seems to
me wrong for two reasons: there has been no mention of any percipient, let alone
a hearer of words, to serve as a reference for ἐκείνου; and there is no reason why
the perceptual stream as such should produce "comprehension." On ἐπαίσθησις,
see further chap. 8 (Perception, Interpretation, and Reason).
22. Sextus Empiricus *Adv. math.* 7.206–9.

recognized, has not been altered. But when a tower is seen from afar, it appears small and round because the edges of the eidola have been knocked off in their journey and accordingly the color has been altered. In either case, Sextus explains, the color, and along with it the shape and size, are seen as they really are. Thus the tower seen from afar really is small and roundish, even though the tower seen from nearby is large and square. Sextus defends this position by pointing out that in hearing, too, we perceive either from nearby or from afar, and that when a sound heard from afar is faint it really is faint, just as we hear it to be.[23]

If we add Sextus' explanation to Epicurus' much more condensed account, it appears that in both sight and hearing there is a perceptual stream, extending from the external source to the percipient, which either preserves its motions unaltered from the source to the percipient or else suffers a disturbance of its motions. The former happens when the percipient is close to the source, the latter when the percipient is far from the source. Whenever the motions remain unaltered, the percipient has a direct acquaintance with the external source, or a perception "on" the source; whenever the motions are altered, the percipient has a direct acquaintance only with what is "outside" the source. The terms "nearby" and "far" apply in the first place, as Sextus shows, to the actual distance of the percipient from the source of perception. But they also imply a cognitive proximity or distance between the knower and the known object. Accordingly, when the percipient is spatially close to the source, the source is directly present to the percipient's awareness; and when the percipient is spatially far away, the source is at a remove from the percipient's awareness.

The distinction between nearby and distant perception may be supposed to apply also to the sense of smell. In his brief discussion of smell in the *Letter to Herodotus*, Epicurus points out that an affection is produced by particles coming from an object and stirring the sense organ, and that these particles are partly "without confusion and suitable" and partly "with confusion and unsuitable."[24] Although Epicurus here seems to be taking into consideration not only the external arrangement of atoms in the perceptual stream, but also the arrangement of atoms once they have entered

23. Lucretius explains similarly to Sextus how a square tower appears round when seen from a distance (4.353–63). He also draws a distinction between distant and nearby perception in his explanation of hearing (553–62).

24. *Her.* 53: οἱ μὲν τοῖοι τεταραγμένως καὶ ἀλλοτρίως, οἱ δὲ τοῖοι ἀταράχως καὶ οἰκείως ἔχοντες. Lucretius explains that one smell is more suitable (*aptus*,

the organ of perception, it seems clear that in smell, as in sight, thought, and hearing, a disarrangement of atoms can occur outside the percipient. It follows that in smelling, too, the percipient may be acquainted directly with the source or may perceive only what is external to it.

Epicurus does not include taste and touch in his discussion of perception in the *Letter to Herodotus.* The reason seems to be that he is here considering only the problem of how we can perceive something when the source of perception is at an interval from the percipient. Epicurus' solution is that whenever the source is at a distance—that is, whenever we see or think, hear, or smell—there is a continuity between the percipient and the source of perception that makes possible a direct acquaintance with the external source. According to Epicurus, whenever there has been no change in the external stream of particles, the external source is just as immediately present as in the case of taste and touch.

So far we have discussed only the process of transmission that occurs outside the percipient. It remains to consider what happens to the continuity of the perceptual stream when it meets the organ of perception. Epicurus indicates the answer very briefly in his explanations of sight and thought and of smell. Concerning sight and thought, he writes that the eidola enter the respective organs "according as the size fits" (κατὰ τὸ ἐναρμόττον μέγεθος); and he also states, as just quoted, that the eidola preserve a sympathy with the underlying object "according to the support derived commensurably from there" (κατὰ τὸν ἐκεῖθεν σύμμετρον ἐπερεισμόν).[25] Both descriptions indicate that there is a match in size between the eidola and the physical makeup of the organ of perception. Epicurus also uses the term "commensurate" (σύμμετρος) in his explanation of smell to signify an adjustment in size between the perceptual particles and the sense organ. As he puts this, there are particles carried from the external object that are "of a measure [σύμμετροι] to stir this sense organ."[26]

The view that the organ of perception admits only particles that

---

4.677) to some animals than to others; for example, the smell of honey is especially suitable to bees and the smell of corpses to vultures (4.677–86). He notes that this difference is due to the shapes of the impinging atoms (4.678); cf. 2.398–443. As in the case of hearing, Epicurus refers to the effect of the particles on the sense organ simply as an "affection" (πάθος, *Her.* 53); but there is no reason to suppose that he did not extend the term φαντασία, used in the case of sight and thought, also to the other senses, as his followers clearly did.

25. *Her.* 49 and 50.
26. *Her.* 53.

correspond to it in size implies not only that each type of organ has its own type of particles corresponding to it, but also that each individual organ admits only the part of a perceptual stream that fits its own individual passages. This aspect of the Epicurean doctrine is discussed at length by Plutarch in his treatise *Against Colotes* (1109a–1110d). Plutarch's discussion complements Sextus' analysis of the perceptual stream. Plutarch likewise presents an Epicurean defense of the claim that all presentations are true; and this also consists in explaining how the same external source can give rise to different perceptions, all of which show what is the case. Instead of explaining, however, how external streams may differ depending on different external circumstances, Plutarch shows how different parts of a perceptual stream may be admitted by the perceptual organ depending on differences in the organ itself. Using the same term, σύμμετρος, as was used by Epicurus, Plutarch points out that only those parts of a perceptual stream that are "commensurate" with it are admitted by the sense organ.[27] As evidence, Plutarch cites an example used by Epicurus himself: wine has a heating effect on some persons and a cooling effect on others, depending on what constituents of the wine enter the body.[28]

Lucretius illustrates further the screening effect of the perceptual organ by giving examples from smell, taste, and sight. Lucretius explains that different species of animals have sense organs that are so composed as to admit different types of perceptual particles; and he also explains that individuals of the same species perceive the same type of thing differently depending on whether or not illness has disarranged the sense organ.[29] According to Lucretius, one illness, jaundice, affects the perceptual stream both from outside the percipient and from within. The reason the jaundiced person sees yellow, Lucretius explains, is that particles of yellow both flow from the person to join the perceptual stream outside and are present inside the eyes so as to join the perceptual stream once it has entered.[30]

In all types of perception, then, the stream of atoms that produces an impression in the perceptual organ admits of varying degrees of continuity with the source, depending on the extent to which the stream has become rearranged either outside or inside

27. Plutarch *Adv. Colotem* 1109d (cf. συμμετρίαι at 1109c).
28. Ibid., 1109e–10b.
29. Lucretius 4.633–86, 706–21.
30. Lucretius 4.332–36.

the organ. Surprisingly, neither type of disturbance makes an impression untruthful. In sight and thought, moreover, the perceptual stream may originate spontaneously in midair, so that there need not be any continuity at all with an external solid. Is an impression produced in this way as truthful as any other? In order to understand what the Epicureans meant by the truthfulness of perceptions, it is necessary to examine not only the external causes of perception but also the contribution made from within the percipient. The next two chapters discuss two distinct kinds of internal contribution: first, the irrational response of the perceptual organ to the influx of particles; and second, the interpretation added by the mind.

# [ 7 ]

# Perceptions: Response by the Organ of Perception

## OBTAINING A PRESENTATION

THE previous chapter examined how particles enter from outside the perceptual organ to produce perception. The influx of particles from outside, however, is only one of two complementary activities required to produce perception. At the same time as the particles flow into the perceptual organ, the organ responds to the particles by an activity of its own. This chapter examines this activity of the perceptual organ; and the first main source for discussion is Lucretius' account of thought, or mental perception.

Lucretius introduces his analysis of mental perception by pointing out that mental presentations are produced by eidola just like those of visual presentations except that they are much finer. Because of their exceptional fineness, Lucretius explains, mental eidola combine readily in midair to form composites, such as eidola of centaurs, which are formed by a combination of horse and man eidola. In addition to such composites, the mind receives eidola showing things just like those we see. Furthermore, unlike sight, the mind may be active during sleep; but dreaming is just like having mental images when one is awake, except that since the senses and the memory are then dormant, the false beliefs prompted by the dream images cannot be refuted.[1]

1. Lucretius 4.724–67; see also U 317 and Cicero's criticisms of the eidolic theory of thought at *Academica* 2.125, *De natura deorum* 1.107–9, and *De divinatione* 2.137–39. In *De divinatione* Cicero attributes the eidolic theory to Democritus, but what he says applies also to Epicurus' theory, which Cicero elsewhere claims to have been derived from Democritus (*De finibus* 1.21; *De natura deorum* 1.107).

Subsequently, Lucretius considers the mind's own activity in response to the eidola as he undertakes to refute two objections to the Epicurean theory of thought. The objections are part of what we know to have been a vigorous attack on Epicurus' materialist explanation of mind.[2] The objections that Lucretius has selected are: how is it possible to think straightway of anything one likes? and how are dream images able to move so very smoothly and rhythmically? Lucretius answers the first question as follows:

> Because in a single perceptible time—that is, when a single utterance is emitted—many times are hidden that reason recognizes to exist, it happens that at any time whatsoever all the eidola are present, ready in their several places. . . . And because they are fine, the mind cannot discern any sharply except those that it strains for. Accordingly, all [eidola] that are additional perish—all except those for which it has prepared itself. The mind itself, furthermore, prepares itself and expects that it will see what follows upon each thing; hence it comes to be. Do you not see that the eyes too, when they begin to discern things that are fine, strain and prepare themselves, and that without this it is impossible for us to see sharply? Moreover, even in the case of things that are plain to perceive, you can know that unless you pay attention, it is just as though the thing were separated by all time and far removed. Why, then, is it strange that the mind loses all things except those to which it is itself given up?[3]

2. Cicero is our main source for criticisms of the Epicurean theory. In *Epistulae ad familiares* 15.16.1–2 he demands to know from his friend Cassius, who is currently in Britain, how an eidolon of him is to appear to Cicero as soon as he wishes to think of Cassius, and, furthermore, how an eidolon of the island Britain is to come flying to him. In *De natura deorum* 1.107–9 Cicero offers a long list of objections, among them how we can have images of men, places, and cities that we have never seen; how an image is present to him as soon as he wishes; and how images come unasked in dreams. A very similar list of objections is found at *De divinatione* 2.137–39. As Kleve suggests, the criticisms may well be derived from the Academic Carneades ("The Philosophical Polemics in Lucretius: A Study in the History of Epicurean Criticism," 67).

3. Lucretius 4.794–815:

>                  . . . quia tempore in uno,
> quod sentimus, id est, cum vox emittitur una,
> tempora multa latent, ratio quae comperit esse,
> propterea fit uti quovis in tempore quaeque
> praesto sint simulacra locis in quisque parata:
>                 .  .  .
> et quia tenuia sunt, nisi quae contendit, acute
> cernere non potis est animus; proinde omnia quae sunt
> praeterea pereunt, nisi ⟨si ad⟩ quae se ipse paravit.
> ipse parat sese porro speratque futurum
> ut videat quod consequitur rem quamque; fit ergo.

As Lucretius outlines it, the solution to the first problem has two components: a distinction between perceptible time and time recognized only by reason, and a mechanism of self-preparation or straining on the part of the mind. The former accounts for a large number of possible presentations within a single perceptible time; the latter allows the mind to make a selection from these possibilities. We have already noted the distinction between the two kinds of time. Lucretius here identifies a single perceptible unit of time with the time during which a single utterance is made. The reason, we may infer from the context, is that Lucretius is specifically concerned with the problem of how we are able to understand what another person is saying, or, in other words, how we are able to fit presumptions to another person's utterances. In order to understand the utterances, we must be able to associate appropriate images with them as soon as they are spoken. Lucretius explains, first, that any single perceptible period of time is divided into many subperceptible periods, so that during the time in which an utterance is made many eidola flow in rapid succession to the mind so as to be available to it. Lucretius then adds that there is a process of self-preparation by which the mind strains to select one or more out of this large available number of eidola. By making an effort of its own, the mind is able to focus on any eidolon at all out of the rapid flow of eidola and hence to call up at any time whatever thought it pleases. When the mind does not make this effort, it "loses" (*perdit*) the object, and the object "perishes." This loss is an explanation for both forgetfulness and complete ignorance.

Lucretius offers two proofs to show that the mind must make an effort in order to have a distinct awareness. First, he compares thought with the experience of seeing tiny objects: just as the eyes strain to see what is tiny (as we know by direct sensory experience), so, we must infer, the mind strains in order to see the very fine objects to which it directs itself. The second proof is also an infer-

> nonne vides oculos etiam, cum tenuia quae sunt
> cernere coeperunt, contendere se atque parare,
> nec sine eo fieri posse ut cernamus acute?
> et tamen in rebus quoque apertis noscere possis,
> si non advertas animum, proinde esse quasi omni
> tempore semotum fuerit longeque remotum.
> cur igitur mirumst, animus si cetera perdit
> praeterquam quibus est in rebus deditus ipse?

I agree with Lachmann that ll. 799–801 ( = 774, 771, 772) do not belong to this passage. For the rest of the text, I have followed Bailey.

ence from our own experience: just as we are barely conscious of
the clearly perceptible objects around us whenever we do not pay
attention, so, we must suppose, the mind cannot have a clear
awareness of its objects whenever it does not pay attention. The
two proofs show that the distinction between a possible presentation and an effort by which a possible presentation becomes actual
applies to all cases of perception. Although Lucretius does not
make clear in his second proof that the perceptual organ itself
must engage in a process of straining in order to have a distinct
impression, he shows clearly in his first proof that every perceptual organ has a capacity for straining, by which it sharpens its
apprehension.

Lucretius' answer to the second question, that regarding the
movement of dream figures, sheds more light on the difference
the mind's effort makes. The solution to this problem consists,
like the solution to the first problem, in the large availability of
eidola in any perceptible time together with an effort on the part
of the mind. Lucretius explains the appearance of moving dream
figures as follows:

> For the rest, it is not surprising that eidola move and toss their
> arms and other limbs rhythmically; for it happens that during sleep
> an image appears to do this. The reason is that when the first image
> perishes and another next arises with a different posture, the earlier
> one seems to have changed position. To be sure, this must be sup-
> posed to occur quickly; so great is the mobility, so great the abun-
> dance of things, and so great the abundance of particles in any
> single perceptible time that it can keep up the supply.[1]

4. Lucretius 4.768–76:

> quod superest, non est mirum simulacra moveri
> bracchiaque in numerum iactare et cetera membra.
> nam fit ut in somnis facere hoc videatur imago;
> quippe ubi prima perit alioque est altera nata
> inde statu, prior hic gestum mutasse videtur.
> scilicet id fieri celeri ratione putandumst:
> tanta est mobilitas et rerum copia tanta
> tantaque sensibili quovis est tempore in uno
> copia particularum, ut possit suppeditare.

I propose that these lines were originally placed after line 815 (see my article
"Lucretius' Explanation of Moving Dream Figures at 4.768–76"). They are an
answer to the second problem raised by Lucretius (at 788–93), and they cannot be
said to be "not surprising" or to be comprehensible at all unless they follow the
explanation that begins at l. 794. Moreover, unless ll. 768–76 are relocated as suggested, the second question receives no answer after being asked, since ll. 794–815
are an answer to the first question. Also, ll. 768–76 are only loosely connected

Although Lucretius does not mention specifically that there is an act of straining on the part of the mind, we may infer from the fact that the mind has a clear presentation—of a figure that is seen to move its arms and legs in unison—that it does make an effort. This effort consists in an interesting blend of straining and nonstraining, which enables the mind to focus in quick succession on one eidolon after another in order to obtain the appearance of a single moving figure. The mind makes no effort to get hold of any single unchanging appearance; accordingly, the successive eidola "perish" as one yields to the next. Throughout this process, however, the mind is intent on obtaining an overall changing appearance; accordingly it makes an effort to select in quick succession precisely those eidola that will produce the image of a single, smoothly moving figure.

The mind's effort, therefore, may vary from sustaining an unchanging appearance over a period of time to shifting focus so quickly as to obtain a continuously changing appearance. That this shifting may take unusual turns Lucretius shows in a series of examples appended to his discussion of dreams. He notes that "at times an image of the same kind is not supplied, but what was previously a woman seems to have become a man in our very presence, or a different face or age follows one after another."[5] Here the mind does not make an effort to sustain the image of a single individual; rather its degree of attention is such that the dream figure changes bizarrely from one sex or face or age to another. The mind makes an effort even so; if it were to lapse into total inattention, none of the figures would become distinct at all.

Lucretius' explanation of mental vision indicates that although eidola may fail, through the mind's lack of attention, to produce a distinct impression corresponding to their configuration, they may yet contribute to a presentation as components of it. As parts of a presentation, these eidola are not discernible in themselves; rather they are individually indiscernible components that merge in imperceptibly fast succession into a single overall presentation.

---

with what precedes in the traditional arrangement; and last, ll. 816–22 follow logically upon 768–76. Lucretius uses both *simulacrum* and *imago* to translate εἴδωλον; the former term corresponds closely to the Greek.

    5. Lucretius 4.818–21:

> fit quoque ut interdum non suppeditetur imago
> eiusdem generis, sed femina quae fuit ante,
> in manibus vir uti factus videatur adesse,
> aut alia ex alia facies aetasque sequatur.

Lucretius' example of seeing tiny objects shows further how these components may contribute to a final overall presentation. A presentation may gain in precision through a gradual intensification of effort, so that what was not discerned initially at all finally comes into focus.

By including dreams in his discussion of mental perception, Lucretius makes clear that the effort or preparation of the mind is not necessarily a deliberate act. In the case of dreams, the effort clearly consists in the existence of a certain physical condition that has nothing to do with deliberate choice. Lucretius explains this physical condition later in his discussion of sleep by relating it to efforts undertaken during the day. Whatever the mind most strained for during the day, he points out, is what it generally experiences in its dreams; the reason is that passages remain open in the mind at night to receive the same images that were received during the day.[6] The mind, then, focuses on certain images rather than on others during sleep because the state of tension that it experienced during the day persists during the night. When awake, the mind is likewise in a certain state of tension, which causes it to admit certain eidola rather than others out of the large number that are continually bombarding it from outside. This state of tension may be conditioned by previous experiences just as much as the state of the mind during dreams; hence the act of selection by the mind may be just as involuntary as in dreams. When the mind is awake, the act of selection is deliberate only when the mind has, in addition, made a resolve to make the selection. Lucretius is quite emphatic that the effort made by the mind in selecting images is an act of self-preparation, undertaken of its own accord. What he stresses here, however, is not that the mind is acting deliberately, but rather that it is an agent that makes a response of its own to forces that come upon it from outside. This response, Lucretius insists, is not imposed by external forces, but is due to the nature of the mind itself.[7]

6. Lucretius 4.973–1037, esp. 976–97. See also Diogenes of Oenoanda, new fr. 5 col. 3.6–14 (Smith, "New Fragments of Diogenes of Oenoanda," 360; and Clay, "An Epicurean Interpretation of Dreams," 363).

7. It is to this act of the mind in response to external forces that Carneades seems to refer in Cicero's *De fato* 23 when he criticizes the Epicurean theory of the swerve as follows: "since they [the Epicureans] taught that there can be a kind of voluntary motion of the mind, it would have been better to defend this than to introduce the swerve" (cum docerent esse posse quemdam animi motum voluntarium, id fuit defendi melius quam introducere declinationem). As Carneades' criticism indicates, there is no reason to suppose that the mind's capacity to have certain presentations rather than others is dependent on there being a swerve.

Both Cicero and Philodemus give evidence of the same capacity of the mind to select its images. Cicero shows that it is an important part of Epicurean hedonism that the mind should have the power to repress unpleasant thoughts and to focus on thoughts that are pleasant, including both memories of past events and expectations for the future.[8] In agreement with Cicero, Philodemus speaks of an intense concentration upon past, present, and future goods, and he gives some specific examples of the suppression of unwelcome thoughts. He also uses the technical Epicurean term ἐπιβολή to refer to the act by which the mind focuses on its objects. According to Philodemus, we should make the "most intense application [συνεχεστάτην ἐπιβολήν] to past, present, and future goods."[9] As an example of a subject that is shunned by many, Philodemus mentions death: people who love life and fear death, he notes, "push aside applications [ἐπιβολάς] to it [death]," with the result that "when the contemplation of it becomes evident [ἐναργής]," it is contrary to expectations.[10] Similarly, Philodemus charges that music makes the misfortunes of love "unattended" (ἀνεπιβλήτους), just as sexual passion and drink do.[11] These uses of the term ἐπιβολή are consistent with Epicurus' own extant uses. In his introduction to the *Letter to Herodotus*, for example, Epicurus invites the student to make a comprehensive "application" (ἐπιβολή) to his physical theory, and in general to make a "keen use of applications."[12]

As we have seen, Epicurus assigns "applications," ἐπιβολαί, not only to the mind but also to the senses; and he demands in his second rule of investigation that we observe in accordance with these applications. Scholars have widely recognized the importance of the notion of ἐπιβολή in Epicurus' methodology, but, as previously indicated, there is no agreement about what the term means. Bailey has argued that ἐπιβολή consists in the straining activity described by Lucretius; but he has denied that this activity occurs in all cases of perception. Relying on the claim that the straining activity of the perceptual organ, as discussed by Lucretius, produces a sharp and distinct presentation, Bailey proposes that ἐπιβολή is a special act of attention that, in the case of sense

8. Cicero *De finibus* 1.57 and 2.104–05; see also *Tusculanae Disputationes* 3.33, 35.

9. Philodemus *De dis* 3 col. 2.25–27 Diels (p. 18).

10. Philodemus *De morte* 4 col. 39.8–11 (see Marcello Gigante, "Filodemo De morte IV 37–39," 371).

11. Philodemus *De musica* 4 col. 15.5–7 Kemke (p. 80).

12. *Her.* 36.

perceptions, results in presentations that are not only sharp but also "near" and are for this reason faithful to the external object, and analogously, in the case of thought, results in "clear" and truthful mental images, whether they are perceived directly through an influx of eidola (as in the contemplation of the gods) or are scientific concepts. Accordingly, Bailey interprets the phrase "and simply the present applications, whether of the mind or of any of the criteria," in Epicurus' statement of his second rule of investigation to refer, in the case of the mind, to the direct intuition of scientific truths, and in the case of the other criteria, to those select sense perceptions that are from nearby and that show the external object without any distortion or falsehood.[13]

Bailey is opposed by those who deny that ἐπιβολή, as the term is used by Epicurus, necessarily involves straining or concentration. These scholars maintain that it is a passive process by which the senses or the mind "get hold" of anything at all (as Furley suggests), or, in other words, make a "contact" (as Rist translates) or obtain a "view" (according to DeWitt).[14] The main evidence cited in support of this position is that in *Letter to Herodotus* 51 Epicurus speaks of dreams and other allegedly deceptive presentations as appearances obtained by "applications," ἐπιβολαί.[15] According to this second view, ἐπιβολή does not guarantee a veridical presentation, and consequently the term ἐπιβολή in the procedural note does not pick out a certain group of perceptions as veridical.

The preceding examination of Lucretius' account of mental

13. See Bailey's essay "On the Meaning of ἐπιβολὴ τῆς διανοίας," both in *Greek Atomists* (559–76) and in *Epicurus* (259–74); see also his commentary on Lucretius, 1275. Concerning the applications of the mind, Bailey proposes that, although in the Κανών Epicurus may have viewed them as a "form of sensation," in *Her.* 38 (and possibly 62) and in *KD* 24 he regards them as apprehensions of scientific truths (*Greek Atomists*, 250–52).

14. Furley writes: "The word *epibletikos* means no more than 'by the apprehensive process,' the process by which the mind or the senses 'get hold of' something" ("Knowledge of Atoms and Void in Epicureanism," in *Essays in Ancient Greek Philosophy*, 611). He argues similarly in his *Two Studies* (208) that "ἐπιβολή is *not* necessarily an act of concentration or deliberate attention," and that apprehension is something passive. DeWitt previously rejected Bailey's interpretation of ἐπιβολή, taking it to mean "view" or "incidence, onfall" of the mind or senses ("Epicurus, Περὶ Φαντασίας," 421–23). Rist agrees with Furley that ἐπιβολαί or "contacts" (as Rist translates) are not necessarily acts of concentration (*Epicurus*, 25); and he suggests in addition that acts of concentration tend to mislead a person more than simple sensory contacts do, on the ground that opinion is involved in the process of selection (ibid., 86–87).

15. Both Furley ("Knowledge of Atoms," 609–11) and DeWitt ("Epicurus, Περὶ Φαντασίας," 420) cite *Her.* 51 as evidence that there are ἐπιβολαί relating to deceptive images as well as to truthful images.

perception indicates, it seems to me, that just as every act of mental perception involves some straining by the mind, so every act of perception whatsoever involves some straining by the perceptual organ. It is clear from Lucretius' discussion that the act of straining does not serve to mark off veridical from deceptive presentations. Rather, it serves to bring an object into focus; and the more intense the straining, the more distinct the object. We feel this effort, Lucretius shows, whenever we direct our senses at an object that is tiny or otherwise elusive. But we may suppose that in all cases of perception an object is brought into focus as the result of some straining by the perceptual organ. An ἐπιβολή, "application," therefore, is a response by which the perceptual organ makes an effort to bring an object into focus; and it is neither a guarantee of a truthful presentation nor simply a passive submission to external influences. Although the response is involuntary, the perceptual organ engages in an activity of its own; and it is in this capacity that it serves as a "criterion" (κριτήριον) that judges what is real.[16]

In his procedural note, then, Epicurus demands that we observe everything in accordance with the acts of attention by which the mind or the senses obtain any presentation at all. No group of perceptions is picked out as veridical, nor is there any reference to a special kind of scientific intuition. But this conclusion does not imply that Epicurus does not set out a criterion of truth. As shall be discussed next, the perceptual organs themselves judge what is real by their own active response to external influences.

### COMPACTING AND REMAINING

In his account of sense perception in the *Letter of Herodotus*, Epicurus introduces the notion of "application" in the following sentence, immediately after the sentence on the formation of a presentation quoted on page 112.

And whatever presentation we obtain by application [ἐπιβλητικῶς] by the mind or [the sight], whether of a form or of its concomitants, this is the form of the solid, generated in accordance with succes-

16. Epicurus' division of perception into an impact from outside the organ and a response from within is not new. His term ἐπιβολή corresponds closely to προσβολή at Plato's *Theaetetus* 153e; here Socrates explains that, according to those who hold that knowledge is perception, a color is produced "by the application [προσβολῆς] of the eyes to the appropriate motion." Similarly, in explaining his own theory of vision at *Timaeus* 64e, Plato describes the sight as "applying" (προσβαλοῦσα) to the things with which it is in contact.

sive compacting [κατὰ τὸ ἑξῆς πύκνωμα] or a residue of the eidolon [ἐγκατάλειμμα τοῦ εἰδώλου].[17]

After showing how a solid acts upon the sight or mind from outside to produce a presentation, Epicurus now explains what makes a visual or mental presentation identical with the form of a solid. This explanation has generally been regarded as crucial to an understanding of Epicurus' epistemology. For here Epicurus seems to set out a criterion of truth, as he identifies a certain type of presentation with a certain state of affairs. He describes the presentation as showing a form or its concomitants, and specifies that we obtain it "by application" of the perceptual organ; and he describes the state of affairs as the form of a solid, with the explanation that it is produced by successive compacting or by a residue of the eidolon.

As the controversy about ἐπιβολή indicates, the interpretation of this sentence has been much debated. According to Bailey, Epicurus here proposes ἐπιβλητικῶς, "by application," as the condition that ensures that a presentation shows an object as it exists in the external world. Others have also held that Epicurus here sets out the condition under which a presentation shows an external object without any distortion; but they have maintained that this condition lies in the two alternative methods—successive compacting and a residue of the eidolon—by which the form is said to come into being.[18]

17. *Her.* 50: καὶ ἣν ἂν λάβωμεν φαντασίαν ἐπιβλητικῶς τῇ διανοίᾳ ἢ * εἴτε μορφῆς εἴτε συμβεβηκότων, μορφή ἐστιν αὕτη τοῦ στερεμνίου, γινομένη κατὰ τὸ ἑξῆς πύκνωμα ἢ ἐγκατάλειμμα τοῦ εἰδώλου. The text presents one major difficulty. The manuscripts vary between τοῖς στερεμνίοις and τοῖς αἰσθητηρίοις after τῇ διανοίᾳ ἤ. The first reading is clearly impossible. The second, which is adopted by all the editors, is very doubtful and should probably be replaced by τῇ ὄψει; for Epicurus is still confining the discussion to sight and thought, as shown by the reference to εἰδώλου at the end of the sentence and by the description of the presentation as being either "of the form [μορφῆς] or of its concomitants [συμβεβηκότων]." Apart from touch, which apprehends its own type of form, that of body, the other senses do not apprehend the form of a solid, nor do their objects qualify as concomitants of form. I suggest that τοῖς αἰσθητηρίοις was an attempt to correct an already corrupt text and was inspired by the later reference to κριτηρίων (*Her.* 51).

18. Furley has argued for this second view ("Knowledge of Atoms," 608–11). Kleve suggested previously that in the case of thought a continuous stream of eidola produces a reliable presentation, whereas a single eidolon is unreliable (*Gnosis Theon*, 78–79). Kleve subsequently elaborated this view by outlining a scale of reliability: most reliable are images produced by a constant stream of eidola from nearby objects; next are images produced by a constant stream of eidola from distant objects; and least reliable are images produced by a single eidolon ("Empiricism and Theology in Epicureanism," 47).

A difficulty that confronts both interpretations is that Epicurus describes the state of affairs as an effect produced within the perceptual organ. Hence it is not at all clear that Epicurus is explaining under what circumstances a presentation corresponds to an independently existing object of perception. Moreover, there is good evidence that Epicurus held that any presentation obtained by an application of the mind or sight is obtained by one of the two stated methods, and that in general any presentation at all is produced by successive compacting or by a residue of perceptual particles.

For successive compacting, there is, first, a brief report by Augustine. He writes that, according to Democritus and Epicurus, a single image is produced by a kind of compacting of countless images flowing continuously from a body:

> When they are asked why there appears a single image of a body from which countless images flow, they reply that for the very reason that images flow and pass by continuously, it happens by a kind of compacting and condensation of them [*quadam earum constipatione et densatione*] that one image appears out of many.[19]

Augustine here considers the same problem treated by Epicurus—how we obtain a presentation of an external solid—and he supplies as an answer one of the two explanations given by Epicurus. Augustine's *constipatione et densatione* corresponds exactly to Epicurus' πύχνωμα. What Augustine makes clear in addition is that this compacting consists in the merging of successive eidola into a single eidolon.

A second piece of evidence is provided by Lucretius. Although Lucretius does not use the term "compacting," he describes the process itself as he undertakes to explain why it is that "things themselves" (*res ipsae*) are seen even though eidola cannot be seen individually. Lucretius' answer is that the cumulative effect of the successively impinging eidola produces a perception of "things themselves":

---

19. Augustine *Epistulae* 118.30: Cum autem quaeritur ab eis, quare una imago videatur corporis alicuius a quo innumerabiliter imagines fluunt, respondent eo ipso, quo frequenter fluunt et transeunt imagines, quasi quadam earum constipatione et densitate fieri ut ex multis una videatur. Augustine betrays some confusion here, for he takes this explanation to apply also to the formation of the concept of god, even though in this case the images do not flow from a single source. Augustine seems to have drawn his information from some well-known Epicurean explanation of successive compacting as set out at *Letter to Herodotus* 50.

In this it must not be considered strange at all that although the eidola that strike the eyes cannot be seen singly, things themselves [*res ipsae*] are discerned. For when the wind too lashes us little by little and when bitter cold flows, we are not accustomed to perceive each individual particle of wind and its cold, but rather [we perceive the wind] as a whole [*unorsum*] and we notice blows occurring on our body just as if some object were lashing it and providing a perception of its own external body. Moreover, when we strike the stone itself with the finger, we touch [*tangimus*] the outermost color of the rock at the very surface, yet we do not perceive this by touch [*nec sentimus eum tactu*] but rather we perceive the hardness itself deep within the rock.[20]

Comparing sight with touch, Lucretius makes a distinction between the immediate cause of perception and the object perceived. Whenever we see anything, he explains, the immediate cause of vision is the impact of eidola on the eyes, just as when we feel the cold wind the immediate cause of perception is the impact of particles of wind on our body, and when we feel the hardness of the

His apparent aim is to shed light on Cicero's account of the Epicurean concept of god in book 1 of *De natura deorum*, and in particular to explain Cicero's statement at 1.109: fluentium frequenter transitio fit visionum ut e multis una videatur ("there is a passage of visions flowing continuously, so that a single vision appears out of many"). Here *transitio* probably refers to the movement of eidola, and not to the logical process of inference that Cicero designated earlier by the term (see chap. 4); in Augustine's explanation, *transeunt* quite clearly refers to the movement of eidola.

20. Lucretius 4.256–68:

illud in his rebus minime mirabile habendumst,
cur, ea quae feriant oculos simulacra videri
singula cum nequeant, res ipsae perspiciantur.
ventus enim quoque paulatim cum verberat et cum
acre fluit frigus, non privam quamque solemus
particulam venti sentire et frigoris eius,
sed magis unorsum, fierique perinde videmus
corpore tum plagas in nostro tamquam aliquae res
verberat atque sui det sensum corporis extra.
praeterea lapidem digito cum tundimus ipsum,
tangimus extremum saxi summumque colorem,
nec sentimus eum tactu, verum magis ipsam
duritiem penitus saxi sentimus in alto.

Unlike Lachmann, Bailey, and others, I take *ipsum* in line 265 with *lapidem* instead of with the following line. This is easier grammatically, and it makes excellent sense, since Lucretius is concerned to show that what we experience is the "thing itself" (cf. lines 258 and 267). At 4.87–89 Lucretius also points out that the thin eidola that fly about in space cannot be seen singly, and at 104–07 he similarly states that the thin eidola that produce mirror images are not seen singly but yield a presentation (*visum*, 107) by repeatedly bouncing off the mirror.

rock the immediate cause is the contact with the surface color of
the rock. We do not, however, perceive the particles with which
we are immediately in contact; rather what we perceive is an independently existing external object, and we perceive it all at once
(*unorsum*), as the result of an accumulation of successively arriving
particles. Thus the object that we see is not an eidolon or eidola,
but a "thing itself"—an object viewed as existing outside ourselves
and independently of ourselves—just as the object that we perceive
by the sense of touch is the external wind or rock. Toward the
end of the passage, Lucretius states the distinction between the
immediate cause of perception and the object of perception by
using *tangimus*, "we touch," to refer to the causal process of contact,
and *sentimus . . . tactu*, "we perceive by [the sense of] touch," to
refer to the perception. Lucretius sharpens the distinction by contrasting the surface color with the inner hardness of the rock. We
certainly do not perceive color by the sense of touch; we may be
said to be in contact with this when we touch the rock, but what
we perceive is the three-dimensional hard object that is external
to ourselves.

Two aspects of Lucretius' detailed explanation of successive
compacting deserve special notice. One is that the theory is not
new in Epicureanism. Among earlier proponents of the theory was
Democritus, who proposed very similarly that perception occurs
"all at once" as the cumulative effect of successively arriving, individually imperceptible particles.[21] The other point, which is of fundamental importance for Epicurus' epistemology, is that successive compacting results in the perception of objects as existing
outside and independently of ourselves—of "things themselves,"
as Lucretius calls them. Lucretius shows clearly that what we perceive is not a sense datum or any interior mental object at all,
but an object that we view as existing in the external world. It is
important to note that this external object is given directly by perception: we do not infer that what we perceive is external to ourselves, but we have an immediate awareness of the object as being
external to ourselves.[22]

21. According to Theophrastus *De sensu* 63 (DK 68 A 135), Democritus held that
"whatever is a collective whole is strong in each, but that which is spread at large
intervals is imperceptible" (ὅ τι γὰρ ἂν ἀθροῦν ᾖ τοῦτ' ἐνισχύειν ἑκάστῳ, τὸ δ' εἰς
μακρὰ διανενεμημένον ἀναίσθητον εἶναι). Cf. ibid., 56 and 67. Lucretius' *unorsum*
(4.262) renders ἀθροῦν.
22. This interpretation is contrary to that of Bailey, who claims without explanation that Lucretius is not being strictly accurate when he says that "things
themselves are discerned." Bailey maintains that, according to the Epicureans, we

Lucretius' analysis sheds considerable light on Epicurus' own very condensed sentence on the form of the solid. Epicurus states in brief the doctrine explained in detail by Lucretius. In identifying the presentation of the form with the form of the solid, Epicurus maintains, like Lucretius, that what we see is an external object; and in adding that the form of the solid is produced by successive compacting or by a residue of the eidolon, Epicurus shows likewise that the external object of perception is the effect of particles impinging on the perceptual organ. Epicurus is not describing any correspondence between what is presented and some hypothetical, independently existing object of perception. Rather, in identifying the presentation with the external object, he eliminates the distinction between an inner and an outer object of perception. The external object of perception is just what we perceive by a response of the perceptual organ to particles entering from outside. Consequently, a perceptual presentation cannot be untruthful, for there is no perceptual object, existing apart from the presentation, to which the presentation might correspond.

Lucretius designates the objects of sight simply by the general term res, "things," corresponding to Greek πράγματα; he also singles out coldness and hardness as objects of the sense of touch. Epicurus identifies the objects of sight and thought as form and its concomitants; the latter, we may suppose, include color and size. Thus the objects of perception may be said to be properties. These properties, however, must not be thought of as properties of some underlying subject that differs from them. The things that we perceive consist entirely of properties such as color, shape, hardness, and coldness, individually or in combination.

Important additional information about successive compacting is found in two lengthy criticisms of the eidolic theory by Alexander of Aphrodisias.[23] In one of these discussions, Alexander summarizes the eidolic theory of sight as follows:

---

do not see "the things themselves" but only the image (Lucretius, 1214). Glidden has previously shown very convincingly, by comparing the Epicurean position with that of the Cyrenaics, that Epicurus did not hold that what we perceive is a sense datum ("The Epicurean Theory of Knowledge," 29–50). Glidden has also argued forcefully (5–21) against Solmsen's contention that by αἴσθησις Epicurus means "feeling" (Solmsen, "αἴσθησις in Aristotelian and Epicurean Thought," 252–62). For Glidden's own view, see chap. 8, n. 26. Edward Lee has also rejected the view that the objects of perception are eidola; he concludes that "for Epicurus, the object of perceptual awareness is the physical object itself" ("The Sense of an Object: Epicurus on Seeing and Hearing," 43). ̇

23. Alexander In librum De sensu commentarium, pp. 56–63 Wendland; and De anima libri mantissa, pp. 134–36 Bruns. When I first came across these texts, they

Since the sight comes to see little by little according to these people
(for the pupil sees as much of the eidolon at each impact as it is
capable of receiving), and [the sight] seems to see the seen object as
though at once and by a single application and as one thing, it is
necessary that such impacts occur in imperceptible times and escape
notice, so that [the sight] may seem to see the object not piece by
piece but as a whole [ἀθρόον].[24]

Elsewhere Alexander mentions that according to this view "seeing
is not due to the impact of a single eidolon."[25] Alexander's account
agrees with Lucretius' claim that sight is produced by the cumulative impact of successively arriving imperceptible eidola. What
Alexander adds to Lucretius' discussion is that only a part of an
eidolon enters the pupil at a time. The reason, Alexander notes,
is that the pupil admits only as much of an eidolon as fits the
small size of the pupil. Alexander thus reveals the answer to a
problem that is not discussed elsewhere with any explicitness:
how can an eidolon, which may be very large, fit into the tiny
aperture of the pupil?[26] The solution, as reported by Alexander,
lies in the process of successive compacting: small parts of eidola
enter successively and combine in the eye to form a single presentation of an object.

---

seemed to have been overlooked completely by Epicurean scholars. After developing the conclusions presented here, I learned that Ivars Avotins had also discovered this important evidence. Avotins has published his findings in "Alexander
of Aphrodisias on Vision in the Atomists." The article contains the two basic texts
(*In librum De sensu commentarium* 56.6–58.22 and *De anima libri mantissa* 134.28–
136.28) with translations and a detailed analysis. There is substantial agreement
between his conclusions and mine, most importantly on the claim that the process
described by Alexander is that of ἑξῆς πύκνωμα (448–49). See also below, nn. 30
and 33.

24. Alexander *In librum De sensu commentarium*, p. 60.3–7 Wendland: ἐπεὶ γὰρ
κατὰ βραχὺ γίνεται τῇ ὄψει κατὰ τοὺς οὕτω λέγοντας τὸ ὁρᾶν (ὅσον γὰρ οἷά τε
δέξασθαι ἡ κόρη τοῦ εἰδώλου τοσοῦτον καθ' ἑκάστην ἔμπτωσιν ὁρᾷ), δοκεῖ δὲ ὡς
ἅπαξ καὶ μιᾷ προσβολῇ καὶ ὡς ἓν ὁρᾶν τὸ ὁρώμενον, δεῖ ἐν ἀναισθήτοις χρόνοις τὰς
τῶν τηλικούτων ἐμπτώσεις γινομένας διαλανθάνειν, ἵνα μὴ κατὰ μικρὰ ἀλλ' ἀθ-
ρόον αὐτὸ ὁρᾶν δοκῇ. Alexander uses Plato's term, προσβολή, for "application"
(cf. *De anima libri mantissa*, p. 136.9); see above, n. 16.

25. Alexander *De anima libri mantissa*, p. 136.17 Bruns: οὐ γὰρ ἑνὸς εἰδώλου
ἐμπτώσει τὸ ὁρᾶν.

26. The objection that the pupil is too small to receive a complete image goes
back at least as far as Theophrastus' *De sensu* (36). Theophrastus notes with reference to Anaxagoras' theory of vision that he and all others who explained vision
as ἔμφασις ("mirroring") did not notice that seen objects are not of the same size
as the reflections in the eye. Augustine raises the same difficulty when he objects
that eidola cannot touch the eye or the mind as wholes (*Epistulae* 118.29).

Alexander shows in the following series of objections how this process of combination was thought to occur. His general aim is to show that it is impossible to obtain a grasp of the shape or size of an object by such a piecemeal process:

> If [the sight] receives many [parts] repeatedly, how and for what reason will it receive different parts of the eidolon at different times, and not always the same part, as well as parts at a distance from one another? Even if it always receives the adjacent part, how are they put together in the sight, so that [the sight] seems to have seen a theater or temple through the impact of such small parts of an eidolon that travels from them [that is, the theater or temple]? How is it that some parts from some other eidola that impinge upon the sight will not intervene and disrupt the continuity of seeing the first object, if it is necessary that so many eidola be carried so often from a thing to the sight, so that by receiving [parts] that correspond to the size of the pupil it always receives something whole from them [that is, the eidola], as it receives different parts from different eidola?[27]

As these rather cumbersome questions show, the proponents of the eidolic theory answered the problem of how we can see the complete shape or size of an object by proposing that the pupil receives in quick succession many different parts of eidola coming from the same object, and that these parts combine into a whole that presents a complete object. Alexander objects that even if the sight receives different parts of eidola one after another, there is no guarantee that it will receive all the parts without missing any intermediate parts; and he objects further that, even if the sight receives all the right parts, it is not clear how they all fit together, nor is there any guarantee that the continuity of the seen object will not be broken by interference from other eidola. In another place Alexander calls the internal process of recomposition "too mythical":

27. Alexander *In librum De sensu commentarium*, p. 58.3–12 Wendland (cf. *De anima libri mantissa*, p. 135.6–18 Bruns): καὶ γὰρ εἰ πολλάκις καὶ πολλὰ δέχεται, πῶς καὶ διὰ τί ἄλλοτε ἄλλο μέρος τοῦ εἰδώλου δέξεται καὶ οὐχὶ ἀεὶ τὸ αὐτὸ καὶ ἐκ διαστημάτων; εἰ δὲ καὶ ἀεὶ τὸ παρακείμενον, τίς ἡ σύνθεσις τούτων ἐν τῇ ὄψει, ὡς θέατρον ἢ ναὸν δοκεῖν ἑωρακέναι διὰ οὕτω μικρῶν μορίων τῶν ἐμπιπτόντων ἀπὸ τοῦ ἀπ' αὐτῶν εἰδώλου φερομένου; πῶς δὲ οὐ μεταξὺ ἀπ' ἄλλων τινῶν εἰδώλων ἐμπιπτόντων τῇ ὄψει τινὰ διασπάσει τὴν τῆς ὄψεως τῆς τοῦ πρώτου συνέχειαν, εἰ δεῖ τοσαυτάκις καὶ τοσαῦτα εἴδωλα ἐνεχθῆναι ἀπό τινος πρὸς αὐτήν, ὡς κατὰ τὸ τῆς κόρης μέγεθος δεχομένην ἀπ' αὐτῶν τι ὅλον ἀεὶ δέξασθαι, ἄλλο ἀπ' ἄλλου εἰδώλου μέρος λαμβάνουσαν;

In sum, what happens to the [parts] that entered before? For to say that they are preserved, as they sink in, and that they are put together in the eye is too mythical. For where do they sink in or remain, and who is it who builds them into a surface and puts them together?[28]

Here Alexander objects, first, that the parts of the eidolon cannot remain long enough in the sense organ to combine with subsequently arriving parts; and, second, that the process of combination cannot occur mechanistically but would—absurdly—require a builder inside the sense organ.

Although Alexander does not name the Epicureans, there is no reason to suppose that he does not include them among those who adopted the solutions that he outlines.[29] We may infer from his discussion that the Epicureans solved the problem of eidolic size by the theory of successive compacting, and not by claiming that the eidolon shrinks between the external object and the eye, as has been suggested by a number of scholars.[30] Contrary to Alexander's objections, there is nothing inherently implausible about the claim that parts of eidola combine in succession to form an impression of an external object. The Epicureans have no need of a

28. Alexander *De anima libri mantissa* (p. 135.18–21 Bruns): ὅλως δὲ τί γίνεται τὰ προεισελθόντα; τὸ γὰρ φυλάσσεσθαι αὐτὰ λέγειν καταβυσσούμενα καὶ συντίθεσθαι ἐν τῷ ὀφθαλμῷ λίαν ἐστὶ μυθῶδες. ποῦ γὰρ καταβυσσοῦται ἢ μένει, τίς δὲ ὁ οἰκοδομῶν αὐτὰ ἐμβαδὸν καὶ συντιθείς; The passage contains the technical term καταβυσσούμενα; Democritus seems to have used the verb ἐγκαταβυσσοῦσθαι to describe the entry of the eidola into the body (DK 68 A 77).

29. In *In librum De sensu commentarium* (p. 56.13–16 Wendland), Alexander names Democritus and Leucippus, as well as Empedocles, as adherents of the eidolic theory; he does not mention Epicurus because Epicurus is not a target of Aristotle's criticism. Most of the details mentioned by Alexander in his criticism are found in Epicurean writings and are not attested for the earlier thinkers.

30. The chief spokesmen for this view are Bailey (*Greek Atomists*, 412–13) and Kleve (*Gnosis Theon*, 17). Bailey proposes that the eidola are compressed as a result of being bombarded continually from outside; against Bailey, Kleve suggests that the collapse of the eidolon is due to an internal loss of atoms. Both interpretations rely on the reading δι[ὰ τὰς σ]υνιζήσε[ις] τὰς ε[ἰς κ]εν[ό]τητα καὶ λεπ[τότ]ητα καὶ μι[κρότη]τα in PHerc. 993/1149 fr. 18 col. 2 (Arr. 24.43.11–15), which occurs in a discussion of the speed of the eidola in book 2 of Epicurus' *On Nature*. Συνίζησις is explained by these authors as the collapse of the eidolon into itself. Adelmo Barigazzi, following Bailey, takes the view that the συνιζήσεις are "i cedimenti che avvengono nei simulacri per la loro vuotezza interna" ("Cinetica degli ΕΙΔΩΛΑ nel ΠΕΡΙ ΦΥΣΕΩΣ di Epicuro," 266). The text, however, is too obscure to support these interpretations of συνίζησις. It is not at all clear how the proposed collapse is related to the ἐξωστικὸς τρόπος, which is the subject of discussion in the surrounding passages. Nor does there seem to be any reason why the term should designate a collapse that is internal to an eidolon rather than a fusion of eidola resulting in a composite eidolon. For further doubts about Bailey's position in par-

craftsman inside the sight any more than they have need of a craftsman in the world at large. There is, to be sure, no guarantee that the whole that is constituted in the sight organ out of successive eidolic parts will have just the same arrangement of atoms as the eidola that have just been released from the surface of the object. Epicurus himself points out that the arrangement of atoms coming from a solid is sometimes disturbed; and, as we have seen, there is much scope for a disarrangement of atoms both inside and outside the perceptual organ. Hence the process of composition does sometimes result in presentations that have little relationship to the external source. But this is not a defect in the theory. What matters is that the sight organ should be complex enough to admit a large variety of eidolic parts in rapid, cumulative succession, and that the composite eidolon produced by this cumulative succession should have an arrangement of its own that can result in a presentation.

Alexander's testimony, along with Lucretius', shows that successive compacting is an essential feature of the process of coming to see any object at all, no matter how large or how small. It follows that successive compacting cannot be a criterion by which a supposedly truthful presentation is distinguished from a supposedly deceptive presentation. Nor indeed is there anything about the process of successive compacting that can ensure that the presentation is free of distortion. For eidola that come in succession are just as vulnerable to disturbance, both individually and in their entirety, as an eidolon that comes by itself.

Both Lucretius and Alexander link the successive compacting of eidola explicitly only with sight. Does the same process of compacting apply also to mental perception, διάνοια? Given that mental perception is also produced by eidola, and that a similar problem of size applies to these eidola, it seems reasonable to suppose that mental perception too is produced by a succession of eidola. Furthermore, the fact that in the *Letter to Herodotus* Epicurus does not single out successive compacting as applying only to sight suggests that the process applies no less to thought.

The traditional view of mental perception, on the other hand,

---

ticular, see Rist, *Epicurus*, 85. Giussani long ago hit upon the right explanation (*De rerum natura*, 3: 285, n. 1). Giussani proposed, apparently without knowing Alexander's testimony, the very solution described by Alexander, that is, that the eidola of sight enter part by part. Recently Avotins has also argued on the basis of Alexander's testimony that there is no diminution in the size of the eidola ("Alexander of Aphrodisias on Vision," 440–45).

has been that mental objects may be produced by the single impact of a single eidolon coming from without.[31] This view is based
primarily on the following argument by Lucretius on composite
mental eidola such as those of centaurs or Scyllas: "When these
[the composite mental eidola] travel with mobility as a result of
extreme lightness, as I showed before, any single subtle image
easily stirs our mind with a single blow; for the mind is itself fine
and marvelously mobile."[32] Lucretius here says quite unambiguously
that a single mental eidolon is sufficient to make an impact on the
mind; but he does not say, as he has generally been interpreted,
that a single eidolon is sufficient to produce a mental presentation
of an object. Lucretius' point is that even though a mental eidolon
is extremely fine and thus very mobile, it has sufficient power to
move the mind; and he cites as the reason that the mind, too, is
extremely fine and hence very mobile. Lucretius, then, claims that
there is a correlation in fineness between a mental eidolon and the
mind, so that it is possible for a mental eidolon to move the mind
with a single blow.[33] It is understood that there is a similar correlation between a sight eidolon and the organ of sight. Accordingly,
there is no reason to suppose that in mental perception, any more
than in sight, a single eidolon impinging on the perceptual organ
from outside has the power to produce a presentation all by itself.

Lucretius' explanation of moving dream figures, which was
examined earlier in this chapter, provides further evidence that
mental presentations are produced by a succession of eidola.
These figures, Lucretius maintains, are formed by a succession of
eidola merging imperceptibly quickly with one another. Admittedly, this succession serves to explain the appearance of change;
but there is no reason why the same principle should not also
apply to the presentation of unchanging objects. In the former
case, the successively merging eidolic components vary in arrangement from one another; in the latter case, they have the same

31. See, for example, Philippson ("Zur epikureischen Götterlehre," 569), Bailey
(*Greek Atomists*, 414), and Kleve (*Gnosis Theon*, 21).

32. Lucretius 4.745–48:

> quae cum mobiliter summa levitate feruntur,
> ut prius ostendi, facile uno commovet ictu
> quaelibet una animum nobis subtilis imago;
> tenuis enim mens est et mire mobilis ipsa.

33. Avotins has also dissented from the standard interpretation by arguing that
Lucretius' aim is to show how a mental eidolon can make any impact at all ("Alexander of Aphrodisias on Vision," 447).

arrangement. Another distinctive feature of Lucretius' dream figures is that some are clearly not produced by eidola coming from a single external solid, but by eidola coming from various sources. These figures therefore do not fit the category of presentations that Epicurus considers in the sentence on compacting. If, however, even presentations that do not come from a single external solid are produced by a succession of eidola, then there is so much more reason to suppose that figures produced from a single external source, which is continually emitting eidola in rapid succession, are produced by a succession of eidola.

A possible objection against the view that all mental presentations, like all sight presentations, are the result of a merging of successive eidola is that composite eidola or eidola formed spontaneously in midair are not likely to come in streams. But there is no reason why they should not. It is entirely plausible, given the eidolic theory, that when we have a presentation of a centaur, for example, two streams of eidola have merged in midair, one coming from a horse, another from a man, and that the combined stream of eidola then enters the mind in a continuous flow to produce the appearance of a centaur.[34] Lucretius himself indicates that spontaneously formed eidola gather in continuously flowing streams when he compares the spontaneous formation of eidola to the gathering of ever-changing clouds in a previously clear sky.[35] All around us are streams of eidola coming from solid objects, gathering spontaneously in midair, or combining at random; and these streams are continually bombarding the eyes and the mind to produce a perception through successive impacts.

Granted that successive compacting applies no less to thought than to sight, what place is there for the other method listed by Epicurus, ἐγκατάλειμμα τοῦ εἰδώλου, "a residue of the eidolon"? It has generally been held that this method applies to thought, whereas successive compacting applies to sight. Unfortunately, the

---

34. Lucretius explains the composite nature of a centaur eidolon at 4.739–43, esp. 741 (*verum ubi equi atque hominis casu convenit imago*). Lucretius' reference to a single image here as elsewhere (esp. 4.782) in his account of thought may seem to support the view that the impact of a single eidolon creates a mental presentation. Lucretius, however, also speaks of *an* eidolon (*imago*) as appearing in sight or as entering our eyes to create an appearance (see 4.156, 269–88, and 302–17; in each case, the eidolon is one that produces a mirror appearance). The reason that Lucretius consistently uses the singular is that a presentation is formed in every case by a single eidolon, as produced by the merging of successive parts. In the same way, Cicero speaks of an eidolon (in the singular) as producing thought images (*Epistulae ad familiares* 15.16.2; *De divinatione* 2.137–39; *De natura deorum* 1.107).

35. Lucretius 4.129–42.

evidence for the method of residue is not nearly as good as for successive compacting. Lucretius provides a clue to the meaning, however, when he explains that the reason that humans, but not cocks, can stand the sight of lions is that the harmful particles coming from lions either do not enter human eyes or else have a free exit once they have entered, so that they do not harm the eyes "by lingering" (*remorando*).[36] This explanation confirms, as one would expect, that particles may remain in a sense organ for varying periods of time after they have entered. Accordingly, whereas some particles leave the organ and need to be reinforced by newly arrived particles in order to produce a presentation, others may stay on and make a continued impact by their own continued reverberation. These remaining particles may properly be called an ἐγκατάλειμμα, that is, something left behind in the organ; and it is reasonable to suppose that this remainder, or residue, may continue to produce a presentation after successive compacting has stopped.

This interpretation derives some support from Aristotle's notion of a residue that remains after an act of sense perception. Aristotle held that motions that occur in a perceptual organ during an act of perception may persist after the perception has stopped, and that these motions are responsible for recollection and dreams. In his discussion of dreams, Aristotle notes that these residual motions are a ὑπόλειμμα of the perception;[37] and he cites as evidence of their existence the lingering effect of some perceptions after the perceptual organ has been directed elsewhere.[38] One example of such an aftereffect is the experience of continuing to see a color that we have long gazed on after we have turned to look at another color.

Epicurus, I suggest, also explained the immediate continuation of a perception, after the perceptual organ has shifted focus, by a residue remaining from the perception, although he differed from Aristotle in supposing that this residue consists of particles that have entered from outside. Unlike Aristotle, moreover, Epicurus restricted the operation of the residue to immediate aftereffects of perception. As attested repeatedly and emphasized particularly

36. Lucretius 4.718–21 (*remorando*, 720). Democritus also distinguished between particles that leave immediately and those that remain. According to Theophrastus, Democritus held that hearing is sharpest if the voice enters all at once (ἀθροῦν) and is quickly and evenly scattered through the body without "falling through to the outside" (διεκπίπτειν ἔξω) (*De sensu* 56).

37. Aristotle *De insomniis* 461b21.

38. Ibid., 459b8–23.

in Cicero's *On Divination*, Epicurus agreed with Democritus that all mental images are produced by eidola that have newly entered from outside.[39] Although the ability of the mind to focus on certain eidola rather than others depends on past experience, each mental image is formed anew by particles from outside. Thus in mental perception as well as in sense perception, presentations are formed either by the compacting of particles that continually enter the organ or by a residue of particles that have just entered; and the latter type of presentation is an aftereffect of perception. When an aftereffect occurs, a presentation is sustained by the continued presence of perceptual particles in the organ after the incoming flow of particles has stopped, and the continued internal reverberation compensates for the continued replenishment of particles from outside.[40]

In summary, whenever a presentation is obtained by an application of the sight or mind, it is the effect either of a succession of eidola entering the perceptual organ and merging into a single eidolon or of parts of an eidolon remaining within the perceptual organ after they have merged into a single eidolon. The application, ἐπιβολή, of the perceptual organ is thus a response either to a continuous bombardment of particles from outside or to a continued reverberation of particles within the organ. In the first case, the response of the perceptual organ causes the particles to merge successively so as to form a single presentation; in the second, it causes the presentation to remain. Accordingly, in the sentence on the form of the solid, Epicurus is proposing a single criterion of perceptible reality: the direct response of the perceptual organ to particles that have entered from outside. Instead of drawing a distinction between truthful and deceptive presentations, he eliminates this distinction by identifying the external object of perception with the content of a perception.

Lucretius' discussion of dreams suggests that although in the

39. Cicero *De divinatione* 2.137–40.

40. This interpretation of ἐγκατάλειμμα τοῦ εἰδώλου is opposed to the commonly accepted view that it is an effect left by an eidolon and applies to mental perception only. Bailey suggests that it is "the impression left by" an eidolon that has penetrated the mind, in contrast to the "successive repetitions" (τὸ ἑξῆς πύκνωμα) of the eidolon in sight (*Epicurus*, 197); and Furley, who also takes τὸ ἑξῆς πύκνωμα in the sense of "successive repetitions" but extends it to mental perception along with sight, understands ἐγκατάλειμμα as a "pattern left behind as a memory by previous sense-experience" ("Knowledge of Atoms," 610, 611). DeWitt takes a view very different from anyone else's; he proposes that an ἐγκατάλειμμα τοῦ εἰδώλου is a residue that reaches the eyes after a process of detrition, and that if the detrition of eidola is uniform, the result is ἑξῆς πύκνωμα, that is, an "orderly reduction" of eidola ("Epicurus, Περὶ Φαντασίας," 417–18).

*Letter to Herodotus* Epicurus gives special attention to presentations formed by eidola from a single external solid, the method of compacting applies also to cases in which the eidola do not come from a single external solid. Since there is no reason why the method of residue should not also apply to these presentations, it appears that the two methods apply to both sight and thought. In addition, although Epicurus speaks of the two methods only in connection with sight and thought, we may suppose that the four remaining senses also obtain their presentations by both successive compacting and a residue. In his comparison between sight and touch, as previously examined, Lucretius shows clearly that touch too occurs by successive compacting; and since all senses receive streams of particles, successive compacting applies to all senses. It follows that in every case of perception what we perceive is an object obtained by the perceptual organ through successive compacting or a residue of particles.

# [ 8 ]

# Perception and Opinion

## TRUTH, FALSEHOOD, AND EVIDENCE

EPICURUS made a strict distinction between perception and belief. He sets out this distinction in the *Letter to Herodotus* just after the sentence on the form of the solid. Because this sentence is linked closely with the explanation that follows, it is quoted again here. The entire text is as follows:

> And whatever presentation we obtain by application by the mind or [the sight], whether of a form or of its concomitants, this is the form of the solid, generated in accordance with successive compacting or a residue of the eidolon. But falsehood and error always lie in that which we additionally believe [or "opine"] will be witnessed or not counterwitnessed [ἐν τῷ προσδοξαζομένῳ . . . ἐπιμαρτυρηθήσεσθαι ἢ μὴ ἀντιμαρτυρηθήσεσθαι] and then is not witnessed ⟨or is counterwitnessed⟩. For appearances obtained as if in a copy, or formed in sleep or in accordance with some other applications [ἐπιβολάς] of the mind or the other criteria, would not have a similarity with the things called "existent" and "true" if these [appearances] were not also certain things that we encounter. There would be no error if we did not also take some other motion within ourselves that is attached [to the application] but has a distinction [συνημμένον μὲν διάληψιν δὲ ἔχουσαν]. In accordance with this motion, if there is no witnessing or if there is counterwitnessing, falsehood comes into being; if there is witnessing or no counterwitnessing, truth [comes into being]. It is necessary to hold on strongly to this opinion, so that neither the criteria in accordance with the evidence may be

destroyed nor error may confuse everything by being upheld in the same way.[1]

Epicurus now explains that a presentation obtained by an application of the perceptual organ is one that has not been joined by any opinion and consequently cannot be false or mistaken. The force of the term ἐπιβλητικῶς in the first sentence now becomes clear: together with the description of the cause of the presentation as compacting or residue, ἐπιβλητικῶς distinguishes the presentation as a direct response by the perceptual organ to external stimuli, free from any interpretation from within.[2] By distinguishing between the act of perception, which is a response to external influences, and the act of opinion, which is an addition made from within, Epicurus attempts to secure a factual basis, free from the possibility of error, by which all opinions may be judged true or false.

Epicurus defends the distinction between a perceptual presen-

---

1. *Her.* 50–51: καὶ ἣν ἂν λάβωμεν φαντασίαν ἐπιβλητικῶς τῇ διανοίᾳ ἢ * εἴτε μορφῆς εἴτε συμβεβηκότων, μορφή ἐστιν αὕτη τοῦ στερεμνίου, γινομένη κατὰ τὸ ἑξῆς πύκνωμα ἢ ἐγκατάλειμμα τοῦ εἰδώλου. τὸ δὲ ψεῦδος καὶ τὸ διημαρτημένον ἐν τῷ προσδοξαζομένῳ ἀεί ἐστιν ἐπιμαρτυρηθήσεσθαι ἢ μὴ ἀντιμαρτυρηθήσεσθαι εἶτ᾽ οὐκ ἐπιμαρτυρουμένου (ἢ ἀντιμαρτυρουμένου). ἥ τε γὰρ ὁμοιότης τῶν φαντασμῶν οἱονεὶ ἐν εἰκόνι λαμβανομένων ἢ καθ᾽ ὕπνους γινομένων ἢ κατ᾽ ἄλλας τινὰς ἐπιβολὰς τῆς διανοίας ἢ τῶν λοιπῶν κριτηρίων οὐκ ἄν ποτε ὑπῆρχε τοῖς οὖσί τε καὶ ἀληθέσι προσαγορευομένοις, εἰ μὴ ἦν τινα καὶ ταῦτα πρὸς ἃ βάλλομεν. τὸ δὲ διημαρτημένον οὐκ ἂν ὑπῆρχεν, εἰ μὴ ἐλαμβάνομεν καὶ ἄλλην τινὰ κίνησιν ἐν ἡμῖν αὐτοῖς συνημμένην μὲν διάληψιν δὲ ἔχουσαν. κατὰ δὲ ταύτην, ἐὰν μὲν μὴ ἐπιμαρτυρηθῇ, ἢ ἀντιμαρτυρηθῇ, τὸ ψεῦδος γίνεται, ἐὰν δὲ ἐπιμαρτυρηθῇ ἢ μὴ ἀντιμαρτυρηθῇ, τὸ ἀληθές. καὶ ταύτην οὖν σφόδρα γε δεῖ τὴν δόξαν κατέχειν, ἵνα μήτε τὰ κριτήρια ἀναιρῆται τὰ κατὰ τὰς ἐναργείας μήτε τὸ διημαρτημένον ὁμοίως βεβαιούμενον πάντα συνταράττῃ. Usener, followed by Bailey and others, supplies ἐπὶ τοῦ προσμένοντος after ἀεί ἐστιν in the second sentence. The addition is both unnecessary and a misuse of the term προσμένον, for something προσμένον cannot be counterwitnessed. The addition of ἢ ἀντιμαρτυρουμένου, also proposed by Usener, does seem to be necessary. I follow Usener, Bailey, and others, in omitting a section of text after ἐπιμαρτυρουμένου, for it is almost wholly repeated a little later. Arrighetti prefers to excise the preceding part of the sentence as well, beginning with τὸ δὲ ψεῦδος; but this creates the problem that γὰρ of the next sentence hangs loose. It is unnecessary to add τῇ φανταστικῇ ἐπιβολῇ after συνημμένον μὲν (as proposed by Usener and Bailey), although the meaning is appropriate. The expression πρὸς ἃ βάλλομεν (the reading of F; the other mss. have πρὸς ὃ βάλλομεν) is not very convincing, although I accept it. Usener's emendation προσβαλλόμενα (which most editors accept) is just as clumsy; Arighetti (following Schneider) writes πρὸς ἃ ⟨ἐπι⟩βάλλομεν. The emendations φαντασμάτων or φασμάτων for mss. φαντασμῶν are suggested below, n. 12.

2. This is recognized by Vlastos in his review of Cornford's *Principium Sapientiae*: he notes that "to get it [the φαντασία] ἐπιβλητικῶς is to apply the mind or sense to just this image, without going beyond it to a προσδοξαζόμενον" (71 n. 1).

tation, which cannot be false, and an opinion, which may be false, by considering apparently deceptive presentations, such as copies (as shown in pictures, statues, mirrors and so on) and dreams. He points out that these are produced, like other presentations, by a contact of the sense organ or mind with things that are real. Accordingly, insofar as these presentations too are produced entirely from outside without the addition of opinion, they cannot be false. Where we go wrong is in adding an opinion to the presentation.

Epicurus also shows very briefly how the truth or falsehood of an opinion is determined. An opinion becomes true whenever there is either direct confirmation, that is, "witnessing" (ἐπιμαρτύ-ρησις), or an absence of counterevidence, that is, "no counter-witnessing" (οὐκ ἀντιμαρτύρησις); and it becomes false whenever there is either no direct confirmation, that is, "no witnessing" (οὐκ ἐπιμαρτύρησις), or counterevidence, that is, "counterwitnessing" (ἀντιμαρτύρησις). Epicurus ends the whole discussion with pointed emphasis by stating a dilemma that would result from our not making a distinction between presentation and opinion.

The first step in examining Epicurus' distinction between perception and opinion is to sort out his and his followers' use of the terms "true" and "false." Our Hellenistic sources impute to Epicurus the view that all presentations (φαντασίαι) are true, or, alternatively, that all presentations through perception (αἱ δι' αἰσθήσεως φαντασίαι) or all perceptions (αἰσθήσεις) or all objects of perception (αἰσθητά) are true.[3] In addition, Sextus Empiricus reports that Epicurus held that all objects of perception are "true" (ἀληθῆ) and "existent" (ὄντα), and that he did not recognize any distinction between saying that something is "true" and saying that it is "real" (ὑπάρχον).[4] Another way of stating Epicurus' view was to say that the senses "never lie."[5] All these formulations signify an absolute reliance on sense perception, in contrast to the Stoic view that the senses sometimes misrepresent the external object

3. Sextus Empiricus *Adv. math.* 7.203 (τὴν φαντασίαν . . . διὰ παντὸς ἀληθῆ) and 8.9 (τὰ μὲν αἰσθητὰ πάντα . . . ἀληθῆ καὶ ὄντα); Plutarch *Adv. Colotem* 1109a–b (πάσας εἶναι τὰς δι' αἰσθήσεως φαντασίας ἀληθεῖς); Aetius (U 248) (πᾶσαν αἴσθησιν καὶ πᾶσαν φαντασίαν ἀληθῆ); and see U 247–54 (also Cicero *De finibus* 1.22, 64). This use of "true" appears to have been common both to Epicurus' followers and to his critics. Lucretius, for example, claims that whatever is presented (*visum*) to the senses at any time is true (4.499).
4. Sextus Empiricus *Adv. math.* 8.9.
5. Ibid., 8.185 (μηδέποτε ψευδομένης τῆς αἰσθήσεως) and Cicero *Academica* 2.79.

and to the Academic position that it is possible in every case for the senses to misrepresent the external object.

In the cited passage, Epicurus distinguishes allegedly deceptive appearances, occurring to the mind or the senses, from things "called existent and true"; and he argues that the former are without falsehood. His argument shows that the phrase "existent and true" is a concession to ordinary usage. Epicurus does not go so far as to call apparently deceptive presentations "true," as the later sources did. Rather, his analysis of truth and falsehood as "coming into being" in connection with opinions suggests that he held that truth and falsehood belong properly to opinions, not to presentations.[6] There appears to be, then, a discrepancy between Epicurus' view and the later wide use of the term "true" to apply to all objects of perception. But the later usage is readily explained as a concession to standard philosophical usage. As has been noted repeatedly, there was a strong trend toward a uniform philosophical vocabulary in the Hellenistic period. In particular, we know that Stoic presentations were divided into "true" and "false," contrary to the strict Stoic application of these terms to propositions only. Likewise, we may suppose, the term "true" was commonly used to apply to Epicurean objects of perception, although Epicurus had previously proposed to restrict the pair of properties truth and falsehood to opinions.[7]

Concerning the truth and falsehood of opinions, Epicurus' own very condensed explanation may be supplemented by a much more detailed analysis by Sextus Empiricus. Sextus shows that what distinguishes the two alternative methods of verification and

6. Epicurus apparently uses "true" in a wide sense to apply to all perceptual presentations at *Letter to Herodotus* 62: "everything that is viewed, or obtained by application by the mind, is true" (τό γε θεωρούμενον πᾶν ἢ κατ' ἐπιβολὴν λαμβανόμενον τῇ διανοίᾳ ἀληθές ἐστιν). Although it is not inconceivable that Epicurus admitted such a wide use of "true," this statement should probably be attributed to a later interpreter who used the term "true" in the standard wide sense. The claim is entirely parenthetical in the context, and looks like a gloss prompted by the expressions οὐκ ἀληθές and προσδοξαζόμενον in the preceding sentence. It may also be noted that θεωρούμενον is here used in the narrow sense of "what is viewed by perception"; Epicurus elsewhere adds the modifier κατὰ τὴν αἴσθησιν to distinguish empirical viewing from contemplation by reason (*Her.* 59 and *Pyth.* 91). The Empiricists used θεώρημα by itself in the narrow sense (Galen *Subfiguratio empirica* 3, p. 46.3 D).

7. For the Stoics, see, for example, *SVF* 2.193, 195. Sextus Empiricus conjectures at *Adv. math.* 8.13 that the Epicureans associate truth and falsehood with the voice, since they do not recognize propositions. This conjecture seems to reflect the view that truth and falsehood belong to opinions, although Sextus is clearly offering an interpretation of his own rather than repeating Epicurean doctrine.

of falsification is that they belong to two different types of opinion: opinions about what is yet to appear (τὸ προσμένον), and opinions about what is nonapparent (τὸ ἄδηλον). Thus, opinions of the first type are verified by "witnessing" (ἐπιμαρτύρησις) and falsified by "no witnessing" (οὐκ ἐπιμαρτύρησις); and opinions of the second type are verified by "no counterwitnessing" (οὐκ ἀντιμαρτύρησις) and falsified by "counterwitnessing" (ἀντιμαρτύρησις).[8]

To illustrate opinions of the first type, Sextus takes the example of a figure approaching from a distance. One guesses and forms the opinion that it is Plato. This opinion is verified when, after the figure has come close and the spatial interval is eliminated, there is "evidence" (ἐνάργεια) that it is Plato. The opinion is falsified, as Sextus explains, when after the spatial interval has been eliminated, we know also by evidence that the figure is not Plato. According to Sextus, then, opinions about what is yet to appear are verified by a presentation (evidence) of what was expected, and falsified by a presentation (evidence) of something other than was expected. As for opinions of the second type, Sextus explains that οὐκ ἀντιμαρτύρησις, "no counterwitnessing," is the "consequence" (ἀκολουθία) of the nonapparent entity upon a phenomenon, and that ἀντιμαρτύρησις, "counterwitnessing," is the "elimination" (ἀνασκευή) of the phenomenon along with the nonapparent entity. He illustrates no counterwitnessing by the Epicurean belief that there is void; the existence of the void follows, he says, upon the evident occurrence of motion. Correspondingly, Sextus illustrates counterwitnessing by the falsification of the Stoic claim that there is no void in the physical world; this claim is falsified by the elimination of motion along with the void.

Sextus concludes that every opinion is judged true or false on the basis of "evidence," a term that Sextus claims was used by Epicurus as a synonym for "presentation." Sextus sums up this conclusion by the ringing motto "evidence is the base and foundation of all things."[9] The terms chosen by Epicurus to state his theory of verification and falsification reflect this reliance on perception: the component -μαρτύρησις, "-witnessing," in each case suggests that the ultimate authority by which an opinion is judged true or false is the immediate acquaintance of perception. It is therefore essential to Epicurus' theory of verification and falsifi-

8. Sextus Empiricus *Adv. math.* 7.211–16.
9. Ibid., 7.216 (πάντων δὲ κρηπὶς καὶ θεμέλιος ἡ ἐνάργεια); cf. Lucretius 4.505–6.

cation that the presentation obtained directly by the senses or the mind show in every instance what is real.

In the cited passage, Epicurus explains the difference between a perceptual presentation and an opinion as a difference between two kinds of motion. The opinion consists in taking "some other motion also within ourselves that is attached [συνημμένον] but has a distinction [διάληψιν]." The prior motion to which the motion of opinion is "attached" is clearly that of taking a presentation "by application." In contrast to this motion, which is imposed from outside, the motion of opinion is initiated from within ourselves. Plato had previously used the noun "attachment" (σύναψις) to refer to the combination of a sense perception with a thought.[10] Plato used this analysis, similarly to Epicurus, to sketch a theory of truth and falsehood that preserves the truthfulness of all sense perception by assigning falsehood to the "attached" thought. The contrasting term in Epicurus' explanation, "distinction" (διάληψις), is employed later in the *Letter to Herodotus* to refer to differences among properties.[11] Since, according to Epicurus, what we add to a presentation by an opinion are physical features that differ from those that are presented, it is reasonable to suppose that the distinction that belongs to the added movement consists in the difference of the added features from those that are presented. As Sextus' analysis indicates, these added features are of two kinds: observable features that may subsequently either become manifest or fail to become manifest, and nonobservable features that may be shown by a process of reasoning either to follow upon observed features or to be in conflict with them.

The test of Epicurus' theory of verification comes in the third sentence of the cited passage, where he argues that apparently deceptive presentations are not false or deceptive. Epicurus exemplifies these presentations by copies (such as artistic representations and mirror images) and dreams, and characterizes them as resemblances of things called "existent and true." It is very possible that Epicurus has in mind here Plato's distinction between resemblances and originals.[12] Plato made prominent use of this dis-

---

10. Plato *Theaetetus* 195d. Epicurus appears to mention the same "attachment" as in *Her.* 51 at PHerc. 1431 fr. 6 col. 4 (Arr. 36.16.3–5): τῆς συνα[π]τομέν[ης δι'] ἡμῶν αὐτῶν κεινήσεως.

11. *Her.* 69; cf. 57–58, where Epicurus uses διαληπτόν and διαλήψεσθαι to signify the ability to distinguish a unit of magnitude from another. Long takes "having a distinction" to mean that the movement of opinion "admits of the distinction between truth and falsehood" ("*Aisthesis*," 118); but what is needed is a distinction between the two types of movement.

12. See esp. *Republic* 509e–10a, where Plato divides the perceptible realm into

tinction to develop an ontological hierarchy having three main levels: resemblances of resemblances; resemblances; and, finally, the only real entities, the Forms, of which all the rest are resemblances. In contrast, Epicurus uses the distinction between resemblances and originals precisely to deny that there are ontological gradations.

The objection raised by Epicurus about resemblances was previously addressed by Socrates in the *Theaetetus* as part of his explanation of the claim that knowledge is perception. In response to the objection that in dreams and illnesses we have false perceptions that are remarkably similar to truthful perceptions, Socrates points out that the apparent misperceptions are different perceptions, produced by the action of an external force on a different percipient, and hence are as valid as the perceptions they resemble.[13] Epicurus appeals to the same kind of causal process to show that apparent misperceptions are without falsehood; but his proof rests on the manifest resemblance of the presentations to the things they resemble. There would not be any similarity to so-called existent and true things, he argues, unless the resemblances were not also certain "things that we encounter" (πρὸς ἃ βάλλομεν).[14] Although the text is suspect, the general sense is assured by the description of the resemblances as appearances obtained by an application of the mind or the senses. Epicurus' argument is that since the resemblances are just like so-called real things, they exist likewise as objects encountered by the perceptual organ. Hence, because they are imposed from outside and not produced by some inner movement of opinion, they are likewise without any falsehood. We may fill out the explanation by saying

---

copies (εἰκόνες), consisting of shadows and appearances (φαντάσματα) in water and other reflecting materials, and the things that the copies resemble. Cf. *Sophist* 236a–c, where imitation is divided into two types, that which produces an exact copy (εἰκόνα) and that which produces an illusory copy (φάντασμα); the latter is created by the art of illusion (φανταστική). Mss. φαντασμῶν (*Her.* 51) is suspect because φαντασμός is not attested anywhere else. I suggest that it be emended either to φασμάτων, a noun used by Plutarch (*Adv. Colotem* 1123d) and Diogenes of Oenoanda (fr. 7 cols. 1.6–7 and 2.12–13 Chilton; and new fr. 5 col. 1.6 Smith, "New Fragments of Diogenes of Oenoanda," 359) to refer to apparently illusory presentations; or else to φαντασμάτων, used by Diogenes Laertius to refer to hallucinations and dreams (10.32) and by Epicurus to designate any kind of perceptual presentation, as it seems, including apparently deceptive appearances in the sky. Examples of Epicurus' use of φάντασμα are at *Her.* 75 (twice; here the plural form is conjoined with πάθη), *Pyth.* 88 (τὸ . . . φάντασμα ἑκάστου τηρητέον), *Pyth.* 102 (τὸ τῆς ἀστραπῆς φάντασμα), and *Pyth.* 110 (τὸ . . . τῆς περιφερείας τοῦτο φάντασμα).

13. Plato *Theaetetus* 157e–60c.
14. For the reading, see above, n. 1.

that pictures, statues, reflections, dreams, and so on are all real
things—resemblances—appearing just as they are; falsehood and
error occur when we take the resemblance for the thing it resembles.

We have several later versions of Epicurus' defense of apparently deceptive presentations. Plutarch accuses the Epicureans of
assembling the strangest visions of dreamers and madmen, and of
saying that there is nothing false about these, but that they are "all
true presentations and bodies and shapes arriving from the environment."[15] Diogenes explains succinctly: "The appearances that
occur to madmen and in dreams are true; for they move [κινεῖ
γάϱ]."[16] The things that "move" are objects of perception—appearances—understood as consisting of particles that make contact
with the perceptual organ. As Sextus Empiricus reports, the Epicureans also developed a more methodical explanation, based on
a commonly accepted definition of "true presentation." In an attempt to establish a common ground with their opponents, the
Epicureans proposed that a presentation is true whenever it is
"from a real thing and in accordance with the real thing itself."[17]
They then argued that just as pleasure and pain are affections
that are produced from and in accordance with certain causes, and
these causes must be pleasant and painful in reality, so the presentations that occur in perception are in every case produced from
and in accordance with certain causes, which must be in reality
just as they appear.[18] The Epicureans are here adopting the standard distinction between a presentation and the object of perception in order to argue that since the object of perception acts
directly on the perceptual organ in such a way that the effect,
the presentation, always corresponds exactly to the cause, the object of perception cannot be other than as it appears.

Sextus Empiricus puts the Epicurean position in perspective by
distinguishing the following three positions concerning sense perception: there are those who hold that none of the things that

15. Plutarch *Adv. Colotem* 1123c: φαντασίας ἀληθεῖς ἁπάσας καὶ σώματα καὶ
μορφὰς ἐκ τοῦ περιέχοντος ἀφικνουμένας. A similar defense is given by the Epicurean Diogenes of Oenoanda at fr. 7 cols. 1–2 Chilton. Diogenes argues that
these appearances are not "empty," as the Stoics hold, because they consist of
bodies even though these are very fine.

16. DL 10.32. Sextus Empiricus *Adv. math.* 8.63 offers the same type of explanation; he points out that Orestes' perception of the Furies is true, because it is
"moved by eidola" that "underlie."

17. This definition is the same as the Stoic definition of "apprehensive [κατα-
ληπτική] presentation" except that it does not include the qualification "such that
it could not come from that which is not real" (*SVF* 1.59).

18. Sextus Empiricus *Adv. math.* 8.203.

are perceived "underlie" (ὑποκεῖσθαι), but that the perceptions are empty feelings (κενοπαθεῖν τὰς αἰσθήσεις); those who claim that all things that are perceived, or, in other words, all things by which they think they are moved (κινεῖσθαι) in perception, "underlie"; and those who hold the intermediate position that some of the things that are perceived "underlie" and some do not. Sextus exemplifies the first position by Democritus' claim that nothing is sweet or bitter, and so forth, externally to us; he attributes to Epicurus the second position, that all perceptible things "underlie" just as they appear; and he cites the Stoics and Peripatetics as proponents of the third view.[19] In his classification, the word "underlie" signifies that there is a real object of perception corresponding to the presentation; when there is no underlying object of perception, the perceptual presentation is "empty." Cicero expressed the same distinction by contrasting truthful movements with empty movements, and describing the object shown by a truthful movement as "evident" (*perspicuum*).[20]

Although Sextus' terminology appears to be Stoic, the Epicureans used it themselves to explain their position. As just noted, Diogenes Laertius claimed that since there is something that "moves" a person who has a hallucination or dream, the appearance is true. The Epicureans also used the expression "underlie" to refer to objects seen in mirrors and to the apparently unmoving sun.[21] As Sextus indicates, the Epicurean view is directly opposed to that of Democritus, who inferred from the same causal process proposed by Epicurus that nothing of what we perceive "underlies." The Epicurean position is also opposed to that of the Stoics, not only insofar as the Stoics held that only some of the things of which we have sensory awareness "underlie," but also in that the Stoics maintained that all visions classified by Epicurus as mental visions—among them dreams, hallucinations, and general concepts—are "empty presentations," caused by an inner movement of the mind without any underlying object.[22]

According to Epicurus, then, even in the case of the presen-

19. Sextus Empiricus *OP* 2.49 and *Adv. math.* 8.184–85.
20. Cicero *Academica* 2.34 and 51; cf. n. 22 below.
21. See PHerc. 1013, fr. 11.7–8 Scott (p. 311) ( = col. 21.7–8 in Costantina Romeo, "Demetrio Lacone sulla grandezza del sole," 20); and Diogenes of Oenoanda, new fr. 5 col. 2.13 (Smith, "New Fragments of Diogenes of Oenoanda," 359). Examples of Stoic usage are at *SVF* 2.54.
22. The Stoics called these mental visions φαντάσματα and held that they are due to an "empty pulling" within the mind called φανταστικόν (*SVF* 2.54; cf. 2.55, 83). In explaining Antiochus' epistemology, which is derived from the Stoics, Cicero describes φαντάσματα as "empty presentations" (*inanium visorum*) that lack "evidence" (*perspicuitas*) (*Academica* 2.51; cf. 2.88–90).

tations that we ordinarily call deceptive, there is a real, or underlying, object of perception. All presentations therefore qualify
as "evidence" (ἐνάργεια); and for this reason, as Sextus attests,
Epicurus used the term "evidence" as a synonym for "presentation." Plutarch confirms Sextus' testimony when he points out
that, according to the Epicureans, "neither a presentation nor a
perception is more evident [ἐναργέστερον] than a different one."[23]
One presentation cannot be more evident than another, because
*all* are evident, that is, all show an object of perception as it really
is.

As one might expect, this extreme position of the Epicureans
was strongly attacked by their contemporaries. In reporting that,
according to the Epicureans, all presentations are equally evident,
Plutarch objects that this involves the Epicureans in a contradiction. He notes that the Epicureans claim that their position differs
from the Cyrenaic position in that they will assert that the tower
is angular after going up close to it and that the oar is straight
after feeling it, whereas the Cyrenaics hold that even when they
come up close there are only "opinion and seeming" (τὸ δοκεῖν
καὶ τὸ φαίνεσθαι). Plutarch maintains that whereas the Cyrenaics
are logically consistent in holding that we cannot know what is the
case, the Epicureans are inconsistent: for even though they claim
that there is no difference among presentations but all are equally
trustworthy, they in effect make a distinction between presentations by selecting certain presentations—those obtained from
nearby—as showing what is the case, and rejecting others—those
from afar—as not showing what is the case.[24]

In this criticism, Plutarch fails to take into account the Epicurean
distinction between presentation and opinion. Although the Epicureans held that all presentations show what is real, they also held
that opinions are true when they are confirmed by the appropriate presentation, and, moreover, that all opinions about perceptible objects are expectations that are verified when what was
expected becomes manifest. Let us suppose, then, that one forms
the opinion that the tower, which now appears roundish from a
distance, is square. This opinion is an expectation that, when one

---

23. Plutarch *Adv. Colotem* 1121d–e. The complete sentence is: εἰ δὲ γίνεται δια-
φορὰ τοῦ πάθους ἀποστᾶσι καὶ προσελθοῦσι, ψεῦδός ἐστι τὸ μήτε φαντασίαν
μήτε αἴσθησιν ⟨ἑτέρας⟩ ἑτέραν ἐναργεστέραν ὑπάρχειν ("If there is a difference in
the affection of those who stand afar and those who have come close, it is false
that neither a presentation nor a perception is more evident than a different one").
24. Plutarch *Adv. Colotem* 1121c–d and 1124b.

comes close, a square tower will appear; and this opinion is verified subsequently when, upon coming close, one has a presentation of a square tower. At the time of the distant presentation, there really is a roundish tower, not a square tower; and hence one is not justified in asserting that there is a square tower. At the time of the nearby presentation, on the other hand, there really is a square tower, not a roundish tower, so that one is justified in asserting that there is a square tower. The presentations do not differ in validity; rather there is a difference in opinion, and the distinction between presentations that verify and those that do not is entirely dependent on this difference. The Epicureans, therefore, did not single out nearby presentations as inherently truthful, as Plutarch suggests; instead they held that all presentations show what is real, but that only nearby presentations confirm an opinion about a nearby object. What differentiates the Epicurean position from that of the Cyrenaics is that the Epicureans held that all presentations show, by being present, what is real, whereas the Cyrenaics maintained that none do.

Modern interpreters have generally held, as Plutarch objects, that Epicurus and his followers did make a distinction between truthful and deceptive presentations. Accordingly, it is widely held that only some presentations were recognized by Epicurus as ἐνάργειαι. These are identified by some scholars as nearby presentations (as Plutarch suggests in his criticism of the Epicurean doctrine); and they have been understood by others in a more general sense as presentations that, by virtue of being ἐνάργειαι, are sufficiently "clear" or "distinct" to show an external object as it really is. In addition, it is widely held that Epicurus and his followers did not understand a "true" or nondeceptive presentation to be a presentation that shows something externally real, but to be either a presentation that is itself a real event or a presentation that corresponds to the atomic configuration that produces it.[25] It has also

25. Bailey proposes that Epicurus distinguishes the "near" view (as opposed to the distant view), which is a view obtained by giving attention (through ἐπιβολή), as the true view that shows the external object as it is; the "near" view, he holds, is called ἐνάργεια (*Greek Atomists*, 242–43, 254–57). Bailey also suggests that "by the truth of a sensation Epicurus meant and could only mean its truth to the external object which it represented" (ibid., 257), and that Epicurus' followers undermined this position by maintaining that all sensations are true for the reason that the image always corresponds to the eidolon that reaches the eye (and similarly for the senses other than sight) (ibid., 256). DeWitt argues that "true" (ἀληθές) has three meanings in Epicureanism as applied to sensations: "real or self-existent" (signifying that the sensation is a real event); "relatively true" (signifying that the sensation corresponds to an atomic configuration); and "absolutely true" (signify-

been suggested by some that Epicurus made a distinction between perceptions that have as their object certain "proper" objects of perceptions (such as color and hardness), and perceptions concerning states of affairs, such as the perception that this tower is round. The former perceptions, it is suggested, are infallible, while the latter are fallible.[26] According to this last view, Epicurus' theory of confirmation breaks down because the infallible type of perception does not show a state of affairs.

These interpretations are all, it seems to me, just like Plutarch's criticism, critical opinions about what Epicurus should be saying rather than explanations of what he is saying. Epicurus held that the object of perception is precisely what is present in an act of perception, and that this is necessarily a real object of perception. It makes no sense, according to Epicurus, to look for perceptible reality apart from this. Each act of perception, therefore, is an ultimate authority concerning the reality of what is perceived. As Lucretius and Diogenes Laertius explain, a perception cannot re-

---

ing that there is a faithful representation of an external object) ("Epicurus: All Sensations Are True"). Rist holds that Epicurus' contention that all sensations are true means that "a real event takes place in the act of sensing" (*Epicurus*, 19–20). Furley, on the other hand, takes "true" to signify a correspondence between the image and the atomic configuration ("Knowledge of Atoms," 616; cf. Tohte, *Kriterien*, 10). Long agrees with this latter interpretation and proposes that an ἐνάργεια is a "clear" view (gained by nearness to the object or through other circumstances) that, in contrast to other presentations, shows the object as it really is ("Aisthesis," 117). C. C. W. Taylor throws important doubts on both of the commonly held interpretations of "true" in "'All Perceptions Are True'" (in *Doubt and Dogmatism*, 105–124).

26. Louis Bourgey suggests briefly that Epicurus shared Aristotle's view of the infallibility of the "proper" object of perception ("La doctrine épicurienne sur le rôle de la sensation dans la connaissance et la tradition grecque," 254). Striker divides propositions about perceptible objects into three types: propositions such as "this is hard," which are about the proper objects of perception, as previously distinguished by Aristotle; propositions about states of affairs such as "that is a horse," "this tower is round"; and empirical generalizations such as "bodies move in space" (Κριτήριον, 65–66). According to Epicurus, Striker proposes, "all sense impressions are true" means that all propositions of the first type are true; in the other cases, there is an addition made by opinion. Striker recognizes that there is a difficulty about distinguishing proper objects of perception from opinions, but suggests that Epicurus held that this is "in principle" possible ("Epicurus on the Truth of Sense Impressions," 140). Along the same lines, Glidden suggests that Epicurus singled out "presentations" as a species of perception, and that these, having qualities such as shape and color for their intension, and the state of affairs that caused them as their extension, cannot be false ("The Epicurean Theory of Knowledge," 55–57 and 86–128). As for the remaining perceptions, Glidden follows Bailey and others in proposing the method of the close look (along with other aids such as memory and attention) as a means of judging their fidelity to external objects (ibid., 140–46).

fute another that belongs to a different sense; for they have different types of objects. Nor can a perception refute another that belongs to the same sense, because the one is as valid as the other. Nor can reason (λόγος) provide a criterion by which to distinguish between presentations; for it is entirely dependent on perceptions.[27]

This is not to say that there is not a serious difficulty about Epicurus' theory of perception and verification. As Epicurus explains, what is perceived is the result of an interaction between the percipient and the environment. It may be objected, therefore, that the perceptible object is nothing but a subjective impression. Epicurus and his followers attempted to meet this objection by pointing out that every act of perception consists in a response of the perceptual organ to an external object; in the case of sight, for example, there is an immediate contact with the seen object, which exists as an external stream of particles arranged as surfaces. Consequently, even though the perceptible object exists only in relation to a percipient, it has existence externally to the percipient. It would be a subjective impression, having no external reality, if it were were produced by an inner, or "empty," movement; but since it is produced by the impact of external particles, it is externally real.

This explanation invites the charge that Epicurus is confusing two kinds of reality, that of the object as perceived and that of the immediate, unobserved causes of perception. Surely the shape of a tower is not the same as the accumulation of eidola that have streamed from the tower to the eyes? Epicurus fails, I think, to offer a satisfactory answer to this objection: but his strategy seems clear. He made it an initial assumption of scientific inquiry that whatever is perceived directly by the senses or the mind is real; and subsequently, when the theory developed on the basis of this assumption showed that these direct objects of perception do not exist independently of the observer, he attempted to save the initial assumption by arguing that perceptible objects have external reality nonetheless.

It is important, therefore, to distinguish between the initial rule of investigation and the theory that follows from its use. Epicurus commits the investigator to the reality of perceptible objects from the very beginning of the investigation by making it a rule of inquiry that the presentations obtained directly by the senses or

27. DL 10.32 and Lucretius 4.482–99.

the mind be used as the basic facts of inference. The beginning investigator has an ordinary, pretheoretical understanding of the difference between perception and opinion, and takes all objects of perception to have the external reality that they appear to have. By relying on this understanding, the investigator learns that what exists externally is very different from what appears to exist. The problem arises: are the objects of perception then *not* real? But in that case, how can the theory be valid, since it was based on the assumption that the objects of perception are real? Epicurus attempted to save the theory along with the phenomena by continuing to maintain the validity of the initial rule of investigation. The theory, he argued, does not show that the objects of perception are not real. On the contrary, the theory confirms the view that the objects of perception are real: for even though it shows that the objects of perception are effects produced in us from outside, it also shows that they are caused by real constituents of the external world. The critic might object that Epicurus has shifted ground—from maintaining the existence of perceptible objects as perceived to maintaining the existence of the immediate, unobserved causes of perception. Epicurus himself, however, is satisfied that the causal analysis of perception, far from undermining the view that the perceptible object is real, in fact confirms the view that the perceptible object is real by showing that it is reducible to bodies that are real.

Although Epicurus refused to distinguish between truthful and deceptive perceptions, or between perceptible appearance and perceptible reality, it may be said that his own distinction between perceptible reality and nonperceptible reality takes the place of this distinction. As a result of scientific investigation, it turns out that perceptible reality exists only in relationship to us, whereas nonperceptible reality exists independently of us as the objective cause of perceptible reality. Lucretius sets out this distinction very clearly in his defense of the truthfulness of the senses. In a long series of examples, which appear to have been commonly used by philosophers to show the deceptiveness of the senses, Lucretius admits that the sense of sight gives evidence that appears to clash with the facts; these facts concern shape, sameness, movement and rest, direction of movement, distance, size, number, and existence.[28] Lucretius' claims that the eyes do not lie with respect to

28. Lucretius 4.353–468. For similar examples see Cicero *Academica* 2.81–82, 88.

any of these features, for it is not within the authority of the senses to judge them. The features belong to "the nature of things" (*naturam . . . rerum*): and this is judged by reason (*ratio*).[29] According to Lucretius, there is no clash between the judgment of the senses and objective reality, because the type of fact that seems to be in conflict with sense perception does not fall within the province of sense perception at all, but belongs to an entirely distinct domain of reality, one that is judged by reason. This analysis is an elaboration of what Epicurus himself maintains. Epicurus too asserts that "the nature of things," ἡ τῶν ὄντων φύσις, is known only by reason;[30] and he states the distinction between ontological realms very clearly in section 91 of the *Letter to Pythocles*. Epicurus here opposes "what is relative to us," τὸ πρὸς ἡμᾶς, to "that which exists by itself," τὸ καθ᾽ αὑτό, as he claims that the size of the sun and of the other heavenly bodies is exactly as it appears (φαίνεται) "with respect to its relation to us" (κατὰ μὲν τὸ πρὸς ἡμᾶς), but is larger or a little smaller or the same "with respect to what it is in itself" (κατὰ δὲ τὸ καθ᾽ αὑτό).

Some of the later Epicureans attempted to make clear the dif-

29. Lucretius 4.384–85: hoc animi demum ratio discernere debet,/nec possunt oculi naturam noscere rerum. There is a difficulty in Lucretius' account of the veracity of the senses. At 4.464–66, after giving a large number of examples of apparent illusions, Lucretius writes that "the greatest part" of these appearances deceive "because of the opinions of the mind that we add ourselves, so that what is not presented to the senses is taken as presented" (quoniam pars horum maxima fallit/propter opinatus animi quos addimus ipsi/pro visis ut sint quae non sunt sensibu' visa). Why does this explanation not apply to all appearances? Lucretius is surely not conceding that some perceptions are false; he fully supports Epicurus' position that every perception is free from falsehood (see esp. 4.499: proinde quod in quoquest his visum tempore verumst), and he introduces his examples by claiming that the eyes are "not deceived at all" (nec . . . falli . . . hilum, 4.379). Bailey is prompted to ask "why this limitation? . . . Is there perhaps a confusion of thought?" (*Lucretius*, 1236). I suggest that the limitation is due to a recognition of indiscernibles (ἀπαράλλακτα), which formed a major subject of controversy between the Academics and the Stoics (see below, ch. 11). Lucretius seems to have held that in most cases there is a difference in presentation between an object and another that resembles it; the distant tower, for example, does not appear truly round, as does the nearby tower, but as a shadowy imitation of something round (non tamen ut coram quae sunt vereque rutunda,/sed quasi adumbratim paulum simulata videntur, 4.362–63). There are cases, however, in which the presentations of an object and of a resemblance are completely alike. For example, a person may show us an egg, remove it, and subsequently show us a different egg, which however looks exactly the same. In this case, the presentation is ambiguous, and accordingly it misleads us into picking out one of two alternative opinions as true, when in fact it verifies both opinions. The fault, therefore, lies with the presentation rather than with the opinion that was added.

30. See *Her.* 45 for Epicurus' use of the expression ἡ τῶν ὄντων φύσις; cf. Plutarch *Adv. Colotem* 1112e and 1114a.

ference between their own view of perceptible reality and that of other philosophers by pointing out that their use of the terms φαίνεσθαι and φαντασία is restricted to perceptual appearances, as obtained directly by the senses or the mind. Plato had previously used the terms to designate the combination of perception (αἴσθησις) and opinion (δόξα); and although the Stoics later distinguished presentation (φαντασία) from assent (συγκατάθεσις), they held that whenever one assents to a presentation, one regards the cause of the presentation as something that exists objectively.[31] Cicero heaps scorn on one Epicurean, Timagoras, for claiming that there never "appeared" ("were presented," *esse visas*) to him two flames from a single lamp when he put pressure on his eye, but that the falsehood is due to opinion, not to the eyes.[32] What Timagoras claims is that the judgment that there are, objectively, two flames is not a judgment made by the eyes, but an opinion added by ourselves. Objective existence does not "appear" at all, as the Stoics supposed; hence in recognizing the reality of whatever "appears," the Epicureans are not forming any opinion about objective reality, as both the Stoics' and Plato's analyses imply. The same distinction between appearance and opinion is made in another Epicurean text in which a critic imputes to the Epicureans the inference: "the sun appears [φαίνεται] to stand still; therefore the sun does stand still." The author replies that "the sun does not appear to stand still, but is thought [δοκεῖ]" to appear to stand still.[33] The Epicurean is denying that a perceptual appearance implies objective existence; and he points out, similarly to Timagoras, that to suppose that what is presented by the senses is objectively real is to form an opinion. In both examples, the critic is using the term φαίνεσθαι to imply a judgment about objective reality; and the Epicurean protests that such a judgment implies the addition of opinion.

In the final sentence of the cited passage, Epicurus argues for the distinction between presentation and opinion on the ground

---

31. Plato *Sophist* 264a–b; and for the Stoics, see esp. *SVF* 2.54, 63, 65.

32. Cicero *Academica* 2.80 (negat sibi umquam . . . duas ex lucerna flammulas esse visas). The controversy seems to go back to Aristotle's use of the same example to illustrate the difference between appearance and opinion at *De insomniis* 461b30–62a8. The example occurs also at Lucretius 4.447–52.

33. PHerc. 1013 fr. 10.2–6 Scott (p. 310); see also the edition by Romeo, "Demetrio Lacone . . . ," 20. The objection to the Epicurean position is: φαίνεται δ' ὁ ἥλι[ος] ἑσ[τηκ]ώς, ἐστιν ἄρα ὁ ἥλιος ἑστ[η]κώς. The answer is: ο[ὐ] φαίνεται μ[ὲ]ν ὁ ἥλιο[ς] ἑσ[τ]ηκώς, δοκεῖ δὲ φαι. . . . The example of the sun also occurs at Cicero *Academica* 2.82 and Lucretius 4.395–96.

that otherwise knowledge is impossible. He states this argument as a dilemma: if we do not make the requisite distinction, either the criteria that show what is evident are eliminated, or false judgments are as valid as the judgments made by these criteria. It is clear that the criteria are the senses and the mind. Since these criteria judge equally correctly whenever they are used, it follows that if any one of the criteria is thrown out on any occasion, all criteria are eliminated. Hence the dilemma is that either every criterion is eliminated or every judgment is valid. Epicurus states this more pointed version of the dilemma in *Authoritative Opinion* 24:

> If you simply throw out some perception and do not distinguish between an opinion made in accordance with what is expected [to appear] [τὸ δοξαζόμενον κατὰ τὸ προσμένον] and that which is already present [τὸ παρόν] in accordance with the perception and the affections and every presentational application of the mind, you will confuse also the remaining perceptions with your futile opinion, so that you will throw out every criterion. But if you uphold also everything that is expected in your opinions [to appear] and that has not been witnessed, you will not escape falsehood, so that you will have preserved every dispute and every judgment whether correct or not.[31]

Here Epicurus considers specifically opinions concerning future appearances, as he states the consequence of not differentiating between a presentation and an opinion concerning a future appearance. The same dilemma, however, results as that stated in the *Letter to Herodotus*. The alternative to differentiating between a presentation and an opinion concerning a future appearance is either to reject some perceptions as false, in which case all per-

---

34. KD 24: εἴ τιν᾽ ἐκβαλεῖς ἁπλῶς αἴσθησιν καὶ μὴ διαιρήσεις τὸ δοξαζόμενον κατὰ τὸ προσμένον καὶ τὸ παρὸν ἤδη κατὰ τὴν αἴσθησιν καὶ τὰ πάθη καὶ πᾶσαν φανταστικὴν ἐπιβολὴν τῆς διανοίας, συνταράξεις καὶ τὰς λοιπὰς αἰσθήσεις τῇ ματαίῳ δόξῃ, ὥστε τὸ κριτήριον ἅπαν ἐκβαλεῖς. εἰ δὲ βεβαιώσεις καὶ τὸ προσμένον ἅπαν ἐν ταῖς δοξαστικαῖς ἐννοίαις καὶ τὸ μὴ τὴν ἐπιμαρτύρησιν * οὐκ ἐκλείψεις τὸ διεψευσμένον ὥστε τετηρηκὼς ἔσῃ πᾶσαν ἀμφισβήτησιν καὶ πᾶσαν κρίσιν τοῦ ὀρθῶς ἢ μὴ ὀρθῶς.
There is some corruption in the text at τὸ μὴ τὴν ἐπιμαρτύρησιν. Bailey keeps the text and takes ἐπιμαρτύρησιν as direct object of προσμένον, but this construction is very harsh. Perhaps a participle should be supplied with ἐπιμαρτύρησιν (Arr. supplies ἔχον). I follow Bailey in keeping τετηρηκὼς in the last sentence, but I change ὡς to ὥστε (following Merbach); −τε could easily have dropped out before τετηρηκὼς, and ὥστε preserves the symmetry with the first half of the statement.

ceptions, and hence all criteria, are equally rejected; or to admit all opinions as true, in which case conflicting judgments will be admitted. Either consequence is unacceptable. In the first case, no criterion is left by which to judge an opinion as true or false; in the second case, all opinions are equally true and hence equally false.

The second alternative is a consequence traditionally associated with Protagoras from the time of Plato. In the *Theaetetus* Plato assigns to Protagoras the view that every "appearance," φαντασία, is true. Here Plato uses the word "appearance" to denote anything that appears to one to be the case; this includes both immediate objects of sense perception, such as the coldness of the wind, and opinions that exceed what is immediately given by sensory perception. As Plato argues in the *Theaetetus*, it follows from Protagoras' position that contradictory opinions are true, including the contradictory of Protagoras' own claim that every appearance is true; hence Protagoras' claim would be disputed by everyone (including himself), so that it would be true for no one.[35] Sextus Empiricus follows Plato in imputing to Protagoras the view that "all presentations [φαντασίας] and opinions [δόξας] are true"; and he mentions that both Plato and Democritus criticized Protagoras for holding a self-refuting position.[36] In the second part of his dilemma, Epicurus sets out the Protagorean position in order to draw the same general conclusion that no dispute could be resolved.

In the *Theaetetus* Plato also considers the very solution later proposed by Epicurus, and rejects it. Like Epicurus, Plato draws a distinction between what is present in perception and what is expected for the future, and points out that opinions about the future are not all equally valid.[37] But Plato then goes on to reject the position that what is present can be known by perception; and this is a view that Epicurus embraced. In Plato's words, according to this view "the perceptions and the opinions in accordance with them," both of which arise from an "affection that is present [παρόν] to each person," are "evident" (ἐναργεῖς) and "instances of knowledge" (ἐπιστήμας), or "true."[38] Plato opposes this view by

35. Plato *Theaetetus* 170a–71c.
36. Sextus Empiricus *Adv. math.* 7.60 and 389–90 (cf. Plutarch *Adv. Colotem* 1109a). Sextus also associated Protagoras with Epicurus as having held that all "phenomena" (φαινόμενα) are true (see for example, *Adv. math.* 7.369).
37. Plato summarizes this argument at *Theaetetus* 178b–79b.
38. Ibid., 179c (περὶ δὲ τὸ πάρον ἑκάστῳ πάθος, ἐξ ὧν αἱ αἰσθήσεις καὶ αἱ κατὰ ταύτας δόξας γίγνονται, χαλεπώτερον ἑλεῖν ὡς οὐκ ἀληθεῖς . . . καὶ οἱ φάσκοντες αὐτὰς ἐναργεῖς τε εἶναι καὶ ἐπιστήμας τάχα ἂν ὄντα λέγοιεν). Plato's answer extends to 186e (see esp. 186d: οὐσίας γὰρ καὶ ἀληθείας ἐνταῦθα μὲν ὡς ἔοικε δυνατὸν ἅψασθαι ἐκεῖ δὲ ἀδύνατον).

arguing that the senses are not in touch with being and hence are not in touch with truth, but that these are the province of the soul reflecting by itself. Epicurus later maintained that through present affections the senses are in touch with reality, so that both the perceptions are "evident" and the opinions confirmed by them are "true." In adopting the position rejected by Plato, Epicurus took over the same key term "evident," as well as the distinction between perceptions and opinions in accordance with them.

## PERCEPTION, INTERPRETATION, AND REASON

In proposing perception as the ultimate criterion of truth, Epicurus was engaging in a debate that not only went back to a time before Plato but was also to continue with great vigor in the Hellenistic period. In agreement with the criticisms made by Plato in the *Theaetetus*, the Platonists distinguished between "evidence," ἐνάργεια, as provided by the senses, and "truth," and claimed that evidence is not sufficient to show what is true, since what appears as evident is not necessarily real. According to the Platonists, reason, λόγος, must join evidence in order to judge whether what is evident is true. The Platonists called this type of reason, which is directed jointly at evidence and truth, "comprehensive reason," περιληπτικὸς λόγος, as comprehending both evidence and truth; and they considered it the equivalent of Stoic "apprehension," κατάληψις.[39]

This Platonist view was vulnerable to the objection, made not only by the Epicureans but also by the skeptical Academy, that reason is ultimately dependent on the senses indicating, by themselves, what is real. The Academic Carneades, for example, argued in detail that since the presentations that occur to the senses could all be false, not only is sense perception (which is without reason) not a criterion of truth, but also reason, which is dependent on the presentations of sense perception, cannot be a criterion of truth.[40]

The Stoics tried to solve the problem of securing a criterion of truth by dividing all presentations, beginning with presentations that occur to the senses, into those that necessarily show what is real and those that do not; they called the former "apprehensive" (καταληπτικαί). Whenever these presentations, which are imposed from outside, are joined from inside by an assent of the

39. Sextus Empiricus *Adv. math.* 7.141–44.
40. Ibid., 7.159–65; see also the detailed discussion in Cicero's *Academica* 2, esp. 40–44 and 77–78.

mind, an "apprehension" (κατάληψις) is produced; in the case of apprehensive presentations that occur to the senses, the apprehension is said to be made "by the sense" (*sensu*) and is called "perception" (*sensus*).[41] The earlier Stoics held that assent cannot be withheld from apprehensive presentations, and accordingly proposed apprehensive presentations as the criterion of truth. The later Stoics added the refinement that only apprehensive presentations that involve no obstacle compel assent, so that only this type of presentation is evident and serves as a criterion of truth.[42] Antiochus expressed the general Stoic position by saying that "evidence" (*perspicuitas*) is sufficient to indicate by itself things as they really are, and that the mind cannot help but assent to what is evident, just as a balance must sink under a weight.[43] Although the Stoics avoided the rationalism of the Platonists, they were no more successful in escaping Academic criticism than the Platonists. Indeed, the Academics made the Stoics the primary target of their criticism when they argued that it is possible for all presentations to be false.

The Epicurean position in this debate was that the evidence obtained directly by the perceptual organs is sufficient to show what is real, and moreover that all, and only, presentations obtained directly by the perceptual organs show perceptible reality; consequently, whenever the mind responds to the perceptual presentations by a movement of its own, its judgment is entirely dependent on the direct evidence of perception. The distinctiveness of this position may be illustrated by using Antiochus' analysis of empirical cognition as a framework for discussion. According to Antiochus, there are four stages of empirical cognition: (1) an apprehension of sensory properties; (2) an apprehension of propositions in which a single sensory property is predicated of a subject, such as "This is white"; (3) an apprehension of propositions that state a more complex predicate, such as "This is a horse"; and (4) an apprehension of general propositions, such as "If it is a man, it is a mortal, rational animal." The last type of apprehension results in concepts, the starting point of investigation. The first type differs from the others in that it is obtained "by the senses" (*sensibus*), whereas the others are obtained "by the mind" (*animo*) and "not by the senses themselves . . . but in a

41. *SVF* 1.60 and 2.53, 71–75; on the assent that occurs in perception, see esp. Cicero *Academica* 1.40–41, 2.37 and 108.

42. Sextus Empiricus *Adv. math.* 7.253–57; cf. 7.405.

43. Cicero *Academica* 2.45 and 38.

certain way by the senses" (*non sensibus ipsis . . . sed quodam modo sensibus*).[44] The same distinction is rendered in Greek by the expressions αἰσθήσει ("by sense perception") and δι' αἰσθήσεως μὲν διανοίᾳ δὲ ("through sense perception but by the mind"). Sextus explains that in the former case the faculty is irrational (ἄλογος), whereas in the latter it is rational (λογική) and involves memory.[45]

Like Antiochus, the Epicureans made a clear distinction between apprehensions obtained by the perceptual organs and judgments made by the mind in reliance on perceptions; and they might well have accepted Antiochus' general division of empirical cognition into four stages. But their interpretation of each stage is unique. First, they maintained that perception is accomplished entirely by the perceptual organ, acting as a part of the body, without any contribution by a central soul or mind. This view differs most conspicuously from that of Plato, who proposed in the *Theaetetus* that perception is accomplished in every case by the soul (as expressed by the dative case) through (διά) the sense organ, and not by the sense organ itself.[46] Although the Stoics modified this position to admit apprehension by the senses, they agreed that the senses are united in a central power, the mind; and they held that sense perception does not occur without an assent by the mind. Against both Plato and the Stoics, the Epicureans insisted that the perceptual organs themselves apprehend perceptible reality through their affections.[47] Lucretius seems to attack Plato in particular when he ridicules the notion that the mind perceives through the eyes as though through some doors;[48] and Aetius

44. Cicero *Academica* 2.19–21 (with a summary at 2.30). Antiochus contrasts only the second type of apprehension explicitly with the first; but since the third and fourth types are also empirical judgments, the same contrast may be supposed to apply to them.

45. Sextus Empiricus *Adv. math.* 10.63–64. In his outline of Stoic epistemology, Diogenes Laertius describes the apprehension of white things (and so on) as occurring αἰσθήσει, "by sense perception," in contrast with the apprehension of the conclusions of demonstrations, which occurs λόγῳ, "by reason" (7.52). Diogenes also draws a distinction between perceptual (αἰσθητικαί) and nonperceptual presentations, and describes the former as obtained "through [δι'] a perceptual organ or perceptual organs" and the latter as obtained "through the mind" (διὰ τῆς διανοίας); presumably the first type corresponds to all of Antiochus' four stages.

46. Plato *Theaetetus* 184b–d.

47. PHerc. 19/698 col. 9.1–10 Scott (p. 265): . . . δ⟨ι⟩όπερ οὐδ' ὅταν φῶμεν τ(οῖ)ς πάθεσι καταλαμβάνεσθαι τὰς ποιότητας, αὐτοῖς ἀποδίδομεν τοῖς πάθεσιν ἰδίας καταλήψεις, ἀλλὰ τοῖς αἰσθητηρίοις διὰ τῶν παθῶν. οὐδ' ὅταν ἑαυτῶν ἐπαισθήσεις εἶναι τὰ πάθη. . . . ("Therefore, when we say that qualities are apprehended by the affections, we do not assign apprehensions of their own to the affections, but [we assign them] to the perceptual organs through the affections; nor when [we say that] the affections are perceptions of themselves . . .").

48. Lucretius 3.350–69.

shows the difference between the Epicurean and Stoic positions when he points out that the Stoics held that "the affections are in the affected places, but the perceptions are in the mind," and that Epicurus maintained that "both the affections and the perceptions are in the affected places and the mind is unaffected."[49]

Since perception, according to the Epicureans, is an act of the perceptual organ, it is "irrational [ἄλογος] and receptive of no memory," as Diogenes notes.[50] It also provides the evidence by which all mental judgments, or beliefs, are verified or falsified. Contrary to all other philosophers of the Hellenistic period, the Epicureans held that all apprehensions that are not made directly by the perceptual organs are opinions that are verified by the direct apprehensions of the perceptual organs. Accordingly, the mental judgment that "this is white" is an opinion that consists in adding the notion of white to a present perception, and it becomes true when there is a perception of white; and similarly for the third and fourth stages of Antiochus' analysis, except that what is presently known and what is added by opinion become increasingly complex collections of observations. The Epicurean position implies that concepts are produced directly by a repetition of perceptions; and it also excludes the use of propositions or definitions. The function of the mind in the last three stages is: first, to form opinions; and, second, to judge their truth, not by virtue of any special insight belonging to it or any special presentation corresponding to the opinion, but by accepting the judgment of the perceptual organs.

The Epicureans used the term ἐπαίσθησις as a synonym for αἴσθησις in order to show by the use of the prefix ἐπ- that perception consists in a direct acquaintance by the perceptual organ with the external object of perception. The term ἐπαίσθησις, which occurs frequently in Epicurean writings, has traditionally been interpreted as denoting a secondary type of perception involving some mental interpretation or understanding, as opposed to a purely irrational sensory response.[51] An examination of its occur-

49. [Plutarch] *Epitome* 4.23 (*Dox.* p. 414).
50. DL 10.31.
51. This traditional interpretation has the authority of Bailey, who proposes that ἐπαίσθησις is the element of mental recognition or understanding in perception (*Greek Atomists*, 420). DeWitt supports this interpretation by the suggestion that ἐπ- in ἐπαίσθησις has "perfective" force (*Epicurus*, 205). Similarly, Long suggests that ἐπαίσθησις probably is perception in a sense that includes mental judgment or recognition ("*Aisthesis*," 130 n. 11); and Rist tentatively takes ἐπαίσθησις as the act of comprehension supervening on sensation (*Epicurus*, 89). Among

ences, however, reveals that the Epicureans used the term precisely to signify an irrational activity. We have already encountered one use of the term in the discussion of hearing at *Letter to Herodotus* 52. Here the use is not unambiguous, although it makes good sense to take the expression τὴν ἐπαίσθησιν τὴν ἐπ' ἐκείνου to denote an immediate acquaintance of the sense organ with the external source of sound.[52] Two quite unambiguous uses are, first, a contrast made by Philodemus between "irrational ἐπαίσθησις" and opinions;[53] and, second, the claim by an anonymous Epicurean that the perceptual affections bring it about that the sense organs have an ἐπαίσθησις of properties.[54] In addition, Aetius correlates ἐπαίσθημα with αἴσθησις, describing the former as an actualization and the latter as the corresponding power.[55] Finally, Diogenes shows in the following remark that an ἐπαίσθημα consists in a direct apprehension of the perceptible object: "The fact that there are underlying ἐπαισθήματα confirms the truth of perceptions; our seeing and hearing are underlying [experiences], just like having a pain."[56] Like Sextus Empiricus in his discussion of Epicurean methodology, Diogenes cites the immediate presence of the perceptible object, which he compares to the occurrence of a pain, as the reason that the senses are always truthful. It is this immediacy that the prefix ἐπ- is intended to convey.

Whereas the Epicureans used the term ἐπαίσθησις to designate only the irrational stage of empirical cognition, they might well have subsumed all four stages of empirical cognition under the general description "viewing in accordance with perception" (κατὰ τὴν αἴσθησιν θεωρεῖν), a phrase used by Epicurus in contrast with "viewing through reason" (διὰ λόγου θεωρεῖν).[57] The latter type of contemplation applies to imperceptible things, ἄδηλα, which are known by calculation (λογισμός) on the basis of what is per-

---

the few who have challenged the traditional interpretation, Edward N. Lee proposes that the term ἐπαίσθησις, as indicated by the prefix ἐπ-, involves a "directness," as well as intensity, of the perception with respect to the perceived object ("The Sense of an Object," 38–40).

52. See above, ch. 6 (The Perceptual Stream and the External Source).

53. Philodemus *De musica* 4 col. 2.18 Kemke (p. 64).

54. PHerc. 19/698 col. 10.1–4 Scott (p. 266): τὴν ἐπαίσθησιν αὐτὰ παρ[έ]χειν τοῖς αἰσθητηρίοις τῶν ποιοτήτων. Cf. col. 12.7–8, where the direct object of the verb is "pleasure" (ἐπ[αισθ]άνεσθαι τ[ῆς ἡ]δονῆς); and passim.

55. Aetius *Placita* 4.8.2 (*Dox.* p. 394) : τὸ μόριόν ἐστιν ἡ αἴσθησις, ἥτις ἐστὶν ἡ δύναμις, καὶ τὸ ἐπαίσθημα, ὅπερ ἐστὶ τὸ ἐνέργημα, ὥστε διχῶς παρ' αὐτῷ λέγεσθαι, αἴσθησιν μὲν τὴν δύναμιν, αἰσθητὸν δὲ τὸ ἐνέργημα.

56. DL 10.32: καὶ τὸ τὰ ἐπαισθήματα δ' ὑφεστάναι πιστοῦται τὴν τῶν αἰσθήσεων ἀλήθειαν. ὑφέστηκε δὲ τό τε ὁρᾶν ἡμᾶς καὶ ἀκούειν ὥσπερ τὸ ἀλγεῖν.

57. *Her.* 47, 59, 62, and *Pyth.* 91.

ceived.[58] The entire cognitive process may be summed up as follows: the foundation of all cognition consists in the presentations obtained by the applications of the perceptual organs (including the mind acting as a perceptual organ); next are opinions added by the mind and verified directly by presentations of the perceptual organs; and finally, there are scientific opinions, which are verified by the use of reason on the basis of presentations obtained by the perceptual organs. Lucretius likens this structure to an edifice built by the use of certain measuring instruments: just as the edifice would collapse if the measures were faulty, so the structure erected by reason would collapse if the perceptions on which it is based were false.[59]

Epicurus uses the term ἐπιβολή, "application," not only to refer to the acts by which the perceptual organs direct themselves to perceptible reality, but also to designate any grasp of reality. Although the mind needs to have a perceptual presentation, produced from outside, to think of anything at all, it may direct itself, through its perceptual applications, to imperceptible reality. Epicurus uses the term ἐπιβολή in a comprehensive sense, signifying a grasp of reality in general, at the beginning of the *Letter to Herodotus* (36), where he claims that a study of his summary will produce an "application to things" (ἐπιβολὴ ἐπὶ τὰ πράγματα); and he seems to designate the apprehension of scientific truths in particular at the end of the *Letter to Herodotus* (83), when he claims that in analyzing the problems of physics into such "applications" as have been made, the student will be able to discover the remaining details. The progress from perception to scientific knowledge thus consists in a series of applications to reality. As Bailey maintained, the mind does engage in applications directed at scientific entities. The apprehension of scientific truths, however, is not an immediate intuition, but a judgment verified through a process of reasoning by applications of the perceptual organs.

From the time of Aristotle, at least, the terms ἐπιβολή and ἐπιβάλλειν were used by philosophers to signify "hitting upon" the truth or reality; and the Epicurean use conforms to this standard usage.[60] In addition, Epicurus promoted the notion of ἐπιβολή to special prominence in his epistemology; and in doing so he may well have promoted the use of a term that is at least as notorious

58. *Her.* 39.
59. Lucretius 4.513–21.
60. Aristotle *Metaphysics* 993b2–3. For the later period, see, for example, Sextus Empiricus *Adv. math.* 7.51–52, 251, 371, and n. 66 below.

as ἐπιβολή. It seems to me no accident that ἐποχή, signifying a "withholding of judgment," was introduced as a technical term of epistemology about the time that Epicurus elaborated the concept of ἐπιβολή. The Academic Arcesilaos, a slightly younger contemporary of Epicurus, argued against the Stoics that nothing can be apprehended, not even the proposition that nothing can be apprehended, so that the wise man will always refuse assent (ἀσυγκαταθετεῖν), that is, withhold judgment (ἐπέχειν).[61] In more general terms, Arcesilaos' position was that since nothing can be known, one must never affirm or deny anything, but always resist a presentation and withhold approval. Carneades and other members of the Academy subsequently defended Arcesilaos' position that one should never assent to a presentation.[62] The Pyrrhonist Skeptics also embraced ἐποχή, defined by Sextus Empiricus as a "standing" (στάσις) of the mind by which "we neither deny nor affirm anything."[63] The Pyrrhonists differed from Arcesilaos and his followers in admitting assent to presentations: but since they understood this as an assent to the appearance alone, and not to the underlying reality, their notion of ἐποχή is roughly the same as that of Arcesilaos.[64]

The term ἐποχή is directly opposed in both linguistic shape and meaning to ἐπιβολή: ἐποχή is a resistance against accepting anything as real, whereas ἐπιβολή is a thrust toward something recognized as real. This terminological opposition became obscured in the ensuing debate on ἐποχή because Epicurean ἐπιβολή was not recognized by the Academics or any other Hellenistic philosophical school as an apprehension of reality. In preference to devising arguments against Epicurean ἐπιβολή, the Academics attacked Stoic apprehension and assent. As a result, ἐποχή was generally viewed as the opposite of Stoic assent; and even the Epicureans argued against ἐποχή by using the Stoic terminology of assent.[65] The

---

61. Sextus Empiricus *Adv. math.* 7.153–57. See also Cicero *Academica* 1.45 and 2.59, 66–67, 77; and Plutarch *Adv. Colotem* 1122a–d. Pierre Couissin argues that Zeno originated the concept of ἐποχή and that Arcesilaos developed it into a philosophical position ("L'origine et l'évolution de l'ΕΠΟΧΗ," esp. 396). Zeno's role, however, is extremely doubtful, and there is too little evidence to allow us to exclude Pyrrho as a proponent of ἐποχή. Whatever its antecedents, the concept is not found in Aristotle or Theophrastus and it is well attested for Arcesilaos.

62. On Carneades, see Sextus Empiricus *Adv. math.* 7.159–65 and Cicero *Academica* 2.28, 59, 108–10; see also Cicero *De finibus* 3.31.

63. Sextus Empiricus *OP* 1.10: ἐποχὴ δέ ἐστι στάσις διανοίας δι' ἣν οὔτε αἴρομεν τι οὔτε τίθεμεν.

64. On Pyrrhonist assent, see Sextus Empiricus *OP* 1.19–20 and 2.10, 232.

65. The Epicurean Colotes is accused by Plutarch of using the Stoic arguments on inaction against Arcesilaos' notion of ἐποχή (*Adv. Colotem* 1122a); Colotes does

Pyrrhonists accommodated ἐπιβολή to the attitude of ἐποχή, just as they admitted assent: as Sextus Empiricus points out, the mind "applies" (ἐπιβάλλει) to presentations and not to external things.[66] In this reinterpretation of both Epicurean application and Stoic assent there is a hint of the original fundamental opposition between the concepts of ἐποχή and ἐπιβολή.

In conclusion, in stating that we must "observe all things in accordance with the perceptions and simply the present applications, whether of the mind or of any of the criteria," Epicurus demands the investigator have observations that consist in presentations obtained directly by the mind or the senses from outside, without the addition of any interpretation. These presentations show in every case what is real; and therefore they serve as a means of inferring what is not observed.

---

use the Stoic term συγκατατίθεσθαι in claiming against Arcesilaos that "it is impossible not to assent to what is evident" (ἀδύνατον τὸ μὴ συγκατατίθεσθαι τοῖς ἐνάργεσι) (ibid., 1122f). In the latter part of bk. 28 of *On Nature,* Epicurus seems to defend his theory of action against the position of ἐποχή (PHerc. 1479/1417; see esp. fr. 19 col. 1, Arr. 31.20); Epicurus here uses his own term ἐπιβλητικῶς.

66. Sextus Empiricus *Adv. math.* 7.383–84.

# [ 9 ]

# Affections

IN his second rule of investigation, Epicurus pairs the affections (or "feelings," πάθη) with the perceptions as providing a basis of inference concerning what is not observed. I argued in Chapter 5 that although Epicurus recognized the perceptions and affections as joint standards of truth, Epicurus' followers later subsumed the function of the affections as a standard of truth under that of the perceptions. I also suggested that Epicurus distinguishes between the perceptions and the affections on the ground that the former consist in an awareness of objects external to ourselves and the latter in an awareness of an inner condition. This chapter examines in more detail what the affections are, and how they are related to opinions.

Lucretius explains that pain is produced as the result of some force that disturbs the bodily motions, and that pleasure comes into being when the disturbed motions of the body return to their previous settled condition.[1] This type of pleasure is called "catastematic" (καταστηματική) because it consists in a restoration of the body's harmonious condition. Catastematic pleasure may be joined by a variety of pleasures, called "kinetic," which result from the impact of smooth and round atoms upon the various senses.[2] For example, the pleasure we feel when smelling perfume or when

1. Lucretius 2.963–66. This Epicurean position seems indebted to the theory outlined by Plato at *Philebus* 31d–32b and 42c–d.
2. On the difference between catastematic and kinetic pleasures see esp. Cicero *De finibus* 1.37–39 and Diano's explanation in "Note epicuree II," in *Scritti epicurei*, 36–56. Diano is followed by Rist (*Epicurus*, 101–15) and myself. Lucretius explains

eating honey is a kinetic pleasure produced by the impact of round and smooth particles upon a sense organ that is in an orderly condition. In contrast, the impact of rough and angular atoms upon a sense organ causes pain by disturbing the arrangements of atoms in the sense organ. For example, a feeling of pain accompanies the bitter taste of wormwood in a healthy person or the bitter taste of honey in a sick person. In both of these cases a stream of rough atoms has been admitted by the sense organ, causing a disturbance in the sense organ; in the latter case the disturbing particles were admitted because the sense organ was already in disarray. However much pleasures may vary, there is no greater pleasure, according to Epicurus, than catastematic pleasure.[3] It follows from the very nature of catastematic pleasure that there is no intermediate state of feeling between pleasure and pain.[4]

Since pleasures and pains are a kind of perception, we may infer that they are produced just like the perceptions of seeing, hearing, and so on, by successive compacting or by a residue of particles. Epicurus mentions a compacting of pleasure in *Authoritative Opinion* 9: if every pleasure were "compacted" (κατεπυκνοῦτο) over a period of time and over the whole creature or the most important parts, he points out, there would never be any difference in pleasures.[5] This compacting consists in the intensification of pleasures to their highest degree, the attainment of an undifferentiated state of catastematic pleasure. Although Epicurus' statement suggests that there is no compacting of pleasure beyond the attainment of catastematic pleasure, we may suppose that each kinetic pleasure is nonetheless produced, along with the perception that it accompanies, by successive compacting or a residue of particles. The maximum of pleasure is attained by compacting before the formation of a kinetic pleasure; but each variety of pleasure is due to further compacting or to a residue. Like every perception, every pleasure, catastematic or kinetic, is produced by successive compacting or a residue; and the limit of compacting coincides with a limit in the intensity of the awareness.

the pleasure and pain that accompany sense perception at 2.398–443 (for all the senses), and again at 4.622–72 (for taste), 4.673–86 (for smell), and 4.706–21 (for sight); the examples I cite are taken from these discussions.

3. *KD* 3 and 18; also U 417, 419, and 434.

4. See esp. Cicero *De finibus* 1.38 and U 420.

5. See also U 432. I agree with Diano ("Note epicuree II," in *Scritti epicurei*, 56–66) and Rist (*Epicurus*, 114–15) that the compacting of pleasure in *KD* 9 consists in the absence of pain throughout the body and in the mind.

As previously cited, the affections have "the most conspicuous evidence [ἐνάργειαν]."[6] The reason that the affections are evident is that they are exactly as they appear: whenever we feel a pleasure or pain, there really is a pleasure or pain. Epicurus and his followers did not consider it necessary to argue for this claim; rather they took it as given and argued for the evidence of all perceptions on the ground that they are just like affections.

The distinction between evidence and opinion clearly applies to pleasure and pain no less than to the perceptions of external objects. First, we may have opinions about future pleasures and pains. Epicurus held that all mental pleasures and pains are derived entirely from bodily pleasures and pains, and specifically that they consist in the remembrance of past bodily pleasures or pains, in the awareness of present bodily pleasures or pains, or in the expectation of future bodily pleasures or pains.[7] The last type of mental pleasure or pain clearly consists in an opinion concerning a future pleasure or pain, added to a present awareness; this opinion is subsequently verified (or not) by a present evident state of pleasure or pain.[8]

As for opinions relating pleasure and pain to what is nonapparent, we noted previously that Epicurus introduces and concludes his brief account of the soul in the *Letter to Herodotus* by referring to both the perceptions and the affections; and this conjunction suggests that Epicurus viewed the affections as providing a basis of inference in the investigation of the soul.[9] This interpretation is confirmed by Lucretius' more detailed analysis of the soul. In his very first proof on the nature of the soul, Lucretius argues that the mind is not a harmony of the body but a distinct part of the person, on the ground that at times we feel pain in the body whereas "in another part" we feel pleasure, and conversely that we are often miserable in mind although we feel pleasure in the whole body.[10] In these cases it is clear that the feelings of pleasure and pain are viewed as "signs" indicating the unobserved nature of the soul. In his long series of proofs on the mortality of the soul, moreover, Lucretius uses a proof from affection whenever he constructs an argument relating an illness, with

6. See chap. 5, n. 37.
7. Cicero *De finibus* 1.55–57; also Plutarch *Non posse suaviter vivi* 1088e.
8. Plato, too, distinguishes between presently experienced pleasure or pain and opinion, in *Philebus* 32b–c and esp. 39d–40e.
9. *Her.* 63 and 68.
10. Lucretius 3.106–9.

its accompanying pain, to the nature of the soul.[11] One conspicuous example is the spread of gangrene from the toes through the entire leg and to the rest of the body, with an accompanying loss of sensation.[12] Here the progressive loss of feeling shows, according to Lucretius, that the soul is itself diminished little by little and hence is mortal.

We also have a papyrus text in which the Epicurean Demetrius of Laconia discusses inference from the affections in connection with the problem of knowing where the rational part of the soul is.[13] We know that the Stoics used inference from the affections to show that the rational part of the soul is located in the chest. They argued that since the affections—which they classified as pleasure, pain, fear, and desire—are manifestly felt in the chest, the rational part is situated here.[14] It is not clear from the papyrus text whether Demetrius is referring to the Stoic argument or to an Epicurean inference. Lucretius, however, seems to be using the same type of argument when he claims, with reference to the chest, "here trepidation and fear throb, and about this place joys are soothing; therefore, this is where the mind and reasoning are."[15]

Our sources do not discuss the epistemological status of the affections separately from the perceptions; and indeed the epistemological importance of the feelings falls into place once the perceptions have been explained. Both the affections and the perceptions consist in an immediate acquaintance with reality—the former with inner conditions, the latter with external objects—and as such they serve as a means of inferring the rest of reality.

To summarize the preceding discussion of Epicurus' second rule of investigation, Epicurus demands that we use the evidence furnished directly by the perceptual activity of the senses or the mind, consisting in both external objects of perception and inner conditions, as the means of inferring what is not observed. This evidence must be distinguished from any opinions added to them. Whatever appears directly through perception is a real feature of the world; and it serves as the evidence by which any opinion

11. Lucretius 3.459–547 and 824–29.
12. Lucretius 3.526–47. The term *livescere* (3.528) shows that this is a case of gangrene (see Celsus *De medicina* 5.26.31).
13. PHerc. 1012 cols. 27–30 De Falco (pp. 37–39); = cols. 42–47, in Enzo Puglia, "Nuove letture nei PHerc. 1012 e 1786 (Demetrii Laconis opera incerta)," 40–42.
14. See *SVF* 2.881, 886, 899, and 900.
15. Lucretius 3.141–42: hic exsultat enim pavor ac metus, haec loca circum/ laetitiae mulcent; hic ergo mens animusquest.

about what does not appear directly through perception is verified or falsified. All scientific knowledge, therefore, depends on taking whatever appears directly through perception, without exception, as a real feature of the world.

# PART III

*Signs*

# The Use of Observations as Signs

## AN OUTLINE OF EPICURUS' THEORY OF SIGNS

EPICURUS' statement of his second rule of investigation has two parts: first, he demands that we have observations in accordance with the perceptions and feelings; and second, he explains why we must have observations of this sort. The preceding section examined the first part of this rule. It now remains to examine Epicurus' statement that we must observe in the way specified "so that we may have the means to infer [ἔχωμεν οἷς σημειωσόμεθα] both what is expected [to appear] [τὸ προσμένον] and what is nonapparent [τὸ ἄδηλον]."[1] This chapter introduces Epicurus' method of inference by first presenting a brief outline of the method, together with an indication of the major problems, and then setting Epicurus' method in the general context of Hellenistic theories of signs. The next two chapters explore Epicurus' method of inference in detail by examining Philodemus' defense of the method and showing how Epicurus' use of signs fits into a historical development that began long before Epicurus and continued to be important long afterward.

The key term in Epicurus' explanation of his second rule, σημειοῦσθαι, implies that observations are to be used as "signs," σημεῖα, of what is unobserved. Epicurus states this function of observations explicitly in the *Letter to Pythocles* when he points out that the phenomena must be used as signs (σημεῖα) of what goes

---

1. For the text of Epicurus' second rule, see p. 83, n. 1.

on in the heavens.[2] In one place, Epicurus uses the verb τεκμαί-
ϱεσϑαι, implying a τεκμήϱιον, "token," instead of σημειοῦσϑαι:
he states in *Letter to Herodotus* 39 that "it is necessary to infer
[τεκμαίϱεσϑαι] what is nonapparent by calculation [λογισμῷ] in accordance with perception."[3] Since nonapparent entities are known
by means of conclusive signs, whereas future appearances can be
inferred only by means of inconclusive signs, it appears that Epicurus agreed with Aristotle in using the word τεκμήϱιον to designate the conclusive type of sign and using σημεῖον as a general term embracing both inconclusive and conclusive signs.

In his procedural note, Epicurus gives no explanation of the
distinction between what is expected to appear (τὸ πϱοσμένον)
and what is nonapparent (τὸ ἄδηλον), or of how one is to use
observations as signs in either of these categories. Our discussion of verification and falsification, however, has already supplied some information that provides the basis of an answer.[4] In
the case of πϱοσμένοντα, it was shown, an expectation is added
to a present perception or feeling, and this expectation is subsequently verified or falsified by another perception or feeling
that directly matches the expectation or fails to match it. Whenever we form an expectation, the initial perception or feeling
serves as a sign of what is expected; the subsequent perception
or feeling can hardly be regarded as a sign, since it immediately
transforms the expectation into a present truth or falsehood. In
contrast, whenever we make an inference about what is nonapparent, the same perceptions and feelings that verify or falsify
the opinion also serve as signs of the unobserved state of affairs.
They do so, moreover, by means of a logical relationship worked
out by calculation, λογισμός.

There are three important types of λογισμός, expressed by compounds of the term. One is συλλογισμός (verb form συλλογί-
ζεσϑαι), the combination of concepts by argument. Epicurus does
not offer any technical elaboration of the notion of "syllogism";
nor does he endorse the forms of argument developed by Aristotle

---

2. *Pyth.* 97 (τὰ φαινόμενα ἃ δεῖ σημεῖα ἀποδέχεσϑαι); cf. 87 (σημεῖα . . .
τῶν παϱ' ἡμῖν τινα φαινομένων). Epicurus also uses the verb form at *Pyth.* 104
to state that mythical explanation will be eliminated "if one infers [σημειῶται]
well about nonapparent things, following the phenomena."

3. The verb τεκμηϱιοῦσϑαι is used similarly by Philodemus in connection with
nonapparent entities at *De signis* fr. 2.1–2 De Lacy in the phrase ἀπὸ τούτων
τεκμηϱιοῦσϑαι πεϱὶ τῶν ἀφ[α]νῶν.

4. See Sextus Empiricus *Adv. math* 7.211–16; and chap. 8 (Truth, Falsehood,
and Evidence).

or the Stoics. An example of Epicurus' use of the compound, which appears to be typical, is "to think out [συλλογίζεσθαι] that which is in agreement with the phenomena."[5] Second, there are compounds formed with ἀνα-, among them ἀναλογίζειν. This compound, together with the forms ἀναλογία and ἀνάλογος, is used in the sense of calculating similarities, whether they are similarities among the phenomena or similarities between the phenomena and things that are unobserved. Again, Epicurus does not provide any technical elaboration of this notion; but one example, in which he argues that the size of the atoms must be inferred by analogy with the size of perceptible bodies, shows that analogy is an important means of extending knowledge from what is perceived to what cannot be perceived.[6] Third, there is the compound ἐπιλογισμός (or ἐπιλογίζεσθαι), which I translate, for lack of a better term, by the general term "calculation." This compound is prominent both in Epicurus' writings and later, and it stands out as a term that is not used in connection with scientific inference in Plato or Aristotle.

Probably the most informative use of ἐπιλογισμός in Epicurus' writings occurs in the discussion of time in the *Letter to Herodotus*. Epicurus claims that "it requires no demonstration [ἀποδείξεως], but rather calculation [ἐπιλογισμοῦ], that we attach [time] to days and nights and their parts, and similarly to affections and nonaffections, and to movements and states of rest. . . ."[7] "Demonstration," ἀπόδειξις, is the method of proving by argument what is unobserved.[8] The context makes it clear that ἐπιλογισμός differs from ἀπόδειξις in that it is an analysis of what is observed, as opposed to an attempt to show what is unobserved. Specifically,

5. *Pyth.* 112. See also *On Nature* 14, fr. 14 col. 4; Arr. 29.25.15–17: τἀφανὲς διὰ τοῦ φαινομένου συλλογί[ζ]εσθαι.

6. *Her.* 58 and 59; here the term ἀναλογία is used. At *Her.* 72 and *Men.* 127 Epicurus uses ἀναλογιστέον to designate, respectively, the analysis of periods of time and the analysis of types of desires. At *Her.* 40 Epicurus distinguishes between things that are thought of "comprehensively" (περιληπτικῶς) and those that are thought of "by analogy with things that are comprehended" (ἀναλόγως τοῖς περιληπτοῖς). Epicurus does not explain the contrast; but he uses the term περιληπτόν (and cognates) elsewhere in the general sense of having a comprehensive understanding (*Her.* 36), as well as in the narrower sense of recognizing a definite numerical or spatial limit (*Her.* 42, 46–47, and 56). These uses suggest a distinction between things that are known with precision by being gathered under a certain concept and things that are known only by analogy with things that have been demarcated in this way; an example of the latter category might be the fourth, nameless constituent of the soul, which may be known only by analogy with the other three constituents.

7. *Her.* 73.

8. See chap. 1, n. 32.

ἐπιλογισμός is an analysis of the observed association of time with days and nights, affections and nonaffections, and movements and states of rest; no demonstration is required, because it is an observed fact that we associate time in this way. This meaning of ἐπιλογισμός as an analysis of what is observed is confirmed by the other occurrences of the term in Epicurus' works. Its predominant use is to admonish the student to calculate (ἐπιλογί-ζεσθαι) the natural goal of life, pleasure. In these uses, Epicurus advises the student to analyze the identity of good with pleasure, a fact that is given directly by sensory experience.[9]

In the case of nonapparent things, calculation, λογισμός, shows whether a certain hypothetical state of affairs is, in Epicurus' terminology, in "agreement" or in "disagreement" with what is observed: as Epicurus explains, a theory about what is unobserved must not be rejected as false provided there is an "agreement," συμφωνία, of the theory with the "phenomena", φαινόμενα, (or, alternatively, with the "perceptions," αἰσθήσεσι); and a theory about what is unobserved must be rejected as false whenever the theory "disagrees," διαφωνεῖ, or is "in conflict," μαχόμενον, with the phenomena (or the "evident facts," ἐναργήματα).[10] As Epicurus' usage shows, the phenomena are the uninterpreted facts given to us directly by perception. A scientific theory, therefore, is false whenever it is incompatible with the phenomena; and although Epicurus does not say this explicitly, it seems that a scientific theory is true whenever it is in agreement, or compatible, with the phenomena. As we saw earlier, Epicurus used the technical expressions "no counterwitnessing" (οὐκ ἀντιμαρτύρησις) and "counterwitnessing" (ἀντιμαρτύρησις) to designate respectively the conditions of truth and falsehood for scientific theories. Accordingly, it seems, whenever there is no counterevidence by the phenomena, a theory is true; and whenever there is counterevidence by the phenomena, a theory is false.[11] Since a theory's

9. See esp. *Men.* 133 (τὸ τῆς φύσεως ἐπιλελογισμένου τέλος, "having calculated the end of nature"); *KD* 20 (ἡ δὲ διάνοια τοῦ τῆς σαρκὸς τέλους καὶ πέρατος λαβοῦσα τὸν ἐπιλογισμόν, "the mind having calculated the end [that is, ultimate good] of the flesh and its limit"); and *KD* 22 (τὸ ὑφεστηκὸς δεῖ τέλος ἐπιλογίζεσθαι, "one must calculate the underlying end").

10. For Epicurus' use of the term "agreement," see *Pyth.* 86 (τοῖς φαινομένοις συμφωνίαν and ταῖς αἰσθήσεσι σύμφωνον κατηγορίαν); 87 (συμφώνως τοῖς φαινομένοις and σύμφωνον . . . τῷ φαινομένῳ); and 93, 95, and 112 (τὸ σύμφωνον τοῖς φαινομένοις). The opposite, "disagreement" with the phenomena, is mentioned at *Pyth.* 93 (οὐθενὶ τῶν ἐναργημάτων διαφωνεῖ), 90 (μαχόμενον . . . τοῖς φαινομένοις), and 96 (μαχόμενος τοῖς ἐναργήμασιν).

11. *Her.* 50–51; see chap. 8 (Truth, Falsehood, and Evidence).

agreement with the phenomena implies that there is no counter-evidence by the phenomena, it appears that Epicurus proposed the agreement of a theory with the phenomena as a criterion of truth. The disagreement of a theory with the phenomena complements this criterion as a criterion of falsehood.

Epicurus specifies that the agreement of a theory with the phenomena may be single or multiple. Whenever there is a single agreement, there is only one theory that can explain the phenomena; whenever there is multiple agreement, several theories provide equally valid explanations of the phenomena.[12] An immediate difficulty concerning multiple explanations is that if agreement is indeed a criterion of truth, then all of the multiple explanations must be true; and this would seem to be an intolerable infringement of logical principle.

A related difficulty is raised by the following, tantalizingly brief remark in the *Letter to Herodotus*, in which Epicurus defends the method of alternative explanations:

> We must give explanations about the events in the heavens and everything that is nonapparent [παντὸς τοῦ ἀδήλου] by comparing in how many ways a similar thing [ὅμοιον] happens in our experience, scorning those who know neither what is or comes to be in a single way nor what happens in more than one way. . . .[13]

Although Epicurus is here concerned specifically with the events in the heavens, the reference to "everything that is nonapparent" suggests that he views the method of investigation that applies to the heavens as extending to everything that is unobserved. If this is right, then Epicurus is making the important claim that scientific investigation as a whole consists in recognizing similarities between what is observed and what is unobserved.

Is Epicurus then claiming that all scientific arguments must be inductive inferences? This would be surprising. For although there are numerous examples of inductions in Epicurean science, there are also many cases in which Epicurus proves the conclusion without any apparent inductive process, either by showing an incompatibility with the phenomena or by deducing a consequence directly from what was previously established. Many of these conclusions seem counterinductive. On the other hand, Epicurus' follower Philodemus does argue in his treatise *On Significations* that

12. *Her.* 80 and *Pyth.* 86–88.
13. *Her.* 80; for the text, see below, chap. 18, n. 8.

all these inferences are basically inductive inferences. In the following discussion, therefore, the question needs to be kept in mind whether Epicurus too embraced this view.

A final major problem of Epicurean methodology concerns Sextus Empiricus' explanation of the truth and falsehood of scientific theories. According to Sextus, "no counterwitnessing" consists in the "consequence," ἀκολουθία, of the supposed nonapparent thing upon a phenomenon, and "counterwitnessing" consists in the "removal," ἀνασκευή, of a phenomenon by the supposed nonapparent thing.[14] This terminology is very different from Epicurus' own use of the terms "agreement" and "disagreement" to explain the relationship between what is observed and what is unobserved; and the relationship of consequence, which Sextus illustrates by the claim that the existence of void follows upon the evident fact of motion, seems to consist in an incompatibility between the phenomena and the contradictory of the proposed theory. Is Sextus, then, explaining Epicurus' "no counterwitnessing" by a relationship that is narrower than that of agreement?

Since much of our evidence concerning Epicurus' method of inference is furnished by later authors, who were clearly influenced by contemporary developments in the theory of signs, a first step toward clarifying some of the problems is to set Epicurus' method into the context of other Hellenistic theories of signs.

## OTHER HELLENISTIC THEORIES OF SIGNS

Sextus Empiricus distinguishes between two kinds of signs, the "commemorative" (or "hypomnestic," ὑπομνηστικόν) and the "indicative" (ἐνδεικτικόν). This distinction is accompanied by a division of reality into things that are "obvious" (πρόδηλα) or "evident" (ἐναργῆ) and things that are "nonapparent" (ἄδηλα). The former are known by us through themselves, that is, by occurring directly to the senses or the mind; the latter are not known through themselves. Nonapparent things are in turn subdivided into three types: what is once and for all nonapparent; what is nonapparent under the circumstances; and what is "by nature nonapparent" (φύσει ἄδηλα). The first of these three types consists of things that are not of a nature to be apprehended by us, such as whether

14. Sextus Empiricus *Adv. math* 7.213–14.

the number of stars is even or odd; the second consists of things that are by nature evident but are nonapparent owing to certain external circumstances, such as the city of Athens for me now; and the third consists of things that are not of a nature to be evident to us, such as the invisible pores through which sweat flows. Only the last two types of things are apprehended through signs; the former type is inferred by the commemorative sign, the latter by the indicative sign.[15]

Sextus also distinguishes between the commemorative and the indicative sign by relating them to two different uses of the word "sign," a general or common use, and a narrow, technical use. In the general use, Sextus explains, a sign is anything that is thought to "show" (δηλοῦν) something; in the narrow use, a sign is "indicative" (ἐνδεικτικόν) of what is nonapparent.[16] The commemorative sign is included only in the wider category.

Sextus explains further that the commemorative sign consists in something evident that reminds us of something not presently evident by having been observed with it previously. Smoke, for example, is a sign of fire because it reminds us of something presently not perceived, fire, which has been observed with smoke in the past. A commemorative sign, moreover, may show something contemporaneous with itself (as in the case of smoke signi-

---

15. Sextus Empiricus *OP* 2.97–99 and *Adv. math.* 8.141–51. At *Adv. math.* 8.316–19, Sextus gives a different classification of evident and nonapparent things, which excludes things nonapparent under the circumstances. He divides nonapparent things into things nonapparent by nature (φύσει ἄδηλα) and things designated simply by the general term ἄδηλα. The former, he explains, are nonapparent by nature, not in the sense that they have a nonapparent nature (for in that case we could not even know that their nature is nonapparent), but in the sense that they are nonapparent to our nature. The latter are "hidden with respect to their own nature, but are thought to be known through signs or demonstrations, for example that there are atomic elements moving in an infinite void" (8.319). These two types correspond respectively to things once and for all nonapparent and things nonapparent by nature in Sextus' threefold division of nonapparent things. The use of ἄδηλα (simply) and the example in the alternative classification suggest that this scheme was designed with a special view to Epicurean doctrine (see Estelle and Phillip De Lacy, *Philodemus*, rev. ed., p. 186, n. 8; also n. 56 below).

16. Sextus Empiricus *Adv. math.* 8.143. Sextus uses the terms κοίνως, "in common usage," and ἰδίως, "in a specialized (or particular) sense." Signs were also said to be "common" (κοινά) in the quite different sense of signifying a number of different nonapparent states of affairs in common, and "particular" (ἴδια) in the sense of being peculiar to a single nonapparent state of affairs (ibid., 8.200–02; Cicero *Academica* 2.34; and Philodemus *De signis* cols. 1.1–19 and 14.2–27 De Lacy). These two sets of distinctions must not be confused. However, a sign that is particular in the one sense is also particular in the other; and a sign that is common in the first sense admits of being common in the second sense.

fying fire), later than itself (such as a puncture of the heart signifying death), or earlier than itself (such as a scar signifying
a wound).[17] In contrast, an indicative sign signifies something "out
of its own nature and condition" (ἐκ τῆς ἰδίας φύσεως καὶ κατασκευῆς). The motions of the body, for example, indicate the
existence of a soul in that they show immediately, by their own
nature, that there is a power in the body that creates them.[18] The
Stoics held, in addition, that the indicative sign is in every case
co-present with what is signified, for the reason that the indicative
sign is a proposition.[19] Sextus points out that the Pyrrhonist Skeptics accept only the commemorative sign, on the ground that it is
a useful guide for life even though it cannot show what is real,
whereas the dogmatists all make use of the indicative sign.[20]

Sextus explains the indicative sign in some detail by analyzing
the Stoic definition of the indicative sign. According to Sextus,
the Stoics defined the indicative sign—that is, "sign" in the narrow
sense—as a "true antecedent proposition in a sound conditional,
revealing [ἐκκαλυπτικόν] the consequent."[21] As Sextus explains

17. Sextus Empiricus *OP* 2.100–02 and *Adv. math.* 8.143, 151–53, and 156–58.
18. Sextus Empiricus *Adv. math.* 8.154–55 and *OP* 2.101, including at *Adv. math.*
8.154: ἄντικρυς ἐκ τῆς ἰδίας φύσεως καὶ κατασκευῆς μόνον οὐχὶ φωνὴν ἀφιὲν
λέγεται σημαίνειν τὸ οὗ ἐστιν ἐνδεικτικόν ("straightway out of its own nature
and condition, all but speaking aloud, it is said to signify that which it indicates").
19. Sextus Empiricus *Adv. math.* 8.254–55.
20. Sextus Empiricus *OP* 2.102; *Adv. math.* 8.156–58.
21. Sextus Empiricus *OP* 2.101 and 104: ἀξίωμα ἐν ὑγιεῖ συνημμένῳ προ-
καθηγούμενον ἐκκαλυπτικὸν τοῦ λήγοντος. Cf. *Adv. math.* 8.245. There is a mis-
conception, which goes back to Philippson (*De Philodemi libro*, 58–60) and Paul
Natorp (*Forschungen zur Geschichte des Erkenntnisproblems im Alterthum*, 142–44) and
is repeated by Werner Heintz (*Studien zu Sextus Empiricus*, 46–51) and Charlotte
Stough (*Greek Skepticism*, 128), that this Stoic definition embraces both the indicative and commemorative signs. The basis of this confusion is that at *OP* 2.104,
and again at *Adv. math.* 8.245, Sextus cites the Stoic definition as a definition of
"sign" simply. It is clear, however, that the Stoics are here using the term "sign" in
the narrow sense in which it means "indicative sign." Sextus shows this at *OP* 2.
101, where he cites the definition explicitly as a definition of the "indicative sign."
Natorp excises this definition as an interpolation (*Forschungen*, 142–44); he is followed by Heintz, *Studien*, 50–51), whereas Philippson proposes that Sextus is here
confusing the Stoic sign with the indicative sign (*De Philodemi libro*, 60). Philippson,
Natorp, and Heintz all hold in addition that the Stoics made no distinction between the commemorative and the indicative signs. What this interpretation rests
on, apart from the definitions at *OP* 2.104 and *Adv. math.* 8.245, is the claim
that Sextus illustrates the dogmatists' use of the indicative sign (as Sextus understands it) by what are really commemorative signs, such as "if this woman has
milk in her breasts, this woman has conceived" (*Adv. math.* 8.252; cf. *OP* 2.106).
However, neither Sextus nor the dogmatists are here failing to discriminate between indicative and commemorative signs. The logical form of these signs marks
them clearly as indicative signs. It makes no difference that the type of event
(such as having milk) referred to by an indicative sign may also be used as a

this definition, the conditional in which the sign occurs is not only sound, or true, but also has an antecedent that is true, so that both the antecedent and the consequent are true.[22] Moreover, the antecedent "reveals" the consequent in the sense that the consequent cannot be known by itself (that is, as something evident), but can be known only by means of something else, that is, by the antecedent in the conditional. An example of a conditional that meets this last requirement is: "If this woman has milk in her breasts, this woman has conceived."[23] In this case, the fact that the woman has conceived cannot be known by itself, but is revealed by the fact that she has milk in her breasts.

Sextus treats the Stoic analysis of the indicative sign as representative of the views of all dogmatic philosophers, while at the same time making adjustments for individual differences among philosophers. One important difference recognized by Sextus is that whereas the Stoics claimed that the indicative sign is a proposition and hence something "intelligible" (νοητόν), the Epicureans held that it is something "perceptible" (αἰσθητόν).[24] The Epicureans clearly rejected the logical form with which the Stoics invested the indicative sign; but because they agreed that it is possible to know what is naturally nonapparent by inference from what is evident, Sextus attributes to them a belief in the indicative sign.

Sextus' reliance on the Stoic definition of the indicative sign suggests that he may owe to the Stoics the entire distinction between the commemorative and indicative signs, along with the division of reality into evident reality and three types of nonevident reality. Sextus' discussion of demonstration (ἀπόδειξις) provides further evidence of such a borrowing, by showing that the

---

commemorative sign; what makes the difference is that the event is stated by means of a conditional of the requisite type. (The Stoics themselves allude to this difference at *Adv. math.* 8.254–55, when they insist that although the event known by means of a sign may belong to the past, present, or future, the proposition that is used to state the event is in every case present.) Philippson further argues that the distinction between signs arose when, about the time of Sextus, the Empiricist doctors introduced the commemorative sign and the rationalist doctors introduced the indicative sign (*De Philodemi libro*, 59–67, esp. 66). As Natorp points out, the evidence adduced by Philippson is insufficient (*Forschungen*, 147). Recently Jonathan Barnes has also concluded that Sextus' definition applies only to the indicative sign ("Proof Destroyed," in *Doubt and Dogmatism*, 180 n. 23).

22. *OP* 2.105–06 and 115; also *Adv. math.* 8.248–51. The term προκαθηγούμε-νον, or, alternatively, καθηγούμενον (used at *Adv. math.* 8.245), designates a true antecedent in a sound conditional, whereas the general term for antecedent is ἡγούμενον.

23. Sextus Empiricus *OP* 2.106; *Adv. math.* 8.251–53.

24. Sextus Empiricus *Adv. math.* 8.177 and 244.

Stoic definition of demonstration is based on that of the indicative sign. In this discussion, too, Sextus singles out the Stoic doctrine for special attention and views it as typical of all dogmatic philosophers' theories of demonstration, although he clearly recognizes that the logical form proposed by the Stoics is unique to them.

Sextus asserts repeatedly that demonstration is a type of sign (understood in the narrow sense as an indicative sign); and he explains that the conjunction of premises in a demonstration is a sign that the conclusion obtains, and that the demonstration reveals the conclusion.[25] Sextus' view of demonstration as a type of sign is clearly indebted to the Stoic definition of a "demonstrative" (ἀποδεικτική) argument as a "valid argument that by means of agreed premises reveals [ἐκκαλύπτει] a nonapparent conclusion."[26] If one views the argument as a conditional, with the premises as the antecedent and the conclusion as the consequent, then the premises reveal the nonapparent conclusion in the same way that the indicative sign reveals the nonapparent consequent. Although the Stoics themselves did not regard arguments as conditionals, they appear to have defined demonstration by adapting their definition of the indicative sign, with the consequence that Sextus and others interpreted demonstration as a type of sign.[27]

In defining demonstration, moreover, the Stoics distinguished between valid arguments that yield a nonapparent conclusion by merely "leading up" (ἐφοδευτικῶς) to it and those that do so by both "leading up" to and "revealing" (ἐκκαλυπτικῶς) it.[28] Only the latter qualify as demonstrations. An example of an argument that leads up to its nonapparent conclusion without demonstrating it is: If some god has told you that this man will be rich, this man will be rich; this god has told you that this man will be rich; therefore this man will be rich. Sextus explains that the reason this argument fails to be demonstrative is that we accept the conclusion "this man will be rich" not because of the force of the premises, but because we trust the declaration of the god; the conclusion, Sextus notes, depends "on trust and memory" (ἐκ

25. Ibid., 180 and 277; cf. 8.299 and *OP* 2.134.
26. Sextus Empiricus *OP* 2.135 and 143, and *Adv. math.* 8.314: λόγος δι' ὁμο-λογουμένων λημμάτων κατὰ συναγωγὴν ἐπιφορὰν ἐκκαλύπτων ἄδηλον.
27. Mates warns that although the Stoics supposed that there is a conditional, formed of the premises and the conclusion, corresponding to every argument, the Stoics did not identify this conditional with the argument (*Stoic Logic*, 59).
28. Sextus Empiricus *OP* 2.141–42; *Adv. math.* 8.307–14.

πίστεως καὶ μνήμης).[29] Sextus illustrates the demonstrative type of argument, which not only leads up to but also reveals the conclusion, as follows: If sweat flows through the surface, there are intelligible pores; but sweat flows through the surface; therefore there are intelligible pores. In this case, Sextus states, we know from the nature of the propositions—that is, through their necessity—that there are intelligible pores; and he explains that the flow of sweat reveals the existence of pores because it is presumed (προειλῆφθαι) that it is impossible for moisture to pass through a solid body.[30]

The difference between these two kinds of argument corresponds, it seems to me, to the two types of sign.[31] If we combine the two premises of Sextus' demonstrative argument, it becomes clear that the claim "sweat flows through the surface" is an indicative sign that shows by itself, or "out of its own nature," the nonapparent fact, stated in the conclusion, that "there are intelligible pores." In contrast, if we combine the premises of the nondemonstrative argument, it becomes apparent that the claim "some god has told you that this man will be rich" serves as a commemorative sign reminding us, on the basis of past experience, that "this man will be rich." In the latter case, we believe that a particular divine prediction, spoken about this particular man, will turn out to be true, because we have observed numerous instances of divine predictions turning out to be true; we do not accept the conclusion of the argument on the ground that it is in the nature of divine predictions that they are true.

Sextus' example of a nondemonstrative argument, which at first looks unduly complicated, is indeed carefully chosen to make clear just how it differs from a demonstrative argument. The example illustrates the practice of divination, and in particular, it seems, the interpretation of divine apparitions in dreams. The Stoics regarded divination as an art that uses conjecture (στοχασμός)

29. Sextus Empiricus *OP* 2.141 and *Adv. math.* 8.308.
30. Sextus Empiricus *OP* 2.142 and *Adv. math.* 8.309.
31. In *Stoic Logic*, 61–62, Mates raises the problem of how the two types of argument differ, without proposing a solution. Since I wrote this analysis of the two types of argument, Jacques Brunschwig has also proposed that the difference between the two types of argument corresponds to the difference between the two kinds of signs ("Proof Defined," in *Doubt and Dogmatism*, 135–43 and 159). Brunschwig suggests as part of his analysis that the distinction between the two types of arguments may be due to the Stoic Cleanthes, and he locates this innovation within a complex historical development. In my opinion, the Stoic classification of arguments is much more unified and systematic than Brunschwig supposes; I think that it is likely to have been worked out as a whole by one person, very possibly Chrysippus.

rather than reason (λόγος) to discover what is not evident, and
that relies on frequently repeated observations to make predictions, without any understanding of the cause. Accordingly, the
Stoics held that divination consists in opinion, which is fallible,
rather than in knowledge.[32] In response to the Stoic claim that
the art of divination is successful for the most part, Cicero, who
is here very likely indebted to the Academic Carneades, charged
that the "innumerable" instances of divination collected by the
Stoics "signify nothing except the acumen of men making now
one conjecture, now another, on the basis of some similarity."[33] It
is clear that in relying on past observations to predict the future,
those who practice divination are using the commemorative type
of sign. Sextus illustrates precisely this use of signs with a very
simple example of divination. The divination consists in an argument showing that a particular divine prediction will come true.
We accept the conclusion of the argument not because we recognize it as following from necessary premises but because we trust
the new prediction on the strength of our past experience of similar predictions all turning out to be true. The premise "if some
god has told you that this man will be rich, this man will be rich"
is an inductive inference based on memory, not an assumption that
it is impossible for a divine prediction not to come true; hence the
two premises together show the nonapparent conclusion by reminding us of past observations, but fail to reveal the nonapparent
conclusion through themselves.

An argument, then, that simply leads up to the conclusion without revealing it has a conclusion that follows upon the premises,
but is accepted because of past experience; it may, therefore, be
called an inductive argument. In contrast, an argument that leads
up to and reveals the conclusion has a conclusion that not only
follows upon the premises, but is accepted because of the premises;
the Stoics called this a demonstrative argument. The basic difference between the two arguments is that in assenting to a demonstrative conclusion we do not rely on an accumulation of
individual observations, but we have passed from individual observations to a general concept, πρόληψις. An accumulation of
observations allows us to make a conjecture about what is nonapparent under the circumstances, whereas a general concept

---

32. Cicero *De divinatione*, esp. 1.12–16, 24–25, 34, and 109.
33. Cicero *De divinatione* 2.145.

forms the starting point of an investigation into what is by nature nonapparent.[34]

The Stoics therefore appear to have distinguished between the commemorative and indicative signs as stages in scientific progress. The distinction between signs was also prominent in Hellenistic medicine. One group of physicians, the so-called λογικοί, or "rationalists," followed the Stoics in recognizing the indicative sign. They were opposed by the Empiricists, who recognized only the commemorative sign. The rationalists held that the very nature of what is harmful signifies what is beneficial by "indication" (ἔνδειξις). Galen describes indication as the method of discovering "from the very nature of a thing, without experience, what follows [τὸ ἀκόλουθον]."[35] Galen explains in addition that indication is the "entailment [ἔμφασις] of what follows," and that "what follows is also discovered from experience [πείρας] but not as being entailed by the antecedent [ὡς ἐμφαινόμενον τῷ ἡγουμένῳ]."[36] This use of the term ἔμφασις throws additional light on the connection between medical ἔνδειξις and the Stoic theory of indication. Ἔμφασις is the narrowest of four types of implication described by Sextus Empiricus. It is distinguished from the third, next narrowest, type of implication, "connection" (συνάρτησις), by the fact that "the consequent is contained potentially [δυνάμει] in the antecedent," with the result that duplicated propositions are excluded.[37] It is clear that indication belongs to this fourth type of implication. Since συνάρτησις appears to have been a Stoic criterion of the soundness of a conditional, it seems that the Stoics themselves

34. For the Stoic notion of πρόληψις, see *SVF* 2.83 (and chap. 4), also Cicero *Academica* 2.21 and 30 (and chap. 8, Perception, Interpretation, and Reason).

35. Galen *De methodo medendi* 2.7 (p. 123.28–30 D): τὸ τοίνυν ἐξ αὐτῆς τοῦ πράγματος τῆς φύσεως ὁρμώμενον ἐξευρίσκειν τὸ ἀκόλουθον ἄνευ τῆς πείρας ἐνδείξει τὴν εὕρεσιν ἔστι ποιεῖσθαι (cf. 2.4, esp. Kühn 10:101–02); see also Galen *Institutio logica* 11 (p. 24.14–16 Kalbfleisch): ἔνδειξιν μὲν γὰρ καλοῦσι τὴν ἐκ τῆς τοῦ πράγματος φύσεως εὕρεσιν τοῦ ζητουμένου κατ᾽ ἀκολουθίαν τῶν ἐναργῶς φαινομένων. Similarly, ἔνδειξις is defined as follows by ps.-Galen *De optima secta ad Thrasybulum liber* 11 (Kühn 1: 131): ἔστι τοίνυν ἔνδειξις ἡ συμπροσπίπτουσα κατάληψις τοῦ ὠφελοῦντος ἅμα τῇ τοῦ βλάπτοντος καταλήψει, ἄνευ τηρήσεως ἢ λογισμοῦ ("Indication is the coincident apprehension of what is beneficial together with the apprehension of what is harmful, without observation or calculation"). See further Galen *De sectis ad eos qui introducuntur* 3–4.

36. Galen *De methodo medendi* 2.7 (p. 123.22–24 D): τὴν γὰρ οἷον ἔμφασιν τῆς ἀκολουθίας ἔνδειξιν λέγομεν. εὑρίσκεται μὲν γὰρ κἀκ τῆς πείρας τὸ ἀκόλουθον, ἀλλ᾽ οὐχ ὡς ἐμφαινόμενον τῷ ἡγουμένῳ.

37. Sextus Empiricus *OP* 2.111–12. Estelle De Lacy previously pointed out that the relationship of a Stoic sign to its consequent is that of ἔμφασις ("Meaning and Methodology in Hellenistic Philosophy," 395).

subordinated ἔνδειξις to συνάρτησις by classifying it as a type of ἔμφασις.

In contrast to the rationalists, the Empiricist physicians proposed to rely on experience to conjecture what treatment will benefit a particular patient.[38] Thus the Empiricists regarded any treatment that they prescribed as only possibly correct; whether it is the right treatment, they held, is determined by the actual result.[39] In place of the logical type of consequence recognized by the rationalists, the Empiricists admitted the type of consequence that is discovered by experience. Galen shows that this empirical type of consequence consists in a constant conjunction of one event with another, as discovered through repeated observations of what occurs at the same time as, or before, or after what.[40] Through the use of the commemorative sign, the Empiricist remembers these observations and infers what is not now observed. Sextus Empiricus also contrasts empirical consequence, which he calls τηρητικὴν . . . ἀκολουθίαν, "consequence of observation," with the logical type of consequence; and he explains that the Pyrrhonist Skeptic, who admits only the empirical type of consequence, thinks anew of something that is not presently observed by remembering what has been observed with, or before, or after what.[41]

The Empiricists, who traced their school to Serapion (about 200 B.C.) or Philinus (about 250 B.C.), were keenly interested in methodology and developed an elaborate system of empirical investigation that rivals both the Stoic and the Epicurean methods of inference.[42] They held that directly perceived attributes of the patient, known as symptoms (συμπτώματα) and associated with one another in a syndrome (συνδρομή), serve as signs of what is not presently perceived.[43] The entire art of medicine is based on experience, πεῖρα, which consists in personal acquaintance, αὐτοψία; experience that has been repeated frequently is called ἐμπειρία

38. For the Empiricists' use of the commemorative sign, see frr. 80 and 81 D (p. 141.20, 22). For a detailed comparison of the Empiricist and rationalist methods of inference see Galen *De sectis ad eos qui introducuntur* 3, 4; also ps.-Galen *De optima secta ad Thrasybulum liber*, esp. 8 (Kühn 1: 118–21).

39. Galen *De sectis ad eos qui introducuntur* 2 (Helmreich 3: 4.6–10 [= pp. 95.30–96.1 D]).

40. Galen *De methodo medendi* 2.7 (p. 123.25–27 D).

41. Sextus Empiricus *Adv. math.* 8.288.

42. Frr. 4–9 D (pp. 40–41) and pp. 254–56 D.

43. On the Empiricist notions of syndrome and symptom, see Galen *De causis continentibus* fr. 78 D (p. 140.8–22), also fr. 84 D (p. 143.9–13).

and furnishes the theorems (θεωρήματα) of the art.[44] In addition
to personal experience, the Empiricists admitted the report of
someone else's experience, called ἱστορία;[45] and since past observations are not sufficient to show how every new illness should be
treated, the Empiricists also admitted inference by similarity, καθ'
ὁμοιότητα μετάβασις. This method is used in three ways: a previously unknown illness is treated in the same way as a similar
known illness; an illness occurring in a part of the body in which
it has not been observed previously is treated in the same way as
the same illness previously observed in a different part of the
body; and in place of a known remedy that happens to be un-
available a similar remedy is used.[46] The type of reasoning used to
conjecture what is presently not perceived was called ἐπιλογισμός.
Ἐπιλογισμός is explained consistently in our texts as a type of
reasoning that deals with the phenomena; it is also glossed as
"reasoning of the phenomena," φαινομένων λόγος. In contrast,
the type of reasoning used by the rationalists was called ἀναλογισμός. The function assigned to ἀναλογισμός was the discovery
of things nonapparent by nature, whereas ἐπιλογισμός was regarded as useful for discovering what is nonapparent under the
circumstances.[47]

   Among philosophers, the Pyrrhonist Skeptics endorsed both
the commemorative sign and ἐπιλογισμός.[48] They gave their own
distinctive interpretation to these concepts by holding that only

---

44. See Galen *Subfiguratio empirica* 2–3 (pp. 44.4–49.19 D). See also Heinrich
von Staden, "Experiment and Experience in Hellenistic Medicine," 188, for an
overview of Empiricist methodology.
   45. Galen *Subfiguratio empirica* 3 (pp. 48.8–9 and 49.10–19 D) and 5 (p. 51.20–
22 D); and fr. 15 D (p. 95.19–20).
   46. See esp. Galen *De sectis ad eos qui introducuntur* 2 (Helmreich 3: 3.21–4.6
[= p. 95.21–30 D]).
   47. Galen *Subfiguratio empirica* 7 (p. 62.25–27 D); cf. 8 (p. 68.23–26 D); and
Galen *De sectis ad eos qui introducuntur* 5 (Helmreich 3: 11.4–10 [= pp. 105.33–
106.8 D]). In addition, the difference between ἀναλογισμός and ἐπιλογισμός is
illustrated at length in Galen *On Medical Experience* 24–29 (see esp. pp. 132–35 and
141–49 Walzer). For ἀναλογισμός in particular see also ps.-Galen *De optima secta
ad Thrasybulum liber* 10 (Kühn 1: 128–29). Galen states at *Subfiguratio empirica*
8 (p. 69.1–2 D) that ἐπιλογισμός is φαινομένων λόγος (*sermo eorum que apparent*);
at *De sectis ad eos qui introducuntur* 5 (Helmreich 3: 11.8–9 [= p. 105.36 D]),
ἐπιλογισμός is also called φαινομένων λόγος; and in the same treatise, section 8
(Helmreich 3: 22.4–5 [= p. 110.18–19 D]), this type of reasoning is said to be
ἀνάμνησις τοῦ φαινομένου.
   48. Sextus illustrates the use of ἐπιλογισμός by the Pyrrhonist Skeptics at *OP*
1.40; he also attributes ἐπιλογισμός to other skeptical thinkers, for example Gorgias
at *Adv. math.* 8.66.

appearances as such—that is, as subjective impressions—are apprehended and that external perceptible things are just as nonapparent as the things said to be nonapparent by nature.

## EPICURUS' THEORY OF SIGNS
## IN A HELLENISTIC CONTEXT

Since Sextus' classification of reality and of signs seems to be
based on Stoic theory, we may expect that it fits Epicureanism
rather badly. Indeed, there are clear differences that show that
Sextus' classification is alien to Epicureanism. It is nonetheless
important to determine how Epicurus' views are related to the
scheme, since it had a strong influence on how the critics viewed
the Epicurean theory of signs and how the Epicureans in turn
defended their method.

As we have seen, Epicurus divided reality into what is evident,
ἐναργές, and what is not; and he divided the latter into what
is expected to be evident (τὸ προσμένον) and what is nonapparent
(τὸ ἄδηλον). Of the two subdivisions, τὸ προσμένον corresponds
roughly to Sextus' category of what is nonapparent under the circumstances, and τὸ ἄδηλον to Sextus' category of what is nonapparent by nature. According to Epicurus, the phenomena serve
as signs of both types of entities. The type of sign used to infer
what will be evident corresponds roughly to the commemorative
sign; the type of sign used to infer what is nonapparent corresponds roughly to the indicative sign.

There is an important difference in the ontological status of
προσμένοντα from that of objects correlated by other philosophers
with the commemorative sign. This difference is suggested by the
term itself, which is unique to Epicurean methodology. The technical usage appears to be derived from the ordinary use of the
verb προσμένειν in the sense of "expect," "anticipate." Epicurus
himself uses the verb in this ordinary sense in the rhetorically
pointed exhortation: "One must keep in mind that the future is
neither ours nor wholly not ours, in order that we may neither
wholly anticipate [προσμένωμεν] it as [something] that will be nor
give up hope of it as [something] that wholly will not be."[49] Diogenes Laertius appears to link the technical use of the term with
the ordinary use in the very compressed explanation: "Therefore
τὸ προσμένον was introduced; for example, to expect [προσμέ-
νειν] and come close to the tower and learn how it appears near-

49. *Men.* 127.

by."[50] Diogenes has just set out Epicurus' criteria for the truth and falsehood of opinions; and he is now explaining that some opinions are expectations that one may verify by coming close to an object. Although Diogenes' testimony leaves a large gap of explanation between the technical and the ordinary usage, it appears that a person's expectation, as expressed by the active form of the verb, is viewed as identical with the expected thing, which is therefore also expressed by the active form. Such an identification, though strange, is in keeping with the general Epicurean position that an object of perception does not exist except as a present appearance; accordingly, what is expected does not exist except as a present attitude, that of expecting. Προσμένοντα are not objects that already exist and remain to be recognized; instead, they are expected entities, existing as expectations and "waiting" to come into existence by becoming evident.[51]

The ontological status of προσμένοντα explains a heretofore puzzling pecularity of the Epicurean theory of verification. According to Epicurus, προσμένοντα are verified by "witnessing" (ἐπιμαρτύρησις) and falsified by "no witnessing" (οὐκ ἐπιμαρτύρησις). Sextus explains "no witnessing" as an apprehension, obtained directly through evidence (ἐνάργεια), that what was believed is otherwise than believed; and using as an example the conjecture that the figure in the distance is Plato, he points out that "no witnessing" occurs when "after the removal of the distance we know by evidence that it is not Plato."[52] According to Sextus, then,

50. DL 10.34: ὅθεν ⟨τὸ⟩ προσμένον εἰσήχθη. οἷον τὸ προσμεῖναι καὶ ἐγγὺς γενέσθαι τῷ πύργῳ καὶ μαθεῖν ὁποῖος ἐγγὺς φαίνεται. Προσμένειν occurs also at Philodemus *Rhetorica* PHerc. 1015 col. 14.11−12 Sudhaus (1: 291): "will make [him] expect something that is afar" (προσμεῖναί τι ποήσει τὸ π[ό]ρρωθεν). Another occurrence is at Philodemus *De signis* fr. 4 De Lacy, where προσμένειν is contrasted with being ἄδηλα φύσει. The first of Philodemus' uses is an ordinary one, the second technical. At both *Her.* 38 and *KD* 24 the manuscripts vary between the active and passive forms (προσμένον and προσμενόμενον); elsewhere the active is the only attested form. The passive form is readily explained as an emendation of the peculiar active form.

51. Bailey translates προσμένον loosely as "problem awaiting solution" (*Epicurus*, 177) and explains that in the case of distant views "we must regard our sensation as a 'thing awaiting confirmation'" (*Greek Atomists*, 254). This view is close to that of Merbach, who includes present sensations along with future sensations among προσμένοντα (*Canonica*, 25). Zeller, in contrast, restricts τὸ προσμένον to "Gegenstand unserer zukünftigen Wahrnehmungen" and translates the term as "das Bevorstehende" (*Philosophie der Griechen*, vol. 3, pt. 1, 404 n. 1). I understand τὸ προσμένον as an object that is expected to be perceived in the future; and I agree with Bignone (*Epicuro*, 74 n. 1) that it is an object of opinion added to a present perception.

52. Sextus Empiricus *Adv. math.* 7.215; cf. *KD* 37, where ἐπιμαρτυρούμενον is used, as well as Philodemus *Oeconomicus* col. 20.12−16 Jensen (p. 57), where Philo-

falsification in the case of προσμένοντα is produced by the occurrence of a presentation different from the one expected. On
the other hand, the expressions "witnessing" and "no witnessing,"
which are contradictories, suggest that falsification occurs simply
whenever there is *not* a presentation that matches our belief.[53] Is
there a conflict here? The answer to the problem lies, it seems to
me, in the distinctive Epicurean view of perceptible objects as existing only when perceived. Accordingly, if we take the opinion
"this is Plato" to be an opinion about a present state of affairs
and not an expectation about the future, then the opinion is
falsified at once by the present nonappearance of Plato. In this
case, since there is no appearance of Plato, there is "no witnessing"
of the opinion "this is Plato." If, on the other hand, the opinion
"this is Plato" is viewed as an expectation about the future—that
is, as something προσμένον—then the opinion is in effect "there
will be an appearance of Plato when the distance is removed"; and
this opinion cannot be falsified except when the future circumstances under which the appearance was expected to occur have
become present. Supposing, then, that we have formed the opinion
that a presently indistinct figure will become distinct as Plato when
the distance has been removed, this opinion is falsified precisely
when the figure does *not* become distinct as Plato when we come
close. The opinion is falsified in the same way as all opinions
about perceptible objects, by the *non*appearance of what a person
believes to be the case. What constitutes this nonappearance is
the failure of an object to be evident just when, according to our
opinion, it should be evident.

There is no conflict, then, in our testimonies. In the case of
προσμένοντα, an opinion is falsified by nonappearance, and this
nonappearance consists in the appearance of something other
than expected. The opinion, moreover, is possibly true or false
whenever the conditions under which it is expected to be true

---

demus writes that we must consider what our presumption of "good businessman"
is, and then apply the term to the person for whom the appropriate features are
"witnessed" (ἐπιμαρτύρηται).

53. Striker has analysed this difficulty and concludes, by arguing for a corresponding category intermediate between οὐκ ἀντιμαρτύρησις and ἀντιμαρτύρησις,
that Epicurus admitted an intermediate category of opinions about perceptible
things; these, Striker proposes, are beliefs not only about the future but also
about the present and the past, and are possibly true (Κριτήριον, 74–80). I argue
below that Epicurus did not admit such an intermediate category of possibly true
opinions in the case of ἄδηλα any more than he did in the case of προσμένοντα.

have not yet been realized. This possibility is in agreement with Epicurus' notorious claim that, of two contradictory statements, it is not necessary that one is true and the other false.[54] In the case of προσμένοντα, the opinion is neither true nor false until such time as the expected thing must, in accordance with the expectation, be present.

As for the sign of the future occurrence, although there is no explicit testimony, there is no reason to suppose that the original presentation does not function similarily to the commemorative sign by reminding us of observations frequently made in the past. To take Sextus' example, the indistinct figure appearing now under these circumstances reminds us of previous observations of the same indistinct figure, under the same circumstances, becoming distinct as Plato.

Epicurean nonapparent things (ἄδηλα) have generally been divided by scholars into two kinds: things that are imperceptible in themselves, such as the atoms; and things that cannot be perceived by us from nearby, but are not imperceptible in themselves, such as the heavenly bodies. This distinction has been thought to be accompanied by a difference in the validity of the inferences: whereas claims concerning the former kind of nonapparent things, it is proposed, can be demonstrated to be true, claims concerning the latter admit only of being shown to be possibly true.[55]

This division of nonapparent things rests on a confusion between the two categories of προσμένοντα and ἄδηλα. Although certain astronomical and meteorological features, which are inferred through the use of reason, could be perceived directly if only we could come closer, they are not treated by the investigator as προσμένοντα, that is, as things expected to be perceived. They are treated as ἄδηλα, for the reason that it is inconceivable that we should ever perceive them. In classifying them as ἄδηλα, the investigator relies on past experience: because they have been inaccessible to our perception in the past, they are regarded as imperceptible by us in the future. Thus the reverse side of the moon, the edge of our world, other worlds, are all investigated alike as ἄδηλα; for they are assumed to be forever hidden from us. According to Sextus' classification, all Epicurean ἄδηλα for

---

54. Cicero *De fato* 18–19, 37; *De natura deorum* 1.70; and *Academica* 2.97.
55. This is proposed by Bailey (*Greek Atomists*, 253 and 264–65) and Rist (*Epicurus*, 37–40); see also Striker (Κριτήριον, 75–80) and Domenico Pesce (*Saggio su Epicuro*, 38).

which there are signs fit the single category of what is "nonapparent by nature," since they all have a nature that will be forever nonevident to us.[56]

Since, therefore, there is no distinction among nonapparent entities that might make a difference to the method of investigation, it seems to follow that all valid inferences concerning nonapparent entities are equally valid. This does pose a serious problem, however. As noted previously, Epicurus held that a scientific theory is true whenever there is "no counterwitnessing," οὐκ ἀντιμαρτύρησις, and false whenever there is "counterwitnessing," ἀντιμαρτύρησις. Epicurus also seems to have held that "no counterwitnessing" consists in there being compatibility, or "agreement," between what is unobserved and what is observed, and that "counterwitnessing" consists in there being incompatibility, or "disagreement," between what is allegedly unobserved and what is observed. This view of "no counterwitnessing" explains how it is possible for there to be multiple explanations of an event; for a number of alternative explanations can all be equally compatible with the phenomena. On the other hand, since "no counterwitnessing" is a criterion of truth, it seems that we must recognize all of the alternative explanations as true; and this appears to be in conflict with the principle of noncontradiction, which no ancient critic accuses Epicurus of rejecting.

The general response to this difficulty has been to interpret "no counterwitnessing" loosely, so that it is a criterion of possible truth as well as of truth. This interpretation derives some support from the fact that in verifying the fundamental theories of his physics Epicurus makes very prominent use of the criterion of counterwitnessing. In these cases, Epicurus shows not just a compatibility of the theory with the phenomena, but an incompatibility of the contradictory of the theory with the phenomena. From this it appears that "no counterwitnessing" serves as a criterion of truth whenever the contradictory of the claim is disproved by counterwitnessing, and not otherwise.

An important aid to sorting out this problem is Sextus Empiricus' analysis of οὐκ ἀντιμαρτύρησις and ἀντιμαρτύρησις, although at first it seems to complicate matters further. Sextus explains οὐκ ἀντιμαρτύρησις as "the consequence [ἀκολουθία] of the supposed and opined nonapparent entity upon the phenomenon";

---

56. At fr. 4 of *De signis* (De Lacy), Philodemus appears to adopt standard terminology in contrasting προσμένειν with ἄδηλα φύσει. Sextus' alternative classification of nonapparent things (see n. 15 above) fits Epicurus' usage more closely.

the claim "there is void," for example, is "proved by the evident fact of motion."[57] In this case, Sextus points out, supposing there is no void, there is no motion; hence the phenomenon of motion "does not counterwitness" the alleged nonapparent entity. 'Αντι-μαρτύρησις, in contrast, is the "removal [ἀνασκευή] of the phenomenon by the supposed nonapparent entity." Here Sextus illustrates the "supposed nonapparent entity" by the Stoic claim "there is no void" (understood in the sense "there is no void interspersed with bodies"); and he points out that this claim is false for the reason that the phenomenon of motion is "removed jointly" (συνανασκευάζεσθαι) with the alleged nonapparent entity.[58] Throughout his explanation, Sextus proceeds as though he were using the conditional 'if there is motion, there is void' with its contrapositive 'if there is no void, there is no motion.' Accordingly, in his explanation of counterwitnessing, Sextus views the Stoic claim "there is no void" negatively as a removal, which is accompanied by another removal, the "joint removal" of motion.

Neither the term ἀκολουθία nor ἀνασκευή is used by Epicurus to define the conditions of truth for scientific inferences; and Sextus' definition of "no counterwitnessing" as a relationship of consequence is a clear departure from Epicurus' own explanation of this criterion as a relationship of agreement. Sextus' entire analysis, it appears, is guided by the Stoic notion of the indicative sign. Although Sextus avoids the use of conditionals, his explanation could readily be reformulated by using the conditional 'if there is motion, there is void,' and taking the antecedent as an indicative sign that reveals the consequent, with ἀκολουθία and ἀνασκευή expressing the logical relationship between the antecedent and the consequent. As a result, Sextus saves the logical coherence of Epicurus' theory of verification: for every claim proved by "no counterwitnessing" must be true, just as every claim disproved by counterwitnessing must be false. But is this account faithful to Epicurus' own notion of "no counterwitnessing"? Or is it a partial account and a distortion, prompted by contemporary theories of the indicative sign?

Although Sextus' account is influenced by the Stoic notion of the indicative sign, it also seems designed to show up the differences between the Epicurean and Stoic positions. True to his own testimony that the Epicureans viewed the sign as something per-

57. Sextus Empiricus *Adv. math.* 7.213.
58. Ibid., 214. Heintz convincingly defends the mss. readings ἀνασκευή and συνανασκευάζεσθαι (*Studien*, 103–13).

ceptible rather than as a proposition, Sextus scrupulously refrains
from stating the Epicurean position by means of conditionals and
he presents the sign throughout as a phenomenon. The relationship of ἀκολουθία must therefore be understood as a relationship between physical conditions; and this difference from the
Stoic position suggests that the Epicureans may have understood
ἀκολουθία in a wide sense as a relationship of agreement, even
though claiming for their type of sign the validity assigned by the
Stoics to theirs.

The examination of Philodemus' *On Significations* in chapter
11 explores further the Epicurean notions of ἀκολουθία, "consequence," and ἀνασκευή, "removal."

# [ 11 ]

# Philodemus: Inference
# by Similarity

**P**HILODEMUS is the author of a remarkably well-preserved
papyrus roll that was probably titled *On Phenomena and Significations* (Περὶ φαινομένων καὶ σημειώσεων).[1] The treatise is a
compilation of answers to objections directed against the Epicurean method of inference. Most of the answers seem to have
originated with the Epicurean Zeno, who headed the Epicurean
school toward the beginning of the first century B.C.; others were
formulated by the Epicurean Demetrius of Laconia, who was contemporary with or a little older than Zeno.[2]

Philodemus' treatise begins with a series of objections to the
Epicurean method of inference, including some criticisms by a
certain Dionysius, who has been identified by scholars as the Stoic

1. Only the first and final words of the title, περὶ and σημειώσεων, are fully
preserved; the remaining letters, of which a few remnants can be made out, have
been plausibly restored by Scott (p. 37) to yield the title Περὶ φαινομένων καὶ
σημειώσεων. I use the conventional Latin title *De signis*.

2. The treatise seems to be divided as follows: cols. 1–7.5 state a number of
objections to the Epicurean method of inference; cols. 7.5–11.26 are an answer to
Dionysius' rebuttal of an Epicurean defense of their method; cols. 11.26–19.9
are Philodemus' defense of the Epicurean method based on Philodemus' conver-
sations with the Epicurean Zeno; cols. 19.9–27.28 are an outline by Zeno of the
objections to the Epicurean method, together with Zeno's answers, as reported
by the Epicurean Bromius; cols. 27.28–29.19 begin with a few remarks on the
methodical presentation of objections and answers, and continue with the replies
of the Epicurean Demetrius the Laconian; and col. 29.20 to the end of the text
presents another defense of the Epicurean method, possibly by Demetrius. The
beginning and end of the treatise are lost. De Lacy and De Lacy, *Philodemus*,
rev. ed., 157–62, provide a detailed analysis.

Dionysius of Cyrene.[3] Accordingly, Philodemus' work has generally been described as a response to Stoic criticisms of the Epicureans, and the method of inference that is held up as valid by the critics, the so-called method of "removal," ἀνασκευή, has been regarded as Stoic. The method of removal, however, is presented throughout Philodemus' treatise as a method used by the Epicureans in common with other philosophers; and some of the criticisms of the Epicurean method have a strong Academic coloring. The entire attack on the Epicureans fits the Academic practice of using concepts applicable to all their dogmatic opponents in order to find incoherencies in their opponents' theories. Thus, if the Dionysius in question is a Stoic, he is joined by non-Stoic critics of the Epicureans, or else he is not promoting a Stoic method of inference as such and is taking a decidedly Academic perspective on the Epicureans.

In his edition of Philodemus' treatise, Gomperz calls it "the first sketch of an inductive logic . . . inspired and sustained by the breath of the truest Baconian spirit."[4] What prompts Gomperz's enthusiasm is Philodemus' attempt to show that all scientific truths are inductive inferences, and that the logical link by which what is unobserved is said to follow upon the phenomena is inductively determined. As Philodemus argues, the method of ἀνασκευή, "removal," is not the only valid method of proving a claim about what is nonapparent; nor indeed is it, according to Philodemus, an independently valid method at all. There is also another method, Philodemus contends, the method of "similarity" (ὁμοιότης), which is a valid method of inferring what is unobserved, and this indeed underlies the method of removal and makes it valid.

We have already encountered the term ἀνασκευή in Sextus Empiricus' analysis of the Epicurean method of inference.[5] Sextus uses the term to explain ἀντιμαρτύρησις, "counterwitnessing," the method of falsification for nonapparent entities. This method, ac-

---

3. See Philippson, *De Philodemi libro*, 4; also A. Schmekel, *Die Philosophie der mittleren Stoa*, 16–17; and De Lacy and De Lacy, *Philodemus*, rev. ed., 98 n. 28 and 159 n. 5. A Stoic by the name of Dionysius is mentioned by Philodemus in *De dis* 1 cols. 9A and 9B Diels; he is identified by Wilhelm Crönert with the Stoic Dionysius of Cyrene (*Kolotes und Menedemos*, p. 113 n. 512). Most recently, the view that the critics of the Epicureans in Philodemus' treatise are Stoics has been supported by David Sedley in "On Signs," in *Science and Speculation*, ed. Jonathan Barnes et al.

4. Theodor Gomperz, *Philodem: Über Induktionsschlüsse*, xi: "Es ist der erste Entwurf einer induktiven Logik . . . belebt und getragen von dem Hauche des echtesten baconischen Geistes."

5. Sextus Empiricus *Adv. math.* 7.214.

cording to Sextus, consists in the removal of a phenomenon by the removal of something nonapparent, as exemplified by the removal of the phenomenon of motion by the removal of the nonapparent existence of the void. As used by Sextus, ἀνασκευή denotes the Epicurean method of falsifying a scientific inference and hence of verifying a scientific theory by the falsification of its contradictory. Philodemus uses the term in the same way in arguing that ἀνασκευή is not the only way of proving a scientific theory.

Philodemus' strategy is to show, in the first place, that the method of similarity is just as valid as the method of removal. He explains as follows:

Supposing that 'if the first, the second' is true whenever 'if not the second, neither the first' is true, this does not prove that only the method of removal [ἀνασκευή] is cogent. For 'if not the second, neither the first' becomes true sometimes insofar as, when the second is removed by hypothesis, by its very removal the first too is eliminated, as in the case of 'if there is motion, there is void.' For when by hypothesis the void is eliminated, by its mere elimination movement too is eliminated; so that this fits the category of removal. But sometimes [the contrapositive becomes true] not in this way but by the very impossibility of conceiving that the first is or is of a certain kind and the second is not or is not of a certain kind. Take, for example, 'if Plato is a man, Socrates too is a man.' If this is true, it becomes true also that 'if Socrates is not a man, Plato is not a man,' not by virtue of the fact that by the removal of Socrates Plato is jointly removed [συναvασκευά-ζεσθαι], but by virtue of the fact that it is impossible that Socrates is not a man and Plato is a man. And this depends on the method of similarity.[6]

6. Philodemus *De signis* cols. 11.32–12.31 De Lacy:

              . . . τιθεμ[έ]νου γὰρ
         τοῦτό τε ἀληθεύ[εσθα]ι, τὸ εἰ τὸ
         πρῶτον τὸ δεύτε[ρο]ν, ὅταν ἀ-
    35   ληθὲς ἦι τὸ εἰ μὴ τ[ὸ δ]εύτερον
         [οὐ]δὲ τὸ πρῶτον, οὐ [κα]τὰ τοῦτο
         [συν]άγεται τὸ μόνον εἶναι τὸν
         [κατὰ τ]ὴν ἀνασκευὴν τρό-
    [XII] πον ἀναγκαστικόν. τὸ γὰρ εἰ μὴ
         τὸ δεύτερον οὐδὲ τὸ πρῶτον ἀ-
         ληθὲς [γ]ίνεται ποτὲ μὲν παρό-
         σον τοῦ δευτέρου καθ' ὑπόθεσιν {σθ}
    5    ἀνασκευασθέντος, παρ' αὐτὴν
         τὴν ἀνασκευὴν αὐτοῦ καὶ τὸ πρῶ-
         τον ἀναιρεῖται, καθάπερ [ἔ]χει

Philodemus here uses conditionals to defend Epicurean induction. In doing so, he is not abandoning the Epicurean view that a sign is not a proposition, but establishing a common ground of argument by adopting a formulation that was commonly used to explain scientific inference. He argues that a conditional is true not only whenever the elimination of the consequent is accompanied automatically by the elimination of the antecedent, but also whenever it is impossible to conceive of the antecedent being true and the consequent not being true. In the first case, the method of inference is that of ἀνασκευή, "removal"; in the second, it is that of ὁμοιότης, "similarity."

Like Sextus, Philodemus illustrates ἀνασκευή by the negation of the Epicurean claim 'there is void.' In this example, the removal of the claim 'there is void' carries with it the removal of the claim 'there is motion.' Philodemus exemplifies the method of similarity by the claim 'if Plato is a man, Socrates too is a man.' In this case, the contrapositive is true not by the joint removal of 'Plato is a man' along with the removal of 'Socrates is a man' but because it is impossible, as shown by the method of similarity, that Socrates is not a man and Plato is a man.

In the cited passage, then, Philodemus recognizes two valid methods of scientific inference, the method of similarity and the method of removal. In defending the two methods, Philodemus is

καὶ ἐπὶ τοῦ εἰ ἔστι κίνησ[ις] ἔστιν
κενόν· ἀναιρεθέντος γὰ[ρ] καθ᾿ ὑ-
10   πόθεσιν τοῦ κενοῦ, παρὰ ψιλὴν
τὴν ἀναίρεσιν [αὐτ]οῦ καὶ ἡ κίνησις ἀναιρεθή[σεθ᾿], ὥστ᾿ εἰς τὸ
κατ᾿ ἀνασκευὴ[ν γένος ἐναρμότ-
τειν τὸ τοιοῦτ[ο· ποτὲ] δ᾿ οὐχ οὕ-
15   τως ἀλλὰ παρ᾿ [αὐτὸ τὸ μὴ] δύνα-
[σ]θαι τὸ μέν π[ρῶτο]ν ὑπά[ρχ]ον ⟨ν⟩ο-
[εῖ]ν ἢ τοιοῦτον [ὑπάρ]χον τὸ δὲ
[δ]εύτερ[ον] μὴ [ὑπά]ρχον ἢ μ[ὴ] το[ι]-
οῦτον, ο[ἷο]ν ε[ἰ] Π[λά]των ἐστὶν ἄν-
20   [θρωπος], καὶ Σωκ[ράτ]ης ἐστὶν ἄν-
[θρ]ωπ[ος]· τούτου γὰρ ἀληθοῦς
ὄντ[ος ἀλη]θὲς [γ]ίνετα[ι] καὶ τὸ
εἰ Σωκράτ[η]ς οὐκ ἔστιν ἄνθρωπος,
οὐδὲ Π[λάτ]ων ἐστὶν ἄνθρωπος,
25   οὐχὶ [τ]ῶι τ[ῆι] Σωκράτους ἀναιρέ-
σει συνανα<σκευ[ά]ζεσθα[ι] τὸν Πλά-
τωνα, ἀλλὰ τῶι μὴ δυν[α]τ[ὸν]
εἶναι τὸν μὲν Σω[κ]ράτη[ν εἶναι]
οὐκ ἄνθρω[πον, τ]ὸν δὲ Π[λάτω]-
30   να ἄνθρωπον, [δ] δὴ τοῦ κ[αθ᾿] ὁμοι-
ότητ[α] ἔχεται τ[ρό]που.

defending the Epicurean use of both induction and counterwitnessing (ἀντιμαρτύρησις) to verify scientific claims. The critic accepts only the method of counterwitnessing, which alone qualifies as a method of removal. Since removal applies not only to Epicurean counterwitnessing but also to the Stoic method of scientific inference, the critic may be assumed to endorse the Stoic method of inference. This approval, however, is incidental to the debate with the Epicureans. Here the critic's aim is to show that the Epicurean method of inferring what is nonapparent is faulty for the reason that it comprises an invalid type of inference along with a type that is valid.

Philodemus indicates in a rather obscure sentence later on that the method of ἀνασκευή depends on a physical link between the evident entity and the nonevident elements that compose it or produce it in some other way.[7] Ἀνασκευή therefore appears to consist in the elimination of an evident effect together with the elimination of the nonapparent physical constituents that are required to produce it. In the case of the conditional 'if there is motion, there is void,' for example, the movement of bodies is eliminated by the elimination of the nonevident empty spaces that, as constituents of the area through which bodies move, produce motion. Whenever the proof is by similarity, there is no such direct causal dependence of the phenomenon on what is nonapparent. Philodemus several times uses the term "inconceivable" to explain the connection between the antecedent and the consequent in this method of proof.[8] The inconceivability in these cases is determined entirely by empirical investigation. It is observation alone that makes it inconceivable, and hence impossible, that the antecedent should be true and the consequent false.

Just as Philodemus uses conditionals to defend the Epicurean method of similarity, so he appropriates other distinctions and expressions that were regularly associated with the indicative sign. He claims, first of all, that not only the method of removal but also the method of similarity employs a particular (ἴδιον) sign.[9]

---

7. Philodemus describes the connection at col. 37.1–7 as one that is due to the fact that "all things are products of elements or of things made of elements or [products] connected [συνηρτημ[έ]να] [with the elements] in some other way." The use of the term συνηρτημένα suggests that Philodemus is here using Stoic terminology to explain ἀνασκευή.

8. Ἀδιανόητον is used at *De signis* cols. 14.17, 15.37, and 21.29; νοεῖν is used equivalently at cols. 12.16–17, 14.23–26, 19.3, 24.7, 28.22, and 37.22; and the noun form ἀδιανοησία occurs at col. 38.7 De Lacy.

9. *De signis* col. 14.2–27 (cf. the objection at 1.1–19).

In conformity with the standard view, Philodemus explains that a particular sign occurs only when the nonapparent thing that it signifies is the case, whereas a common (κοινόν) sign occurs whether or not the nonapparent thing is the case. Philodemus is here stating the difference, as commonly recognized, between the indicative and commemorative signs; and what he is claiming in effect is that inference by similarity has the validity of the indicative sign.

In addition, Philodemus points out that ἀκολουθία, "consequence," applies to inferences made by the method of similarity no less than to inferences made by the method of removal.[10] This claim is implicit in Philodemus' use of the conditional 'if Plato is a man, Socrates is a man' to state an inductive truth; and it underlies all of Philodemus' defense of the method of similarity. As we saw earlier, Sextus Empiricus explains "no counterwitnessing," οὐκ ἀντιμαρτύρησις, Epicurus' criterion of truth for scientific claims, as the "consequence," ἀκολουθία, of what is nonapparent upon a phenomenon.[11] Although Sextus illustrates his explanation by the claim that the nonapparent existence of void follows upon the evident occurrence of motion, and this claim is proved by removal, there is no reason to suppose that Sextus does not assign to ἀκολουθία the same wide extension that Philodemus assigns to it. As Philodemus and his circle argued, scientific claims are verified by either removal or inductive reasoning; and in both cases what is nonapparent follows upon what is evident. Sextus does not mention induction in his brief outline; but he provides an accurate summary of Philodemus' general position by explaining "no counterwitnessing" as consequence, ἀκολουθία, and "counterwitnessing" as removal, ἀνασκευή. It remains for us to supply that consequence embraces both the method of removal and the method of similarity.

Last, Philodemus associates the Epicurean theory of signs with the notion of the indicative sign by using the term συνάρτησις, "connection," to describe the relationship between both types of sign, as used in induction and removal, and what is signified.[12] We noted in the preceding chapter that the criterion of truth for the type of conditional to which an indicative sign belongs is that of ἔμφασις, "entailment"; this criterion appears to be a subdivision of συνάρτησις, according to which a conditional is true "when-

10. Ibid., col. 37.11–13.
11. Sextus Empiricus *Adv. math.* 7.213.
12. *De signis* cols. 33.28 and 35.5; see also n. 7, above.

ever the contradictory of the consequent is in conflict [μάχεται] with the antecedent."[13] Both criteria seem to have been defined in the first place by the Stoics, to be adopted later by other thinkers. In applying the term συνάρτησις to conjunctions that are inductively determined, Philodemus is asserting that these conjunctions, like the connections known by the indicative sign, are linked in such a way that it is impossible for what is evident to be the case and what is nonapparent not to be the case.

Philodemus justifies the method of similarity by showing in detail how it is used to arrive at valid conclusions. His favorite example of inference by similarity is the claim that since all human beings in our experience are mortal, humans who have not been observed, and hence all humans everywhere, are mortal. In this case, Philodemus explains, the inference is valid for the reason that "all men, both those of whom inquiry has been made [καθ' ἱστορίαν γεγενότας] and those who have come into one's own experience [ὑπὸ τὴν πεῖραν πεπτωκότας], are mortal, there being nothing that pulls one to the opposite [εἰς τοὐναντίον μηδενὸς ἀνθέλκοντος]."[14] Philodemus here states the two basic requirements of a valid inductive inference: first, we must have made a thorough examination of observed similarities, using not only our own experience but also reports of others' experience; and second, there must be no hint of any evidence to the contrary.[15]

In stating the first of these requirements, Philodemus is addressing the charge that the Epicureans rely only on their own sensory experience. This charge is made by the Academic Cotta in Cicero's *On the Nature of the Gods*. Cotta attributes to Epicurus the view that because "I have never seen a rational soul except in a human form," there is no rational soul except in a human form; and he claims that according to this line of reasoning we must eliminate "all new things that inquiry [*historia*] or reason [*ratio*] brings." To illustrate the former alternative, he claims that inland people would not believe in the sea, nor would inhabitants

---

13. Sextus Empiricus *OP* 2.111–12. William and Martha Kneale argue convincingly that συνάρτησις was a criterion adopted by Chrysippus (*The Development of Logic*, 161–62). This, of course, does not exclude the possibility that Chrysippus used the fourth criterion, ἔμφασις, to apply to the indicative sign.

14. *De signis* cols. 16.35–17.2 (cf. 34.34–35.22). The example occurs first at 2.25–4.10 as an objection (cf. 19.37–20.4) and is discussed at 16.5–17.11; 22.28–23.7; 34.11–15; and 34.34–35.22.

15. The first requirement is stated also at cols. 20.35–39 and 32.13–18. The second requirement occurs also at 8.2; 13.4–8; 21.13–14; 32.21–27; 33.13; and 36.7–17. Except at 32.24–25 and 36.16, where Epicurus' term μάχεσθαι is used, the term used to signify a conflict of the theory with the phenomena is ἀντιπίπτειν.

of Seriphus (a notoriously insignificant island in the Aegean) believe in lions or panthers or elephants.[16] Philodemus points out that the Epicureans accept the observations of others, so that they too believe, without ever having been there, that Crete and Sicily are islands.[17] Galen cites the same two islands to illustrate the Empiricist reliance on ἱστορία.[18] The Empiricists, as discussed in the preceding chapter, joined inquiry, ἱστορία, with personal experience, πεῖρα, as the two methods of acquiring observations. Philodemus adopts these Empiricist distinctions as part of his general strategy of defending Epicurus' method by using the opponents' concepts.

What has invited Cotta's charge concerning inquiry is that the Epicurean theory of verification demands, strictly speaking, that the observed facts that are used to verify an opinion be self-evidently present to the person who judges the opinion to be true. By admitting inquiry, Philodemus indicates that the observations of other persons may be treated as though they were self-evidently present to oneself. The other part of Cotta's charge, that discoveries made by reason are eliminated, is directed against the Epicurean reliance on induction. Cotta supports his accusation by pointing out that Epicurus has never seen anything like the sun, or moon, or five planets; it follows (Cotta implies) that since Epicurus has no evidence on which to base an inductive inference, he must deny the existence of these heavenly bodies. This attack on induction depends on the assumption of unique entities. Philodemus responds to this general line of argument by contending that in the case of unique entities, such as the sun, the moon, and the magnet, a careful analysis of both similarities and differences among the phenomena enables us to make valid inferences.[19]

Philodemus' two requirements for valid inductive inferences—careful observation and the absence of any evidence to the contrary—may be summed up by a single requirement, the use of ἐπιλογισμός, "calculation." Like the Empiricists, Philodemus de-

---

16. Cicero *De natura deorum* 1.87–88.

17. Philodemus *De signis* col. 32.13–21.

18. Galen *Subfiguratio empirica* 8 (p. 68.7–10 D); Galen here adds Sardinia as a third island. There appears to have been considerable controversy among philosophers and physicians about the validity of secondhand evidence. In *Subfiguratio empirica* Galen sets out three criteria used by the Empiricist physicians to judge the truthfulness of written records: one is the agreement of all the sources; another is the wisdom and character of the writer; and third is the similarity of the reported facts with what is known from one's own experience (8, pp. 67.18–69.28 D).

19. Philodemus outlines the objection concerning unique entities at cols. 1.19–2.3 and answers it at cols. 14.28–16.1 and 24.10–25.23.

scribes ἐπιλογισμός as a calculation "of the phenomena."[20] According to Philodemus, we may obtain valid inferences by "calculating [ἐπιλογιζόμενος] the similarity and difference among the phenomena"; and this is the method of "drawing a conclusion by ἐπιλογισμός."[21] As Philodemus explains, this method does not demand, as the critic charges, that we examine all the phenomena, which is impossible. Nor does this impossibility entail, according to Philodemus, that we rely on chance encounters; what is required is that we examine "many and varied instances of the same kind."[22]

We have already noted Epicurus' use of the term ἐπιλογισμός. This usage is in agreement with Philodemus' explanation of ἐπιλογισμός as an analysis of the phenomena. It is true that Epicurus nowhere in his extant writings presents ἐπιλογισμός as a means of inferring what is unobserved; but his use of induction implies that he, too, regarded ἐπιλογισμός as a means of knowing what is unobserved. This view of ἐπιλογισμός is in striking contrast with that of the Empiricists; although the Epicureans agreed with the Empiricists in using ἐπιλογισμός as a means of inference, the Epicureans held, contrary to the Empiricists, that it is a means of discovering what is nonapparent by nature.[23]

20. The expression τῶν φαινομένων ἐπιλογισμοῦ occurs at col. 22.38–39; cf. col. 27.22–23. At col. 24.34–35 the same type of reasoning is described simply as ὁ τῶν φαινομένων λόγος.

21. *De signis* col. 13.30–32: τὴν ὁμοι[ό]τητα καὶ διαφορὰν τὴν ἐ[ν τ]οῖς φαινομένοις ἐπιλογιζό[με]νος; cf. col. 17.32–34: περιοδευόντ[ων] ἡμῶν τῷ ἐπιλογισμῷ δεό[ν]τω[ς τ]ὰς ὁμοιότητας; and col. 23.5–6: ἐπιλογισμῷ συνβιβάζων. Demetrius uses the verb in the same sense when he accuses the critics of failing to take proper account (ἐπιλελογίσθαι) of the facts (col. 28.15–16, 26, and 37–38).

22. Ibid., col. 20.32–36, including, at ll. 35–36, πολλοῖς ὁμογενέσι καὶ ποικίλοις.

23. For Epicurus' use of ἐπιλογισμός, see chap. 10 (An Outline of Epicurus' Theory of Signs); for the Empiricists, see chap. 10 (Other Hellenistic Theories of Signs). I disagree, therefore, with Arrighetti, who proposes that ἐπιλογισμός is an immediate understanding—something like intuition—and not a reasoning process ("Sul valore di ΕΠΙΛΟΓΙΖΟΜΑΙ ΕΠΙΛΟΓΙΣΜΟΣ ΕΠΙΛΟΓΙΣΙΣ nel sistema epicureo," 123: ἐπιλογισμός has "un senso di immediatezza quasi intuitiva"). De Lacy has argued against Arrighetti that ἐπιλογισμός signifies inductive inference ("Epicurean ΕΠΙΛΟΓΙΣΜΟΣ"). De Lacy concedes to Arrighetti that ἐπιλογισμός sometimes seems to be the "process of extracting truths from experience" rather than the "extension of these truths to things outside experience," but he maintains that these are aspects of the same thing and that ἐπιλογισμός is basically the formulation of a generalization extending to what is unobserved (see esp. 182). Although I agree with Arrighetti that the prefix ἐπ– suggests immediacy, I take this to consist in the direct acquaintance of the reasoning mind with the phenomena; thus ἐπιλογισμός is not an intuition without calculation but an application of one's reasoning powers to the facts that are immediately available. This brings my interpretation closer to De Lacy's than to Arrighetti's. The many uses of ἐπιλογισμός by the Epicureans and others show clearly, however, that ἐπιλογισμός is a calculation performed on phenomena and does not itself extend beyond them, even

Because ἐπιλογισμός is a sufficiently powerful tool of inquiry, Philodemus contends, it is not necessary to presuppose in the argument on human mortality either that unobserved men are similar to observed men not only in other respects but also in respect to mortality, or that observed men are mortal insofar as (ᾗ or καθό) they are men.[24] Instead, Philodemus claims, both of these general truths are conclusions obtained by the use of ἐπιλογισμός. He defends this claim by analyzing in detail general statements expressed by ᾗ, καθό, and παρό. Treating the three terms as synonymous, Philodemus distinguishes four kinds of statements: (1) this accompanies (συνέπεται) that by necessity— for example, men, in respect of (ᾗ) being men, are made of flesh and are receptive of illness and old age; (2) this is a proper account (λόγον ἴδιον) of that, and a presumption (πρόληψιν)—for example, body, according as (καθό) it is body, has bulk and resistance, and man, in respect of (ᾗ) being man, is a rational animal; (3) this is a concomitant (συμβεβηκέναι) of that—for example, man, according as (καθό) he is man, dies; and (4) this is a concomitant (συμβεβηκέναι) resulting from a concomitant of that— the atoms, for example, according as (καθό) they have weight, move downward.[25] In all four cases, Philodemus argues, the feature that is conjoined with another "in respect of" (ᾗ), "according to" (καθό), or παρό (which is not exemplified in the extant text) the other, attends the other by necessity; and this necessity is proved by the method of similarity.[26]

A major objection to the Epicurean use of induction was the claim that there is nothing to prevent us from making an infer-

---

though the Epicureans used ἐπιλογισμός as a means of demonstrating what is unobserved. Philippson rightly takes ἐπιλογισμός as the "Erwägung von Tatsachen," and hence as an empirical method. However, Philippson also denies that ἐπιλογισμός has any connection with ἀπόδειξις at all; he identifies the latter with the "dialectical–syllogistic" method of Plato and Aristotle ("Epikurs Buch 28 Περὶ φύσεως," 1458–59). Sedley shares the view that ἐπιλογισμός is an appeal to experience; and he holds, against De Lacy, that it is a process "not necessarily involving analogy or induction" ("Epicurus, *On Nature* Book XXVIII," 27–28).

24. For the first type of presupposition, see *De signis* cols. 2.26–3.26, 19.36–20.1, and 22.29–35; for the second, cols. 3.29–35 and 6.31–7.2.

25. *De signis* cols. 33.33–36.7. The text breaks down when Philodemus comes to describe the fourth category. Philippson's restoration . . . [καὶ τὸ] [συμβε]βηκ[έναι τόδε ἐκ τ]ουδ[ε . . . at col. 34.15–16 seems to capture the general meaning ("Zur Wiederherstellung von Philodems sog. Schrift ΠΕΡΙ ΣΗΜΕΙΩΝ ΚΑΙ ΣΗΜΕΙΩΣΕΩΝ," 35). The examples show that the concomitant in the fourth category differs from that of the third category in that it is related to another concomitant rather than directly to the subject.

26. *De signis* cols. 34.24–26 and 35.4–6, 27–29.

ence on the basis of an irrelevant similarity.[27] One way in which this objection was elaborated is as follows: the "similars" of Epicurean inference must be either "indistinguishables" (ἀπαραλλακτά), that is, things that are indistinguishable in themselves and differ only in number, or things that differ from one another. If they are indistinguishables, there is no inference, since in that case the supposed nonapparent thing is just as evident as the phenomenon; and in the case of things that differ, the inference is invalid since the similars may differ in respect to the inferred feature.[28] This objection looks Academic, for the Academics used indistinguishables, which they exemplified by twins, eggs, seal imprints, and so on, very conspicuously in their arguments against the dogmatists. The Stoics, against whom these arguments were chiefly directed, did not recognize indistinguishables.[29]

Philodemus answers this objection by saying that in some cases the similar entities are indeed indistinguishables, but that this does not mean that they are equally evident. Inference concerning indistinguishables may occur, Philodemus claims, when there is some circumstance that is evident in the one case and not in the other.[30] Although Philodemus offers no examples, we might illustrate his answer by inferring, in the case of two indistinguishable twins, that the persons whom we know to be the parents of one are also the parents of the other. As for things that differ in some respect, Philodemus sets out a carefully graduated hierarchy of inferences, which is intended to assure the closest possible similarity. Philodemus specifies that we must infer from individual men to men most like them, and from the genus of men to an attribute of the entire genus; from animals of a certain kind to animals most like them, and from the genus of animals to an attribute of the genus; from a body of a certain kind to a body of a certain (very similar) kind, and from generic body to a generic attribute of body; and from a certain kind of existent to existents most like this, and from generic existence to a generic attribute.[31] Again, Philodemus offers no examples with his answer; and there

27. Ibid., cols. 5.1–6.31.
28. Ibid., cols. 5.37–6.31 and 19.25–36.
29. See Cicero *Academica* 2.54–58, 84–86.
30. *De signis* cols. 22.2–11 and 37.24–29; cf. 25.18–23.
31. Ibid., cols. 18.17–19.4. The two subdivisions in each category appear to be specific signs (εἰδικά) and generic signs (γενικά), respectively. These two divisions are distinguished by Philodemus at col. 36.17–21 and fr. 2.7–10. In accordance with this division, Philodemus regards individual human beings as εἴδη, "species," and the general type, to which these species belong, as a γένος (see also Sextus Empiricus *Adv. math.* 8.41).

is some obscurity in his scheme. But it is reasonable to suppose
that the inductive progress begins with such inferences as 'if Plato
is a man, Socrates is a man,' in which individual human beings
(each viewed as a species) are compared with one another, and
then continues with inferences concerning the attributes of the
genus, such as the attribute of mortality in the case of men. The
inductive progress then goes on to successively higher classes as
illustrated by animals, bodies, and existents, with a distinction
made at each level between the species into which the genus is
divided and the genus itself. By establishing a hierarchy of inductive levels, Philodemus attempts to show that a careful analysis
of the phenomena, ἐπιλογισμός, allows us to find exactly the right
degree of similarity on which to base our inferences.

The type of objection to which Philodemus is here responding
is also voiced by the Academic Cotta in Cicero's *On the Nature
of the Gods*.[32] Cotta charges that the "similarity that delights you
[the Epicureans] exceedingly" is beside the point, citing among
other examples that men who are most similar in shape may differ in character, and that men who are most similar in character
may differ in shape. Cotta then attempts to turn the Epicurean
method of similarity against the Epicureans by constructing a typical Academic sorites: why should someone hold that rationality
can exist only in a being of human shape (as the Epicureans
hold in assigning human shape to the gods) and does not exist
instead only in a terrestrial thing, which was born, which has
grown up, which has learned, which has a mind and a body subject to decay, and finally which is a mortal human being. Cotta's
conclusion is that since rationality is observed to be conjoined not
only with human shape, but also with all the properties in this
sequence, it is arbitrary to suppose that god is rational without
possessing all of these properties. Philodemus attempts to disarm
this kind of attack by constructing an inductive progression of
his own, which is to make clear at what level an inference is to
be made.

The clinching argument that Philodemus uses to defend the
inductive method of inference consists in the claim that removal
is not an independent method of inference at all, but a special
form of the method of similarity. He describes this relationship
by saying that the method of similarity "extends through" (διήκει)
the method of removal, and that the latter is "confirmed" (βε-

32. Cicero *De natura deorum* 1.97–98.

βαιοῦται) by the former.[33] As a result, he maintains, if the method of similarity does not have the power to "demonstrate" (ἀπο-δεῖξαι), neither does the method of removal.[34] In one place, he claims outright that there is just one correct method of inference, that of similarity, and that only this method assures that the sign and what is signified are joined by necessity in such a way as to demonstrate.[35] To illustrate the subordination of the method of removal to that of similarity, he takes the prime example of removal, the claim that if there is motion, there is void. He contends that "we apprehend the conditional 'if there is motion there is void' in no other way than by proving by the method of similarity that it is impossible for motion to occur without void"; and he explains that we do this "by calculating [ἐπιλογισάμενοι] all the properties that accompany the moving things of our experience, without which we see nothing moving."[36] This calculation shows, according to Philodemus, that "all moving things of our experience differ in other respects, but have in common that they move through empty spaces"; and this conclusion justifies the inference that unobserved moving things, too, move through empty spaces.[37] According to Philodemus, therefore, what justifies an inference by removal is that it can be reformulated as an inductive inference.

Whereas the critics, then, made a distinction between inductive and demonstrative arguments, Philodemus claims that all demonstrative arguments are basically inductive arguments. To make sure that there is no misunderstanding on this point, he rejects the view that the method of removal "depends on" (ἠρτῆσθαι) the method of similarity. This position, he points out, is in effect the same that he advocates, but it leaves the suspicion that there are two distinct methods of inference.[38]

The critics attempted to undermine the claim that all scientific inferences are inductions by pointing out that induction results in conclusions opposed by the Epicureans themselves. According to this criticism, we should infer from the fact that all bodies in our experience are destructible that atomic bodies too are destructible, and from the fact that all bodies are observed to have color that atoms too have color.[39] Philodemus replies by pointing out that

33. *De signis* col. 7.8–11; cf. cols. 8.22–9.8.
34. Ibid., col. 9.3–8.
35. Ibid., cols. 30.37–31.9.
36. Ibid., col. 8.26–36.
37. Ibid., cols. 35.36–36.2.
38. Ibid., col. 31.8–17.
39. Ibid., col. 5.1–7.

the bodies in our experience are destructible insofar as they partake of a "nature that is opposed to a corporeal nature and that yields," and that bodies likewise do not have color insofar as they are bodies. In both cases, Philodemus maintains, corporeality is a chance similarity between what is observed and what is nonapparent.[40] Here and throughout the treatise, Philodemus indicates that science consists in distinguishing chance similarities from those that are connected by the necessity of scientific law.

Philodemus' expression for "inference by similarity" is ἡ καθ' ὁμοιότητα μετάβασις or ἡ κατὰ τὸ ὅμοιον μετάβασις.[41] The locution is not found in Epicurus' extant writings. Since it is an important feature of Empiricist methodology and, as we have noted, there are other similarities between Empiricist and Epicurean methodology, it has been proposed that Philodemus owes his inductive system largely to the Empiricists.[42] The chief source of Philodemus' methodology, however, is clearly Epicurus. Philodemus' distinction between the method of removal and the method of similarity corresponds to Epicurus' use of counterwitnessing and induction to prove his physical theories; and although there is doubt about how Epicurus viewed the relationship between the two methods of verification, it is clear that he used induction widely in the development of his theories. Ἐπιλογισμός, the analysis of phenomena, is prominent in Epicurus' writings. Most important, it was Epicurus who established the basic principle on which all of Philodemus' analysis depends, that the observed facts, and they alone, serve as signs of what cannot be observed. This principle, moreover, was directly opposed by the Empiricists. Whereas the Epicureans claimed that the phenomena provide conclusive signs of what is nonapparent, the Empiricists held that the phenomena provide signs only of what may be observed in the future.

Although Philodemus' methodology is based on that of Epicurus, his manner of defending it is strongly influenced by contemporary thinkers. The Empiricists, Stoics, Academics all made a contribution to the debate; and there is some reason to sup-

40. Ibid., cols. 17.30–18.10.
41. Ibid., cols. 32.22–23; 15.5–6; and 18.14–15.
42. This is the suggestion of Philippson, *De Philodemi libro*, 56–57. It is opposed by Schmekel, who suggests that Philodemus' inductive theory is derived from Carneades (*Philosophie*, 346–50). Estelle and Phillip De Lacy agree with Philippson that Philodemus' theory of signs is indebted to the Empiricist physicians; they also hold, however, that Epicurean methodology underwent no fundamental change after Epicurus but was only elaborated by his followers (*Philodemus*, rev. ed., 175–76, 195–96, 205).

pose that the Academics, using concepts from other philosophical schools, were the leaders in the debate and the main influence on the Epicureans. Cicero reports that the Epicurean Zeno heard the Academic Carneades and "disagreed very much with him, yet admired him above all others."[43] It is tempting, therefore, to suppose that Zeno, who was the chief Epicurean participant in the debate, was stimulated by criticism from Carneades to use all the conceptual tools currently available to defend the method of inference that had been handed down by Epicurus.

In conclusion, Philodemus attempted to show that Epicurus' method of using observations as signs of what is nonapparent is a valid, indeed the only valid, method of making scientific discoveries. Using as a model the contemporary theory of the indicative sign, he argued that scientific—that is, demonstrative—knowledge not only depends on induction but consists entirely in inductive inferences. In agreement with Philodemus, Sextus Empiricus later explained Epicurus' criterion of truth for scientific inferences, "no counterwitnessing," οὐκ ἀντιμαρτύρησις, as the "consequence," ἀκολουθία, of what is nonapparent upon the phenomena; this "consequence" may be assumed to embrace, as Philodemus argues, both induction (in the narrow sense in which it is distinct from proof by counterwitnessing, or removal) and proof by counterwitnessing. What remains unclear is whether Epicurus himself held that induction is as cogent a method of inference as counterwitnessing—especially in view of the fact that induction may result in multiple explanations (a problem not treated by Philodemus)—and whether he went so far as to subordinate the method of counterwitnessing to that of induction. The following, wider view of the historical context to which Epicurus' theory of signs belongs will help to focus the problem. Subsequently, a detailed examination of Epicurus' own scientific proofs will furnish more evidence of his position.

43. Cicero *Academica* 1.46.

# [ 12 ]

# The Continuing Debate
# on Signs

## ARISTOTLE AND EARLIER

THE discussion of signs so far has aimed at elucidating Epicurus' theory of signs by considering developments in the theory after his time. The problem may also be approached by an examination of the theory and use of signs in the period before Epicurus. Aristotle and earlier writers provide ample evidence of a use of signs that was well developed long before Epicurus' time. Aristotle is an especially helpful source, because he both analyzes the use of signs in some detail and employs signs himself in support of his theories.

In the *Prior Analytics* Aristotle gives the following explanation of "sign":

A sign [σημεῖον] is meant to be a demonstrative [ἀποδεικτική] premise that is either necessary or commonly accepted. For this is a sign of [a thing] having come to be or being: when it is, a thing is, or when it has come to be previously or later, a thing has come to be.[1]

Aristotle goes on to explain with examples that the use of a sign corresponds to the use of the middle term in each of the three syllogistic figures. First, he explains, in showing that this woman is pregnant because she has milk in her breasts, one uses the middle of a first figure syllogism; the middle term is "having

1. Aristotle *Prior Analytics* 70a6–9: σημεῖον δὲ βούλεται εἶναι πρότασις ἀποδεικτικὴ ἢ ἀναγκαία ἢ ἔνδοξος. οὖ γὰρ ὄντος ἔστιν ἢ οὖ γενομένου πρότερον ἢ ὕστερον γέγονε τὸ πρᾶγμα, τοῦτο σημεῖόν ἐστι τοῦ γεγονέναι ἢ εἶναι.

milk" (B), while the other two terms are "to be pregnant" (A) and "woman" (C). An example of the use of a middle in the second figure is the inference that since this woman is sallow, she is pregnant; in this case, the middle term is "sallow" (A), while the other two terms are "to be pregnant" (B) and "woman" (C). The use of a middle in the third figure is illustrated by the inference that since Pittacus is good, the wise are good; here the middle term is "Pittacus" (C) while the other two are "good" (A) and "wise" (B). Aristotle adds that if only one premise is used, a sign is used; if the other premise is used as well, a syllogism is formed. However, Aristotle points out, only a sign of the type that corresponds to the middle term of a first figure syllogism can form a valid syllogism, and so only this type can constitute conclusive proof.[2] In the *Rhetoric* Aristotle calls this conclusive type of sign τεκμήριον, "token," to distinguish it from nonconclusive signs.[3]

In illustrating the type of sign that corresponds to the middle term of a second figure syllogism, Aristotle points out the fallacy involved in using a sign of this sort: "since sallowness attends those who are pregnant, and it follows also upon this woman, they think that it has been shown that she is pregnant."[4] The fallacy is that of affirming the antecedent on the ground of affirming the consequent. In *On Sophistical Refutations* Aristotle extends this charge to the rhetorical use of signs in general when he claims that in rhetoric "demonstrations by sign" are inferences from consequents; and he uses as an example the inference that a person is an adulterer because he is nice looking or is seen wandering about at night.[5] This general charge presupposes that all inferences by signs, at least as used by the rhetoricians, conform to syllogisms of the second figure.

The fallacy that belongs to signs of the third figure is that a universal conclusion is based on a claim that is not universal or relevant. It is not the case, Aristotle notes, that if Pittacus is good, all wise men are good. This type of sign differs from that of the second figure in that the inference is from particular to universal, whereas in signs of the second figure it is from universal to particular.[6]

Signs that may be formulated as first figure syllogisms are rec-

---

2. Ibid., 70a11–38.
3. *Ars rhetorica* 1357b3–21; cf. 1402b18–19.
4. *Prior Analytics* 70a21–22.
5. *Sophistici Elenchi* 167b8–12.
6. *Prior Analytics* 70a30–34; and *Ars rhetorica* 1357b10–21.

ognized as valid by Aristotle for the reason that the premise that
states the sign (such as "she has milk") is joined by a universal
statement that justifies the inference (in this case, "all women who
have milk are pregnant").[7] In effect, the sign is an antecedent
from which what is signified follows as a consequent. Thus it
follows from the fact that this woman has milk that she is pregnant; for it is the case that all women who have milk are pregnant.

Although signs joined by the appropriate covering generalization are conclusive, Aristotle explains in the *Posterior Analytics* that
such signs are not "demonstrative" in the strict sense in which
this term signifies scientific demonstration. For although the attribute that is asserted of the subject may always accompany it,
the attribute does not belong to the subject essentially (καθ' αὐτό)
and hence does not belong by necessity, so that we do not have an
explanation for why the conclusion obtains.[8] If we take the example of the woman who has milk, we may illustrate Aristotle's
criticism by noting that pregnancy does not belong essentially to
women who have milk, although it belongs always; hence, in concluding that this woman is pregnant, one does not have an explanation for why she is pregnant.

Aristotle also notes that since in the case of signs the attribute
does not belong essentially to its subject, it is possible for there to
be different explanations of the same fact. The reason is, according to Aristotle, that the middle term does not constitute the
definition of the major term.[9] Aristotle offers no illustrations. But
suppose we take another of Aristotle's examples of signs belonging to the first figure: Pittacus is free; for those who love honor
are free, and Pittacus loves honor.[10] Here love of honor admits
of being one of several explanations of freedom, since it is not a
definition of freedom. Strictly speaking, Aristotle does not recognize this type of explanation as a real explanation.

In his analysis of signs, Aristotle makes clear how inference by
signs falls short of his own requirements for scientific argument—
that is, demonstration—but reveals little of how the use of signs
may have been justified by others. Although his illustrations and
his own use of signs throughout his works show that inference by

7. *Prior Analytics* 70a29–30. Strictly, the universal statement should be: "All
women who have milk have conceived." But since the aim is to discover an unobserved fact (pregnancy) through an observed fact (having milk), the possibility
that a woman with milk has already given birth is left out of account.

8. *Posterior Analytics* 75a28–37.

9. Ibid., 99a1–4.

10. *Prior Analytics* 70a26–27.

signs consists in using observed facts as evidence of what is un-observed, Aristotle does not indicate to what extent inferences by signs were supported by analogy, or induction in general, or rea-soning establishing a causal link between what is observed and what is unobserved. Aristotle himself points out in his discussion of "physiognomy"—the use of signs to infer a mental character-istic from a physical characteristic—that we must presuppose a causal connection in order to make a valid inference from a physi-cal to a mental characteristic. This presupposition is that the soul and body undergo joint physical alteration. Only if this is granted, Aristotle maintains, may we infer, for example, that those who have large extremities have courage.[11]

Thus, although Aristotle knows nothing of the later termino-logical distinction between the commemorative and the indicative signs, his criticisms anticipate the later debate on the validity of signs. It may be noted, too, that his analysis of a sign as something that occurs at the same time as that which is signified, or earlier, or later, agrees with the Hellenistic analysis of the commemora-tive sign as having these three distinctions.

Aristotle not only distinguishes the use of signs from his own method of scientific demonstration, but also dissociates it from his method of induction (ἐπαγωγή). This is implied by his clas-sification of signs as attempted demonstrations, as well as by his classification of rhetorical arguments. Aristotle divides rhetorical arguments into two types, the enthymeme (ἐνθύμημα) and the example (παράδειγμα), which correspond respectively to syllogism and to induction; and he classifies inference by signs under the enthymeme, distinguishing it consistently from the use of ex-amples.[12] However much, then, inference by signs is an inductive process, it must be distinguished from Aristotle's own method of induction. The two methods are indeed fundamentally different: inference by signs is based on a distinction between observed particulars and unobserved particulars, and attempts to demon-strate the latter by showing that they follow from the former, whereas Aristotelian induction is based on a distinction between

11. Ibid., 70b7–38. For further details about physiognomy, see also the Peri-patetic work *Physiognomica* and Ross's comments in his annotated edition of Aris-totle's *Prior and Posterior Analytics*, 501–02.

12. *Ars rhetorica* 1357a22–1357b36 and 1402b13–1403a10. In the former dis-cussion Aristotle admits only signs (and tokens) and likelihood under syllogisms, and contrasts syllogisms with examples; in the latter he includes examples ex-ceptionally under syllogisms. In both discussions, signs are distinguished from examples.

the particulars of sense perception and the universals that apply to them, and attempts to pass from the former to the latter by a direct intuition of the universal as it exists in the particular.

Although Aristotle does not admit inference by signs as a method of scientific demonstration, he makes surprisingly frequent use of signs in his own investigations. He explicitly endorses the use of signs in the *Nicomachean Ethics* when he claims that "it is necessary to use evident things [φανεϱοῖς] in witness [μαϱτυϱίοις] of nonevident things [ἀφανῶν]."[13] In this brief injunction, Aristotle sums up the key features of the method of signs—the distinction between what is evident and what is nonevident, and the use of the former as a "witness" of the latter. An example of Aristotle's own use of signs in the *Nicomachean Ethics* is the claim that the pleasure or pain that accompanies deeds is a sign of dispositions; another example from the *Nicomachean Ethics* is that it is a sign of pleasure being the supreme good that all animals and men pursue pleasure.[14] Other of Aristotle's books furnish many more examples from every field of inquiry, including medicine, meteorology, zoology, psychology, physics, and metaphysics. An example of a sign used in medicine is that roughness of the tongue is a sign of fever;[15] an example from meteorology is that the large size of hailstones is a sign of their having been formed close to earth.[16] In some cases, the use of the sign consists in drawing an analogy between what is observed and what is unobserved. In the *Meteorologica*, for example, Aristotle notes that it is a sign that flames in the sky, including shooting stars, are formed below the moon, rather than farther away, that "their speed is similar to that of objects thrown by us, which seem to move much faster than the stars, sun, and moon because they are close to us."[17] Here, the sign is the observed fact that the objects thrown by us move much faster than the moon and the other heavenly bodies. It follows by

13. *Nichomachean Ethics* 1104a13–14: δεῖ γὰϱ ὑπὲϱ τῶν ἀφανῶν τοῖς φανεϱοῖς μαϱτυϱίοις χϱῆσθαι.
14. Ibid., 1104b3–5; and 1153b25–26.
15. *De divinatione per somnum* 462b26–32.
16. *Meteorologica* 348a33–36. Examples from the other cited fields occur at *De generatione animalium* 760b33, *De divinatione per somnum* 463b23, *Physics* 219b3, and *Metaphysics* 980a21.
17. *Meteorologica* 342a30–33. Cf. 358a4, where the saltiness of the sea is explained by signs consisting of analogies with urine, sweat, and ash. Aristotle makes frequent use of analogies (see G. E. R. Lloyd, *Polarity and Analogy*, 361–77); although he does not usually refer to them as "signs," they are clearly intended as such.

analogy that the flames in the sky, which also move very fast, are close to us.

Both Aristotle's theory and his practice, therefore, indicate that his predecessors had developed a method of inference by signs that rivaled his own method of inductive and syllogistic inference. Direct evidence of such a method is, moreover, plentiful. We may turn in the first place to the Hippocratic corpus. This contains many examples of signs, most conspicuously prognostic signs, such as that the contortion of the eyes is a sign of coming death.[18] We also find in the Hippocratic corpus, and especially in the three works *On the Seed, On the Nature of the Child,* and *Diseases* 4, numerous examples of analogies by which an unobserved condition is inferred on the basis of a known similarity with one or more observed processes.[19] One elaborately developed analogy is that between the growth of a child in the mother's womb and the growth of a plant in the surrounding soil.[20] At times the comparison that is offered is described as an ἀνάγκη, "compelling proof," and in general the comparisons seem to be viewed in the three cited works as conclusive proof of the unobserved condition.[21]

The Hippocratic corpus also contains some methodological remarks on the use of signs. The author of the treatise *On the Art* notes that there are things that escape the sight of the eyes, called ἄδηλα, "nonapparent," and that these things have been "conquered by the sight of intelligence" (τῇ τῆς γνώμης ὄψει κεκράτηται) and are investigated "by calculation" (λογισμῷ).[22] Moreover, the author identifies the means by which the physician learns what is invisible as signs, citing, among other examples, the clarity or roughness of the voice[23] In the treatise *On the Nature of Man,* a distinction is drawn between signs common to many individuals and signs peculiar to one individual. The author claims that there

---

18. *Prognostic* 2.
19. Otto Regenbogen has a very valuable discussion of the analogies used in treatises *On the Seed, On the Nature of the Child,* and *Diseases* 4 in "Eine Forschungsmethode antiker Naturwissenschaft."
20. See, for example, *Diseases* 4.33–34 Littré (7:544.17–548.10). See further Lloyd, *Polarity and Analogy,* 347–48; Regenbogen, "Eine Forschungsmethode," 134–38; G. Senn, "Über Herkunft und Stil der Beschreibungen von Experimenten im Corpus Hippocraticum," esp. 228–31; and William Arthur Heidel, *Heroic Age of Science,* 147–50.
21. See Regenbogen, "Eine Forschungsmethode," 140–41.
22. *On the Art* 11; cf. the cryptic discussion at *On Regimen* 1 chaps. 11–12, and *Breaths* 3 (τῇ μὲν ὄψει ἀφανής, τῷ δὲ λογισμῷ φανερός).
23. *On the Art* 13.

are two causes of disease, air and regimen; these differ in that air is a common cause, which affects many persons of different regimens with the same disease at the same time, whereas regimen is a particular cause, which affects people of different regimens with different diseases at any given time.[24] It is clear from the details cited by the author that the physician is expected to balance similarities and differences carefully against each other in order to make the right inference. We also find a number of anticipations of the Empiricist position. In the treatise *On Ancient Medicine* the author claims that a person cannot make an assertion about what is unobserved without using a hypothesis, and a hypothesis cannot be known to be true or false since there is nothing against which it can be checked.[25] Likewise, the author of *On the Art* points out that in order to discover the correct treatment the physician must compare the present case with past cases and determine what past treatments were effective.[26]

Among other groups that used signs are the historians. A conspicuous example is Herodotus' inference that the Nile is of the same length as the Danube.[27] Making the standard distinction between what is evident and what is nonevident, Herodotus notes that he is making a conjecture "by inferring [τεκμαιρόμενος] the unknown by means of what is evident"; and he bases his inference on the known similarities between the two rivers, especially the fact that they transect continents located opposite one another. Thucydides uses inference by signs frequently, particularly in his introductory section on the early history of Greece. Using the verbs τεκμαίρεσθαι and τεκμηριοῦν among others to denote the process of inference, and the nouns σημεῖον, τεκμήριον, παράδειγμα, and μαρτύριον to denote the sign, he repeatedly infers a past event from a presently observed event, and on occasion he also infers a future event. His first chapter contains an example of each kind of inference: he says that he expected from the very beginning that the Peloponnesian War would be important,

---

24. *On the Nature of Man* 9.
25. *On Ancient Medicine* 1.
26. *On the Art* 7.
27. Herodotus 2.33 (τοῖσι ἐμφανέσι τὰ μὴ γινωσκόμενα τεκμαιρόμενος); see also Lloyd, *Polarity and Analogy*, 342–44; and Hans Diller, "ΟΨΙΣ ΑΔΗΛΩΝ ΤΑ ΦΑΙΝΟΜΕΝΑ," 16–17. In his article, which is intended as an extension of Regenbogen's "Eine Forschungsmethode," Diller demonstrates the wide use of analogy and signs in a variety of early thinkers, especially the physical philosophers. Diller distinguishes between analogy and the use of signs, although he thinks that signs originated as analogies (23).

"inferring" (τεκμαιρόμενος) this from the fact that the parties involved were then at the height of their power; and he claims that earlier events were hard to discover clearly, but that by investigating these as far as possible through "tokens" (τεκμήρια) he has confidence in the conclusions he has reached.[28]

The importance of signs in rhetoric is well attested by Aristotle. One example of many from the rhetoricians themselves is found in Gorgias' *Defense of Palamedes*, where Palamedes cites his inventions as a "sign" (σημεῖον) of the fact that he abstains from ugly and evil deeds.[29]

Last, and most important from our point of view, the method of using observed facts as signs of what is unobserved is amply attested for the pre-Socratic philosophers. To Anaxagoras we owe the well-known dictum "the phenomena are a view of what is nonapparent" (ὄψις ἀδήλων τὰ φαινόμενα).[30] The experiment of the inflated bladder, which Anaxagoras appears to have devised, may be said to provide a sign of the substantiality and strength of air.[31] Anaxagoras' dictum, we are told, was approved by Democritus.[32] We have certain obvious examples of Democritus' use of observed facts as signs of what is unobserved. In one of his fragments Democritus points out that we observe both living and lifeless things gathering together according to similarity: for example, we see animals, such as doves and cranes, forming groups; we see grains of the same kind collecting in the same place when passed through a sieve; and we see similarly shaped pebbles washed up in the same place on the seashore.[33] These observations are intended by Democritus as signs of the grouping of atoms. Further, Democritus is said to have explained the formation of wind by comparing it to the movement of a crowd in the marketplace: just as the turmoil of a crowd is due to the confinement of a large number of individuals within a small space, so the formation of wind is due to the gathering of a large number of particles in a small space.[34] Democritus also likened the umbilical cord to the cable that anchors a ship, as well as to the cutting from which a

28. Thucydides 1.1.1–3; see also in book 1: 2.6, 3.3, 6.2, 8.1; and Diller, "ΟΨΙΣ," 22.
29. DK 82 B 11a.31.
30. Sextus Empiricus *Adv. math.* 7.140 (DK 59 B 21a).
31. Aristotle *Physics* 213a22–27; Aristotle also mentions the use of the clepsydra to prove the same point (cf. DK 59 A 69).
32. See n. 30, above, for the reference.
33. DK 68 B 164; cf. DK 68 A 128.
34. DK 68 A 93a.

plant grows.[35] In all these Democritean examples, there is a clear use of analogy to obtain a view of what is unobserved. We shall return to Democritus later. The use of signs is also attested for Anaximenes, Empedocles, Alcmaeon, and Diogenes.[36] A final example in this brief suvey is Diogenes' claim that one important sign that everything is air is that men and the other animals live by breathing air.[37]

## EPICURUS AND HIS FOLLOWERS

The preceding discussion indicates that the method of using observations as signs flourished in the fifth century, but suffered a period of decline in the fourth. Plato developed an approach to scientific inquiry that is wholly antithetical to this method of inference. Aristotle continued to oppose it; but he also made a considerable concession to the method of "signs" (as he called it simply) by frequently using signs in his own investigations.

After Aristotle, the method of signs enjoyed a resurgence. This resurgence consists in part in an energetic revision of the method, designed to withstand the sort of criticisms made by Aristotle. The Stoics were the leaders in this enterprise. By defining "sign" as a true antecedent proposition, revealing what is nonapparent, in a sound conditional, they ensured that a sign is conclusive and that it has demonstrative validity when reformulated as an argument consisting of the conditional as one premise and of its antecedent as the other. Through their redefinition of sign, the Stoics developed a theory of demonstration that not only is as rigorous as that of Aristotle but also preserves the notion that scientific progress begins with observations and ends with the discovery of what cannot be observed.

In part, too, the revival of the method of signs consists in a return to the earlier method of signs, with an attempt to strengthen it against its opponents. Epicurus and his followers took this approach. Epicurus himself does not appear to respond directly in his extant writings to the criticisms made by Aristotle, although he insists throughout his work that scientific discovery consists in using the phenomena as signs. Epicurus' followers later de-

---

35. DK 68 B 148; and Lloyd, *Polarity and Analogy*, 337 n. 1. See also Lloyd's general discussion of Democritus' use of analogies at 339–41.

36. See Diller, "ΟΨΙΣ," 35–42; and Lloyd, *Polarity and Analogy*, 315–19, 322–36, and 337 n. 1.

37. DK 64 B 4.

fended his method by taking into consideration the objections and revisions of contemporary thinkers. As Philodemus shows, they argued that observations furnish conclusive signs of what is nonapparent provided that a careful account has been taken of observed similarities and differences; and they contended that scientific demonstration consists in using observations as signs. Philodemus, moreover, offers an implicit reply to Aristotle's criticisms. Aristotle had maintained that a sign is conclusive only when, as part of a first figure syllogism, it is joined by a covering generalization, and that a sign cannot in any case be demonstrative, since the attribute does not belong essentially to the subject. Philodemus' response is that there is no need to use any kind of general claim as a premise, and that there is a variety of essential connections between things, all of which are determined by the method of using the phenomena as signs. The demonstrative validity of signs is thus, according to Philodemus, prior to the alleged validity of an Aristotelian demonstrative syllogism.

Although the Epicureans, then, embraced a method of inference that originated in a much earlier period and had been under strong attack when Epicurus adopted it, it would hardly be correct to characterize the Epicurean method as archaic. The method was in continuous use from the fifth century, and even Aristotle resorted to it as a means of exploring scientific problems. By the first century B.C., the method had acquired a new look. This new look is essentially faithful to Epicurus' position, but relies on standard contemporary concepts to present his method as a rival to other methods.

In his discussion of Epicurean ethics in *On Ends*, Cicero shows in brief how the Epicureans fitted their theory into a standard framework in order to defend it. The Epicurean Torquatus begins his argument by claiming that it is a judgment of "nature" (*natura*), made by each animal from birth, that pleasure is the supreme good and pain the supreme evil. He continues:

> Therefore [Epicurus] denies that there is any need for argument or debate as to why pleasure is desirable and pain is to be avoided. He thinks that this is perceived, just as it is perceived that fire is hot, snow is white, and honey is sweet, none of which needs to be supported by subtle arguments; a mere reminder [*admonere*] is enough. For there is a difference between demonstration on the one hand and ordinary notice and reminding on the other [*inter argumentum conclusionemque rationis et inter mediocrem animadversionem*

*atque admonitionem*]. By the former, certain hidden and as though shrouded things are revealed [*occulta quaedam et quasi involuta aperiri*]: by the latter, obvious and open things [*prompta et aperta*] are judged.[38]

Torquatus here uses contemporary terminology to render Epicurus' distinction between what is evident (ἐναργές) and what is nonapparent (ἄδηλον). He calls evident things "obvious and open," *prompta et aperta*, a conjunction of terms that renders Greek πρόδηλα; and he calls nonapparent things "hidden and as though shrouded," *occulta . . . et quasi involuta*, terms that correspond closely to ἀποκεκρυμμένα, a synonym for ἄδηλα.[39] Both sets of terms are linked to the use of *aperiri*, "to be revealed." This term is a translation of Stoic ἐκκαλύπτειν; the Stoics held that what is nonapparent is "revealed" through an indicative sign or, equivalently, through a demonstrative argument.[40] In presenting Epicurean nonapparent things as things that are hidden and need to be brought out into the open through demonstration, Torquatus gives clear evidence of Stoic influence.

Torquatus' distinction between nature and argument—that is, between the admonition of nature and the use of demonstrative argument—was also commonplace. In the case of evident things, it was thought, we need merely to be reminded of a fact that we know immediately by nature, whereas in the case of nonapparent things we need to be taught by demonstrative argument.[41] In the expression *mediocrem animadversionem atque admonitionem*, *admonitio*

---

38. Cicero *De finibus* 1.30: Itaque negat opus esse ratione neque disputatione quamobrem voluptas expetenda, fugiendus dolor sit. Sentiri haec putat, ut calere ignem, nivem esse albam, mel dulce, quorum nihil oportere exquisitis rationibus confirmare, tantum satis esse admonere. Interesse enim inter argumentum conclusionemque rationis et inter mediocrem animadversionem atque admonitionem: altera occulta quaedam et quasi involuta aperiri, altera prompta et aperta iudicari.

39. Sextus uses ἀποκεκρυμμένον at *Adv. math.* 8.146 and 324 to describe nonapparent things; cf. his description at 8.320.

40. See chap. 10, nn. 21 and 26.

41. At *Adv. math.* 8.327, Sextus Empiricus mentions that we do not need many arguments, but "a short and ready reminder," that demonstration is nonapparent. Cicero uses the contrast between the two methods of cognition repeatedly in both Epicurean and non-Epicurean contexts. At *De finibus* 3.3 he summarizes Torquatus' position as follows: there is no need to offer proof of the desirability of pleasure, since this fact is judged by the senses, "so that it is enough for us to be reminded, and it is beside the point to be taught" (ut commoneri nos satis sit, nihil attineat doceri). The Epicurean spokesman Velleius makes the same contrast in Cicero's *De natura deorum* 1.46 with respect to the shape of god; he points out that "partly nature reminds us, partly reason teaches" (partim natura nos admonet, partim ratio docet). The distinction occurs in a non-Epicurean context at *Tusculanae disputationes* 1.29. Here Cicero writes that men of an earlier age, since they had not yet learned physics, "persuaded themselves only of as much

("reminding") is a translation of ὑπόμνησις, and *mediocris* ("ordinary" or "slight") is intended to make a contrast between the ease with which we recognize what is evident with the effort required to uncover what is nonapparent. The contrasting phrase *argumentum conclusionemque rationis*, literally "proof and conclusive argument," corresponds to the single Greek term ἀπόδειξις, "demonstration."[42]

Within this commonly accepted framework, Torquatus introduces a claim that is unique to Epicurus and his followers, that it is judged directly by sense perception that pleasure is desirable and pain is to be avoided. The desirability of pleasure and undesirability of pain are thus among things obvious and do not need to be proved by argument. This claim was highly controversial; and Torquatus goes on to show how the Epicureans responded to the criticisms. He mentions two types of response, each a refinement of Epicurus' position. One group of Epicureans, Torquatus points out, held "that it is not sufficient for what is good and bad to be judged by perception, but that it is understood also by the mind and reason" that pleasure is to be sought and pain avoided; this rational type of cognition is a presumption, or initial concept.[43] This revision of Epicurus' doctrine is a reply to the criticism made by Cicero later in his book, that it is not within the province of the senses to judge whether pleasure is good and pain bad, but that this judgment must be made by reason; the senses, he claims, can judge only the properties bitter, sweet, and so on.[44] In proposing to add the judgment of reason to that of the senses, these Epicureans are not abandoning Epicurus' view that the goodness of pleasure and badness of pain are judged directly

---

as they learned by the admonition of nature, and did not grasp explanations and causes of things" (tantum sibi persuaserant quantum natura admonente cognoverant, rationes et causas rerum non tenebant); cf. 5.19 (where *argumentis et admonitionibus* renders the two kinds of cognition); also *De divinatione* 1.5 (*magis eventis moniti quam ratione docti*).

42. *Argumentum* is "proof" (see, for example, Cicero's *Topica* 8, where Cicero defines *argumentum* as *rationem quae rei dubiae facit fidem*, "an argument that makes a doubtful thing to be believed"). Cicero appears to use *rationem concludere* to translate Stoic συνάγειν λόγον (for example, at *De natura deorum* 2.20: *conclusae rationis*; ibid., 2.22: *rationem conclusit*; cf. Sextus Empiricus *Adv. math.* 8.411–15 and *OP* 2.137). At *Academica* 2.26 Cicero points out that he is translating ἀπόδειξις by *argumenti conclusio* (cf. 2.27 and 2.40). The two methods mentioned by Torquatus have been interpreted very diversely in the past. Philippson identifies *argumentum conclusionemque rationis* as ἐπιλογισμός (*De Philodemi libro*, 30, and "Epikurs Buch 28 Περὶ φύσεως," 1459), whereas Arrighetti takes *mediocrem animadversionem atque admonitionem* to represent ἐπιλογισμός ("Sul valore di ΕΠΙΛΟΓΙΖΟΜΑΙ," esp. 123).

43. Cicero *De finibus* 1.31.

44. Ibid., 2.36–37.

by sense perception; but they concede that in order to make judgments corresponding to the sentences "pleasure is good" and "pain
is bad," we need to have concepts formed by a process of reasoning. It is understood that since initial concepts are derived from
perceptual impressions, the ultimate foundation of knowledge is
nonetheless perception.

The second refinement of Epicurus' position is the view, which
Torquatus says he shares, that since many philosophers have argued against the claim that pleasure is good and pain bad, the
Epicureans should offer arguments in support of their position.[45]
This group of Epicureans, too, seeks to strengthen Epicurus' position by taking into account contemporary criticism. But their
strategy is to add argument to the evidence of sense perception,
without forfeiting the claim that perception is sufficient to show
that pleasure is desirable and pain to be avoided.

Torquatus does not discuss how nonapparent things are revealed through demonstration; but he mentions at the end of his
exposition that only if all sense perceptions are true can anything
be known.[46] It is a basic assumption of Epicurean methodology
that all perceptions alike serve as evidence of what is unobserved
by showing what is real. Philodemus, as we have seen, argued
that the phenomena reveal what is nonapparent through inductive
inference. What is preserved of Epicurus' writings on his methodology suggests that this position may be a refinement of Epicurus' own position, similar to the two refinements mentioned by
Torquatus. Whether or not this is the case needs to be examined
further through an analysis of Epicurus' physical doctrines.

This discussion of signs closes our examination of Epicurean
canonic as such. Epicurus' canonic, it has been argued, consists of
two rules of investigation, as set out in the *Letter to Herodotus.*
Epicurus demands, first, that we have concepts, corresponding to
the words that we use, as a means of judging a problem; and
second, that we have facts, as shown directly by perception, as a
means of inferring what is not presently known. The two rules
together make up the method of using the phenomena as signs of
what is unobserved.

It now remains to test this interpretation of Epicurus' canonic,
as well as his consistency in applying the rules, by examining a
large body of evidence that has barely been touched upon—Epicurus' own scientific inferences.

45. Ibid., 1.31; see also chap. 2 (Demonstration).
46. Ibid., 1.64.

# PART IV

*Epicurus' Scientific Doctrines:*
*Fundamental Theories*

# [ 13 ]

# Generation and Destruction

ACCORDING to the preceding discussion, Epicurus proposed an empirical method of investigation that consists in using the phenomena as the facts on which scientific theories are based. This conclusion now needs to be tested by an examination of Epicurus' own scientific inferences. How closely does Epicurus' own procedure conform to the rules as they have been analyzed, and in general how consistent and systematic is Epicurus in the way in which he proves his theories?

The following discussion of Epicurus' scientific doctrines is divided into two main parts, the first dealing with the fundamental theories of Epicurus' physics, the second with the elaboration of these theories. The fundamental theories are treated separately from the rest because they pose a special problem. It has been held that they originated as predominantly rationalist speculations of the early atomists, and that many of the claims remain as non-empirical assumptions in Epicureanism, even though Epicurus tried to add to them some empirical support.[1] If this view is cor-

1. Natorp claims that although Epicurus tried to base his atomic theories on the evidence of sense perception, he could not free himself from the rationalism of the early atomists (*Forschungen*, 234–35). Bailey argues in detail that although Epicurus adopted the main principles of the early atomists, which are rationalist, he added empirical support (*Greek Atomists*, 275–99). Cornford takes the extreme position that the "atomic theory is not a hypothesis which can be checked by sensation" (*Principium Sapientiae*, 27) and that Lucretius "deduces it from a few axioms" (28) while adding from observation some "vague, unanalyzed analogies which prove nothing and serve only to illustrate foregone conclusions" (19). Against this trend of interpretation, Estelle and Phillip De Lacy suggest briefly that Epicurus' atomic theory is "an hypothesis based on inference from empirical obser-

rect, then Epicurus' two rules of investigation, as analyzed in the preceding chapters, not only are an incomplete guide to scientific investigation, but also are joined with an incompatible method of investigation.

A second difficulty concerning the fundamental theories is that even when they seem to exemplify the method of using the phenomena as signs of what is unobserved, this use seems to consist entirely, or almost entirely, in the reduction of the contradictory of a hypothesis to an incompatibility with the phenomena. The method of verification seems to be that of "counterwitnessing" (ἀντιμαρτύρησις), or "removal" (ἀνασκευή, the later Epicurean term), rather than that of induction (or "similarity"). Are we to infer from this use of counterevidence that Epicurus considered it a more powerful method of proof than induction? Such a position would be in conflict with later Epicurean methodology.

Because Epicurus' fundamental theories thus provide an important test of the consistency of Epicurean methodology, they warrant more detailed examination than the rest of Epicurus' physical doctrines. This examination, involving as it does a comparison of Epicurus' method of investigation and that of the early atomists, will also test the alleged rationalism of the early atomists and, in particular, the relationship of the early atomists to the Eleatics. In tracing the origins of Epicurus' doctrines to a period of great innovation and controversy in the development of scientific method, the discussion will offer some new conclusions on atomist scientific method in general.

Epicurus presents his fundamental physical theories in sections 38 through 44 of the *Letter to Herodotus*, immediately after his methodological note. He begins with the remark: "Having made these distinctions, we must now consider things nonapparent [ἀδήλων]." He completes his presentation at section 45 with the statement: "This much speech, when all of this is memorized, affords a sufficient outline of an understanding of the nature of what there is."[2] This sentence marks a division between Epicurus' fundamental physical doctrines, which have just been set out in outline, and the more detailed theories that follow.

The word "nonapparent" in Epicurus' introductory statement

---

vation, and indirectly verified by lack of evidence to the contrary" (*Philodemus*, 1st ed., p. 145; see also rev. ed., pp. 188–89); this general position seems to me correct, but the authors do not support it by an analysis of Epicurus' arguments.

2. *Her.* 45: ἡ τοσαύτη δὴ φωνὴ τούτων πάντων μνημονευομένων τὸν ἱκανὸν τύπον ὑποβάλλει τῆς τῶν ὄντων φύσεως ἐπινοίας.

signals the beginning of his presentation of his physical doctrines. Thereupon Epicurus states his first physical doctrine, together with a brief proof:

Nothing comes to be from nonbeing [ἐκ τοῦ μὴ ὄντος]. For everything would come to be from everything without requiring seeds.[3]

By itself, this argument is too abbreviated to show whether Epicurus is appealing to sense perception as proof of his claim. Fortunately, in his poem *On the Nature of Things* Lucretius gives a much more elaborate version of Epicurus' single proof, and adds five other detailed proofs as well. He begins by translating Epicurus' proof:

If [things] came to be from nothing, every kind would be born from all things, without requiring a seed.[4]

In his subsequent development of this proof, as well as in his five other proofs, Lucretius shows that supposing it is *not* the case that nothing comes to be from nonbeing, our observations would be otherwise than they are.

Lucretius' six proofs are, in outline: if something came to be from nonbeing, everything would come to be from everything; everything would come to be at every time; everything would grow within every period of time; plants and animals would be nourished from everything; men would grow to superhuman size, having superhuman strength and living for a superhuman lifetime; and all the produce of the fields would become better without our labor. The last two consequences may be regarded as special cases of the more general claims that everything would grow to every extent and that everything would grow in every place.[5] As Lu-

---

3. *Her.* 38: . . . οὐθὲν γίνεται ἐκ τοῦ μὴ ὄντος. πᾶν γὰρ ἐκ παντὸς ἐγίνετ' ἄν σπερμάτων γε οὐθὲν προσδεόμενον.

4. Lucretius 1.159–60: Nam si de nilo fierent, ex omnibu' rebus/omne genus nasci posset, nil semine egeret. Lucretius' translation of μὴ ὄν by *nil* is not strictly accurate, since if things came to be from nonbeing, they would still come to be from *something*; for everything would come to be from everything. Lucretius excuses himself in advance for this type of inaccuracy by citing the inadequacy, *egestas*, of the Latin language (1.139).

5. Lucretius 1.159–214. The first argument begins at line 159; but since the claim made at 159–60 is basic to all six arguments, Lucretius begins the first argument anew with the word *primum* in line 161. Sextus Empiricus cites a Stoic version of the Epicurean argument at *Adv. math.* 9.202–03; in this version, the proposition "there is a cause" is proved by means of the conditional "if there is no cause, all things will necessarily come to be from everything and in every place and moreover at every time."

cretius states explicitly and shows by his examples, "everything" stands for "every kind." In addition, as illustrated by his examples, Lucretius uses the term "seed" in the ordinary sense in which it designates the stuff from which biological entities—humans, other animals, and plants—grow. His argument is: supposing that something comes to be from nonbeing, then all things could and would come to be from nonbeing, without any need for fixed seeds, with the consequence that all things would come to be from all things and without any other restrictions on their growth.

In his six arguments, Lucretius draws six observational consequences and shows in each case that these are false. For example, the first consequence is shown to be false by the failure to observe men coming to be from the sea, or fish coming to be from the earth, or birds coming to be from the sky; the second is shown to be false by the failure to observe a rose coming to be at another season than springtime; and so forth. Lucretius thus reduces the contradictory of the hypothesis "nothing comes to be from nonbeing" to an incompatibility with the phenomena. This is a clear use of counterwitnessing (ἀντιμαρτύρησις), the method of falsifying a scientific hypothesis through the evidence of perception and thereby verifying its contradictory. At the same time, Lucretius shows how the verification and falsification of scientific inferences are related to the verification and falsification of opinions about observable entities. Each of Lucretius' consequences is false for the reason that it is *not* observed to be the case. In Epicurus' terminology, the observational consequence is falsified by οὐκ ἐπιμαρτύρησις, "no witnessing." Accordingly, it is beside the point to ask whether our observations might be different at some future time. For the present, it is false that everything comes to be from everything, and so on; and this present set of observations is taken as authoritative. Epicurus himself demands this type of verification in his second rule of investigation when he specifies that present observations be used as a basis of inference.

Since Lucretius' sequence of proofs follows logically upon Epicurus' own brief proof and exemplifies in detail Epicurus' own theory of verification and falsification, we may suppose that Lucretius either derived his proofs from Epicurus or else modeled them closely on proofs supplied by Epicurus. His proofs thus confirm that, starting with the very first doctrine of his physics, Epicurus puts into practice the rule that the phenomena must serve as signs of what is unobserved. Epicurus does not hold "nothing comes to be from nonbeing" as a self-evident axiom or as a conclusion derived from nonempirical assumptions, but proves it by inference from the observation that not everything comes to be from everything.

This finding is in conflict with the widely held belief that the claim "nothing comes to be from nonbeing" is an Eleatic claim, proved by means of rationalist assumptions that have nothing to do with observation, and that the early atomists, along with other contemporary thinkers, took over this rationalist claim from the Eleatics, to be passed on as an Eleatic proposition to Epicurus.[6] This traditional view needs to be revised; and a short sketch of Parmenides' arguments will help to show how different Epicurus' method of argument is from that of Parmenides.

Parmenides held that "it is" is conceivable, whereas "it is not" is inconceivable; and on this premise he based a sequence of deductive arguments proving that being is ungenerated and undestroyed, indivisible, without motion, and complete like a sphere. In the first section of argument, on generation and destruction, three arguments may be distinguished. First, Parmenides argues that since generation would be from nonbeing, and nonbeing is inconceivable, there is no generation. Second, he argues that if there were generation from nonbeing, there would be no need for generation to occur at one time rather than at another. The text and interpretation of the third argument are controversial. It is likely that Parmenides here argues that there can be no increase in being, since this would come to be from nonbeing; but it is also possible that he is arguing against the complementary possibility that generation might be from being. In any case, his follower Melissus makes explicit that on this alternative assumption, too, there would be no generation; for there would be nothing but being.[7]

An immediately conspicuous difference between Parmenides' arguments and Epicurus' argument as elaborated by Lucretius is that Epicurus does not use the assumption that nonbeing is inconceivable. For Epicurus, nonbeing is entirely conceivable; for the concept is empirically acquired, and we observe things and their attributes passing in and out of existence. The investigator

6. Bailey claims that the doctrine "nothing is generated from nonbeing" is "practically implied in the Parmenidean conception" along with the next two doctrines set out in the *Letter to Herodotus* (*Greek Atomists*, 278). Similarly, Rist writes that the doctrine on generation is one of the canons of Parmenides (*Epicurus*, 41). See also above, n. 1, and chap. 14, n. 12.

7. Parmenides DK 28 B 8.6–13. For Melissus see DK 30 B 1, together with the paraphrase furnished by Simplicius (*In Aristotelis Physica*, p. 103 Diels).

uses this concept of nonbeing to ask whether at the subperceptible level, too, the process of generation begins with nonbeing or whether nothing is ultimately generated from nonbeing. The observed alternation of being with nonbeing cannot be denied. But observation alone cannot tell us whether or not a process of generation begins ultimately with nonbeing: this must be determined by the use of reason, through an analysis of the evidence presented by perception.

Along with an empirically acquired concept of nonbeing, Epicurus uses an empirically acquired concept of being. He assumes as the underlying premise of his whole argument that there are things just as we observe them to be: there are things that are generated, and they are generated from fixed sources, at fixed times, and so on, just as observed. This empirical concept of being implies nonbeing, whereas Parmenides' concept of being excludes nonbeing; nor does this empirical concept allow Epicurus to conclude, as Parmenides must do, that since there is no generation from nonbeing and since the only alternative is generation from being, there is no generation. Epicurus' distinction between observed and unobserved being allows him to hold that there is generation and that it is not from nonbeing.

Epicurus' method of inference, then, is directly opposed to that of Parmenides. Using empirical concepts of being and nonbeing, Epicurus seeks to discover the unobserved origin of the observed process of generation and deduces from the observational evidence that nothing is generated from nonbeing. Parmenides, in contrast, starts with a concept of being that excludes nonbeing, and deduces that there is no generation. Accordingly, Parmenides uses the claim that "nothing is generated from nonbeing" as a step toward proving that nothing is generated, whereas Epicurus proves that "nothing is generated from nonbeing" by using as a premise that there is generation.

Parmenides' second argument on generation has a special link with Lucretius' second argument. Although there is much debate about the exact force of Parmenides' argument, it is clear that both arguments rely on the claim that if there is generation from nonbeing, nothing comes to be at a definite time. This claim is used to opposite purposes by Parmenides and Lucretius: whereas Parmenides affirms the antecedent (for the sake of argument) and hence the consequent, in order to draw the conclusion that there is no generation, Lucretius denies the consequent, on the assumption that there is generation as observed, and so denies the antecedent. This opposition between the two arguments strongly suggests a historical connection between them.

The basic difference between the Epicurean and the Eleatic methods of argument is that Epicurus begins with the assumption that the phenomena are real, and infers what there is beyond the phenomena, whereas Parmenides begins with the assumption "it is," quite apart from the phenomena, and infers the unreality of the phenomena. Both thinkers use a deductive method of argument: as Parmenides deduces the unreality of generation from a concept of being, so Epicurus deduces unobserved being from a concept of generation. Each thinker admits into his deductive sequence the proposition that "nothing is generated from nonbeing." This proposition, however, is embedded in two very different sequences of argument: whereas Parmenides affirms the proposition on the basis of an a priori concept of being in order to show that the phenomena are not real, Epicurus uses the claim that the phenomena are real to show that the proposition is true.

Epicurus' second opinion, as stated in the *Letter to Herodotus*, complements the first. It is that nothing is destroyed into non-being. Epicurus presents it very briefly by stating only the proof:

> And if that which disappears were destroyed into nonbeing, all things would be destroyed, there not being [things] into which they would be dissolved.[8]

Just as in the preceding argument on generation Epicurus considered whether anything can be generated in such a way that there is not an underlying continuity of being, so now he considers whether anything can be destroyed without an underlying continuity of being. As before, the problem concerns what is unobserved; and it is solved by taking what is observed as fact. In this case, the senses show us things vanishing. What they do not show directly is whether what vanishes is obliterated even beyond the level of perception, in such a way as to be dissolved into nonbeing. The question, then, is whether or not at the subperceptible level something is ever destroyed into nonbeing, or in other words whether or not the process of destruction ever ends with a final dissolution of being into nonbeing. Lucretius puts the problem clearly by asking what would happen "if anything were mortal in all its parts" and, as a special case of this, what

---

8. *Her.* 39: καὶ εἰ ἐφθείρετο δὲ τὸ ἀφανιζόμενον εἰς τὸ μὴ ὄν, πάντα ἂν ἀπω-λώλει τὰ πράγματα, οὐκ ὄντων εἰς ἃ διέλυετο.

would happen "if old age utterly destroys, consuming all its matter, everything that it eliminates."[9] Epicurus' short proof consists of the claim that everything would perish. It is understood that if something is destroyed into nonbeing, then there is no reason why it is not possible for everything whatsoever to be destroyed into nonbeing, so that everything would in fact be destroyed into nonbeing.

Lucretius offers four detailed proofs of Epicurus' claim on destruction, of which the second seems to be a special case of the general proof offered by Epicurus. The proofs are all proofs by counterwitnessing, like the six proofs on generation. Hypothesizing that something is destroyed into nonbeing, Lucretius infers the following consequences, which are contradicted by observation: everything would perish all of a sudden, since there would be no need for any force to dissolve the parts; supposing that things would last long enough to be destroyed by old age, nothing would now be left from which things would grow; the same amount of force would destroy all things; and rain would not make plants grow, once it has sunk into the earth and perished, nor would plants, upon their destruction, make animals grow.[10] The fourth proof forms a fitting conclusion to the entire preceding series of arguments on both generation and destruction; for it binds generation and destruction into a single cyclical process by showing that the end of destruction is the beginning of generation.

In claiming that "nothing is destroyed into nonbeing," Epicurus opposes Parmenides in the same way as in the preceding claim that "nothing is generated from nonbeing." By using the phenomena as signs of what is unobserved, he argues that what we observe to be destroyed is not destroyed into nonbeing. Contrary to Parmenides, who assumes that nonbeing is inconceivable and deduces that there is no destruction, Epicurus assumes that there is destruction, as observed, and deduces that destruction is not into nonbeing. Just as Epicurus and Parmenides agree that "nothing is generated from nonbeing," so they agree that "nothing is destroyed into nonbeing"; but this agreement covers a fundamental difference. Unlike Parmenides, Epicurus proves the propositions by deduction from the phenomena; and accordingly he did not take over the propositions from the Eleatics. Epicurus owes a debt to the Eleatics, but it is a debt of opposition. In place of a rationalist method of inference, Epicurus uses an empirical method of inference; and by this method he reaches con-

9. Lucretius 1.217 and 225–26.
10. Lucretius 1.215–49.

clusions that display a similarity with Eleatic doctrine but are fundamentally different in meaning and implication.

As his third opinion about what is nonapparent, Epicurus states a logical consequence of the preceding two conclusions:

> The universe [τὸ πᾶν] was always such as it is now and always will be such. For there is nothing into which it changes. For there is nothing besides the universe that by entering into it would make the change.[11]

The universe, or "all," is the totality of being. This "all" always was and will be as it now is, Epicurus claims in the cited text, because there is nothing apart from it that could, by entering, make a change.[12] The conclusion depends on the concept of "all," together with the premise, demonstrated by the preceding two arguments on generation and destruction, that there is no internally initiated change. Because there is no generation from or destruction into nonbeing, and because there is nothing apart from all that is, the totality of being is without change in time.

Epicurus' third opinion closes his sequence of arguments on generation and destruction in a way that corresponds quite remarkably to Parmenides' conclusion to his arguments on generation and destruction. According to Parmenides, it follows from the denial of generation and destruction that being is so unchanging that it does not even admit of a past or a future, but "it is now all together."[13] Epicurus, who affirms generation and destruction, concludes that there is a totality of being that always was and

11. *Her.* 39: καὶ μὴν καὶ τὸ πᾶν ἀεὶ τοιοῦτον ἦν οἷον νῦν ἐστι, καὶ ἀεὶ τοιοῦτον ἔσται. οὐθὲν γάρ ἐστιν εἰς ὃ μεταβάλλει. παρὰ γὰρ τὸ πᾶν οὐθέν ἐστιν ὃ ἂν εἰσελθὸν εἰς αὐτὸ τὴν μεταβολὴν ποιήσαιτο. Giussani proposed the following reading after τοιοῦτον ἔσται: παρὰ γὰρ τὸ πᾶν οὐθέν ἐστιν εἰς ὃ μεταβαλεῖ ἢ ὃ ἂν εἰσελθὸν εἰς αὐτὸ τὴν μεταβολὴν ποιήσει (*De rerum natura*, 2: 197). This reading introduces a clear distinction between the two alternative methods of change, loss and increase: see also the next note. Bignone emends to ὅ⟨ποι ἄν τι ἐξέλθοι ἢ ὃ⟩ ἂν εἰσελθὸν (*Epicuro*, 256).

12. There are, however, good reasons for supposing that the text should be emended to yield the two complementary explanations, first, that there is nothing apart from the "all" into which something could depart so as to make a change, and second, that there is nothing apart from the "all" that could enter so as to make a change. Such an emendation would offer a clear distinction between the two ways—loss and acquisition—in which the sum total of being could change. The main support for such an emendation is an argument by Lucretius at 2.303–07; this argument is constructed on the model of Epicurus' third opinion, and in it the two alternatives are clearly distinguished. The two alternatives are also mentioned by Lucretius at 5.359–63 (= 3.814–18).

13. DK 28 B 8.5; cf. 8.11, 8.19–21, and 8.22. I leave aside the difficult question whether Parmenides eliminated time altogether along with generation and destruction.

always will be as it now is. Common to both thinkers is the claim that there is a totality, "all," that is without change. But whereas Parmenides understands this totality as something that excludes all generation and destruction and so does not have a past or future, Epicurus views it as the unchanging ground of all generation and destruction and therefore assigns to it everlasting duration in the past and future.

All three of Epicurus' doctrines so far are very striking in that they resemble Parmenidean assertions, but are incompatible with them. This incongruity appears most plainly in the third opinion. Epicurus has now deduced the unchangeability of being throughout time from the very changeability of things as observed. Although Epicurus' conclusion is partly similar to Parmenides' conclusion on unchangeability, it is incompatible with it, derived as it is from the assumption that there are generation and destruction. Epicurus' conclusion looks like a tour de force, aimed directly at Parmenides; for he shows that by making an assumption denied by Parmenides—that there is change as observed—one may reach a conclusion that resembles, but is fundamentally different from, Parmenides' assertion that there is no change.

The question therefore arises whether this opposition between Epicurus and Parmenides can be traced back to the early atomists, Leucippus and Democritus. There are good general grounds for such a supposition. By the time of Epicurus, the controversy provoked by the Eleatic arguments on being had subsided; the early atomists, on the other hand, were clearly at the center of the controversy. Moreover, it is clear that Epicurus took over most of his fundamental physical doctrines from the early atomists; and it is reasonable to suppose that along with the conclusions, he took over some of the arguments. We have no direct evidence concerning the early atomists' arguments on generation and destruction. Although we know that the early atomists held that nothing comes to be from nonbeing and nothing is generated from nonbeing, no proof for these claims is recorded.[14] Democritus is also said to have maintained that the "all" is unchanging; but no context is supplied to clarify the meaning.[15] We do have a great deal of highly controversial evidence about the early atomists' method of proof, including a claim by Aristotle that the early atomists held that "the truth is in the phenomena."[16] But before

14. DL 9.44 (DK 68 A 1); cf. Plutarch *Adv. Colotem* 1111a (DK 68 A 57).
15. [Plutarch] *Stromateis* 7 (DK 68 A 39).
16. For a detailed discussion of this testimony and Democritus' epistemology in general, see below, chap. 20.

any of these reports can be used to shed light on the atomist method of inference, it is necessary to examine the available evidence for the rest of the early atomists' basic physical doctrines. This evidence, fortunately, is much more plentiful than the evidence concerning generation and destruction; and it indicates that Epicurus' arguments form a pattern of confrontation with the Eleatics that goes back to the early atomists.

Lucretius omits Epicurus' third opinion and offers instead an argument showing that there are invisible things.[17] Here he addresses the objection that there are no invisible things, and that consequently there can be no invisible bodies from which things are generated and into which they are destroyed. Lucretius answers this objection by citing numerous observed facts, including the action of strong winds, the drying of garments in the sun, and the gradual attrition of a ring worn on the finger, of a rock hollowed out by dripping water, and of pavement stones worn away by footsteps. All of these observed events, Lucretius argues, must be supposed to be due to the action of invisible entities. In his introduction to the argument, Lucretius is clearly proposing to refute an objection to the conclusion that has just been reached. His refutation, however, turns out to be an independent, inductive proof for the conclusion. Lucretius now proves in the manner of Philodemus that there are invisible particles from which all things are generated and into which all are destroyed. It looks as though Lucretius is here indebted to contemporary Epicurean efforts to reformulate proofs by counterevidence as inductive proofs. Even though Lucretius does not go so far as to integrate his inductive proof in his series of proofs by counterevidence, it appears that he is at any rate familiar with the issue debated by Philodemus.

17. Lucretius 1.265–328.

# [ 14 ]

# Bodies and Void

## THE EXISTENCE OF BODIES AND VOID

AFTER concluding that the universe is unchanging in what there is, Epicurus undertakes to show that this universe consists of bodies and void:

> The universe [τὸ πᾶν] is [bodies and a nature without touch]. For that there are bodies is witnessed in all cases by perception itself, according to which it is necessary to infer by calculation what is nonapparent, as I said before. If there were not what we call void [κενόν] and space [χώραν] and nature without touch [ἀναφῆ φύσιν], there would not be anywhere for bodies to be nor [any space] through which [bodies] would move, as they have the appearance [φαίνεται] of moving. Besides these, nothing can be conceived comprehensively or by analogy with comprehensively grasped things, such as may be grasped as whole natures and not as so-called accidents [συμπτώματα] or concomitants [συμβεβηκότα] of these.[1]

1. *Her.* 39–40: ἀλλὰ μὴν καὶ τὸ πᾶν ἐστι ⟨σώματα καὶ ἀναφὴς φύσις⟩. σώματα μὲν γὰρ ὡς ἔστιν, αὐτὴ ἡ αἴσθησις ἐπὶ πάντων μαρτυρεῖ, καθ' ἣν ἀναγκαῖον τὸ ἄδηλον τῷ λογισμῷ τεκμαίρεσθαι, ὥσπερ προεῖπον τὸ πρόσθεν. εἰ ⟨δὲ⟩ μὴ ἦν ὁ κενὸν καὶ χώραν καὶ ἀναφῆ φύσιν ὀνομάζομεν, οὐκ ἂν εἶχε τὰ σώματα ὅπου ἦν οὐδὲ δι' οὗ ἐκινεῖτο, καθάπερ φαίνεται κινούμενα. παρὰ δὲ ταῦτα οὐθὲν οὐδ' ἐπινοηθῆναι δύναται οὔτε περιληπτικῶς οὔτε ἀναλόγως τοῖς περιληπτοῖς ὡς καθ' ὅλας φύσεις λαμβανόμενα καὶ μὴ ὡς τὰ τούτων συμπτώματα ἢ συμβεβηκότα λεγόμενα.

The first sentence is incomplete in the manuscripts: what the "all" is must be supplied. Usener (followed by Bailey) proposes σώματα καὶ τόπος; Usener also reads τόπος at the beginning of the third sentence, emending to . . . ὥσπερ

238

The argument has three parts. First, Epicurus claims that it is verified directly by perception that there are bodies. Second, he infers from the perceived existence of bodies that there is void. And third, he claims that there is no third type of self-subsistent entity in addition to bodies and void.

That there are bodies is said to be confirmed directly "in all cases," ἐπὶ πάντων, by perception (αἴσθησις). Lucretius writes in his corresponding account that *communis sensus*, "common perception," shows that there are bodies.[2] Since "common perception" cannot signify anything else in Epicureanism than perception that is common to all percipients, Lucretius' expression confirms that ἐπὶ πάντων means "in the experience of all." In agreement with other philosophers, the Epicureans held that bodies are the object of the sense of touch, and that all percipients have at least the sense of touch. It follows that anyone at all who has perception perceives bodies. What is distinctive about Epicurus' position is that he holds that perception by itself is sufficient to show that there *are* bodies. According to Epicurus' theory of verification, the opinion that there are bodies is confirmed directly by the sense of touch by the criterion of ἐπιμαρτύρησις, "witnessing." Epicurus alludes to this criterion, which he explains later in the *Letter to Herodotus*, by the use of the verb "witness" (μαρτυρεῖ).

Epicurus uses three different expressions, "void," "space," and "nature without touch," to refer to the type of entity that is not a body. These expressions pick out different aspects in which the nonbodily entity differs from body. As void ("the empty"), the nonbodily entity is a three-dimensional interval that is without the fullness of body; as space, it receives body, as opposed to obstructing body; and as nature without touch, it lacks the capacity

---

προεῖπον. τόπος δὲ εἰ μὴ ἦν, ὃν κενόν. . . . I have supplied σώματα καὶ ἀναφὴς φύσις, since Epicurus uses this conjunction at *Letter to Pythocles* 86 (where σώματα is Usener's emendation for mss. σῶμα) to state what the universe is. There is also, however, good authority for Usener's conjecture. David Sedley has shown that Usener's emendation for the end of the second sentence and beginning of the third agrees closely with the reading of the best manuscript, B ("Two Conceptions of Vacuum," 183–84); and there are testimonies that conjoin bodies and place (U 76; see below, n. 3). Κενόν is also a plausible alternative to ἀναφὴς φύσις or τόπος; it is opposed by Epicurus to σώματα in the later argument on infinity.

2. Lucretius 1.422–23. Bailey rightly translates ἐπὶ πάντων as "in the experience of all men" and points out that this is a frequent legal usage (*Epicurus*, 23 and 181). Implied in the use of the term *communis* is the sense "ordinary person's" as opposed to "technical." Aristotle uses κοινὰς αἰσθήσεις in the same way at *Metaphysics* 981b14.

of a body to make contact.[3] All of these concepts apply, in the first place, to perceptible reality: thus void is what is perceived to lack the fullness of body; space is perceptible room for bodies to move into; and nature without touch is what is not perceived to make contact. Once these ordinary concepts have been extended to nonperceptible reality and it has been demonstrated by calculation (λογισμός) that there is subperceptible void, they are transformed into technical, or scientific, concepts, expressing a technical distinction between body and nonbody. According to this technical distinction, what is empty is a three-dimensional interval that is absolutely free of the fullness of body, whether perceptible or subperceptible, and what is full is correspondingly a three-dimensional interval that is absolutely free of void; and similarly for space and nature without touch.

The problem that Epicurus considers after pointing out that bodies exist is: does the universe consist only of bodies, or is there also what is nonbodily? Sense perception shows directly that there are bodies; and it also presents areas that are empty of bodies. Does an alternation of body and nonbody occur also at

3. Sextus Empiricus writes at *Adv. math.* 10.2 that Epicurus assigned different names to "nature without touch," depending on different ways of looking (ἐπιβολαί) at it: the same nature is called "void" (κενόν) when destitute of every body, "place" (τόπος) when occupied by a body, and "space" (χώρα) when bodies move through it. Similarly, Aetius reports that void, place, and space differ only in name (*Placita* 1.20.2; *Dox.* p. 318 [ = U 271]; cf. U 74). As for nature without touch, Sextus adds at *Adv. math.* 10.2 that it is so called "because it is deprived of the contact by resistance"; similarly Lucretius claims that only body can "touch and be touched" (1.304; cf. 434). Although the manuscripts of Epicurus' writings do not contain any clear mention of τόπος as a synonym for void (see above, n. 1), the term occurs joined to σώματα in Plutarch *Adv. Colotem* 1112e and in a scholion on *Her.* 39 (both at U 76); and Lucretius uses the Latin version *locus* along with translations of the other terms. I take τόπος, "place," to be the void that surrounds a body; Brad Inwood has recently defended this view in "The Origin of Epicurus' Concept of Void" (esp. 275–77 and 280), although I do not agree with Inwood that Epicurus is indebted for this notion to Aristotle's view of place as the immediate container of a body. Epicurus' notion of void seems to me identical with that of the early atomists: this is the notion (imputed to Democritus and Leucippus, along with others, by Aristotle at *Physics* 213a32–b1) that void is an incorporeal, three-dimensional interval that separates bodies. David Sedley differs from both Inwood and myself in proposing that the early atomists viewed void as an occupant of place, whereas Epicurus identified void with spatial extension ("Two Conceptions of Vacuum"). Sextus' explanation of Epicurean place is a little misleading, though not incorrect (as Inwood charges, 280–81). As I understand Sextus' explanation, Sextus views the "untouched nature," which he subsequently describes as "place," as an expanse whose boundaries exceed those of the body that may come to occupy it. Immediately after outlining the Epicurean view, Sextus describes the Stoic notion of place by pointing out not only that place is what is occupied, but that it is equal to the occupier; this added specification serves to distinguish the Stoic from the Epicurean view.

the subperceptible level that is known only through reason, or is the universe packed absolutely full of bodies? Epicurus' proof that there is void interspersed with bodies is very brief. He offers two "signs," the location and the movement of bodies. Epicurus describes the latter specifically as a phenomenon; and since the location of bodies, too, is a perceived fact, we may suppose that his method of proof is that of "counterwitnessing." In claiming, then, that there would be neither location nor movement as perceived unless there were void, Epicurus offers an empirical proof for the existence of void, just as he did for the earlier propositions that "nothing is generated from nonbeing" and "nothing is destroyed into nonbeing."

As before, Lucretius provides further details about Epicurus' method of proof. In addition to translating Epicurus' own brief proof, Lucretius offers an expanded version of the proof from motion and two other detailed arguments. His argument on motion includes the following explanation:

> If it [the void] did not exist, things could in no way move. For that which is the office of bodies, to hinder and be in the way, would apply to all things at every time. Therefore nothing could proceed ahead, since nothing would make a beginning of yielding.[4]

The explanation is that if there were only bodies, every body would be blocked by another body at all times, with the consequence that nothing could ever begin to move. Lucretius later elaborates upon this explanation when he answers the objection that bodies could move without void as a result of one body taking the place of another.[5] This manner of moving is impossible, according to Lucretius, since one thing must previously have given way, and yielding can occur only if there is void for a body to move into in the first place.

Lucretius' second and third detailed arguments are also clearly arguments by counterwitnessing. In the second argument, Lucretius uses the perceived passage of one body through another as a sign of the existence of void. Citing as examples the passage

4. Lucretius 1.335–39 (the full argument occupies 1.335–45):

quod si non esset, nulla ratione moveri
res possent; namque officium quod corporis exstat,
officere atque obstare, id in omni tempore adesset
omnibus; haud igitur quicquam procedere posset,
principium quoniam cedendi nulla daret res.

5. Lucretius 1.370–83. Aristotle makes the objection at *Physics* 214a29–32.

of water through rocks, the dispersal of food through the bodies of animals and through plants, the passage of voices through walls, and the flow of cold into one's bones, he concludes that none of these things could happen unless there were void mixed with body.[6] In the third argument, Lucretius uses as a sign the perceived difference in weight of various bodies of the same size. There would be no such difference, he claims, unless there were void mingled with body in various proportions.[7]

These arguments for the existence of the void afford the first opportunity for a direct comparison between the Epicurean and the early atomist methods of argument, for in this case we have good evidence about how the early atomists themselves argued. Our main source is Aristotle, who reports four arguments for the existence of void interspersed with bodies. Just before outlining these arguments, Aristotle singles out Democritus and Leucippus by name as proponents of the view that there is void interspersed with bodies. He then presents the first argument as follows:

> They [those who hold that there is void] claim, for one thing, that [otherwise] there would not be local movement, that is, translation and increase. For there would not seem to be motion if there were not void. For the full is unable to receive anything. Suppose that it will receive something, and that there will be two [bodies] in the same [place]; then any number of bodies would admit of being together. For it is impossible to state the difference why what has been said should not be the case. But if this is admissible, the smallest will receive the largest; for a large thing is many small things, so that if many equals admit of being in the same [place], so do many unequals.[8]

The argument is, in outline, that if there were not void, then there would not be locomotion, since the full cannot receive anything; but there is locomotion; hence there is void. Most of the reported argument consists in proving that the full cannot receive anything. This is done by showing that if the full, which is as-

---

6. Lucretius 1.346—57. Related examples are supplied at 6.942–58.
7. Lucretius 1.358–69.
8. Aristotle *Physics* 213b4–12: λέγουσιν δ' ἓν μὲν ὅτι κίνησις ἡ κατὰ τόπον οὐκ ἂν εἴη (αὕτη δ' ἐστὶ φορὰ καὶ αὔξησις). οὐ γὰρ ἂν δοκεῖν εἶναι κίνησιν, εἰ μὴ εἴη κενόν· τὸ γὰρ πλῆρες ἀδύνατον εἶναι δέξασθαί τι. εἰ δὲ δέξεται καὶ ἔσται δύο ἐν ταὐτῷ, ἐνδέχοιτ' ἂν καὶ ὁποσαοῦν εἶναι ἅμα σώματα· τὴν γὰρ διαφοράν, δι' ἥν οὐκ ἂν εἴη τὸ λεχθέν, οὐκ ἔστιν εἰπεῖν. εἰ δὲ τοῦτο ἐνδέχεται, καὶ τὸ μικρότατον δέξεται τὸ μέγιστον· πολλὰ γὰρ μικρὰ τὸ μέγα ἐστίν· ὥστε εἰ πολλὰ ἴσα ἐνδέχεται ἐν ταὐτῷ εἶναι, καὶ πολλὰ ἄνισα.

sumed to be body without any void whatsoever, were to receive another body, then two bodies would be in the same place, and (since there is no reason to suppose a difference) any number of bodies would be in the same place, with the consequence that the smallest body would receive the largest. After setting out this argument, Aristotle adds immediately:

> Melissus in fact shows from this that the universe [τὸ πᾶν] is unmoved. For if there will be movement, he says, it is necessary for there to be void, and the void is not among existent things [τῶν ὄντων].[9]

Melissus' argument is that since there is no void, and since void is a necessary condition of motion, there is no motion.

Because Aristotle names the atomists Leucippus and Democritus just before the cited passage, and because in his treatise *On Generation and Destruction* Aristotle attributes explicitly to Leucippus the argument that since there is motion there is void, it is reasonable to suppose that the cited argument for the void was used by the atomists.[10] This supposition has important implications concerning the early atomist method of reasoning that have not been sufficiently noticed in the past.

The basic assumption in the argument reported by Aristotle is,

9. Ibid., 213b12–14: Μέλισσος μὲν οὖν καὶ δείκνυσιν ὅτι τὸ πᾶν ἀκίνητον ἐκ τούτων· εἰ γὰρ κινήσεται, ἀνάγκη εἶναι (φησί) κενόν, τὸ δὲ κενὸν οὐ τῶν ὄντων. Cf. DK 30 B 7.7 and 7.9. Melissus takes the same position concerning the remaining three arguments of Aristotle; he rejects the existence of rarity and density on the ground that these entail the existence of void, which is impossible (DK 30 B 7.8).

10. Among modern critics who assert explicitly that the atomists used the first argument are R. Mondolfo (*L'infinito nel pensiero dell'antichità classica*, 397–98), Theodor Gomperz (who suggests that Leucippus is responsible for the first argument and Democritus is likely responsible for the fourth, in *Griechische Denker*, 291–92), and Enrico Berti (who supposes that Aristotle assigns all four arguments to the early atomists, in "La critica di Aristotele alla teoria atomistica del vuoto," 146–49). W. D. Ross suggests that the first two arguments may well have been used by Leucippus (*Aristotle's Physics*, 582). All four of Aristotle's arguments are cited by Luria (fr. 255) as testimonies for the early atomists. The only scholar, as far as I know, who has claimed that the first argument was not used by the early atomists is Jonathan Barnes, who would deny all four to the atomists (*The Presocratic Philosophers*, 2: 102). Barnes adopts a position similar to that of Charles Mugler, who suggests that the atomists used the Eleatic principle that whatever one thinks of "is"; hence, by the "no more" principle, being and nonbeing, both of which are thought of, "are" equally ("L'isonomie des atomistes," 239). Although this position seems to me untenable, it is at any rate consistent with the generally alleged rationalism of the early atomists, whereas the arguments cited by Aristotle are not.

quite clearly, that there are moving bodies. This plurality of bodies cannot already be viewed, as some have interpreted, as a plurality of atoms.[11] For the existence of atomic bodies presupposes the existence of void, since void is required as a means of separating the bodies from one another; and the existence of the void is the very thing that the argument is designed to prove. On the other hand, plurality and movement were commonly recognized, from the time of the Eleatics, as two of the fundamental properties of perceptible things. Moreover, Aristotle reports in *On Generation and Destruction* (325a23–26) that Leucippus endeavored to save the phenomena of plurality and movement along with the phenomena of generation and destruction. It therefore appears that the early atomists, like Epicurus, based their argument for the existence of the void on the assumption that there are moving bodies, as perceived.

If, then, both Epicurus and the early atomists inferred the existence of void from the existence of bodies as perceived, it is clear that not only their conclusion but also their method of argument is anti-Parmenidean. It has been a source of confusion in the past that in the argument reported by Aristotle the void ("empty") is opposed to the "full." This looks as though the atomists are already referring to the atoms, or as though they are adopting the Parmenidean concept of being as something that is full. The atomists are arguing indirectly, however, about what would result *if* everything were full. In the atomists' argument, the full is the hypothetical existence of nothing but bodies; by means of this hypothesis the atomists aim to show precisely that the universe is *not* full. In the same way, Epicurus argues that if the universe were completely corporeal, without any void, then there would be no motion. The early atomists take the additional step of demonstrating by argument that if everything were entirely corporeal, without void, then motion could not occur: for if there were nothing but bodies, motion could occur only as a result of one body receiving another, with the consequence that the smallest would receive the largest. Epicurus shares the assumption that no body can receive another body, and draws the same conclusion that the universe is not full. Subsequently—once it has been shown

11. Mondolfo, for example, holds that the purpose of the argument is to demonstrate the absurdity of one atom containing all the others (*L'infinito nel pensiero*, 397–98). He offers this interpretation against Gomperz, who charged the atomists with fallaciously assuming from the start what needs to be proved, that is, that bodies are incompressible (*Griechische Denker*, 291–92). Both interpretations mistakenly attribute a *petitio principii* to the early atomists.

that the universe is not full—further argument shows that there is indeed something full in the universe: although the universe contains void, each ultimate body is full, without any void.

The early atomists, therefore, did not make it an initial assumption, taken over from the Eleatics, that being is full; nor do they seem to have taken over, on the authority of the Eleatics, anything of the Eleatic concept of being, contrary to the traditional interpretation.[12] Quite the opposite. The atomists assumed, against the Eleatics, that what is perceived is the case; thus there *is* a plurality of bodies that move. From this it follows that the universe is *not* full, contrary to the Eleatic assumption that being is full. It also follows that there is *non*being, contrary to the Eleatic concept of being: for it is assumed to begin with, in accordance with the direct evidence of sense perception, that there *are* bodies; but the argument shows, on the basis of what is perceived, that in addition to this bodily being, there *is* also nonbody, or in other words nonbeing. The atomists put this by saying that "being is no more than nonbeing," a statement that Aristotle explains to mean that "bodies are no more than void."[13] The paradoxical phrasing is intended to show that if there are bodies, as observed, then there is also nonbody, as demonstrated by argument.

The atomist claim about nonbeing and the entire relationship of the early atomists to the Eleatics may be elucidated further by Aristotle's analysis of the relationship between Leucippus and

12. Zeller, who sets out the main outlines of this traditional view, holds that the atomists borrowed the concepts of being, nonbeing, fullness, void, and so on from the Eleatics (*Philosophie der Griechen*, 1: 952–53). The atomist theory of being, according to Zeller, differs in principle from the Eleatic theory only insofar as it transfers to the many individual existents, the atoms, the attributes of Parmenides' one existent (851–55). Natorp endorses the main features of Zeller's interpretation; he maintains that although the atomists went beyond the Eleatics in checking their concepts against the data of the senses and in attempting to explain the phenomena, they accepted the basic Eleatic concept of being and used a rationalist method of inquiry (*Forschungen*, 171–72). Vittorio Enzo Alfieri interprets Democritus' atomism as a "razionalismo di tipo matematico" in which the single Eleatic existent is converted into infinite atomic existents (*Atomos idea*, rev. ed., 203; "L'atomo come principio intelligibile," 66). Bailey also upholds the traditional interpretation that the atomists transferred the Eleatic attributes of being to their plural existents (*Greek Atomists*, 71–76). Similarly, W. K. C. Guthrie presents atomism as satisfying in large part the Eleatic conditions of being (*History of Greek Philosophy*, 2: 390–91). Many more similar opinions could be cited. Among the very few who have raised doubts about this line of interpretation, Gomperz stands out; he argues for a strongly empirical approach on the part of the early atomists and suggests that they were less influenced by the Eleatics than by the preceding physicists (*Griechische Denker*, 286–89).

13. For the atomist saying, see Aristotle *Metaphysics* 985b4–10; also Simplicius *In Aristotelis Physica* p. 28 Diels ( = DK 67 A 8) and Plutarch *Adv. Colotem* 1109a.

the Eleatics in *On Generation and Destruction*. This analysis has indeed been interpreted in the past as a major support for the view that the early atomists took over, on the authority of the Eleatics, certain of the Eleatic propositions about being. A closer examination, however, shows that although Aristotle recognizes certain similarities between Eleatic and atomist doctrine, he nowhere implies that the early atomists were followers of the Eleatics. Indeed, Aristotle indicates that the atomists took a course directly opposed to that of the Eleatics. He writes:

> Leucippus thought he had arguments that by asserting what agrees with perception would not eliminate generation or destruction or movement and the multitude of existents. Agreeing in this with the phenomena, and [agreeing] with those who support the one that there would not be motion without void and that the void is nonbeing [μὴ ὄν], he says that nothing of being is nonbeing; for that which is properly being is fully being. But this [he says] is such as to be not one, but infinite in number and unseen because of the smallness of the masses. These are carried about in the void, for there is void [κενὸν γὰρ εἶναι], and by combining they effect generation, and by being dissolved, destruction.[14]

According to this analysis, Leucippus held that there are generation, destruction, movement, and plurality as perceived; and he also agreed with the Eleatics that there is no motion without void, that void is nonbeing, and that nothing of being is nonbeing, since being is "fully being." Aristotle does not explain on what grounds Leucippus agreed to these Eleatic claims; but he also makes clear that there was a fundamental disagreement between Leucippus and the Eleatics, since Leucippus supposed not only that there is what is "fully being," but also that there is nonbeing.

14. *De generatione et corruptione* 325a23–32: Λεύκιππος δ᾽ ἔχειν ᾤήθη λόγους, οἵτινες πρὸς τὴν αἴσθησιν ὁμολογούμενα λέγοντες οὐκ ἀναιρήσουσιν οὔτε γένεσιν οὔτε φθορὰν οὔτε κίνησιν καὶ τὸ πλῆθος τῶν ὄντων. ὁμολογήσας δὲ ταῦτα μὲν τοῖς φαινομένοις, τοῖς δὲ τὸ ἓν κατασκευάζουσιν ὡς οὐκ ἂν κίνησιν οὖσαν ἄνευ κενοῦ, τό τε κενὸν μὴ ὂν καὶ τοῦ ὄντος οὐθὲν μὴ ὂν φησιν εἶναι· τὸ γὰρ κυρίως ὂν παμπλῆρες ὄν. ἀλλ᾽ εἶναι τὸ τοιοῦτον οὐχ ἕν, ἀλλ᾽ ἄπειρα τὸ πλῆθος καὶ ἀόρατα διὰ σμικρότητα τῶν ὄγκων. ταῦτα δ᾽ ἐν τῷ κενῷ φέρεσθαι (κενὸν γὰρ εἶναι), καὶ συνιστάμενα μὲν γένεσιν ποιεῖν, διαλυόμενα δὲ φθοράν.

It should be noted that although most scholars accept this analysis of Leucippus' method as historical fact, Cherniss cautiously suggests that it may be a "logical reconstruction" of Aristotle's rather than "a real historical tradition" (*Aristotle's Criticism of Presocratic Philosophy*, 95 n. 401). Herman De Ley supports this suggestion in some detail ("Aristotle, *De gen. et corr.* A8, 324b35–325b11: A Leucippean Fragment?").

How, then, is Leucippus' agreement with the Eleatics to be reconciled with his disagreement? It makes little sense, I think, to view Leucippus as a partial adherent of Eleaticism who accepted some of the Eleatic doctrines only to reject others. For in affirming that "nonbeing is," he repudiates the basic assumption, on which all Eleatic arguments depend, that "it is." The argument on motion in Aristotle's *Physics* suggests an answer to our problem. Although there is no explicit identification of the void with nonbeing in this argument, this identity is implied by the assumption that there are bodies as perceived. Void is nonbeing in the sense of being nonbody. This concept of nonbeing differs from the Eleatic concept in that nonbeing is not the negation of a type of being divorced from perceptible reality, but rather the negation of a type of being, body, that is recognized directly by perception. It is this difference that allows Leucippus to assert that "nonbeing is." Although perception is the basic criterion of what there is, it cannot show all that there is. As it turns out, argument based on perception shows that there must also be the opposite of the bodily existence shown directly by perception; otherwise bodies themselves could not be as they are perceived to be. Hence, the justification for supposing that there is nonbeing is that only by supposing this is it possible to save being, as shown by sense perception.

When Leucippus, therefore, claims that "nothing of being is nonbeing," he is not endorsing the Eleatic view of being but is stating a self-evident truth about the relationship of body to nonbody: clearly, nothing of body is nonbody. By identifying body with being, moreover, he obtains an argument showing that nonbeing is, and so opposes the Eleatics on their most fundamental doctrine, while agreeing with them that there is no motion without void and that void is nonbeing. All three of the apparently Eleatic claims assigned by Aristotle to Leucippus turn out to be propositions that are based on the assumption that the phenomena are real; and Leucippus' position, as analyzed by Aristotle, turns out to be consistently anti-Eleatic. Although Aristotle may be faulted for misleading one into thinking that Leucippus designed his atomism as a compromise between the demands of the phenomena and the rationalism of the Eleatics, there is really no inaccuracy in his testimony. For even though Leucippus does assent to a number of propositions that were affirmed by the Eleatics, this assent is not an agreement in principle, but one that proclaims its opposition to Eleatic rationalism by the very similarities that it displays.

It is frequently claimed that the atomists justified the claim that "being is no more than nonbeing" by using the term "be" in two different ways.[15] If what I have suggested above is correct, this difference in usage corresponds to the two ways in which sense perception serves as a criterion of what there is. In the first place, sense perception shows directly that there is body. In the second place, sense perception shows indirectly by means of argument that there is nonbody as well as body. In this second use, the phenomena serve as a sign of what is not perceived. The two uses complement each other in that the use of the phenomena as signs is intended to save the phenomena as shown directly by sense perception. Epicurus later adopted the same method of inference to obtain the same conclusions, except that he dispensed with the terms "being" and "nonbeing" as no longer having philosophical relevance.

The other three arguments cited by Aristotle in the *Physics* for the existence of void illustrate the same method of inference as the first.[16] Aristotle presents the second and fourth arguments explicitly as arguments resting on the evidence of sense perception. He sums up the second argument by stating that some things "have the appearance" (φαίνεται) of contracting. As an example, he notes that wine jars receive their full capacity of wine together with the wineskins that contained the wine; the reason is that "the condensed body [that is, the wine transferred into the wine jar] contracts into the empty spaces within it." The fourth proof consists in the claim that ashes are a "witness" (μαρτύριον) to the existence of void; and the reason is that a container receives as much water when filled with ashes as it does without the ashes. Aristotle's third proof also clearly consists in using a phenomenon as a sign of what is unobserved; in this case, the phenomenon is the increase that results from nourishment. In stating that nourishment is a body and "two bodies cannot be together." Aristotle reiterates the claim elaborated in the first argument, that one body cannot receive another. It is understood that the nourishing body cannot join the body that is to be nourished unless there is void.

It is clear that all four of Aristotle's arguments rest on the claim that two bodies cannot be in the same place. All four also

15. See, most recently, Barnes, *The Presocratic Philosophers*, 2: 101–02.
16. The three arguments are at *Physics* 213b15–22. That all three proofs are based on the evidence of sense perception is pointed out by Ross (*Aristotle's Physics*, 582–83) and Berti ("La critica di Aristotele," 149).

conform to the general pattern of deducing what is unobserved by inference from what is observed. In view of this similarity it is plausible that not only the first, but all four arguments were used by the early atomists.

If we return now to the Epicureans, we find that there is nothing in Lucretius' detailed argument on motion that might not have been derived from the early atomists. In place of the claim that it is impossible for a body to receive another, Lucretius makes the equivalent claim that a body always obstructs another. Lucretius omits to prove his claim; but there is no reason why he might not have used the early atomist proof. The principle of indifference, which assures that if one body is received by another any number of bodies may be received, as well as the assumption that what can be will be, have already been exemplified by the Epicurean arguments on generation and destruction. As we shall see, they pervade all of Epicurean science. As for the consequence that the smallest will receive the largest, this is an extreme consequence of the same type as "everything would be generated from everything"; and it is similarly counterwitnessed by perception.

Lucretius' second detailed argument, the argument from the observed interpenetration of bodies, explicitly includes Aristotle's third argument, the argument from nourishment, and could readily be elaborated to embrace also the remaining two arguments of Aristotle. Although Lucretius does not state that two bodies may not coincide, this assumption operates in his second argument as it does in his first. Lucretius' third argument, on the other hand, is not included by Aristotle among the arguments for the void; and there is considerable doubt whether this might also have been used by the early atomists. The argument rests on the claim that objects having the same volume would not differ in weight unless there were void; and this claim depends on the assumption, as Lucretius puts it, that "it is the office of body to press downward in every case."[17] It is very debatable whether this assumption was shared by the early atomists.[18]

In their arguments for the existence of the void, neither Epicurus nor Lucretius uses the inductive form of the argument from motion that Philodemus offers as an alternative to the argu-

17. Lucretius 1.362.
18. On the question of the atoms' weight and their downward motion, see further chap. 16. Aristotle does not cite the perceived difference in weight as an argument for the existence of the void, although he does mention that the void was offered as an explanation of perceived differences in weight (*De caelo* 309a2–11).

ment by counterwitnessing. As discussed earlier, Philodemus argues that the claim "if there is motion, there is void" is an inductive generalization obtained by an analysis of observed instances of motion.[19] Lucretius' failure to use an inductive argument here, as well as his procedure in the preceding arguments, indicates that he gave preference to arguments by counterwitnessing whenever these were available.

After proving that there is void in addition to bodies, Epicurus draws the conclusion that there is no third self-subsistent entity apart from bodies and void. The rest of what there is, he explains, consists of attributes of bodies and void; and he divides these into "accidents" (συμπτώματα), or temporary properties, and "concomitants" (συμβεβηκότα), or permanent properties. Epicurus does not himself provide any proof or explanation at this stage of the argument, although later he offers a detailed analysis of the two kinds of attributes.[20] Lucretius outlines two arguments to show that there is no third self-subsistent entity. In each case the conclusion follows from the notion of self-subsistence together with the previously established existence of bodies and void; the arguments conform thus to the type of argument used previously by Epicurus to conclude that the universe is always the same. Lucretius also adds a detailed analysis of the two types of attributes.[21]

Epicurus' sequence of argument on bodies and the void, leading to the conclusion that the universe contains no third self-

19. See above, p. 209.
20. *Her.* 68–71. As for the distinction of terms, most interpreters hold that Epicurus used συμβεβηκότα to designate everlasting properties as opposed to συμπτώματα, which designates temporary properties. Munro, however, argues that the two terms were used interchangeably (in his commentary on Lucretius 1.449, pp. 69–71); he is followed by Bignone (*Epicuro,* 101 n. 2). Munro points out that Sextus Empiricus uses the term συμβεβηκότα to denote both essential and accidental properties in his report of the Epicurean doctrine at *Adv. math.* 10.221; and he also cites Aristotle and Galen for the indifferent use of the two terms. It may well be, however, that the later Epicureans' use of συμβεβηκότα to embrace both permanent and temporary properties does not correspond to Epicurus' own usage, but was intended to agree with standard contemporary philosophical usage. Epicurus' careful explanation of the technical term σύμπτωμα as a derivative of the term συμπίπτειν (*Her.* 70) suggests that he used σύμπτωμα to designate temporary properties only. On the other hand, Philodemus' use of σύμπτωμα at *De signis* cols. 23.3 and 35.19 (cf. 20.9–10) to refer to the mortality of humans suggests that this is a contemporary use, agreeing with Empiricist usage.
21. Lucretius 1.430–82. The two arguments are at 433–39 and 440–48. The first (which should be read in the order of the mss.) is based on the claim that everything self-subsistent has spatial extension; the second is based on the claim that everything self-subsistent acts or suffers or is a place for acting or suffering.

subsistent entity, continues the opposition to Parmenides that began with the preceding sequence of arguments on generation and destruction. After concluding in his arguments on generation and destruction that the universe is unchanging throughout time in what there is, Epicurus now argues that this unchanging universe is divided into two kinds of things, bodies and void, both of which "are."[22] This new conclusion adds precision to the previous conclusion on the universe and is likewise obtained by inference from sense perception. Parmenides follows up his sequence of arguments on generation and destruction, leading to the conclusion that being is without differentiation in time, by arguing that being is not divided but full. Whereas Epicurus concludes that the universe is discontinuous, since void separates bodies from one another, Parmenides argues that since there is no "more" or "less" that might prevent it from clinging together, being is all continuous (ξυνεχὲς πᾶν ἐστιν).[23] As in the preceding arguments on generation and destruction, there is also a resemblance within this opposition between Epicurus and Parmenides: although Epicurus' universe is divided, its two constituents exist equally— neither more nor less than the other—so that in a sense there is a continuity of being even here.

Since the early atomists seem to have used the same method of argument to reach the same conclusions as the Epicureans, there is good reason to suppose that the entire confrontation with Parmenides originated with the early atomists. The terminology of the early atomists confirms this view by reflecting especially closely an opposition to Parmenides. In dividing the universe into being and nonbeing and asserting that "being is no more than nonbeing," the early atomists not only reject Parmenides' claim that there is a single indivisible being, but also challenge his assertion that being is no more or less in any respect. Against Parmenides, they maintain that even though there is more and less of being in the universe (for being alternates with nonbeing), being is no more (and no less) a part of the universe than nonbeing.[24] The

---

22. Plutarch notes explicitly that Epicurus made a division (διαίρεσιν) of the single nature of existent things into two kinds, bodies and void (*Adv. Colotem* 1114a [ = U 74]). Similarly, Cicero notes that Epicurus "divides" (*dividit*) the nature of all things into bodies, void, and their attributes (*De natura deorum* 2.82, at U 75).

23. DK 28 B 8.22–25.

24. That there is a connection between the atomist "no more" formulation and Parmenides' expression is pointed out by Andreas Graeser in "Demokrit und die skeptische Formel," 301–2.

early atomists thus admit an absence of degrees of being within their universe, even though they wholly reject Parmenides' conception of absoluteness.

## ATOMS

After showing that the universe is divided into bodies and void, Epicurus argues that bodies are ultimately atomic and unchanging:

> Of bodies, some are combinations and the rest are [bodies] from which the combinations have been made. The latter are atomic [ἄτομα] and unchanging [ἀμετάβλητα], if all are not about to be destroyed into nonbeing, but are to remain strong in the dissolutions of the combinations, being full in their nature, not being capable in any respect or in any manner of being dissolved. Hence it is necessary for the beginnings [ἀρχάς] to be atomic natures of bodies.[25]

Epicurus now claims that bodies are either combinations of bodies or atomic (literally, "uncuttable") and unchanging components of the combinations. His explanation is that if the components were not atomic and unchanging, all would be destroyed into nonbeing. Epicurus has previously shown that there is no destruction into nonbeing. It follows that there are atomic and unchanging bodies.

Epicurus supplies no further details about his argument here, but he touches upon the argument twice later in the *Letter to Herodotus*. One of these discussions deals with atomicity. Epicurus explains that since a finite body cannot contain an infinite number of masses (for in that case the finite body would be infinite in extent), we must deny that a body can be cut to infinity into ever smaller pieces "in order that we may not make everything weak and be forced in our comprehension of wholes to use up existent things into nonbeing as we shatter them."[26] Epicurus here

---

25. *Her.* 40–41: καὶ μὴν καὶ τῶν σωμάτων τὰ μέν ἐστι συγκρίσεις, τὰ δ' ἐξ ὧν αἱ συγκρίσεις πεποίηνται. ταῦτα δέ ἐστιν ἄτομα καὶ ἀμετάβλητα, εἴπερ μὴ μέλλει πάντα εἰς τὸ μὴ ὂν φθαρήσεσθαι, ἀλλ' ἰσχύοντα ὑπομένειν ἐν ταῖς διαλύσεσι τῶν συγκρίσεων, πλήρη τὴν φύσιν ὄντα, οὐκ ἔχοντα ὅπῃ ἢ ὅπως διαλυθήσεται, ὥστε τὰς ἀρχὰς ἀτόμους ἀναγκαῖον εἶναι σωμάτων φύσεις.

I understand πάντα to refer only to the components of bodies. If it is taken to refer to all things in general, then ἰσχύοντα ὑπομένειν must be emended; Usener proposes ἰσχύειν τι, Bignone and Bailey ἰσχύον τι, and Rohde ἰσχύοντα τινά.

26. *Her.* 56: ἵνα μὴ πάντα ἀσθενῆ ποιῶμεν κἂν ταῖς περιλήψεσι τῶν ἀθρόων εἰς τὸ μὴ ὂν ἀναγκαζώμεθα τὰ ὄντα θλίβοντες καταναλίσκειν. I agree with Bailey (*Epicurus*, 205) that Epicurus is here referring to the physical division of a body. For a different view, see Furley, *Two Studies*, 12–13. I take περιλήψεσι to refer to the act of distinguishing the finite entities ("wholes") that are physically separated from the body.

claims that the infinite physical division of a finite body into ever smaller parts would result in the destruction of the body into nonbeing. This is a more elaborate version of the argument used by Epicurus in his outline of his fundamental doctrines. However, it too fails to make clear why Epicurus supposes that the infinite division of a finite body results in nonbeing.

The other reference concerns the unchangeability of the ultimate bodies. Later on in the *Letter to Herodotus* Epicurus uses the claim that the atoms are unchangeable as a premise in an argument showing that the atoms lack all the properties of perceptible bodies except shape, weight, size, and what is entailed by shape: "The atoms change in no way, since in the dissolutions of combinations there must remain something that is solid and indissoluble that will not make changes into nonbeing or from nonbeing. . . ."[27] If the atoms were to change, Epicurus claims, there would not be any ultimate bodies that are exempt from change into or from nonbeing. Epicurus here mentions change from nonbeing along with change into nonbeing because change is a passage from one condition to another; supposing the atoms were to change, he maintains, they would be both destroyed into nonbeing and generated from nonbeing. Lucretius states the same general view in the following criticism of the Heraclitean doctrine that everything is made of fire. Taking fire as the ultimate constituent of the universe, he argues:

> Suppose they believe that fire can be extinguished in some other way when combining and can change its body: if they exempt it in no part from doing this, surely all flame will perish utterly into nonbeing and whatever is created will come to be from nonbeing. For whatever by changing passes out of its own bounds, immediately this is the death of that which was before. Accordingly it is necessary that something should remain safe for them, lest all things revert utterly into nonbeing and the store of things, reborn, come to life from nonbeing.[28]

27. *Her.* 54: αἱ δὲ ἄτομοι οὐδὲν μεταβάλλουσιν, ἐπειδήπερ δεῖ τι ὑπομένειν ἐν ταῖς διαλύσεσι τῶν συγκρίσεων στερεὸν καὶ ἀδιάλυτον, ὃ τὰς μεταβολὰς οὐκ εἰς τὸ μὴ ὂν ποιήσεται οὐδ᾽ ἐκ τοῦ μὴ ὄντος. . . .

28. Lucretius 1.665–74:

> quod si forte alia credunt ratione potesse
> ignis in coetu stingui mutareque corpus,
> scilicet ex nulla facere id si parte reparcent,
> occidet ad nilum nimirum funditus ardor

The assumption that Lucretius rejects, just like Epicurus, is that a body can change in every part. If that were to happen, he argues, each part, and consequently the whole, would be destroyed into nonbeing and would be generated again from nonbeing. It follows that there are bodily parts—the components out of which the combinations are made—that are unchanging.

But granted that there must be an unchanging foundation, why must this foundation consist in bodies that are atomic? It is not at all clear from what has been said why Epicurus joins the demand for atomicity to that of immutability. Lucretius' long series of eleven arguments for the existence of atomic bodies offers some help toward answering this problem. Although none of these arguments is the same as Epicurus' single argument, two of them shed some light on the presuppositions of Epicurus' argument. In one of these, Lucretius maintains that unless matter were everlasting, everything would by now have been destroyed into nonbeing and everything that we see would have been created from nonbeing.[29] In the other, Lucretius argues that if there were no limit to the breaking of bodies, there would still be bodies at present that are intact after an everlasting time; but this is impossible, since bodies that can be broken must be broken at some time in an everlasting time.[30] Both arguments depend on the assumption that a possibility must be realized at some time in an infinite extent of time. Since the time that has already passed is infinite, it follows that if a body is capable of being destroyed or broken, it must by now have been destroyed or broken. Consequently, all bodies would by now have been destroyed or broken up into nonbeing and, as Lucretius makes explicit in the first of

---

omnis et ⟨e⟩ nilo fient quaecumque creantur.
nam quodcumque suis mutatum finibus exit,
continuo hoc mors est illius quod fuit ante.
proinde aliquid superare necesse est incolume ollis,
ne tibi res redeant ad nilum funditus omnes
de niloque renata vigescat copia rerum.

Lucretius directs the same general criticism also against those who propose that the universe consists of the four elements—fire, air, water, and earth—changing from one to another in a continuous cycle of transformation (1.782–802). At 1.753–57, too, Lucretius states the general criticism that other physical systems permit destruction into nonbeing and generation from nonbeing; and at 1.847–58 he addresses this criticism to Anaxagoras in particular. See also 2.751–56 and 842–64.

29. Lucretius 1.540–50.
30. Lucretius 1.577–83.

the two arguments, what we see would have been generated from nonbeing.

We may fill out Epicurus' brief argument, then, by adding to it the assumption that a possibility must be realized at some time within an infinite time. It follows that if it is possible for every body to be cut, then there will be a time at which all bodies will have been cut; and this entails that there remain no bodies at all. Formulated in this way, Epicurus' argument takes on a familiar look, for it agrees in outline with the one presented by Aristotle in *On Generation and Destruction* (316a11–b34) in support of the view that there are atomic magnitudes.

Without specifically attributing it to the early atomists, Aristotle introduces the argument by first rejecting the Platonic argument for atomic magnitudes and then praising Democritus for being persuaded by "appropriate, physical arguments." He promises that this will become clear as he goes on, and then immediately sets out an elaborate chain of reasoning. Aristotle's introduction to the argument is a strong indication that Democritus is responsible for at least the basic outline of the argument; and this likelihood is strengthened by the argument itself.[31]

Briefly, Aristotle's presentation is as follows. Suppose that a body or magnitude is completely divisible. Since complete division is possible, there is nothing impossible in the complete division being carried out. Let this be done. What is left? It will not be a magnitude; for a magnitude may be divided further. Aristotle continues:

> But if there will be no body or magnitude and there will be division, either it will consist of points, and its constituents will be

---

31. The introduction is at 316a11–14. Whether, and to what extent, Democritus is responsible for Aristotle's argument has been a point of controversy. Ingeborg Hammer Jensen proposed that Aristotle is throughout preserving Democritus' own argument for atomic bodies ("Demokrit und Platon," 103–05 and 211–12.). Subsequently most scholars have agreed that Aristotle is rendering an argument of Democritus, although most express caution about the extent to which Aristotle is faithful to Democritus. Alfieri (*Atomos idea*, 1st ed., 57) and Furley (*Two Studies*, 83) hold that the substance of Aristotle's argument, though not the terms in which it is expressed, is Democritean. Mau does not agree that the argument is Democritean (*Studien*, 12; *Zum Problem*, 25–27). He points out that elsewhere Aristotle is much more direct in attributing arguments to others; and he also holds that Aristotle is using his own concepts of actuality and potentiality in the discussion. It seems to me, however, that the early atomists did have the concept of potentiality that is used in the argument; and Aristotle is often very careless about indicating the source of an argument.

without magnitude, or it will be nothing at all, so that it would come to be and would be composed from nothing and all would be nothing but appearance. Similarly, if it consists of points, it will not be a quantity.[32]

After some further argument involving points, Aristotle repeats the argument in brief. He now hypothesizes that "every perceptible body" is divisible at every point at once, and he concludes:

Nothing therefore will be left, and the body will be destroyed into nonbody, and it would come to be again either from points or entirely from nothing.[33]

The argument as a whole may be summarized as follows: supposing that a perceptible body is completely divisible, either it will consist of points, which cannot make up a magnitude, or it will be destroyed into nonbody and hence into nothing, and consequently would be generated from nothing.

Aristotle states explicitly that the argument is about perceptible bodies. Hence the problem being considered is: are perceptible bodies completely divisible, or does the division of perceptible bodies end with ultimate bodies that are indivisible? The method used to solve the problem is to hypothesize that a perceptible body is completely divisible, and then to derive two alternative consequences, each of which is incompatible with the continued existence of perceptible bodies. The impossibility of the two consequences depends on the assumption, stated explicitly for the second consequence, that nothing is generated from nonbeing; it follows that all bodies would be "nothing but appearance." The conclusion of the entire argument, then, is the contradictory of the hypothesis: no perceptible body is completely divisible, but there are ultimate, indivisible bodies into which perceptible bodies are divided.

The whole argument thus rests on the assumption that there are bodies as perceived; and the problem that is being examined is whether these bodies, which are observed to admit of division,

32. Aristotle *De generatione et corruptione* 316a25–30: ἀλλὰ μὴν εἰ μηδὲν ἔσται σῶμα μηδὲ μέγεθος, διαίρεσις δ᾽ ἔσται, ἢ ἐκ στιγμῶν ἔσται, καὶ ἀμεγέθη ἐξ ὧν σύγκειται, ἢ οὐδὲν παντάπασιν, ὥστε κἂν γίνοιτο ἐκ μηδενὸς κἂν εἴη συγκείμενον, καὶ τὸ πᾶν δὴ οὐδὲν ἀλλ᾽ ἢ φαινόμενον. ὁμοίως δὲ κἂν ᾖ ἐκ στιγμῶν, οὐκ ἔσται ποσόν.

33. Ibid., 316b25–27: οὐδὲν ἄρα ἔσται λοιπόν, καὶ εἰς ἀσώματον ἐφθαρμένον τὸ σῶμα, καὶ γίγνοιτο δ᾽ ἂν πάλιν ἤτοι ἐκ στιγμῶν ἢ ὅλως ἐξ οὐδενός.

are completely divisible in such a way that at the subperceptible level there is no part that does not admit of division. The basic problem, therefore, is the same as is found in Epicureanism. Moreover, the development of the argument is the same in outline as in Epicureanism. In both cases, the possibility of complete division is viewed as realized; it is deduced that bodies will be destroyed into nonbeing; and it has previously been established that nothing is generated from nonbeing and nothing is destroyed into nonbeing. It has also been established previously that there is void that separates bodies; otherwise bodies would not be divisible at all.

The early atomists, as discussed previously, held that nothing is generated from nonbeing or destroyed into nonbeing; and they inferred from the perceived motion and interpenetration of bodies that there is void in addition to bodies. It now appears that they followed up these conclusions with an argument attempting to save the existence of perceptible bodies by setting a limit to the divisibility of bodies. Epicurus therefore seems indebted to the early atomists both for his general argument on atomicity and for the entire sequence of argument that has preceded.

It is difficult to determine to what extent the details of the argument on atomicity, as reported by Aristotle, may be traced back to the early atomists. There is some correspondence between the points of Aristotle's argument and the minimal parts in Lucretius' final three arguments for atomic bodies.[34] Lucretius here argues that since all finite bodies, whether perceptible or not, consist of minimal parts, and since minimal parts cannot exist by themselves but only in union with one another, there are ultimate bodies that cannot be separated into parts. Since, however, it is a very controversial and complex question whether the early atomists recognized minimal parts, and this question cannot be treated here, it must be left open whether or not Lucretius is here indebted to the early atomists.[35]

34. Lucretius 1.599–634.
35. The problem whether the discussion concerning points in Aristotle's argument is indebted to the early atomists is complicated by the problem of the early atomists' relationship to Zeno.It has been claimed that Aristotle's argument makes use of Zeno's contention that something without magnitude cannot make another thing larger by being added to it or smaller by being subtracted from it; Zeno concluded from this that an entity without magnitude is nothing (DK 29 B 2). Zeno's argument is, however, quite distinct from the argument at *De generatione et corruptione* 316a14–b34. In Zeno's argument, the entities without magnitude are not viewed as end products of complete division, but as consequences of the hypothesis that a thing is "the same as itself and one." It is true that at *De gen. et corr.* 325a8–10, Aristotle cites the following as an Eleatic argument: "If,

Epicurus' general position, then, like that of the early atomists, is that there must be ultimate bodies that are physically indivisible, if all bodies are not to change into or from nonbeing. Lucretius elaborates this position by presenting a series of arguments that focus on different aspects of the fundamental bodies. Lucretius begins this series with three closely connected proofs, in which he attempts to deduce the indestructibility of bodies from the previously established division of the universe into bodies and void, without making any new appeal to the phenomena as signs. In all three proofs, Lucretius' strategy is to show that there are bodies that are solid. From this conclusion it follows, according to Lucretius, that bodies are everlasting; for solid bodies cannot be dissolved by any outside force or admit anything into themselves or be harmed in any way, such as by being crushed or broken or split, or by admitting moisture or cold or heat.[36] This explanation coincides with an explanation attributed to the early atomists: they are said to have held that the atoms are indivisible, because they are solid and hence impassive.[37] Lucretius adds descriptive detail to this explanation by specifying a number of ways in which a solid is impassive.

Of the remaining eight proofs by Lucretius, three have not yet been touched upon. These proofs appear to rely directly on the phenomena as signs showing that the contradictory of the theory is false. First, Lucretius argues that if there were no limit to breaking, bodies would have been so reduced by now that nothing could ever reach maturity. The reason for this, Lucretius notes, is that everything can be dissolved more quickly than it

---

on the one hand, it is divisible in every way, nothing is one, so that there is also no plurality, but all is empty; but if it is divisible in one respect and not in another, this looks like a fiction." However, although it is possible that this dilemma was fashioned by Zeno, there is no need to suppose that the argument concerning complete divisibility originated with Zeno or with any other of the Eleatics; the whole dilemma may well be an Eleatic response to an atomist position. The atomists, in turn, might well have evaded the dilemma by claiming that partial divisibility is a consequence entailed by the evidence of sense perception, and hence is not an arbitrary assumption. Michael C. Stokes discusses the relationship between Zeno and the early atomists in *One and Many in Presocratic Philosophy*, 222–25.

36. Lucretius 1.503–39.

37. DK 67 A 13; DK 67 A 14, where Simplicius writes that Leucippus and Democritus considered the principles to be "atomic, indivisible, and impassive [ἀπαθεῖς] because they are packed [ναστάς] and without void"; and DK 68 A 43. At *In Aristotelis Physica* p. 82.2–3 Diels, Simplicius reports that an atom is impassive because of "solidity and compactness" (στερρότητα καὶ ναστότητα); similarly, Aristotle writes at *De generatione et corruptione* 326a1–3 that the atom is considered ἀπαθές because nothing can "suffer" (πάσχειν) except through the void.

can be put together again. Consequently, since bodies would continue to be shattered at present as they were shattered in the infinite time that has already passed, nothing could ever be put together as it is observed to be put together.[38] It is interesting to note that Lucretius' conclusion applies to any time at all in the history of the universe. For at any time the process of dissolution would outstrip the process of combination, so that no object could ever have reached maturity in the past any more than it can in the present or in the future.

The second of the remaining arguments is that only solid primary bodies can account for both hard and soft perceptible bodies, whereas soft primary bodies cannot account for hard perceptible bodies. By "soft" bodies Lucretius means bodies mixed with void.[39] Last in this group of arguments is the claim that if all bodies kept on changing, then the perceptible species too would keep on changing instead of remaining constant as observed.[40]

Epicurus' claim that there are atomic and unchanging bodies can be proved entirely by deduction from what has been established previously, together with the concepts of atomicity and changeability. Epicurus' single argument as set out in the *Letter to Herodotus* does not make any new appeal to the phenomena to "counterwitness" the contradictory theory; nor does the majority of Lucretius' arguments. In all of these cases, however, the conclusion rests on the prior use of the phenomena to counterwitness a theory. As for Philodemean induction, neither Epicurus' single argument nor any of Lucretius' arguments is formulated as such. However, Philodemus himself explains how we are to view the equivalent induction. According to Philodemus, an examination of the bodies of our experience shows that, insofar as they are bodies, they are indestructible, so that we may conclude that all bodies as such are indestructible.[41]

In concluding that there are atomic and unchanging bodies, Epicurus completes his discussion of what the universe is. After showing that the universe is divided into bodies and void, he goes on to show that the bodies are ultimately indivisible, so that the universe is divided into indivisible bodies and void. This conclusion in turn completes Epicurus' confrontation with Parmenides on the divisibility of what there is. Epicurus ends by agreeing

38. Lucretius 1.551–64.
39. Lucretius 1.565–76.
40. Lucretius 1.584–98.
41. Philodemus *De signis* cols. 17.37–18.3; cf. 34.22–23.

with Parmenides that there is fullness and indivisibility; but by situating what is full and indivisible in a universe that is divided and contains what is empty, Epicurus shows his fundamental opposition to Parmenides.

There is detailed evidence indicating that Epicurus derived his entire sequence of arguments on the divisibility of the universe from the early atomists. It seems likely, then, that it was the early atomists that first opposed Parmenides by arguing, on the basis of the phenomena, that the universe is divided into indivisible bodies and void.

# [ 15 ]

# Infinity

## THE INFINITY OF THE UNIVERSE

THE next topic to which Epicurus turns is whether the universe has a limit. He argues as follows that it is unlimited:

The universe ["all," τὸ πᾶν] is unlimited [ἄπειρον]. For that which is limited [πεπερασμένον] has an edge [ἄϰρον]. But an edge is viewed alongside something else. Hence, since it does not have an edge, it does not have a limit [πέρας]; and since it does not have a limit, it is unlimited and not limited.[1]

That the universe is unlimited is a conclusion based on the concept of "all," which was introduced previously, and the newly admitted concepts of "limit" and "edge." These new concepts are clearly empirical concepts. It is when we think of perceptible objects as having a limit that we think of the object as having an edge, and accordingly of being alongside something else. Lucretius indicates the empirical origin of these concepts when he points out in the fourth of his arguments for the infinity of the universe that whereas "before our eyes one thing is seen to limit [finire] another," there is nothing outside to limit the universe.[2] By arguing that a limit implies an edge, which in turn implies something beyond it, Epicurus concludes that the universe has no limit.

Epicurus' empirical notion of limit is in marked contrast to that

1. *Her.* 41: ἀλλὰ μὴν καὶ τὸ πᾶν ἄπειρόν ἐστι. τὸ γὰρ πεπερασμένον ἄϰρον ἔχει· τὸ δὲ ἄϰρον παρ' ἕτερόν τι θεωρεῖται. ὥστε οὐϰ ἔχον ἄϰρον πέρας οὐϰ ἔχει· πέρας δὲ οὐϰ ἔχον ἄπειρον ἂν εἴη καὶ οὐ πεπερασμένον.
2. Lucretius 1.998–1001.

of Parmenides, who assigns a "farthest limit [πέρας]" to being and compares being to a sphere.[3] Parmenides uses the term πέρας to signify the completeness of being. Epicurus, too, uses it to signify a type of completeness; but this is a completeness that belongs to perceptible objects, and it consists in being bounded against something else. Accordingly, for Epicurus, it follows that the universe is unlimited, whereas Parmenides concludes that being is limited. Paradoxically, these opposed conclusions have a single underlying explanation: that there is nothing missing from "all" that is. The difference is that for Epicurus "all" is the physical universe, containing bounded perceived objects, whereas for Parmenides "all" is being, abstracted from perceptible objects.

Of Lucretius' four arguments for the infinity of the universe, the first is an elaboration of Epicurus' argument.[4] It adds the following claim:

> It makes no difference in what regions of it [that is, the universe] you take a stand; so true is it that whatever place anyone occupies, he leaves the universe just as much infinite in all directions.[5]

Lucretius here points out that from any place in the universe there is an equal distance in any direction. This is a principle of equilibrium; and it is a counterpart to Parmenides' contention that since being has a final limit, "it is complete in every direction, like the mass of a well-rounded sphere, equally balanced everywhere from the middle."[6] From the conclusion that the universe is infinite Lucretius draws a consequence that is similar to that drawn by Parmenides from his claim that being is finite: both claim that being in its totality is equally balanced in every direction. Again, an Epicurean opposition to Parmenides is accompanied by a similarity.

The use of the concept of limit to demonstrate the infinity of the universe is not new in Epicureanism. Aristotle includes the

---

3. DK 28 B 8.42–43.

4. Lucretius 1.961–67. Another occurrence of the Epicurean argument is at Cicero's *De divinatione* 2.103; here Cicero explains "edge" as something "viewed from another thing from outside" (*cernitur ex alio extrinsecus*). Philodemus explains "edge" similarly to Epicurus and Lucretius as that which we view "alongside something else" (*De signis* col. 24.31–32).

5. Lucretius 1.965–67:

> nec refert quibus adsistas regionibus eius;
> usque adeo, quem quisque locum possedit, in omnis
> tantundem partis infinitum omne relinquit.

6. DK 28 B 8.42–44; cf. 49.

general argument from limit as the fourth in his outline of five proofs for the infinity of the universe. In Aristotle's words, the argument is that "the limited [πεπερασμένον] is always limited against something, so that it is necessary for there to be no limit, if it is always necessary for one thing to have a limit against another."[7] Aristotle does not name any proponents of this or any of the other proofs for infinity; but it is plausible that both Aristotle and Epicurus took this argument from the early atomists, who relied, like Epicurus, on empirically derived concepts to obtain a conclusion opposed to that of Parmenides.[8]

Of Lucretius' remaining proofs for the infinity of the universe, the second is a deduction from the division of the universe into bodies and void as previously demonstrated. It consists of a thought experiment. Suppose, Lucretius says, that there is a boundary of the universe and that you place yourself at this boundary. Now try to shoot a javelin with all your might. Then, either the javelin flies off ahead, in which case there is empty space beyond; or it is stopped, in which case there is body beyond it that stops it; and similarly for whatever new position you may take.[9] The same general proof is attributed to the Pythagorean Archytas, except that a hand and a stick take the place of the powerfully propelled javelin.[10] Since the early atomists held that the universe is infinite and that it consists of body and void, it is quite possible that this argument, too, originated with the early atomists.

Lucretius' third argument on the infinity of the universe is the only one in his series in which a phenomenon is used as counterevidence. If the universe were limited, Lucretius argues, all bodies would by now have collected at the bottom, since it is the nature of all bodies to fall.[11] Like the argument in which Lucretius infers from observed differences in weight that there is void, this depends on the assumption that all bodies have weight, and that weight causes them to fall. As noted previously, it is doubtful whether the early atomists shared this assumption; nor is there any trace of this argument in Aristotle. As for Lucretius'

7. Aristotle *Physics* 203b20–22. Simplicius writes that, as Alexander noted, this is an argument on which the Epicureans relied especially (*In Aristotelis Physica*, p. 467 Diels).

8. Barnes also suggests, though on other grounds, that the argument may be Democritean (*The Presocratic Philosophers*, 2: 60).

9. Lucretius 1.968–83.

10. DK 47 A 24. The attribution is due to Eudemus. The Stoics used the hand version of the argument to show that there is an infinite void beyond the finite world (*SVF* 2.535).

11. Lucretius 1.984–97.

last argument, this has already been touched upon. Lucretius here points out very briefly that things are perceived to bound one another, such as the mountains and the sky, but there is nothing to bound the universe.[12] This argument seems a variation on the first argument.

After showing that the universe is infinite, Epicurus deduces two consequences: first, the universe is unlimited in the number of bodies; and second, it is unlimited in the size of the void. Epicurus' argument for the first claim is: if the void were infinite but bodies were finite, the bodies would not remain anywhere but would scatter throughout the infinite void, since they would not have bodies to "support them and propel them in accordance with collisions." His argument for the second proposition is: if bodies were infinite but the void finite, the bodies would not have any place in which to be.[13] Lucretius gives no separate treatment to the second of these problems. He treats the first in some detail, elaborating on Epicurus' single proof and adding to it a refutation of the view that the world can cohere just because all things tend toward the center.[14] In his more detailed treatment, Lucretius shows that if the number of bodies in the infinite universe were finite, then not only would bodies not be able to combine with one another, but they could not even meet with one another in the first place.

Epicurus' proof for infinite bodies in an infinite universe has a link with the last of Aristotle's five arguments for the infinity of the universe. The argument reported by Aristotle is that since we can always think of more, it follows that number, mathematical magnitudes, and the outside of the world are all infinite. Aristotle continues by setting out two arguments concerning the outside of the world:

> Since the [space] outside [the heavens] is infinite, body too is thought to be infinite, as well as worlds. For why [should something be] here rather than there in the void? So that if bodily mass is in one place, it is everywhere. At the same time, supposing there is void

12. 1.998–1007. Following Bailey, I have distinguished four arguments for the infinity of the universe in Lucretius' text. It is possible to view 1.1008–13 as a fifth argument, although it seems to me more likely that it is the introduction of an argument showing that matter cannot be finite in an infinite universe. The lacuna following line 1013 makes it unclear what the precise purpose of the argument is.

13. *Her.* 41–42.

14. Lucretius 1.1014–1113 (esp. 1014–20 for the elaboration of Epicurus' argument). The refutation appears to be directed against the Stoics (see *SVF* 2.549–51).

[outside the heavens] and infinite place, it is necessary for body, too, to be infinite. For among everlasting things there is no difference between being possible and being.[15]

The first of these two arguments is attributed by Philoponus to Democritus.[16] This argument relies on the principle of indifference to show that since there is no reason for a body, or a world, to be here rather than in any other place of the void, these are everywhere. Since the early atomists endorsed the principle of indifference, as illustrated previously by the claim that there is no reason for a body not to receive any number of bodies if it receives one, its use here supports the suggestion that the argument is an early atomist argument. Moreover, the same principle of indifference is implicit in Epicurus' argument for infinite bodies; for Epicurus' claim that a finite number of bodies would scatter throughout an infinite universe depends upon the assumption that if bodies are in one place in the infinite universe, there is no reason why they should not be everywhere in the infinite universe. A finite number of bodies would forever be scattering throughout the infinite universe to satisfy the requirement that no part of the universe be exempt from bodies. Epicurus uses the principle of indifference also in his argument for infinite worlds later in the *Letter to Herodotus*. He argues here that since the types of atoms that can make up a world are not used up in this one world or in any finite number of worlds, and since the atoms extend throughout the infinite universe, there is nothing to prevent the existence of infinite worlds.[17] Epicurus claims in effect that since there is no reason for a world to be here rather than in an infinite number of places in an infinite universe, there are infinite worlds.

The second of Aristotle's arguments is that since possibility and

15. Aristotle *Physics* 203b25–30: ἀπείρου δ᾽ ὄντος τοῦ ἔξω, καὶ σῶμα ἄπειρον εἶναι δοκεῖ καὶ κόσμοι· τί γὰρ μᾶλλον τοῦ κενοῦ ἐνταῦθα ἢ ἐνταῦθα; ὥστ᾽ εἴπερ μοναχοῦ, καὶ πανταχοῦ εἶναι τὸν ὄγκον. ἅμα δ᾽ εἰ καὶ ἔστι κενὸν καὶ τόπος ἄπειρος, καὶ σῶμα εἶναι ἀναγκαῖον· ἐνδέχεσθαι γὰρ ἢ εἶναι οὐδὲν διαφέρει ἐν τοῖς ἀϊδίοις.

16. Fr. 1 Luria; Luria also cites Simplicius' comment that Democritus seems to have used this argument, and he includes a statement by Lactantius attributing to Leucippus what appears to be a conflation of the two arguments. Luria argues on the basis of these testimonies that the entire fifth argument is Democritean ("Zwei Demokrit-Studien," 37–39). Furley considers it very plausible that the first argument is Democritean ("Aristotle and the Atomists on Infinity," 95); and Ross suggests that Aristotle is here thinking primarily of the atomists (*Aristotle's Physics*, 547).

17. *Her.* 45.

actuality are the same for everlasting things, and since (it is implied) it is possible for void, as place, to receive bodily mass, the infinite void receives an infinite amount of body. This argument is another that is attributed to Archytas.[18] There is probably better reason to attribute it to the early atomists, for there is good evidence that they did maintain that what is possible in the case of everlasting things must be actual at some time; the arguments for the void and for the atomicity of bodies, as we have discussed, both depend on this assumption. Epicurus clearly made a pervasive use of this claim; it is especially conspicuous in Epicurus' and Lucretius' arguments on generation and destruction, as well as in their arguments for the indivisibility of bodies.[19]

Although, then, our evidence concerning the early atomists' arguments about the infinity of the universe is rather tenuous, there is enough to suggest that Epicurus was dependent on the early atomists here too. What makes a connection between Epicurus and the early atomists all the more plausible is that in his arguments on infinity Epicurus continues the pattern of confrontation with Parmenides. Epicurus' arguments on the infinity of the universe begin a third main section of argument in his series of deductions on what there is. After showing, first, that the universe is always the same and, second, that this unchanging universe is divided into indivisible bodies and void, Epicurus now shows that the universe, which is divided into indivisible bodies and void, is infinite and, moreover, is divided into an infinite number of indivisible bodies and an infinite expanse of void. Each of these sections of argument corresponds to a section of Parmenides' series of deductions on being; and each develops conclusions that are fundamentally opposed to those of Parmenides while displaying some similarity.

As for Epicurus' method of argument, his conclusions on in-

---

18. Again, it is Eudemus who assigns this argument to Archytas (DK 47 A 24).

19. There is one other argument on the infinity of the universe that is explicitly assigned to Democritus by an ancient source. In [Plutarch] *Stromateis* 7 (*Dox.* p. 581; = DK 68 A 39) we read that "Democritus . . . thought the universe infinite because it has not in any way been hand-fashioned [δεδημιουργῆσθαι] by anyone." Lucretius uses the same type of explanation to show why there is more than one shape of atom: the reason, he says, is that the atoms are formed by nature and not by hand (2.377–80). The same general explanation is also implicit in Lucretius' claim that because this world was made by nature through the chance collisions of atoms, it is not unique (2.1058–63). In both cases a demiurge would provide a reason why the number of possibilities should be restricted to a single possibility.

finity so far, like his earlier conclusion on atomicity, do not require any new use of the phenomena to counterwitness the contradictory claim, although they clearly rest on an earlier use of the phenomena as counterevidence. Although Lucretius adds an argument by counterwitnessing, the conclusion follows deductively upon the preceding conclusions, together with concepts that are derived from the phenomena. Again, there is no use of Philodemean induction, although Philodemus could easily have defended his case by pointing out that the claims "whatever has a limit has an edge" and "an edge is viewed alongside something else" are inductive generalizations showing that there is always something beyond any finite entity.

## THE SHAPE AND SIZE OF THE INFINITE ATOMS

Epicurus continues his arguments on infinity by arguing that the number of shapes of the ultimate bodies is incomprehensibly large, though not infinite, and that for each shape the number of bodies is infinite. This sequence of arguments affords a major test of the dependence of Epicurus on the early atomists, since the differences between the two schools are well attested.

In Epicurus' terminology, the atoms are "incomprehensible" (ἀπερίληπτά) in the number of their shapes; and the reason, he argues, is that the many differences among things cannot come to be from shapes that are "comprehended" (περιειλημμένων).[20] This explanation indicates that what makes the number of atomic shapes incomprehensible is that the number of perceived differences is too large to permit us to assign a certain number of specific shapes to the atoms. Epicurus is here implicitly rejecting Plato's analysis of solids in the *Timaeus* as having four shapes.[21] He is also correcting the early atomists' view that the number of atomic shapes is infinite. As Epicurus states, the atomic shapes are incomprehensible in number, but not infinite (ἄπειροι). In his extant writings, Epicurus supplies no explanation of why the number of atomic shapes is simply too large for us to know, and not infinite.

Lucretius, who reserves the entire problem of atomic shapes

20. *Her.* 42.
21. Epicurus attacks Plato on the number of corporeal shapes in book 14 of *On Nature* (PHerc. 1148 [ = Arr. 29.22–27]); see W. Schmid, *Epikurs Kritik der platonischen Elementenlehre.*

until after he has discussed the motion of the atoms, explains them in detail. He argues in the first place that there is a difference in atomic shapes. This part of the explanation consists of one very brief initial argument and two detailed arguments.[22] First, Lucretius claims that since there is an infinite number of atoms, there must be a difference in shapes among them. Second, Lucretius adds an argument that stands out because it is our first example of an inductive argument used by him since the arguments on generation and destruction, and because it fits the model of a Philodemean induction extremely well. Lucretius argues that just as within other kinds, such as any animal species or any type of grain or shell, there is some difference in the individuals that make up the kind, so there must be some difference in shape among the individual atoms. Third, and in most detail, Lucretius argues that differences in sensory perception are caused by differences in the shapes of atoms.

Lucretius subsequently qualifies the claim that there are differences among atoms by arguing that the differences in shapes are limited in number. He offers two arguments. The first is that if the number of shapes were infinite, the size of atoms would increase to infinity. The second is that if the shapes were infinite, there would be an infinite variation in sensory experiences, so that there would always be a more pleasant and a more unpleasant experience.[23] In both cases, the consequence is false because it is not observed to be the case. Epicurus includes a version of the first argument in a section on the size of the atoms later on in the *Letter to Herodotus*.[24] He claims that if there were every size of atom, atoms would come to us large enough to be seen, and this is not only not observed but also inconceivable. Epicurus joins this argument with another, by claiming that every size would not be "useful" for the differences in qualities. This additional, bare explanation is perhaps based on the same reasoning used by Lucretius in his second argument on the restriction of atomic shapes. Lucretius himself does not have a separate section of argument dealing with the size of the atoms. Epicurus' general ex-

22. Lucretius 2.333–477. The three arguments are: 337–41, 342–80, and 381–477.

23. Lucretius 2.478–99 and 500–21.

24. *Her.* 55–56, including, at 56: πᾶν δὲ μέγεθος ὑπάρχειν οὔτε χρήσιμόν ἐστι πρὸς τὰς τῶν ποιοτήτων διαφοράς, ἀφῖχθαί τε ἅμ' ἔδει καὶ πρὸς ἡμᾶς ὁρατὰς ἀτόμους· ὃ οὐ θεωρεῖται γινόμενον οὔθ' ὅπως ἂν γένοιτο ὁρατὴ ἄτομος ἔστιν ἐπινοῆσαι.

planation for restricting the number of atomic sizes is "so that the phenomena may not counterwitness."[25]

Concerning the early atomist position that the number of atomic shapes is infinite, there are two sources. One is Simplicius, who writes that Leucippus supposed the number of atomic shapes infinite "because none is more of this sort than of that [διὰ τὸ μηδὲν μᾶλλον τοιοῦτον ἢ τοιοῦτον εἶναι] and because he saw that generation and change are unfailing among existents." Simplicius adds a little later that Leucippus and Democritus "themselves" supplied as the reason for the infinity of atomic shapes that "none is more of this sort than of that."[26] Simplicius offers no further details. The other source is Aristotle; in his treatise *On Generation and Destruction* he explains the atomists' reasoning as follows:

> Since they thought that the truth is in the phenomena [τἀληθὲς ἐν τῷ φαίνεσθαι] and the phenomena [φαινόμενα] are opposite and infinite, they made the shapes infinite, so that as a result of changes in the composite entity the same thing seems opposite to different persons and alters its movement as the result of a small admixture and appears wholly different due to a single transposition. For a tragedy and a comedy come to be from the same letters.[27]

Simplicius' and Aristotle's reports are jointly and individually puzzling. In the first place, it seems that the "no more" argument cited by Simplicius is a quite different type of explanation from that of Aristotle. In the past, scholars have interpreted this argument as one that excludes the evidence of sense perception. Aristotle's argument, in contrast, clearly depends on empirical evidence. Also, Simplicius' additional argument on generation and

25. *Her.* 55: ἵνα μὴ τὰ φαινόμενα ἀντιμαρτυρῇ. We do have a third argument for restricting the number of atomic shapes, which is attributed to Epicurus. This is that there are no "hooklike or tridentlike or ringlike" shapes among the atoms, since "these shapes are easily broken and the atoms are impassive" (Aetius 1.3.18, *Dox.* p. 286a4–9 [ = U 270]). This report appears to be confused: both Epicurus and Lucretius make it clear that the only way in which an atom could suffer alteration is by containing void; and void is necessarily excluded from the atoms.

26. Simplicius *In Aristotelis Physica*, p. 28 Diels (DK 67 A 8 and 68 A 38), including: διὰ τὸ μηδὲν μᾶλλον τοιοῦτον ἢ τοιοῦτον εἶναι καὶ γένεσιν καὶ μεταβολὴν ἀδιάλειπτον ἐν τοῖς οὖσι θεωρῶν.

27. *De generatione et corruptione* 315b9–15: ἐπεὶ δ' ᾤοντο τἀληθὲς ἐν τῷ φαίνεσθαι, ἐναντία δὲ καὶ ἄπειρα τὰ φαινόμενα, τὰ σχήματα ἄπειρα ἐποίησαν, ὥστε ταῖς μεταβολαῖς τοῦ συγκειμένου τὸ αὐτὸ ἐναντίον δοκεῖν ἄλλῳ καὶ ἄλλῳ, καὶ μετακινεῖσθαι μικροῦ ἐμμιγνυμένου καὶ ὅλως ἕτερον φαίνεσθαι ἑνὸς μετακινηθέντος—ἐκ τῶν αὐτῶν γὰρ τραγῳδία καὶ κωμῳδία γίνεται γραμμάτων.

change, which appears to be a summary of Aristotle's argument, relies on empirical evidence.[28] But Aristotle's argument in turn makes no transparent sense. Granted that the phenomena are infinite and always changing, this does not seem to be a sufficient reason for the infinity of atomic shapes; and Aristotle himself indicates that there is no need for an infinite number of shapes. For he explains variations in appearance as resulting from a "small admixture" and a "single transposition"; and this explanation does not necessitate an infinite number of atomic shapes, any more than a change from comedy to tragedy or vice versa, to cite Aristotle's own example, requires an infinite variety of letters. In contrast, Simplicius' "no more" argument, to the effect that there is no reason why the atoms, which are infinite in number, should be a certain shape rather than any shape at all, seems to make good sense; and as we saw in the preceding discussion, it is a type of argument that the early atomists endorsed. The fact that Simplicius points out that the atomists "themselves" used the "no more" argument suggests further that this, rather than Aristotle's, is the argument used by the early atomists.

Is there, then, any possibility of saving Aristotle's testimony? I suggest that the early atomists did argue for an infinity of atomic shapes by the principle of indifference, as Simplicius reports. At the same time, I suggest, the early atomists claimed, first, that perceptible properties would not change to their opposites, or in as many ways as they are observed to do, unless each perceptible thing contained *some* variety of atomic shapes out of the infinite variety of atomic shapes; and, second, that an infinite number of atomic shapes entails infinite variety among the phenomena. The explanation of phenomenal change that Aristotle attributes to the early atomists implies the first claim; a small admixture of atoms having the same shape as any other atom in the complex would not produce a major phenomenal change or indeed any phenomenal change at all. Moreover, Lucretius uses the first claim as the basis of his third argument for a variety of atomic shapes; and as part of his proof, he employs, just like Aristotle, the analogy of letters.[29] The second claim is recognized by Aristotle elsewhere (as we shall see shortly) as a difficulty that applies to atomism;

28. This distinction between an a priori and an empirical proof is made by Bailey (*Greek Atomists*, 81) and Alfieri (*Atomos idea*, 1st ed., 63). Barnes accepts the distinction but suggests that the early atomists used only the οὐ μᾶλλον argument (*The Presocratic Philosophers*, 2: 62–63).

29. Lucretius 2.581–699, esp. 688–94 (cf. 1013–22).

and it was used by Lucretius as a reason for rejecting an infinite number of atomic shapes. It is reasonable to suppose, therefore, that Aristotle has taken the two claims and has conflated them into a single explanation, so as to attribute to the early atomists the view that perceptible change entails that there is an infinite number of atomic shapes. In fact, the early atomists held that any perceptible change entails some variety of atomic shapes, and that there are both infinite perceptible variations and infinite types of atomic shapes; but they did not deduce the infinite variety of atomic shapes from the infinite variety of phenomena.

If this is right, then there is no need to reject Aristotle's claim that the atomists thought that "the truth is in the phenomena." For even though Aristotle misleadingly suggests that the atomists inferred the infinity of atomic shapes directly from the infinite variety of phenomena, the atomists did rely on the phenomena to infer, in the first place, that there are unchanging atomic bodies, and, in the second place, that any perceptible thing contains a variety of atomic shapes.

Granted, then, that the early atomists did argue that, given an infinite number of atoms, there is no reason why the atoms should be of one shape rather than any other, Epicurus later corrected this position by maintaining that there *is* a reason why the atoms should have a finite number of shapes rather than any shape at all. Both of the reasons supplied by Lucretius consist in an appeal to counterwitnessing. In the simpler argument, Lucretius claims that the finite variation in sensory experiences contradicts the view that the atoms have infinite shapes. It is likely that this argument is indebted to Aristotle; for, as just noted, he had previously objected to an infinite number of atomic shapes on the ground that this would result in an infinite range of perceptible properties, such as flavors.[30] The early atomists might have responded to this objection by saying that even though our own sensory experience has a limited range of variation, this is no reason to suppose that in the universe at large sensory variation might not be infinite. Epicurus, on the other hand, takes our own limited sensory experience as representative of all sensory experience. Accordingly, he corrects the early atomist conclusion, which is itself ultimately dependent on the phenomena showing what is the case, by applying anew the principle of counterevidence. Epi-

30. Aristotle *De sensu* 442b21–22 (on flavors); cf. *De caelo* 302b30–303a3. Furley suggests that Epicurus may here be responding to Aristotle's criticism ("Aristotle and the Atomists on Infinity," 92).

curus is not objecting to the early atomist method of inference; rather he is objecting that the early atomists did not apply it thoroughly enough.

There is a hint of the early atomist "no more" argument in Lucretius' argument that the infinite number of atoms entails that there is some variety of shape. This restricted use of the principle of indifference is logically dubious; and indeed Epicurus and Lucretius seem to have replaced the principle of indifference altogether in the case of atomic shapes by appealing to the phenomena as evidence that the number of shapes is incomprehensibly but not infinitely large. It may be objected that just as Epicurus used the principle of indifference to conclude that there are infinite bodies and infinite worlds in an infinite universe, so he must use the principle of indifference to conclude that there are infinite atomic shapes. But even though Epicurus may not have sufficient grounds for supposing that there is a difference that prohibits an infinity of atomic shapes, the use of the phenomena as evidence that there is a difference is consistent with the use of the principle of indifference.

The other argument used by Lucretius to show that the number of atomic shapes is not infinite is more difficult to sort out, for it involves the assumption of minimal parts. The argument is that because the atoms consist of minimal parts, any increase in the number of atomic shapes entails an increase in the size of atoms, with the consequence that unless there is a limit to the number of atomic shapes, there will be atoms of enormous size. Lucretius makes this argument vivid by inviting the reader to line up the minimal parts, as though they were building blocks, to produce a number of shapes. Since any finite number of these parts can yield only a finite number of shapes, Lucretius argues, new parts would need to be added to produce additional shapes, and this increase would go on to infinity. The result is that some atoms would be "monstrously huge" (*immani maximitate*).[31] Epicurus states the consequence by saying that atoms would necessarily be seen by us, and this is not the case, nor is it conceivable that an atom should be seen. According to Epicurus' perceptual theory, it is impossible for individual, absolutely solid bodies to be seen; hence it is inconceivable for atoms to be seen, even though they would have sufficient size to be seen.

Since it is not clear whether the early atomists held that the

31. Lucretius 2.481–99 (*immani maximitate* at 498).

atoms consist of minimal parts, it is doubtful whether they inferred infinite atomic sizes from the infinite number of shapes that they posited. There is some evidence, however, that the early atomists did admit infinitely large atoms. According to Aetius, Democritus held that "it is possible for there to be an atom of world size"; and Dionysius, as cited by Eusebius, claimed that whereas Epicurus posited atoms that were "smallest" and hence imperceptible, Democritus also admitted some atoms of "largest" size.[32] In addition, Diogenes Laertius reports briefly that Democritus held that the atoms are "infinite in size and number."[33] This evidence has been rejected by most scholars on the ground that Aristotle and others claim repeatedly that the atoms of Leucippus and Democritus are too small to be perceived.[34] There is, however, no need to reject any of the testimonies, because, as Mugler has shown, the claim that there are very large atoms is reconcilable with the claim that in any world whatsoever, including our own, the atoms are too small to be perceived.[35] Accordingly, there are atoms that are world size relative to our world; but they have been excluded from our world along with any other atoms that are too large to unite into a single complex with the atoms of this world. These other atoms are, in turn, integrated into complexes that make up other worlds; and these worlds vary infinitely in size. There are thus, according to the early atomists, worlds composed of subperceptible atoms that have the size of our own world.

This vision of ever-larger worlds consisting of ever-larger atoms strains the imagination; but it is comparable to other atomist conclusions on infinity. Moreover, the claim that the atoms are unlimited in size follows just as much, by the principle of indifference, from the infinite number of atoms as does the claim that the atoms have an infinite number of shapes. It seems, therefore, that on the issue of atomic size, no less than on the issue of atomic shapes, Epicurus used the principle of "no counterwitnessing" to revise a conclusion reached earlier by his atomist predecessors by means of the principle of indifference. In both cases,

32. Aetius 1.12.6 (*Dox.* p. 311; DK 68 A 47); Dionysius in Eusebius *Praeparatio evangelica* 14.23 (DK 68 A 43).

33. DK 68 A 1 (DL 9.44).

34. See esp. Aristotle *De generatione et corruptione* 325a30.

35. Charles Mugler, "L'invisibilité des atomes," 399–403; "Sur quelques particularités de l'atomisme ancien," 143–49; and "L'isonomie des atomistes," 242–43. Mugler suggests that Leucippus did assign a limit to the size of the atoms, whereas Democritus did not; but his own arguments show, it seems to me, that we need not suppose a difference between the two atomists.

Epicurus seems to have assumed, by induction, that the range of variations among worlds is very limited.

After concluding that the number of atomic shapes is finite, Lucretius offers a proof showing that the number of atoms for each shape is infinite. This proof relies on the same principle of dispersal used to prove that there are infinite atoms in the infinite universe.[36] Lucretius begins by proposing that either the number of atoms for each shape is infinite or the universe is finite; and after reasserting that the universe is infinite, he goes on to prove the disjunction and to show that the number of atoms for each shape is infinite.[37] He argues that even if a species were to consist of a single individual (which is never the case), yet the atomic shapes that are required to produce this single individual must be represented by an infinite number of atoms; for if the atoms were finite in number, they would forever scatter throughout the infinite universe without ever coming together. It follows that each atomic shape has an infinite number of atoms. It is likely that the early atomists made a similar use of the principle of indifference to show that the number of atoms for each shape is infinite.

Epicurus closes his section of argument on infinity with the conclusion that the number of atoms for each shape is infinite. Throughout this section, he opposes Parmenides on the issue of limit. After showing that the universe is unlimited and that bodies and void are unlimited, he considers whether the infinite bodies in the universe—each of which is individually limited in that it has shape—are limited in the number of shapes and in the number of bodies for each shape; and he concludes that the number of shapes is large but not unlimited and that the number for each shape is unlimited. Epicurus thus opposes Parmenides' single limited being with a plurality of infinities; at the same time, this system of infinities exhibits an equilibrium that is a counterpart to the equilibrium of Parmenides' limited being.

The early atomists proposed the same infinities, except that they also supposed that the number of atomic shapes is infinite. Their system of infinities is thus a perfect counterpart to Par-

36. Lucretius 2.522–68.

37. In framing the disjunction, Lucretius is using (with a reversal of "first" and "second") the fifth Stoic "undemonstrated" form of argument, which is: (1) either the first or the second; (2) not the first; (3) therefore the second. See Mates, *Stoic Logic*, 73, where the same reversal of "first" and "second" is exemplified. This appears to be another example of the later Epicureans' adopting on occasion a form of argument used by their opponents.

menides' limited being. They opposed Parmenides' perfectly balanced spherelike being with a perfectly balanced infinite universe, in which any part of the universe is in perfect balance with any other, consisting as it does of atoms of infinite shapes similarly distributed in the void. Epicurus later introduced an imperfection into the system of infinities by restricting the number of atomic shapes on the ground that there is counterevidence by the phenomena. In using the principle of counterevidence to correct an early atomist conclusion, Epicurus applies the same principle used by the early atomists to construct their entire system of oppositions to Parmenides.

# [ 16 ]

# Motion

EPICURUS concludes his outline of fundamental theories in the *Letter to Herodotus* with a discussion of the motion of the atoms.[1] The claims that he makes here follow upon the previously established claims about the two components of the universe, bodies and void. Epicurus asserts that the atoms move continuously (συνεχῶς), either separated a long distance from each other or entangled with other atoms so as to reverberate with them.[2] Epicurus explains this continuity by pointing out, first, that the void is unable to provide any support, and second, that bodies have solidity, which causes them to rebound after a collision for as long a distance as the surrounding atoms allow. Finally, Epicurus concludes that there is no beginning of these motions, since the atoms and void are responsible for it. It is understood that the atoms and void have existed for all time. It is also understood in the earlier part of the argument that the solidity of the atoms comes in various shapes, and that this variety accounts for the different kinds of entanglement—more or less close—of the atoms with one another.

1. *Her.* 43–44. Since the sense of the first sentence is complete, there is no need to mark a lacuna (as most editors do). Gassendi's emendation of mss. αἰτίων to ἀϊδίων in the last sentence is very plausible.

2. The term συνεχῶς implies that the atoms do not come to a halt, even for a very short time, when they collide. Lucretius states this in a roundabout way: "If you think that the principles of things can rest [*cessare*] and create new motions of things by resting, you stray far from the true explanation" (2.80–82). What makes the hypothetical motions "new" is that they would be preceded by an interval of rest.

As this outline on motion stands, it could well have been derived in its entirety from the early atomists. They held likewise that the atoms are always in motion, that the atoms are either separated a long distance from one another or entangled with another, and that there is no beginning of atomic motion. In addition, the early atomists appear to have given the same explanation for the continuity of atomic motion; for they too held that the void yields to bodies and that the atoms bounce off other atoms.[3]

Later in the *Letter to Herodotus* Epicurus introduces three claims about motion that many scholars have regarded as innovations of his own: he argues that there is an upward and downward direction in the universe; in agreement with this, he holds that the weight of the atoms causes them to move in a downward direction; and he maintains that so long as atoms move without collision in the void, they move with equal speeds.[4] In connection with the last claim, Epicurus also points out that it would be wrong to infer that the atoms that make up a complex have the same continuity of motion as the perceptible object they compose. Although none of the three claims is included in Epicurus' own initial account of motion, Lucretius incorporates the second and third in his much more detailed, corresponding account. Lucretius defends at some length the downward motion of the atoms by weight and in addition argues for an occasional interruption of this motion, the swerve. He also has a section on the speed of the atoms. Moreover, Lucretius adds two sections of argument that have no counterpart anywhere in the *Letter to Herodotus*. First, he concludes his sequence of arguments on motion by showing that the motions of the universe are always the same. Second, as a sequel to the entire discussion of motion he reassures the student by some examples from sense perception that invisible motion is compatible with observed immobility. This sequel corresponds to the section

3. For the claim that the atoms are always in motion, see Aristotle *De caelo* 300b8–10 and *Metaphysics* 1071b29–72a7. There is no evidence for Bailey's suggestion that Democritus thought that the atoms suspend their own motions when gathered in a complex (*Lucretius*, 813–14). For the other claims, see DK 68 A 37, 43, and 57; DK 68 A 56 and 39; and DK 67 A 14, and Aristotle *Physics* 215a22–23, respectively. Simplicius also explains that the atoms "are at strife [στασιάζειν] and move in the void because of unlikeness [ἀνομοιότητα] and the other previously mentioned differences" (DK 68 A 37). The "previously mentioned differences" seem to be the differences in shape and size. As for "unlikeness," this term may well have been used by Democritus himself to denote the dissimilarity between bodies and void, in opposition to the Eleatic claim that being is all "alike" (see DK 28 B 8.22 and 30 B 7).

4. *Her.* 60–61.

on invisible, underlying bodies that Lucretius has previously appended to his arguments on generation and destruction.[5]

Let us first consider Epicurus' three additional claims. Epicurus defends the view that there is an up-and-down direction in the universe by taking the observed position of the human being as a reference point: up stretches infinitely above the head, and down extends infinitely beneath the feet.[6] Although it is difficult to agree with Epicurus on this, it seems that he is projecting the directionality of our own experience to the universe at large. That there should be absolute direction in the universe is required by the doctrine that the weight of bodies causes them to move in the same downward direction throughout the universe. Philodemus explains that this downward motion of bodies by weight is known by induction;[7] and Lucretius appears to be in agreement with Philodemus, for he outlines a thorough process of calculation that supports this induction. Lucretius first points to apparent counterexamples, such as the crops and trees, which grow upward, and flames that shoot up to the roofs of houses; and he explains that in these cases some force has been applied that causes the upward movement. Subsequently, Lucretius confirms the natural downward movement of bodies by citing examples of fires that move either downward or in a slanting direction across the sky, such as meteors, the rays of the sun, and the thunderbolt.[8] As for the underlying claim that bodies have weight, none of our sources offers an explanation of this; but it is reasonable to suppose that the weight of bodies was thought to be known directly by perception.

In proposing that the atoms move downward by weight, it is possible that Epicurus is responding to two objections made by Aristotle to the early atomist theory of motion. In the first place, Aristotle accuses the atomists of not assigning a "natural" motion to the atoms but only a forced motion, the motion of collision; the latter, according to Aristotle, presupposes natural motion.[9] Second, Aristotle notes that if bodies were placed in a void, there

5. Lucretius' entire discussion of motion occupies 2.62–332. This account includes the following divisions: 184–215 on downward motion, 216–93 on the swerve, 142–64 and 225–42 on the speed of the atoms, 294–307 on the sameness of motions, and 308–32 on the invisibility of atomic motion.

6. *Her.* 60. I accept Bailey's general interpretation of Epicurus' argument. David Konstan argues against Bailey that Epicurus is here attacking Aristotle ("Epicurus on 'Up' and 'Down' (*Letter to Herodotus* § 60)").

7. Philodemus *De signis* col. 34.23–24.

8. Lucretius 2.184–215.

9. Aristotle *De caelo* 300b11–16; cf. *Physics* 215a1–14 and *Metaphysics* 1071b34–36.

would not be movement in any direction, since the void admits equally of movement in any direction.[10] In assigning to the atoms a downward motion by weight, Epicurus is clearly assigning to the atoms a motion that is due to themselves, and hence natural. At the same time, he is providing a reason as to why they should move in one direction rather than another.[11] Aristotle's criticisms suggest, although they do not show conclusively, that the early atomists did not suppose that the atoms move downward by weight. The early atomists might well have responded to both criticisms by pointing out that the atoms have always been colliding with one another, so that Aristotle is illegitimately demanding to know what is the beginning of movement.[12]

Lucretius in turn addresses a problem introduced by the theory of a natural, downward motion. If all atoms were always falling straight downward by their own weight, he notes, then nothing would ever be created; instead there would be a kind of eternal rain in which no atoms would ever collide with another.[13] Furthermore, he argues, there would be no free will as observed; for one motion would be linked with another in a necessary chain of causation that would go back infinitely in time.[14] Accordingly, it is necessary that the atoms deviate a little, or, precisely, "no more than the least" (*nec plus quam minimum*), from the straight downward direction "at an indefinite time and in indefinite places."[15]

10. Aristotle *Physics* 214b17–19; cf. 214b31–15a1.

11. Brad Inwood also holds that Epicurus is here responding to Aristotle's two criticisms ("The Origin of Epicurus' Concept of Void," 282–83).

12. There has been a long debate about whether the early atomists assigned weight and downward motion by weight to the atoms. Guthrie provides a concise outline of the problem and concludes that whereas atoms moving freely in a void do not have weight, atoms whirled about in a vortex do (*History of Greek Philosophy*, 2: 400–04). Recently Furley has defended Zeller's view that the early atomists, like the Epicureans, proposed that the atoms move downward by weight ("Aristotle and the Atomists on Motion in a Void," 87). Barnes agrees that the early atomists assigned weight to the atoms (*The Presocratic Philosophers*, 2: 63–65). D. O'Brien attempts to save weight for the early atoms by proposing that the early atomists did not hold that weight causes the atoms to fall ("Two Conceptions of Change and Identity," 68–69; and *Democritus: Weight and Size*). I do not think that the distinction made by Guthrie is sufficiently supported by the evidence; nor is there sufficient evidence, it seems to me, that the early atomists assigned weight to the atoms at all. The best evidence we have is Aristotle *De generatione et corruptione* 326a9–10; but here Aristotle clearly shows ignorance about "heaviness and lightness" in the atoms, since he speculates whether these properties do apply. In this passage Aristotle may well have misinterpreted a claim by Democritus that perceptible heaviness is due to an "excess" in the atoms to mean that the atoms themselves have weight.

13. Lucretius 2.221–24.

14. Lucretius 2.251–93.

15. Lucretius 2.218–19 and 243–44.

I have argued elsewhere that this deviation is a sideways move by a single minimal unit of space at a single minimal unit of time, followed immediately by a renewed, straight downward motion of the atom.[16] As a momentary break in the downward motion of the atom, the swerve is not a continuous oblique motion, as has been thought traditionally, but rather a discontinuity in an otherwise continuous straight downward motion. Accordingly, the existence of a swerve is compatible with the view presented elsewhere by Lucretius and Epicurus that there are just two kinds of continuous motion of the atoms, downward motion by weight and sideways motion as a result of blows. Both of Lucretius' proofs for the existence of a swerve are proofs by counterwitnessing. Lucretius also uses the principle of counterwitnessing in pointing out that the swerve must be as small as it is in order that the phenomena may not contradict.[17]

In arguing for the swerve, Lucretius also considers the problem of the speed of the atoms.[18] He argues that since all atoms move at the same speed, it is not possible for the heavier to fall on top of the lighter and in this way to effect meetings and combinations. He explains that differences in speed are due to differences in the resistance of the medium through which a thing moves, and that since the void offers no resistance whatsoever, all bodies move through the void at the same speed. In his discussion of atomic speed, Epicurus likewise points out that small and large atoms move at the same speed, so long as they do not collide; and he gives as an explanation that the path of the atoms is "commensurate" (σύμμετρος) with themselves, that is, that their path is of a size to let them pass through unobstructed.[19]

As we saw earlier, Epicurus elaborated his views on the speed of the atoms by maintaining that a movement without collision occurs over a "comprehended" (περιληπτόν) length in an "incom-

16. "Epicurus' Theory of Free Will." Evidence for a minimal deviation, apart from Lucretius 2.244 (*nec plus quam minimum*), is found at Plutarch *De sollertia animalium* 964c (ἐπὶ τοὐλάχιστον); and Cicero *De fato* 22 (*intervallo minimo—id appellat* [*Epicurus*] ἐλάχιστον) and esp. 46 (cur declinent uno minimo [intervallo], non declinent duobus aut tribus; "why do they swerve by a single minimal space, and not by two or three?").

17. Lucretius 2.244–250. It may be noted also that Philodemus, in keeping with his general analysis of scientific inferences, presents the theory of the swerve as an inductive generalization that has been tested to make sure that none of the phenomena is incompatible with it (*De signis* col. 36.10–17). Similarly to Lucretius, Philodemus cites chance (τὸ τυχηρὸν) and free will (τὸ παρ' ἡμᾶς) as evidence for the swerve.

18. Lucretius 2.225–42.

19. *Her.* 61.

prehensible" (ἀπεϱινοήτῳ) time.[20] The etymology of the term suggests that a "comprehended" (πεϱιληπτόν) length is one that has been, or can be, surrounded by a perceptual or mental act, and so is a finite quantity that is marked off from a larger, possibly infinite quantity.[21] An "incomprehensible" (or "uncomprehended", ἀπεϱινόητος) time, on the other hand, is a period of time that cannot be marked off conceptually from the rest of time as a finite quantity. Epicurus' discussion of atomic shapes shows that "incomprehensible" (designated here by ἀπεϱίληπτον, a term whose use embraces ἀπεϱινόητον) does not mean the same as "infinite" (ἄπειϱον).[22] To be infinite is to be without boundaries altogether; to be incomprehensible with respect to boundaries is not to have boundaries that admit of comprehension. Thus it seems that just as the number of atomic shapes is too large to be known with precision, though it is not infinite, so the speed of a body moving without obstruction through the void is too fast to be known precisely, though not infinite. Accordingly it is impossible to assign a particular period of time to a movement that occurs without any obstruction over any particular known distance.

As part of his explanation of the incomprehensible time of an unobstructed movement, Epicurus points out that "collision and lack of collision take on a likeness of slowness and quickness." It makes good sense to take this very compressed explanation to mean that the more collisions a body encounters when moving from one point to another, the slower is its movement. This may be illustrated as follows. Suppose an atom moves from A to C in two laps, with a collision at B. Then each of the two movements, from A to B and from B to C, occurs in an incomprehensibly fast time; but the composite movement from A to C occurs more slowly than if the body had traveled without collision from A to C, and faster than if it had suffered an additional collision between A and C. The difference in speed is due to the difference in the cumulative length of the path; for it is understood that collision

20. *Her.* 46; see above, chap. 6 (Formation and Speed of the Visual Stream). My translation fails to reflect the difference in the components –ληπτόν and –νόητον. This difference is not, however, direcly relevant to the argument. I take πεϱιληπτόν to embrace both sensory and mental awareness, so that its contradictory, ἀπεϱίληπτον, includes but is not coextensive with ἀπεϱινόητον.

21. Similarly, at *Physics* 206b9–10 Aristotle uses the verb πεϱιλαμβάνειν to denote the mental act of taking a finite magnitude out of another magnitude. Epicurus uses the noun πεϱίληψις in the same sense at *Her.* 56 (see chap. 14, n. 26).

22. *Her.* 42; and see above, chap. 15 (The Shape and Size of the Infinite Atoms). It should be noted that ἀπεϱινόητον is also to be distinguished from ἀδιανόητον, "inconceivable," which implies absurdity or impossibility.

deflects a body from the direction in which it was traveling. Thus, although there is no difference in speed in the individual components of a movement, which are incomprehensibly fast, the total movement may be slow or fast.[23]

Epicurus' theory of speed in a void contains an answer to a charge made by Aristotle in the *Physics.* Aristotle here argues against movement through a void not only on the ground that everything would move at the same speed, but also on the ground that there is no ratio between movement through a void and movement through a resistant medium, so that there is no period of time in which movement through a void could occur.[24] Aristotle argues that since the speed of a moving body varies with the density of the medium through which the movement occurs, and since there is no limit to the rarity of the medium and hence to the velocity of the moving body, any time whatsoever assigned to movement through a void would be equal to a time taken to move through a medium of some degree of rarity. But this is absurd, Aristotle points out, since movement through a void must be quicker than movement through a medium that has some density. Epicurus meets this objection by assigning a finite speed to movement through a void and making the speed of movements that are obstructed dependent on this speed. It may be objected in turn that since the void is wholly yielding, it is arbitrary to posit any interval of time at all between collisions; or that since it is arbitrary to choose a particular speed rather than a faster speed, the speed must be assumed to be infinitely fast. No response against these objections is preserved; but an argument against infinite speed can be constructed by analogy with the argument for the atomicity of bodies. Suppose that there is no limit to the speed with which a body moves through the void; but let the period of time be reducible to ever smaller periods. What period of time will be left? It cannot be a finite period; hence the movement must be accomplished in no time at all, or at points of time

23. This explanation is also put forward by A. D'Andrea ("Nota ai §§ 61 e 62 dell' 'Epistola a Erodoto' di Epicuro"). Two alternative proposals are that of Bignone, that the atoms are at rest for a moment when they collide (*Epicuro*, 229–31), and that of Israel E. Drabkin, that the atoms slow down for a period of time while they are in contact with one another ("Notes on Epicurean Kinetics," 367–69). Bignone's suggestion faces the serious difficulty, as pointed out by Drabkin (366), that the atoms are said by Epicurus to be in continuous motion; and Drabkin's suggestion implies an entirely new type of movement, that of atoms engaged in collision with each other, which is not attested anywhere else.

24. Aristotle *Physics* 215a24–216a21. Furley also proposes a connection between these arguments and Epicurus' theory of motion ("Aristotle and the Atomists on Motion in a Void," 89–91).

(and points do not make up a continuum). But since there is movement as observed, there must be a limit to the speed of bodies moving through the void. Consequently, there are atomic periods of time and distances, just as there are atomic bodies. We know that Epicurus held that there are minimal parts of time and of distance, just as there are minimal parts of bodies.[25] It seems reasonable to assume that Epicurus viewed these minimal parts of time and distance as making up single, continuous periods of time and distances, and that at the subperceptible level these are times and distances in which an atom travels from one collision to another.

It is not clear to what extent Epicurus is following the early atomists in his arguments on the speed of the atoms, or indeed in any of the details of his theory of motion with the exception of the swerve; the latter is clearly another correction justified by the principle of counterwitnessing. There remains a major topic in Epicurus' theory of motion where Epicurus does seem to be directly dependent on the early atomists. Epicurus ends his outline of motion with the claim that there is no beginning of the motions of the atoms as just described. He might well have added, as a direct consequence of the entire preceding series of deductions, the conclusion that Lucretius adds to his more detailed account of motion. This is the conclusion that the motions of the unchanging atoms in the unchanging universe are always the same, with the result that what is generated is always the same:

> Nor was the supply of matter ever more packed or with greater intervals; for nothing either increases it or perishes from it. Therefore the primary bodies have previously moved with the same motion with which they now move, and will afterward always move in the same way, and the things that have been accustomed to be generated will be generated, and will be, and will grow, and will have power under the same conditions, as much as is granted to each by the laws of nature. Nor can any force change the sum of things; for there is nothing outside where any type of matter could escape from the whole, nor from which a new force might arise and break into the whole and change the whole nature of things and alter its motions.[26]

25. Both Simplicius and Themistius attribute minima of distance, time, and motion to Epicurus (U 278). Also, Sextus Empiricus at *Adv. math.* 10.142 attributes to the Epicureans the view that bodies, places, and times are ultimately partless.

26. Lucretius 2.294–307:

> Nec stipata magis fuit umquam materiai
> copia nec porro maioribus intervallis;

From the impossibility of any increase or diminution in the corporeal constituents of the universe, Lucretius infers that the proportion of bodies to void in the universe is always the same; and from this he infers that the motions of the atoms have always been the same as they now are, and will always be the same, and hence that things will always be generated in the same way as in the past. In the last sentence, Lucretius states the underlying reason why the motions in the universe cannot change: there is nothing outside the universe into which bodies could escape or from which some new force could enter so as to produce a change.

Epicurus had argued in his section on generation and destruction that the universe is always the same in what there is because there is nothing outside the universe that could introduce a change.[27] Lucretius now uses the same type of reasoning to add a final precision to Epicurus' claim that the universe is unchanging. It has previously been established that the unchanging universe is divided into unchanging bodies and void, and that bodies and void are both infinite in an infinite universe. From this last claim (together with the claim that there is nothing outside the universe) it follows that the universe is unchanging in its density; and from this conclusion (again with the assumption that there is nothing outside the universe) it follows that the universe is unchanging in the movements of its unchanging bodies, with the final remarkable consequence that what is generated is ever the same.

There are no testimonies attributing explicitly to Epicurus the view that what is generated is always the same; but two brief reports by late authors help to confirm that Lucretius is here following Epicurus. Pseudo-Plutarch in the *Stromateis* reports that according to Epicurus, "nothing strange is accomplished in the universe considering the infinite time which is already past"; and Justin attributes to Epicurus the view that "since they [that is,

---

nam neque adaugescit quicquam neque deperit inde.
quapropter quo nunc in motu principiorum
corpora sunt, in eodem ante acta aetate fuere
et post haec semper simili ratione ferentur,
et quae consuerunt gigni gignentur eadem
condicione et erunt et crescent vique valebunt,
quantum cuique datum est per foedera naturai.
nec rerum summam commutare ulla potest vis;
nam neque, quo possit genus ullum materiai
effugere ex omni, quicquam est ⟨extra⟩, neque in omne
unde coorta queat nova vis irrumpere et omnem
naturam rerum mutare et vertere motus.

27. *Her.* 39; see chap. 13, nn. 11 and 12.

the atoms] remain indestructible, it is not impossible that by coming together again and adopting the same arrangement and order they produce a body out of themselves which is similar to what had previously come to be".[28] As we have seen in the argument for infinite worlds, for Epicurus it follows that if something can be produced by the atoms, it necessarily is produced by them. Accordingly, the ever unchanging atoms keep on producing ever the same combinations as they have been producing in the past.

How narrowly do Epicurus and Lucretius understand the things that keep on being generated in the same way? None of the testimonies cited so far makes this clear. Later in his poem, however, Lucretius hints that the sameness of generation applies not only to species, such as humankind, that encompass individuals different from each other, but that it extends also to individuals. In an attempt to remove all fear of an afterlife, he argues that if there are future individuals just like ourselves, this matters not at all to our present selves, since our memory will have been severed; and he adds that in the same way our past selves do not matter to us, since we do not remember these. Lucretius explains these past selves by saying that when we consider the infinite time that has passed and the varied motions of the atoms, "one can easily believe" that "these very atoms out of which we are now composed were often previously placed in the same order that they are now."[29] Although Lucretius does not make an outright assertion, it is clear that he is inviting us to believe that there have been many individuals just like ourselves. It follows, since past time is infinite, that there have been infinitely many individuals just like us; and it also follows that there will be infinitely many individuals just like us in the future. Lucretius does not say any of this, but he indicates at least that the Epicureans may well have understood the infinite recurrence of types as extending to individuals, so that the recurring types are ultimately types of individuals, differing from one occurrence to another only in number.

The conclusion that there is an everlasting sameness of gen-

---

28. [Plutarch] *Stromateis* 8 (*Dox.* p. 581 [ = U 266]): οὐδὲν ξένον ἐν τῷ παντὶ ἀποτελεῖται παρὰ τὸν ἤδη γεγενημένον χρόνον ἄπειρον; and Justin *De ressurectione* 6 (U 238a): τούτων μενουσῶν ἀφθάρτων οὐδὲν ἀδύνατόν ἐστι συνελθουσῶν πάλιν καὶ τὴν αὐτὴν τάξιν καὶ θέσιν λαβουσῶν ποιῆσαι ὃ πρότερον ἐγεγόνει ἐξ αὐτῶν σῶμα καὶ ὅμοιον.

29. Lucretius 3.847–61, including, at 3.856–58: facile hoc accredere possis / semina saepe in eodem, ut nunc sunt, ordine posta / haec eadem, quibus e nunc nos sumus, ante fuisse.

erated things comes as a surprise ending to the series of arguments on motion, for it is based directly on the claim that the constituents of the universe are continuously in motion. Within the context of the argument on motion, everlasting sameness is deduced from continuous change. What makes the conclusion even more surprising is that it is the crowning conclusion of a series of arguments that began with the assumption of continuous perceptible change. The everlasting sameness of generated things, it turns out, is deduced from the observed continuous cycle of change from generation to destruction and back again. By assuming from the start that things are generated and destroyed as observed, Epicurus finally concludes that nothing of what we observe to be generated and destroyed really changes: for although each perceptible thing is generated and destroyed through its own lifetime, this process of generation and destruction keeps on recurring, ever the same, throughout an infinite time. Paradoxically, change is always the same, and this sameness is known by inference from the continual changes observed by us.

Like Plato and Aristotle, therefore, Epicurus recognizes unchanging types; and, like them, he differentiates clearly between the fixity of types and the changeability of perceived individuals. But in marked contrast to Plato and Aristotle, Epicurus deduces the former from the latter and holds that the type is not distinct from the individuals that exemplify it, but consists precisely in the everlasting succession of individuals.

There is good evidence that Epicurus owes his theory of types to the early atomists and, in particular, that the early atomists held that the types that keep on recurring are ultimately individuals. We have Cicero's testimony that Democritus maintained not only that are there innumerable humans and gatherings of humans that are entirely alike, but also that there are innumerable worlds that differ in no way from each other. Amazingly, Cicero points out, there are innumerable other groups of people, exactly the same, in exactly the same places, discussing exactly the same topics that Cicero and his friends are discussing now.[30] Cicero seems to have in mind recurrence in space, but his descriptions do not exclude recurrence in time, and the latter follows by the same type of reasoning as the former. Democritus thus seems to have held the staggering but logically consistent view that there is an infinite recurrence of individual entities, including

---

30. Cicero *Academica* 2.55 (DK 68 A 81) and 125; also DK 68 A 82.

not only such beings as humans but also entire worlds, throughout an infinite time and in an infinite space.

Aristotle confirms that Democritus did posit an infinite recurrence of types in time. In his discussion of the growth of the fetus in *On the Generation of Animals,* he criticizes Democritus and others for maintaining that it is a sufficient explanation of an event that it "always" happens in this way:

> All those who say, like Democritus of Abdera, that it always happens so, and think that this is a principle [or beginning, ἀρχή] in them, are wrong and do not state the necessity of why it happens; they claim that there is no beginning [ἀρχή] of the infinite, but that an explanation is a beginning and what is always is infinite, so that to ask for an explanation of such things (Democritus says) is to seek a beginning of the infinite.[31]

As Aristotle outlines Democritus' position, Democritus denied that it is possible to give an explanation of why things keep on occurring in the same way, on the ground that the succession of occurrences is infinite, so that there is no initial event that caused the occurrence. Aristotle's criticism here shows that Democritus held that certain types of things at least, such as a fetus, are always generated in the same way throughout time in an infinite succession. A very similar criticism in the *Physics* indicates that Democritus held that this is true of all generated things. Here Aristotle charges that Democritus reduced all natural causes to the claim that "it always is or happens in this way"—that is, that it happened this way previously, too—with the justification that there is no beginning of what is always.[32] Epicurus later asserts the same position when he claims in the final sentence of his outline on motion that "there is no beginning" of the motions by which the atoms become entangled with one another. Each type of atomic complex has existed for an infinite time; and therefore everything has always happened in the past as it now happens, and will always happen in the same way.

Although there is much uncertainty, then, whether some of the details of Epicurus' theory of motion go back to the early atomists,

31. Aristotle *De generatione animalium* 742b17–23: οὐ καλῶς δὲ λέγουσιν οὐδὲ τοῦ διὰ τί τὴν ἀνάγκην ὅσοι λέγουσι ὅτι οὕτως ἀεὶ γίγνεται, καὶ ταύτην εἶναι νομίζουσιν ἀρχὴν ἐν αὑτοῖς, ὥσπερ Δημόκριτος ὁ Ἀβδηρίτης, ὅτι τοῦ μὲν ἀεὶ καὶ ἀπείρου οὐκ ἔστιν ἀρχή, τὸ δὲ διὰ τί ἀρχή, τὸ δ' ἀεὶ ἄπειρον, ὥστε τὸ ἐρωτᾶν τὸ διὰ τί περὶ τῶν τοιούτων τινὸς τὸ ζητεῖν εἶναί φησι τοῦ ἀπείρου ἀρχήν.

32. *Physics* 252a32–252b1.

it appears that Epicurus did derive from the early atomists the conclusions that are set out in his initial outline, along with the consequence that the motions of the atoms, and accordingly the combinations they produce, are always the same. If we add to this the other correspondences between Epicurus' sequence of arguments and what we know of the early atomists' arguments, there appears to be a substantial overlap, both in method of argument and in conclusions, indicating that Epicurus took the entire basic sequence of arguments, starting with the arguments on generation and destruction and ending with the arguments on motion, from the early atomists.

The early atomist origin of Epicurus' sequence of arguments is strongly confirmed by its direct opposition to the sequence of arguments put forward by Parmenides concerning being. Epicurus' section on motion forms the final part of this confrontation with Parmenides. Whereas Parmenides concludes that being is wholly immovable, Epicurus concludes that the universe is always in motion with respect to each of its corporeal constituents. But like Epicurus' preceding conclusions, this opposition harbors a similarity: the motions of the atoms are always the same throughout time; hence the universe is unchanging with respect to its motions, and everything that happens in the universe is now the same as it always has been in the past and always will be in the future. Epicurus thus admits sameness within change, in the same way as he previously admitted limit within infinity, indivisibility within divisibility, and being within generation and destruction.

Epicurus' entire confrontation with Parmenides may now be set out as follows. Epicurus' argument has four main parts:

1. Nothing is generated from nonbeing and nothing is destroyed into nonbeing, with the consequence that the universe is forever unchanging in what there is.
2. The universe is divided into bodies and void; and the bodies are indivisible and unchanging.
3. The universe is unlimited in itself, and in the number of its bodies and in the extent of the void; and the bodies are incomprehensible in the types of shapes and unlimited in number with respect to each shape.
4. The universe is continually in motion with respect to its bodies; and these movements are forever unchanging, with the consequence that the universe is forever unchanging in the combinations that are formed.

These four sections have a close correspondence with Parmenides' sequence of deductions on being. The first two sections correspond to the first two sections of Parmenides' argument, in which he argues that there is no generation or destruction and that being is undivided. The third section corresponds to the last section of Parmenides' sequence, in which he concludes that since being has a final limit, it is complete and equally balanced like a sphere. The fourth section corresponds to the third section of Parmenides' argument, in which he maintains that being is unmoved.[33] In opposition to Parmenides, Epicurus holds: there is generation and destruction in the universe; the universe is divided; the universe is unlimited; and there is movement in the universe. To these opposed conclusions, Epicurus attaches certain similarities to Parmenides' conclusions, as follows: the universe is unchanging in what there is; the universe is unchanging and indivisible with respect to each ultimate corporeal constituent; the universe is equally balanced in every direction and limited with respect to each ultimate body; and the universe is unchanging in its motions. The similarities are subordinate to the differences and serve to highlight the fact that the whole system of deductions is constructed in opposition to Parmenides.

This opposition in conclusions is based on an opposition in the method of inference. Whereas Parmenides deduces his conclusions from an abstract concept of being as that which excludes nonbeing, Epicurus deduces his conclusions from the assumption that the phenomena are real. Epicurus assumes to begin with that there is generation and destruction as observed, together with a plurality of bodies and movement. Epicurus deduces from this that there is a universe that is forever unchanging in the very changes that occur. Parmenides, in contrast, deduces from his notion of being an absence of all change and, with this, an absence of all phenomenal being.

This confrontation with Parmenides, I have argued, originated with the early atomists. As Aristotle reports of Leucippus, the early atomists held that there are generation, destruction, plurality, and movement, as observed. From these observed facts the early atomists deduced, by a direct response to Parmenides, that

33. DK 28 B 8.6–21 (on generation and destruction), 8.22–25 (on divisibility), 8.26–31 (or 33) (on motion and change), and 8.42–49 (on completeness). It is generally recognized that Parmenides' deductions consist of these four main sections of argument. The first two sections are clearly demarcated; but a long transition between the arguments on motion and completeness makes it doubtful precisely how the rest of the argument is articulated.

there is an unchanging universe, which is divided into being and nonbeing in such a way as to be infinite and engaged in motions which are ever the same. By including certain similarities to Parmenidean being in their set of oppositions, the early atomists pay a fitting tribute to the thinker who inspired their arguments, without forfeiting anything of their opposition.

The method of using the phenomena as "signs" takes on special significance within this Parmenidean context. Parmenides introduces his series of deductions on being with the claim: "There is now left only one way to speak of: it is. On this way there are very many signs [σήματα] that, being ungenerated, it is also undestroyed. . . ."[34] For Parmenides, the claim "it is" furnishes "signs" of the nature of being. The atomists, I suggest, opposed Parmenides by proposing the phenomena as signs of what is. As we saw earlier, the method of using the phenomena as signs of what is unobserved came into prominence in the fifth century. Our new conclusions concerning the early atomists now indicate that the early atomists had an important part in developing this method: whereas Parmenides held that all investigation begins with the concept "it is" (ἔστι), and that this concept provides signs of what is under investigation, the atomists held that all investigation begins with the appearances of sense perception, or, as we might put it, with the claim "it appears" (φαίνεται), and that appearances—the phenomena—provide signs of what is under investigation. Parmenides' term σῆμα was soon replaced by the cognate term σημεῖον, which was used at first to designate both empirical and nonempirical proofs.[35] Eventually the term σημεῖον came to be associated with the method of using the phenomena as signs, so that by the time of Aristotle this method of inference was known as *the* method of signs.

34. DK 28 B 8.1–3.
35. Melissus provides examples of the nonempirical use at DK 30 B 8.1.

# PART V

*Epicurus'*
*Scientific Doctrines:*
*Elaboration of Theories*

# [ 17 ]

# Additional Precision in the Physical Theories

## PROPERTIES OF THE ATOMS

THE next two chapters examine to what extent Epicurus uses his two rules of investigation in the more specialized theories that he develops subsequently to his fundamental doctrines. In these theories, Epicurus clearly makes a wide use of empirical proofs. What is unclear is how these proofs agree with the method of inference used in the fundamental doctrines, and in particular how the inductive method of proof is related to the method of reducing a claim to an incompatibility with the phenomena.

A special problem concerning the more specialized theories is the use of induction to support multiple explanations. In these cases, a number of alternative explanations are proposed, all of which are said to be in agreement with the phenomena, but only one of which can apply to any particular case. As was previously discussed, these explanations have generally been regarded as satisfying a less strict standard of confirmation than the rest. If this is correct, then the agreement of a theory with the phenomena does not, it seems, constitute conclusive proof of a theory, and accordingly inductive proof seems inferior to the method of counterwitnessing.[1]

1. On multiple explanations, see chap. 10. The difficulty posed by multiple explanations has led Wolfgang Detel to suggest that although Epicurus attempts to deduce theories from observed facts, his method is inconsistent; for in offering multiple explanations, he resorts to hypotheses in order to explain the phenomena rather than deriving theories from the phenomena ("Αἴσθησις und Λογισμός: Zwei Probleme der epikureischen Methodologie," 33–34.

The following discussion of Epicurus' elaboration of his theories first treats four main topics—the properties of the atoms, the soul and its functions, worlds, and gods—and then the problem of multiple explanations. In the preceding discussion of Epicurus' fundamental theories, we examined some details that Epicurus reserves for discussion after his outline—in particular, details concerning the topics of motion and of atomic size. These topics are accordingly omitted now. The chapter on multiple explanations will touch on Epicurus' geology, meteorology, and astronomy. Together, the topics that I have mentioned cover roughly the range of Epicurus' more specialized physical doctrines. Although the treatment of these topics will not be comprehensive, the arguments that have been selected are representative of the method of inference that is used throughout.

With regard to the properties of atoms, Epicurus shows in the outline of his fundamental theories that the atoms have a variety of shapes. Subsequently, he discusses what the size and parts of the atoms are, and he also shows what properties the atoms cannot have. In restricting the properties of the atoms, Epicurus argues briefly that if the atoms were to have the qualities of the phenomena, other than shape, weight, size, and what necessarily accompanies shape, they would be changeable, since "every quality changes"; and this is impossible since something must remain through all changes.[2] Although this argument is too compressed to be clear, it makes sense to interpret it to mean that the component atoms must not have any of the perceptible qualities of the particular combinations that they compose, since all of these qualities are observed to change. It follows, by deduction from the previous conclusion that the atoms are unchanging, that the atoms lack all the properties that the phenomena have, although the atoms have their own shape, weight, and size, and necessary accompaniments of shape (such as the arrangement of minimal parts in the atom). Lucretius uses the same argument from change in both sections of his much more detailed account of atomic properties, showing, first, that the atoms lack perceptible qualities, such as color, and second, that the atoms lack perception.[3] Both Epicurus and Lucretius add the explanation that perceptible changes

2. *Her.* 54.

3. The two main divisions of Lucretius' discussion are 2.730–864 and 865–990. Lucretius uses the argument from change at 2.748–56 and 854–64 (in his dission of perceptible properties) and at 904–19 (in his discussion of perception).

are the result of changes in the arrangement of the atoms, incurred through some additions and subtractions of atoms.[4]

Epicurus joins his argument from change with another argument that is clearly inductive. This argument is worth special notice for two reasons: it is our first example of an inductive argument used by Epicurus himself, and it seems to be the only example of an inductive argument being added by Epicurus as a separate argument to a deductive proof. Epicurus' presentation of the inductive proof is very brief. He points out that when things in our experience (παρ' ἡμῖν) change their shape as a result of having parts removed all around, the property of shape remains to the end but other qualities are destroyed.[5] Lucretius permits us to fill in the details; for he offers the same argument as one of a number of arguments dealing specifically with color. He notes that objects lose their color little by little as they are pulled apart into ever smaller bits, until the color is observed to vanish wholly; and he concludes that "particles lose all color before they are separated into atoms."[6] As shown by Lucretius' formulation, the Epicurean argument consists of an analogy, in the form of a continuous progression, between what is observed and what is unobserved: just as perceptible objects have ever less color as they are pulled apart, until they are observed to have no color at all, so these remnants of perceptible objects, which are perceived to have no color, are divided into imperceptible atoms that have no color. The progression is intended to have mathematical certainty. It is claimed that if perceptible objects are separated into bits that have no color (as observed), it is so much more to be supposed that the ultimate, imperceptible remnants of dissolution have no color. This type of argument, as we shall see, is used again and again by Lucretius as a means of proving Epicurus' more specialized doctrines. The underlying justification, which will appear more clearly later on and which applies to all inductive arguments, is that there is no reason why the observed state of affairs should be the case and the unobserved state of affairs should not be the case.

In his series of arguments on color, Lucretius also offers a detailed argument by counterevidence in which he shows that observed changes of color are easily explained if we hypothesize a variety of atomic shapes, all of which lack color, and cannot be

4. *Her.* 54; Lucretius 2.769–71, 1013–18.
5. *Her.* 55.
6. Lucretius 2.826–33.

explained on the supposition that the atoms that constitute the object have color, whether of a single kind or of various kinds.[7] In addition, Lucretius offers another argument by counterevidence that relies on the assumption that if the atoms have color, any shape of atoms may exhibit any color at all; this claim is another Epicurean use of the "no more" principle. The consequence, Lucretius points out, is that individual members of a species would have any color at all; for example, some crows would be white and—just as interestingly—some swans would be black.[8] Of Lucretius' remaining arguments on color, two are deductions based on perceptual theory. One is that since color is not seen except in light, and since the atoms are not reached by any light, the atoms have no color.[9] The other is that color is perceived as the result of a certain kind of blow upon the eye, so that the perception of color does not depend on atoms being colored but on their having a certain shape.[10] The final argument in Lucretius' series of arguments on color is that just as we admit that not all bodies make a sound or emit an odor, and accordingly we suppose that there are some bodies that are without sound or odor, so we must suppose that since we cannot see all bodies, some bodies are deprived of color.[11] This is an inductive argument consisting of an analogy between bodies that lack sound and odor, and bodies that lack color.

In his discussion of the properties of the atoms, Lucretius treats the claim that the atoms lack perceptible qualities as complementary to the claim that the atoms lack perception. Whereas Epicurus offers no distinct arguments concerning perception, Lucretius constructs another detailed series of proofs. His first argument is an inductive proof, and it begins as follows:

> Manifest things do not refute, nor do evident things fight against it [*contra pugnant*], but rather lead one by the hand and force one to believe that, as I say, animate beings are created from things that lack perception.[12]

7. Lucretius 2.757–94.
8. Lucretius 2.817–25.
9. Lucretius 2.795–809.
10. Lucretius 2.810–16.
11. Lucretius 2.834–41.
12. Lucretius 2.867–70:

>            . . . neque id manifesta refutant
> nec contra pugnant in promptu cognita quae sunt,
> sed magis ipsa manu ducunt et credere cogunt
> ex insensilibus, quod dico, animalia gigni.

*Contra pugnant* corresponds to Epicurus' μαχόμενον (*Pyth.* 90 and 96).

In claiming that the phenomena do not contradict the theory, Lucretius announces that his proof is by "no counterwitnessing"; and in adding that the phenomena force us to assent to the theory, Lucretius contends that this method of proof is cogent. Lucretius' assertion is important because it indicates that he agreed with Philodemus and his circle that inductive proof, which shows simply an agreement of the theory with the phenomena, is no less cogent a method of proof than proof by counterevidence. Subsequently, Lucretius cites numerous observed details to support his induction. He points out that we observe worms to be created from dung. He also notes that rivers, leaves, and pasturages turn into cattle, which then turn into human bodies, which sometimes turn into the bodies of wild beasts or birds. In all these cases, Lucretius remarks, food is turned into living bodies and then into the perceptual faculties, just as wood turns into fire.[13] As Philodemus demands, Lucretius here uses a large diversity of examples, illustrating a wide range of transformations, to show that all percipient beings are formed from bodies that lack perception.

Of Lucretius' remaining arguments on perception, one includes the inductive claim that since we always observe perception to be joined to bodily parts—flesh, sinews, veins—which change, the atoms, which must not change, lack perception.[14] Another argument is a reductio ab absurdum: supposing the atoms have perception, Lucretius maintains, they must also be supposed to cry and laugh and think.[15] Lucretius also infers from the observed fact that a heavy blow inflicted on an animate being causes a loss of sensation that sensation is the result of an arrangement of atoms; and he argues similarly that pain and pleasure are due to certain arrangements of atoms.[16] In both of these arguments, Lucretius attempts to show a causal connection between an observed fact and the nature of the atoms. Finally, Lucretius sums up both his arguments against perceptible qualities and his arguments against perception by reverting to the notion of cyclical transformation that he used earlier to summarize the arguments on generation and destruction. Arguing by counterevidence, he maintains that the entire observed cycle of development from the

13. Lucretius 2.871–85.
14. Lucretius 2.904–06. Lucretius continues the argument by supposing that the atoms are sentient and drawing the consequence that they are living beings (907–930). The preceding section of argument at 886–901 does not seem to add anything new to Lucretius' discussion.
15. Lucretius 2.973–90.
16. Lucretius 2.944–62 and 963–72.

earth's reception of rain from the sky to the creation of crops, animals, and humans, followed by the absorption of things back into the earth and the sky, shows that there are unchanging atoms, forming all things through various arrangements of themselves.[17]

In his account of the properties of the atoms, then, Lucretius offers a mixture of proofs by counterwitnessing, by induction, and by deduction from other theories. There is no hint that Lucretius regards any of these types of proof as stronger or weaker than another. Although Epicurus' own extant account of the subject is very brief, his one combination of a deductive with an inductive argument suggests that Lucretius is following Epicurus' lead in joining deductive arguments with inductive arguments in his detailed presentation.

As for the early atomists, we know from Aristotle that they assigned three distinguishing characteristics to the atoms—shape, position, and arrangement—and that, like Epicurus, they explained perceptible change by a change in the arrangements of the atoms.[18] It is therefore clear that Epicurus is indebted to the early atomists for his general view of the properties of the atoms. Unfortunately, we lack any early atomist arguments that would permit a direct comparison with the Epicurean arguments. This lack, however, is compensated in part by a remarkably detailed account by Theophrastus in *On Perception* showing how Democritus explained both perception and perceptible properties by the shapes, sizes, and arrangements of atoms. According to Theophrastus, Democritus explained with especially great precision how the atoms produce the various types of taste and of color. Included in Theophrastus' report is an example of an argument in which the phenomena are used as a sign of what is unobserved. This argument, which seems to have been overlooked in the past, is important confirmation that the early atomists attempted to deduce from the phenomena what is unobserved and in this endeavor made careful observations to support their inferences.

As Theophrastus outlines the argument, Democritus held that red color is produced by the same atomic shapes as fire, except that they are larger, and he adduced as a "sign" (σημεῖον) of this

17. Lucretius 2.991–1022.

18. For the characteristics of the atoms, see Aristotle *Metaphysics* 985b13–19 (DK 67 A 6); cf. DK 68 A 125. On the question of weight, see chap. 16, n. 12. The early atomists seem to have viewed size as a property that follows upon the three differentiae. For their explanation of perceptible change, see Aristotle *De generatione et corruptione* 315b9–15 (and above, chap. 15: The Shape and Size of the Infinite Atoms).

claim that "when we become hot, we become red, and so do all things that catch fire, for so long as they remain fiery."[19] In addition, Theophrastus notes, Democritus maintained that fiery things that come to be from large atoms are redder than those that come to be from small atoms, for example, the flames and coals of green wood are redder than those of dry wood; in general, moreover, things that are hottest and have the finest fire are brightest, and those that are less hot and have coarser fire are more red. As Theophrastus shows, Democritus inferred the shape and size of the atoms that produce a red color by relying on an observed series of conjunctions between redness and fire. These observed conjunctions form a scale of increasing heat, accompanied by decreasing redness; and from this scale Democritus inferred not only that redness is produced by the same atomic shape as fire, but also, since a greater degree of heat is due to a greater fineness of particles, that the redder the color is, the larger are the atoms that produce the color.

The method of inference here used by Democritus is that of counterevidence: we observe, in the case of all things that catch fire (and in certain other cases of heating), that they become red and then stay red for as long as they are fiery (or hot), and that the hotter they are, the less red they are; and this, we must suppose, would not be the case unless redness were produced by the same atomic shapes as fire, though bigger shapes. Thus, although our testimonies are scanty, they indicate that the early atomists, too, inferred the properties of atoms by deduction from the phenomena.

## THE SOUL AND ITS FUNCTIONS

In his outline of physical doctrines, Epicurus argues that all perceptible bodies are combinations of atoms entangled with one another in different ways. One type of perceptible complex is that of animate beings; and the special problem concerning these is what atomic combinations make them animate. Epicurus maintains that the solution to this problem must be inferred from the "percep-

19. Theophrastus *De sensu* 75 (DK 68 A 135), including: σημεῖον δ' ὅτι ἐκ τοιούτων τὸ ἐρυθρόν· ἡμᾶς τε γὰρ θερμαινομένους ἐρυθραίνεσθαι καὶ τὰ ἄλλα τὰ πυρούμενα, μέχρις ἂν οὗ ἔχῃ τὸ τοῦ πυροειδοῦς. I follow A. E. Taylor's interpretation of the reference to green and dry wood (as cited by G. M. Stratton, *Theophrastus and the Greek Physiological Psychology before Aristotle*, 198–99). Theophrastus also discusses the function of atomic shapes in producing perceptible properties in *De causis plantarum*, DK 68 A 129–32.

tions and affections"; but the only precise inference of this sort that he offers is that since it is evident that the soul acts and suffers, and since only what is corporeal can act and suffer, the soul must be corporeal.[20] Epicurus also mentions that "the powers of the soul, its feelings, its mobility and thoughts, and what we are deprived of when we die" show that the soul is a very fine complex of atoms, "most like wind having a mixture of warmth."[21] For more precise details we must turn to Lucretius, who devotes two books to the nature of the soul and its functions.

The first question concerning the soul is whether there is a soul that is a distinct part of the animate being. Lucretius begins his detailed exposition on the soul by offering proofs that the soul exists as a distinct entity. He divides the problem in two, arguing first that the mind is a distinct part of the person and then that the rest of the soul is also.[22] In both discussions, Lucretius aims to refute the claim that the soul is a harmony of the body. He offers two proofs about the mind: that since we often experience joy when the body is in pain, and misery when the body gives pleasure, we must infer that there is a distinct part of ourselves, the mind, which has its own pleasures and pains; and that when we dream and the body is inactive, there is something else, the mind, which is active. With respect to the rest of the soul, he shows that not all parts of the body support life equally. These proofs take their evidence from the phenomena and can readily be formulated as proofs by counterwitnessing.

After pointing out that the mind dominates the soul, Lucretius undertakes to prove that the soul is corporeal. Like Epicurus, he argues that since the soul acts and suffers, as shown by its observed effects, it must be corporeal.[23] Lucretius continues his sequence of arguments by showing that the bodies that make up the soul are very small and very round; as before, his method of proof is that of counterwitnessing. He has two proofs, one depending on the observed quickness with which the mind initiates action, the other depending on the observed sameness of bodily bulk just after a person has died.[24] Lucretius then elaborates upon his conclusion by dividing the small and round atoms into four kinds. He claims,

20. Epicurus' discussion of the soul occupies *Her.* 63–68. The argument concerning corporeality is at *Her.* 67.

21. *Her.* 63 (including προσεμφερέστατον δὲ πνεύματι θερμοῦ τινα κρᾶσιν ἔχοντι).

22. Lucretius 3.94–116 and 117–35. Concerning the mind, see also chap. 9.

23. Lucretius 3.161–76.

24. Lucretius 3.177–207 and 208–30.

first, that the soul contains breath (or wind) mixed with heat; for this is what is observed to depart from the dying person. From this he infers that the soul atoms contain a third kind, air; for wind is always accompanied by air. Last, since these three kinds are not sufficiently mobile to account for the sensory movements of the soul, there is a fourth, nameless kind of extremely small and round atoms. The soul therefore consists of four types of atomic arrangements. This entire explanation adds detail and precision to Epicurus' own brief description of the soul as "most like wind having a mixture of warmth"; and there is no reason to suppose that Lucretius' explanation differs from Epicurus' own theory.[25]

According to Aristotle, Democritus held that the soul's atoms are spherical because this shape is most mobile and capable of moving other things, and the soul is very mobile and moves the whole body; Aristotle also attributes to Democritus the view that the soul is fiery because spherical atoms constitute fire.[26] Like the Epicureans, Democritus inferred the sphericity of the soul's atoms from the soul's mobility; and it is reasonable to suppose that he likewise inferred the mobility of the soul from its observed effects. Although there is no direct evidence, it is plausible that Democritus supposed that the heat of the soul is known not only as a consequence of the sphericity of its atoms, but also by inference from observed effects. In proposing, like Epicurus, that soul particles enter and leave the body as breath, Democritus posited a direct link between an observed entity and the unobserved soul.[27] Democritus also used an analogy between what is observed and what is unobserved in comparing the spherical soul and fire atoms to the dust particles that are seen in beams of sunlight.[28] It is not

25. Lucretius' discussion of the four components is at 3.231–57; see also U 314 and 315. Bailey argues in detail that Lucretius' account is in agreement with Epicurus' (*Greek Atomists*, 388–90). See also G. B. Kerferd, "Epicurus' doctrine of the soul," on the composition of the soul.

26. Aristotle *De anima* 403b28–404a9 (DK 67 A 28) and 405a8–13 (DK 68 A 101); also DK 68 A 102–4. According to a scholion on *Her.* 66, Epicurus held that the soul atoms are "very different" from those of fire. This testimony has led Bignone to suggest that Epicurus is here polemicizing against Democritus (*Epicuro*, 100 n. 4). This is a possibility, although Epicurus may well have misinterpreted Democritus to mean that the soul is like ordinary fire when in fact Democritus may have held, quite similarly to Epicurus, that the soul is a fiery stuff that is very different from ordinary fire.

27. Aristotle *De anima* 404a9–16 and *De respiratione* 471b30–472a16 (DK 68 A 106).

28. *De anima* 404a3–4. There is some unclarity in the text, which makes it possible to take the image of the dust particles to apply not just to soul and fire atoms, but to all atoms in general (as Lucretius uses the image).

clear, however, whether Democritus used this analogy as evidence
for the nature of the soul or simply as an illustration. Lucretius
uses the same image to illustrate the concept of atomic motion, as
well as to prove that there is a continuous, colliding movement
of atoms.[29]

As for the distinction between mind and soul, Aristotle claims
that the atomists identified ψυχή, "soul," with νοῦς, "mind" or
"intellect." But since this verdict is very likely inspired by Democritus' rejection of a mental intuitive faculty of the type that Aristotle later called νοῦς, it cannot be relied upon as evidence that
the early atomists did not recognize mind as a separate part of the
soul.[30]

After discussing the four components of the soul, Lucretius
turns to the relationship between body and soul. This is a topic
that Epicurus also discusses in some detail, emphasizing that the
union of soul and body is responsible for perception as well as for
life.[31] Again, we rely on Lucretius' far more precisely detailed
proofs for an insight into the method of inference. As part of his
discussion, Lucretius shows by counterwitnessing that the soul does
not perceive by itself, but that we perceive by means of the body,
as joined to soul. As proof that the mind does not look through
the eyes, as though they were doors that had been opened, he
suggests, sarcastically, that we should see better when the eyes
have been removed.[32] Lucretius also argues by counterevidence
that the mind contributes more to the preservation of life than
does the rest of the soul; this is shown, Lucretius points out, by
the fact that a person may lose all his limbs and still stay alive.[33]

Most important for our purposes in Lucretius' discussion of the
relationship of body and soul is his correction of Democritus on
the relative distribution of soul and body particles. According to
Lucretius, sense perception shows that soul and body atoms are

29. Lucretius 2.112–41.
30. Aristotle *De anima* 404a27–31 and 405a9 (DK 68 A 101). See also DK 68
A 105. Both Bailey (*Greek Atomists*, 160–61) and Guthrie (*History of Greek Philosophy*,
2: 433–34) think that Democritus, like Epicurus, distinguished between the soul
and the mind (although Guthrie suggests that Democritus placed the mind in the
head rather than in the chest). Maria Michela Sassi follows Guthrie (*Le teorie della
percezione in Democrito*, 68–69). Peter J. Bicknell has an ingenious, though implausible, argument for the view that the soul and mind are literally the same for
Democritus ("The Seat of the Mind in Democritus," 17–19). See further below,
chap. 20.
31. *Her.* 63–66.
32. Lucretius' discussion of the relationship between body and soul occupies
3.323–416. The argument about perception is at 350–69; cf. *Her.* 64–66.
33. Lucretius 3.396–416.

not distributed equally, one next to the other, as Democritus maintained, but rather that there are many more body atoms than soul
atoms. As evidence of this unequal distribution, Lucretius points
out that we do not feel any contact with certain very delicate
bodies, such as dust or spiders' webs; these make contact with us
in spaces where there are no soul atoms.[34]

This correction of an early atomist doctrine appears to be of the
same type as Epicurus' correction of the early atomist doctrine on
the number of atomic shapes.[35] Although we cannot be certain on
what grounds Democritus proposed an equal distribution of body
and soul atoms, it is plausible that he used the principle of indifference to argue that since there is no reason to suppose that
an animate body should not consist of both body and soul atoms
in any part whatsoever, we must suppose that body and soul atoms
are distributed equally. The Epicureans later thought that they
had discovered a reason why soul and body atoms are not distributed equally; as in the argument for the number of atomic
shapes, the Epicureans corrected the earlier conclusion by applying the principle of counterwitnessing. As we noted earlier, the
use of the principle of indifference is not in itself in conflict with
the method of counterwitnessing; and Lucretius' correction does
not imply that Democritus' own argument on the distribution of
soul particles does not rest ultimately on the use of the phenomena as signs. Rather, as heirs of atomist science, the Epicureans
made certain corrections in early atomist doctrine by applying with
special thoroughness a principle developed by the early atomists
themselves.

Lucretius' discussion of the relationship between the body and
the soul leads directly to a long series of arguments showing that
the soul is mortal. These arguments are predominantly inductive,
with some admixture of arguments by counterwitnessing. With
the exception of a reduction to the absurd, in which Lucretius
imagines the souls wrangling with one another just before the
moment of conception about which body to enter at conception,
all of Lucretius' proofs depend on assuming a certain relationship
between the body and the soul. These relationships may be distinguished as follows: the body is the container of the soul; the
chest is the place of the mind; body and mind grow and decline
together; body and soul suffer pain and illness, and are healed,

34. Lucretius 3.370–95.
35. Concerning the number of atomic shapes, see above, chap. 15 (The Shape
and Size of the Infinite Atoms).

together; parts of the body and soul are severed together from the rest of the animate complex; body and soul are joined in sense perception and memory; body and soul combine to produce life; and body and soul combine to produce behavioral characteristics.[36]

A survey of the first three proofs will illustrate the relationship of inductive proofs to proofs by counterwitnessing in the series as a whole. Lucretius' first proof is an example of Philodemean induction. Lucretius argues that just as water disperses when its container is shattered, and mist and smoke disperse in the breezes of the air, so the soul, which is far more finely textured and mobile than any of these substances (for it is moved even by eidola of smoke), disperses once it has withdrawn from the body. Lucretius adds that we can hardly suppose that the air can contain the soul, when the dead body, which is far less fine than air, cannot.[37] In this argument, the observed examples of water on the one hand, and mist and smoke on the other, represent a progression in fineness that ends with the fineness of smoke eidola and of the soul itself. Along with this, there is a progression in the fineness of containers, from solid substances to air. Lucretius infers on the basis of these progressions that the soul must disperse once it has withdrawn from the body.

This argument illustrates the same use of analogy as noted in our previous discussion of the colorlessness of the atoms. A sequence of observed relationships is extended by analogy to what is unobserved, so that we must conclude that what is unobserved is similar to what is observed. Later in his series of arguments on the mortality of the soul, Lucretius adds an argument in which he shows the underlying physical reason why the soul cannot remain as a unified complex once it is released from its container, the body.[38] Lucretius now concludes that the distinctive composition of the body, with its veins, flesh, and so on, forces the soul atoms into a distinctive, life-giving pattern of movement within the body, which the air outside cannot impose on the soul atoms; if the air could do so, Lucretius points out, it would itself be an animate

36. The proofs occupy 3.425–829. Their divisions are approximately as follows: (body as container) 425–44, 558–79; (chest as place of mind) 548–57, 615–23, 784–805; (growth and decline) 445–58; (pain and illness) 459–525, 526–47, 580–614, 806–29; (being severed) 634–69; (sense perception) 624–33, 670–78, 679–712; (life) 713–40; and (behavior) 741–75. These divisions are approximate since there is much overlap and it is often difficult to tell when Lucretius is starting a new argument or reinforcing a preceding line of argument. The reduction to the absurd is at 776–83.

37. Lucretius 3.425–44.

38. Lucretius 3.558–79.

creature. This is an argument by counterwitnessing, in which the manifest difference between an animate body and the surrounding air is a sign of the confinement of the soul within the body. The difference between this and Lucretius' inductive argument illustrates very well Philodemus' distinction between an argument by removal and an argument by similarity. In presenting the two arguments as two separate proofs, Lucretius appears to agree with Philodemus that the two kinds of argument are equally cogent.

Lucretius' second argument in the series also consists, like the first, of an analogy with what is observed, although it is not a progression to something ever smaller. Lucretius argues that just as the mind is observed to be born and to grow and to become old together with the body, so it must die with the body.[39] In this inductive argument, it is inferred from all the observed similarities between body and soul that the soul is similar also in respect to dying.

Lucretius continues to use induction in his third argument, where he claims that just as the body suffers illness and pain that may be so vehement as to result in its destruction, so the mind and soul too suffer illness and pain that may result in their destruction.[40] But in this case Lucretius adds immediately the underlying physical explanation for the conclusion. He points out that since the mind and soul are altered whenever they experience illness or a cure, and whatever is altered is no longer what it was and hence cannot be immortal, the soul and mind cannot be immortal.[41] The same explanation, which constitutes an argument by counterwitnessing (or, in Philodemus' terminology, removal), could have been added to the preceding argument. Together, then, Lucretius' first three arguments on the mortality of the soul exemplify a strong reliance on inductive argument, as well as a tendency to pair an inductive argument, which is considered cogent in itself, with a corresponding argument by counterwitnessing. This mixture of inductive arguments with arguments by counterwitnessing is typical of the series as a whole.

After setting out the nature of the soul, including its mortality, in the third book of his poem, Lucretius discusses the functions of the soul in the fourth book. He presents these, in order, as sense perception, thought, nourishment, movement, sleep and dreaming, and reproduction. Of these, Epicurus deals in the *Letter to*

39. Lucretius 3.445–58.
40. Lucretius 3.459–525.
41. Lucretius 3.513–20.

*Herodotus* only with sense perception and thought. We have already dealt in some detail with the process of perception, including thought and dreaming, though not with a view to the method of inference. The discussion that follows addresses only the topic of the eidola; for this topic presents a number of interesting inductive arguments that promise to throw more light on Epicurus' method of "no counterwitnessing."

In the *Letter to Herodotus* Epicurus mentions "no counterwitnessing," οὐϰ ἀντιμαρτύρησις, twice as the method of verification for a particular theory, both times in connection with his theory of eidola. In section 47, he points out that "none of the phenomena counterwitness that the eidola have unsurpassed fineness." In the following section he states that none of the various ways in which eidola are generated, including the continuous flow of eidola from the surface of bodies, is "counterwitnessed by the perceptions." Although Epicurus gives no further explanation, Lucretius has a number of detailed arguments showing how these two theories are verified by "no counterwitnessing."

To take first the formation of the eidola, Lucretius argues that just as there are perceptible emissions, such as smoke, heat, and skins that are shed, so there are imperceptible emissions, the eidola. After citing the perceptible examples, he writes:

> Since this happens, a fine eidolon must also be emitted from objects from the surface of their body; for it is impossible to tell why those things should be cast from and depart from objects any more than things that are fine. . . .[42]

Lucretius adds immediately that this is especially the case because perceptible objects have at their surface very fine bodies that can be thrown off, keeping the arrangements that they had on the surface and moving much faster than bodies that come from the

---

42. Lucretius 4.63–66:

> quae quoniam fiunt, tenuis quoque debet imago
> ab rebus mitti summo de corpore rerum.
> nam cur illa cadant magis ab rebusque recedant
> quam quae tenuia sunt, hiscendit nulla potestas;

The entire argument occupies 4.54–97. It is joined by a proof by counterevidence concerning mirror images at 98–109: the similarity of mirror images to actual things, Lucretius claims, cannot be explained except by the fact that eidola are emitted from things and are thrown back from the surface that mirrors them.

interior. Lucretius then gives an observed example of a very fine emission from the surface of a body: color is shed from the awnings of a theater over all the spectators below.

Lucretius' argument is an inductive argument on the model proposed by Philodemus, and one that consists, moreover, in a progression from the larger to the smaller. The pattern is the same as in the first argument for the mortality of the soul and in the argument on the elimination of color. In this case, however, Lucretius makes explicit what was implicit in those arguments: that since no reason can be given for supposing that the non-apparent state of affairs is different from the observed state of affairs, the former must be accepted equally with the latter. This justification applies alike to all inductive inferences; and it is an application of the principle of indifference. We have already seen this principle used extensively by Epicurus in his fundamental theories. The same principle is now found to operate in the inductive inferences that are so prominent in the elaboration of his doctrines.

This use of the principle of indifference in inductive inferences has the important consequence that it bestows deductive certainty on inductive inferences. All of Epicurus' inferences, therefore, the inductive inferences no less than the reductions to an incompatibility with the phenomena and the deductions from previous conclusions, may be described as deductions from the phenomena. If someone were to object to the use of the principle of indifference in inductive reasoning on the ground that at some future time, or in some other place, a reason for a difference might be discovered, the answer is that this possibility no more invalidates the induction than the possibility that something may be observed at some unspecified time in the future, which is not presently observed, invalidates an inference by counterwitnessing. The scientist relies on a present analysis of presently known observational facts to frame theories that are true. If one objects that this is to base science on ignorance, the response is that the scientist has no choice but to base all inferences on precisely those facts that are presently known; to do otherwise is to resort to myth.

After showing that eidola are emitted from the surface of bodies, Lucretius explains that there is also a quite different type of eidolic formation, that of a spontaneous combination of particles in midair. As proof he uses an analogy: eidola are formed and change shape in the same way that clouds form in midair and keep changing their appearance.[43] Later Lucretius uses a similar analogy to show how quickly eidola are generated: just as storm clouds gather very rapidly in the sky, so eidola form very quickly, and indeed they form much more quickly because they are many times finer than clouds.[44] In both cases, the proof by analogy is intended as a conclusive proof, based on the principle of indifference. The phenomena fail to counterwitness, and thus serve to verify, the theory of eidolic formation in that they do not provide a reason why the unobserved process should not be similar to the observed process.

As for the fineness of the eidola, Lucretius undertakes to prove this by showing how much smaller the atoms are than the things that are just at the threshold of perception. In this proof, Lucretius outlines a continuous progression in smallness from barely visible animals to invisible parts of the animal (such an the entrails, heart, and eyes) and to the atoms that make up its soul and mind. It is understood that since the atoms are very small, they can combine into very finely textured eidola.[45] Lucretius here depicts an inductive progression, since it must be assumed that the invisible parts of the animal are just like those of visible animals. Yet this progression, like the others, is intended to have the certainty of a mathematical proof; and this certainty is imparted to it by the principle of indifference.

It is perhaps relevant that Democritus claimed that bloodless animals are so small as to have entrails that are invisible.[46] We have much more direct evidence, however, about Democritus' theory of eidola. According to Theophrastus, Democritus held that effluences, called eidola, flow continually from objects and are stamped on the air like impressions on wax; these imprints then produce an appearance, ἔμφασις, in the eyes. Theophrastus criticizes Democritus at length for positing imprints in the air; and he suggests that the eidola by themselves should be sufficient to produce an appearance.[47] Scholars have generally held that Epicurus simplified Democritus' theory by eliminating the intermediate imprints; and in support of their view they cite Epicurus' own

43. Lucretius 4.129–42. Lucretius mentions a third method of eidolic formation in his explanation of mental perception. This consists in the combining of eidola from solids in midair (4.724–43); the explanation for this is that the eidola are so fine as to join easily in midair, like spiderwebs or gold leaves (see chap. 7).
44. Lucretius 4.168–75.
45. Lucretius 4.110–28.
46. Aristotle *De partibus animalium* 665a31–33.
47. Theophrastus *De sensu* 50–51 (DK 68 A 135).

statement denying that color and form are stamped on the inter-mediate air.[48] This simplification appears to be a modification of Democritus' theory rather than a radical departure from it. As Lucretius shows, it is part of the Epicurean theory that eidola may arrive in the pupil mixed with air.[49] Also, Aristotle indicates that Democritus did not consider air necessary for vision, for he re-ports that according to Democritus one would see an ant in the sky if there were no intervening air.[50] The difference between Democ-ritus and Epicurus thus seems to be that whereas Democritus con-sidered air a basic component in the eidola that enter our eyes, Epicurus held that air is an incidental admixture. Since the addi-tion of air may alter the arrangement of eidola, Epicurus may well have drawn the epistemological conclusion that the eidola convey the shapes of external atomic complexes more faithfully than Democritus supposed.

We have some detailed information about Democritus' views of the various functions of the soul, especially of perception, thought, breathing, and reproduction. As noted earlier, in an analogy con-cerning reproduction Democritus compared the umbilical cord to a cable and to the cutting of a plant.[51] This comparison reveals little about Democritus' method of argument; but there is another set of comparisons by Democritus, also mentioned previously, that appears to have been constructed as an elaborate inductive proof. It begins with the claim that animals of the same kind, such as doves and cranes, gather together. Similarly, inanimate things of the same kind, Democritus goes on, collect in the same place; for example, different kinds of grains, such as lentil, barley, and wheat, collect in the same place when they are sifted, and differently

48. *Her.* 49. There is some controversy on what Democritus' position was. John I. Beare (*Greek Theories of Elementary Cognition from Alcmaeon to Aristotle*, 26–27), Bailey (*Greek Atomists*, 167–68), and Guthrie (*History of Greek Philosophy*, 2:443) fol-low Theophrastus closely. In contrast, Richard W. Baldes suggests that the im-pression is stamped upon the air right at the eye as a result of the entrapment of air between the eye and the image ("Democritus on Visual Perception: Two Theories or One?" esp. 99–101).

49. Lucretius 4.246–55.

50. See Aristotle *De anima* 419a13–25. Aristotle here opposes his own theory, which requires air as a medium of vision, to Democritus', which does not. The later sources do not report any difference between Democritus and Epicurus con-cerning the passage of eidola through the air. At *Quaestiones convivales* 734f–35b (DK 68 A 77), Plutarch describes Democritus' and Epicurus' theories as being alike except that Democritus held that the eidola, as though animated, convey an indi-vidual's plans, feelings, and character to the percipient. Diogenes of Oenoanda notes the same difference in new fr. 1, cols. 2.10–3.14 (Clay, "An Epicurean Interpretation of Dreams," 361); see also Augustine *Epistulae* 118.28.

51. DK 68 B 148 (see chap. 12, Aristotle and Earlier).

shaped pebbles, such as elongated and round pebbles, gather in the same place when they are cast up on the shore by the motion of the waves.[52] The sequence of comparisons, involving both animate and inanimate objects, suggests that Democritus used it to infer that in the same way atoms of the same type gather in the same place. Sextus Empiricus cites this set of comparisons as evidence for the general epistemological claim that "like is known by like"; and Aetius, who offers a slightly abbreviated version of the comparisons, uses it to support the claim that an acoustic stream is formed by a mingling of voice particles with similar air particles. From these two testimonies it seems that Democritus used the set of comparisons to argue inductively, among other things, that perception is due to particles of like shape coming together; and although the details are not clearly attested, it is likely that Democritus had in mind both the joining of air particles with the perceptual particles that are emitted from objects, and the joining of such perceptual streams with the particles that make up the sense organ.

Although there is little attested overlap between the Epicurean and early atomist arguments on the soul and its functions, it seems that the early atomists, too, used the phenomena as signs of what is unobserved and in doing so relied on induction. Lucretius uses induction very prominently in his proofs about the soul; and he also justifies its use in claiming that whenever we can give no reason that there should be a difference between what is observed and what is unobserved, we must suppose that they are similar. This use of the principle of indifference assures that inductive inferences have the same deductive validity as inferences by counterwitnessing or deductions from previously established theory. Inductions confirmed by "no counterwitnessing" are therefore as valid as inferences proved by counterwitnessing, or, as Philodemus puts it, the method of similarity is as cogent as the method of removal.

## WORLDS

Immediately after concluding his outline of physical doctrines in the *Letter to Herodotus*, Epicurus continues the discussion of the infinity of the universe by considering the number of worlds in the universe. He argues as follows that the number of worlds is infinite:

52. DK 68 B 164 (Sextus Empiricus *Adv. math.* 7.116–17) and 68 A 128 (Aetius). See also Aristotle's report at *De generatione et corruptione* 323b10–15.

There are infinite worlds, both like and unlike this world. For since the atoms are infinite, as was just demonstrated, they also move farthest. For atoms of the kind from which a world might be generated or by which it might be produced have not been used up either for a single or for finite worlds, or for worlds such as this one or for worlds different from these. As a result, there is nothing that will stand in the way of an infinity of worlds.[53]

According to this argument, the conclusion that there are infinite worlds follows by the principle of indifference from the previously established conclusion that there are infinite bodies in an infinite universe. Lucretius offers two versions of Epicurus' argument: first, he claims that we cannot suppose that the infinite atoms produce nothing outside this world, especially since this world has been made by nature, that is, by the chance movements of atoms, rather than by design; and second, he points out that what can happen must happen.[54] As noted previously, there appears to be a strong connection between these Epicurean arguments and early atomist reasoning.[55]

Lucretius joins his two versions of Epicurus' argument by another argument that fits Philodemus' model of an inductive argument. This is that just as among perceptible things every individual thing is a member of a kind that embraces many individuals, so the sky, earth, sun, moon, and sea that we perceive are not unique representatives of a species but exist in countless numbers; it follows that there are innumerable worlds.[56] This inductive argument is of the same general type as the inductive argument used by Lucretius to show that there is a variety of atomic shapes.[57] Neither argument is found in the extant writings of Epicurus or in the sources for early atomism.

Later in the *Letter to Herodotus*, as well as in the *Letter to Pythocles*, Epicurus explains briefly how worlds come into being and are destroyed.[58] Lucretius develops this theme in the fifth book of his poem by arguing first, mainly by counterevidence, that the gods have nothing to do with the world, whether as parts of it or as

53. *Her.* 45: ἀλλὰ μὴν καὶ κόσμοι ἄπειροι εἰσὶν οἵ θ' ὅμοιοι τούτῳ καὶ οἱ ἀνόμοιοι. αἵ τε γὰρ ἄτομοι ἄπειροι οὖσαι, ὡς ἄρτι ἀπεδείχθη, φέρονται καὶ πορρωτάτω. οὐ γὰρ κατανήλωνται αἱ τοιαῦται ἄτομοι, ἐξ ὧν ἂν γένοιτο κόσμος ἢ ὑφ' ὧν ἂν ποιηθείη, οὔτ' εἰς ἕνα οὔτ' εἰς πεπερασμένους, οὔθ' ὅσοι τοιοῦτοι οὔθ' ὅσοι διάφοροι τούτοις. ὥστε οὐδὲν τὸ ἐμποδοστατῆσόν ἐστι πρὸς τὴν ἀπειρίαν τῶν κόσμων.
54. Lucretius 2.1048–66 and 1067–76.
55. See above, pp. 265–66.
56. Lucretius 2.1077–89.
57. Lucretius 2.342–80.
58. *Her.* 73–74 and *Pyth.* 88–90.

inhabitants of it or as its creators.[59] He then shows that since each of the parts of the world is destructible, so is the whole world;[60] this section of argument displays a mixture of inductive and non-inductive argument similar to that in Lucretius' arguments on the soul. Subsequently Lucretius explains in detail how a world comes into being. Although he presents this for the most part as a consequence that follows upon already established facts about the universe, at times he uses an analogy from sense perception to support a general claim about the behavior of bodies. Thus, after explaining that ether rises from the earth because it consists of much smaller atoms than the earth, he points out that it rises from the earth in the same way that mist may be observed to rise from lakes, rivers, and the earth in the early morning.[61] The argument is that just as the fineness of the mist causes it to rise from the grosser particles of water and earth, so the fineness of the ether causes it to rise from the earth. Similarly, after explaining that as a result of its fineness the ether takes a position above the air and moves with its own smooth motion without ever mingling with the air or being disturbed by it, Lucretius points out that the steady, undisturbed motion of the ether is similar to that of the Black Sea; the latter, he writes, "signifies" the motion of the ether.[62] Lucretius here cites the observation (as was generally believed by the ancients) that the Black Sea always flows in one direction into the Propontis, without any change in tide, as a sign showing by inductive reasoning that the ether flows steadily in a single direction.

Concerning cosmogony, there is evidence that the early atomists also relied on observation to provide analogies with unobserved processes. Leucippus held that in the initial cosmic whirl atoms were sorted out "like to like," and that in this process the small atoms passed to the outside "as though sifted" (ὥσπερ διαττώμενα), that is, as though passed through a winnowing fan or strainer. Also, Leucippus likened the surface of the cosmic complex to a

59. Lucretius 5.110–234. Lucretius also deals with the growth and decline of worlds at 2.1105–74.
60. Lucretius 5.235–415.
61. Lucretius 5.457–70.
62. Lucretius 5.495–508 (with *significat* at 507). Soon afterward Lucretius offers an elaborately developed analogy between the human body and the earth to explain why the earth is at rest in the center of the world (5.534–63). Lucretius asserts that the earth is closely united with the surrounding air, which supports it and moves along with it, just as the body is united with the soul, which supports it and causes it to move.

skin or membrane (ὑμήν), as though of an embryo.[63] As we noted earlier, Democritus appears to have argued for the congregation of like atoms by an elaborately constructed analogy with observed groupings, including the sifting of grains.[64] Democritus' analogy is especially appropriate to the process of world formation, and may be assumed to have been used to explain it, as well as perception. Although it is difficult to tell from Leucippus' analogies whether these were intended as inductive proofs, Democritus' more elaborate comparison suggests that the early atomists may have used induction pervasively in their explanation of the formation of worlds, and indeed in their physical theories as a whole.

An important topic concerning the formation of worlds and their continued existence is the origin and arrangement of the heavenly bodies. Much of Lucretius' and Epicurus' explanations concerning the heavenly bodies is taken up by multiple explanations, which will be discussed later. One notorious explanation may be noted now: the claim that the sun, moon, and stars are "in themselves" (that is objectively) approximately the size that they are seen to have, and that the sun in particular is about a foot across.[65] Both Epicurus and Lucretius support this claim by comparing the heavenly bodies to fires here on earth that we see from a distance. The details of this argument are somewhat obscure. As Lucretius seems to explain, the fires that are seen from a distance here on earth, so long as they are seen distinctly, change the appearance of size very little with increasing distance. In their case, the appearance of size corresponds closely to the size that the fires have "in themselves." The reason for this, we may suppose, is that the eidola that emanate from these fires are so fine as to suffer very little disturbance as they travel over ever larger distances; this preservation of eidolic arrangements may be inferred from the fact that the eidola present a clear, distinct outline of the fires. Similarly, as I interpret Lucretius, the heavenly bodies, since they appear distinctly, are seen by means of very fine eidola that have suffered very little disturbance in traveling over a vast distance, and that therefore present the size of the heavenly bodies approximately as it is "in itself." In developing this explanation, Epicurus may well have had in mind Democritus' claim that we could see an ant in the sky if there were no intervening air.[66]

---

63. DK 67 A 1 (DL 9.31–32); see also DK 67 A 23.
64. DK 68 B 164; and Guthrie's discussion at *History of Greek Philosophy*, 2: 409.
65. Lucretius 5.564–91; *Pyth.* 91; and Cicero *De finibus* 1.20.
66. See above, n. 50, for Democritus' claim on the ant. Democritus, however,

Epicurus introduced some changes into the early atomist view of worlds, although it is sometimes difficult to tell exactly what the change is. In certain cases, Epicurus seems to have narrowed the range of possibilities on the ground of a similarity between the phenomena and what is nonapparent. Although Epicurus acknowledges in the paragraph cited at the beginning of this discussion that worlds may be similar to or different from this world, he seems to have held that every world includes the same kinds of plants, animals, and so on as this world.[67] This contrasts with Democritus' view that worlds do not all contain the same kinds of things, for example, that they do not all contain a sun, or moon, or animals, or plants, or water.[68] We already have reason to suppose that Epicurus narrowed the range of perceptible properties, as well as the range of sizes, in the infinite worlds.[69] Concerning the destruction of worlds, Epicurus rejects the claim of a "certain physicist" that a world increases until it collides with another, on the ground that this is "contrary to the phenomena."[70] Epicurus does not explain why this claim is contrary to the phenomena; but in any case his view, to judge from Lucretius, is that the growth and decline of worlds are similar to the growth and decline of living beings. As Lucretius explains in detail, a world grows so long as it takes in more from outside than it gives off and then declines for the opposite reason.[71] Apparently Democritus pro-

did suppose that the sun is "large" (Cicero *De finibus* 1.20). In denying that eidola are stamped on the air, Epicurus seems to remove an obstacle to the view that the heavenly bodies are objectively about the same size that they appear. Sedley proposes a different explanation for the size of the heavenly bodies. He keeps the reading ἄλλο γὰρ τούτῳ συμμετρότερον διάστημα οὐθέν ἐστι at *Pyth.* 91, instead of excising this as the final part of the preceding scholion (as almost all editors do); and he interprets this text to mean that "you cannot get a better vantage point for viewing the sun's size by moving toward it or away from it" ("Epicurus and the Mathematicians of Cyzicus," 49). Sedley takes this rather than the observed size of fires as proof of Epicurus' claim about the size of the sun (48–53). This would make a reasonable argument, but it is very difficult to get the proposed sense out of συμμετρότερον. I suggest that the use of σύμμετρον at *Her.* 61 provides a good parallel for taking the phrase to mean "there is no path [between the heavenly bodies and the observer] better adapted to transmit it [the size along with the color]"; that is, there is a minimum of collisions along this path. Costantina Romeo discusses the Epicurean view of the size of the sun in a broad historical context, involving Stoic doctrine, in "Demetrio Lacone sulla grandezza del sole (PHerc. 1013)."

67. *Her.* 74.
68. DK 68 A 40 (Hippolytus).
69. See above, chap. 15 (The Shape and Size of the Infinite Atoms).
70. *Pyth.* 90.
71. See esp. Lucretius 2.1105–74. Epicurus touches briefly on the dissolution of worlds at *Her.* 73.

posed destruction by collision, although he seems also to have held a view of cosmic growth and decline similar to that of Epicurus.[72]

In addition to restricting possibilities in the infinite worlds, Epicurus sometimes seems to have widened the range of possibilities by reliance on induction. He allows that a world may have a boundary that is rare or dense, and moving or stationary, and round or triangular or any shape at all; his explanation is that "none of the phenomena in this world counterwitnesses," since it is impossible to know what the termination of this world is.[73] The early atomists seem to have held that this world is spherical and moves with a rotary whirl.[74] It is plausible that Epicurus' opposition is here directed less against the early atomists than against Plato and Aristotle. Also, Epicurus allows that a world comes to be within a world or in a space between worlds or in a relatively empty space; and he rejects the suggestion of "some" that the world comes to be in "a large pure void."[75] Here Epicurus seems to be referring to Leucippus, although in that case he has probably misunderstood the early atomist by placing an extreme interpretation on his claim.[76]

In summary, Epicurus followed the early atomists in deducing from the infinite number of atoms in an infinite void that there are infinite worlds. Lucretius uses inductive reasoning extensively to support his claims about the formation and operation of worlds; and in this he seems to be following Epicurus, who at times appears to rely on induction to reject an early atomist conclusion. The early atomists also used analogies to explain the formation of worlds. Although the evidence for the early atomists is slim, it suggests that their method of using the phenomena as signs included not only the use of the phenomena to refute hypotheses, but extended also, like the Epicurean use of signs, to the use of induction to prove scientific claims.

72. DK 68 A 40; Hippolytus here mentions that worlds are destroyed by collision with one another, and he also notes that worlds grow until they can no longer take in anything from outside. Bailey is, I think, right to propose that Democritus allowed both a gradual decline and a destruction by collision (*Greek Atomists*, 148). In contrast, Friedrich Solmsen suggests that Epicurus' claim that the world declines by a loss of matter is a refinement added by Epicurus to Democritus' doctrine that a world grows by absorbing matter ("Epicurus on the Growth and Decline of the Cosmos," esp. 37–38, 47–51).

73. *Pyth.* 88.

74. DK 67 A 22 and Lucretius 5.621–24 (on the whirling motion of the heavens).

75. *Pyth.* 89.

76. DK 67 A 1 (DL 9.31).

GODS

Epicurus considered it his task to purify the beliefs of mankind about the gods by showing, through scientific investigation, that the gods have nothing to do with anything that goes on in this world. Once the fundamental theories of physics have been set out and the gods have been expelled from the world, little remains to be done except to fill in some details about the life of the gods and, above all, to worship the gods as models of happiness. The expulsion of the gods from the physical world is clearly in marked contrast to Plato's or Aristotle's view of god; it is also in direct conflict with the theology of the Stoics, who held that the study of nature not only begins with god, but is nothing but the study of god, since the physical world *is* god.

Epicurus expelled the gods from the world by situating them in the interspaces between worlds. We have already noted that the existence of god is known directly by means of images that are emitted from the gods and enter our minds both when we are awake and when we are asleep.[77] The Epicureans also held that the gods have a body that, though similar to a human body, is made of much finer stuff.[78] This seems to be an inference from the appearance and fineness of the images. From the fine texture of the gods, as Lucretius shows, the Epicureans in turn inferred that the gods cannot have an abode in this world, since the world is too coarsely textured to support them; thus the gods live in the interspaces between worlds.[79]

As for the life of the gods in these interspaces, the Epicureans were hard pressed by others to explain this in detail, and especially to show how the gods used their human form to live an utterly happy life.[80] Although it is not clear how detailed an explanation Epicurus or his followers gave, it seems that the Epicureans were inclined to answer their opponents in generalities.[81] The Epicurean spokesman in Cicero's *On the Nature of the Gods* responds to the critics by giving only the very general answer that the gods live

77. See chap. 4, n. 41.
78. Cicero *De natura deorum* 1.49 and 1.74–75.
79. Lucretius 5.146–55.
80. See Cicero *De natura deorum* 1.50 and 1.65–114 (esp. 92 and 112–14).
81. Bailey suggests that in setting out details about the gods' way of life Philodemus goes beyond Epicurus (*Greek Atomists*, 469). Rist objects that there is no evidence that Epicurus differed from his followers in this respect (*Epicurus*, 151–52), and he assigns detailed human traits to Epicurus' gods; Kleve proposes a similar interpretation in "On the Beauty of God: A Discussion between Epicureans, Stoics, and Sceptics," 75–77.

a perfectly happy life of complete unconcern for humans or for anything else in the world.[82] Almost as evasively, Philodemus explains in the third book of *On the Gods* that the gods show favor to one another, though without giving gifts, and that they have neither a ceaseless rotary motion nor complete rest.[83] Philodemus also mentions the Epicurean Hermarchus' view that the gods breathe and (as the text seems to indicate) speak. Philodemus goes on to remark that, "by Zeus," they speak Greek; but it is not clear whether this is ironical or not.[84]

The Epicurean answers about the life of the gods did not satisfy the critics; and indeed Epicurean positive theology, as opposed to the negative theology consisting in the expulsion of the gods from the world, is perhaps the least satisfactory of their doctrines. It is obscure how the gods can exist in the interspaces and how each can exist eternally. This difficulty accounts for the suspicion harbored by some ancients that Epicurus retained a belief in the gods only to avoid persecution.[85] It is perhaps fairer to say that Epicurus retained a belief in the gods in spite of his science, and that, like many others, he found the two kinds of beliefs difficult to reconcile. It should be stressed, however, that Epicurean theology is, in a sense, the culmination of all of Epicurean physics: by showing how all events occur by a natural process of causation, science at once expels the gods from the world and frees all mankind to pursue a happiness like that of the gods.

We previously discussed some thorny problems concerning the initial concept of god. Among the remaining problems of Epicurean theology, one is particularly relevant to our concerns here.[86]

82. Cicero *De natura deorum* 1.51.

83. Philodemus *De dis* 3 fr. 85 Diels (pt. 1, p. 17), and cols. 10–11 Diels (pt. 1, pp. 30–32).

84. Ibid., cols. 13–14 Diels (pt. 1, pp. 36–37; see also pt. 2, pp. 49–51). Cf. Sextus Empiricus *Adv. math.* 9.178 (U 357).

85. Cicero *De natura deorum* 1.85.

86. For the earlier discussions of the concept of god, see chaps. 2 and 4. One major problem of scholarship should be mentioned briefly in addition. Did the Epicureans posit two types of gods? I agree with Philippson ("Die Götterlehre der Epikureer"; cf. "Nachträgliches zur epikureischen Götterlehre"), Günther Freymuth (*Zur Lehre von den Götterbildern in der epikureischen Philosophie*, 9–24), Arrighetti ("Sul problema dei tipi divini nell' epicureismo"), and Lemke (*Die Theologie Epikurs*, 77–98) that the available evidence does not support the view that Epicurus believed in two (or more) types of gods. Other scholars have variously identified two types of gods: Hirzel argued that these are gods that live in the interspaces between worlds, and mere images occurring to our imagination (*Untersuchungen zu Ciceros philosophischen Schriften*, 46–84; so Zeller, *Philosophie der Griechen*, 3, pt. 1, 446 n. 1); Hermann Diels held that Epicurus posited both gods of the interspaces and stellar deities such as the Sun and the Moon (*Philodemos über die Götter*, Book 3, pt. 2,

This is the relationship of Epicurus' view of the gods to that of Democritus. Before setting out Epicurean theology in Cicero's *On the Nature of the Gods*, Velleius rejects a number of other theologies, among them that of Democritus. He accuses Democritus of identifying the gods variously with images (that is, eidola) and their movements, with the nature that releases the images, and with opinion and concept.[87] The Academic critic Cotta later lists Democritus' gods as: divine images, mental principles, living images, and huge images that embrace the world from the outside.[88] Although both speakers intend to make a contrast between Epicurean and Democritean theology, there is a common feature in these lists that suggests an underlying similarity between the two theories of god. Democritus' alleged gods are all aspects of thought, whether as images that enter from outside to produce thought, as objects thought of by means of images, or as the thoughts themselves. Democritus, as will be discussed later, denied that what we perceive directly by images exists externally to us, whereas the Epicureans held that it has external reality. Thus for Democritus the object of thought is nothing but the content of a thought, having no external reality, whereas Velleius views it as an external object that emits the eidola through which it is thought of. Accordingly, for Democritus the gods exist only as images or as thoughts; Cotta attests this view when he identifies Democritus' gods with images and mental principles. Sextus Empiricus attributes the same position to Democritus when he reports that according to Democritus the gods are nothing but eidola.[89] The eidola are mental principles insofar as they are elements that, together with soul atoms, produce thought; and they may be described as "living,"

pp. 25–34); and Merlan argued for both the individual gods of popular religion, such as Zeus, and types of gods, such as the Muses and the Graces (*Studies in Epicurus and Aristotle*, 38–72; "Zwei Fragen der epikureischen Theologie," 196–204; Merlan is followed by Rist, *Epicurus*, 172–75). As for Hirzel's view, Epicurus always makes a clear distinction between eidola and the objects from which they come; the textual evidence for Diels's argument is very doubtful; and as for Merlan's position, Epicurus recognizes, it seems to me, a distinction between individual gods and the genus of the gods, without making further subdivisions (see above, chap. 4, n. 44).

87. Cicero *De natura deorum* 1.29 (DK 68 A 74); cf. DK 68 B 166.
88. Cicero *De natura deorum* 1.120 (DK 68 A 74); Aetius' report (at 1.7.16, *Dox.* p. 302; DK 68 A 74) that god is mind (νοῦς) existing as spherical fire may be classified under mental principles in Cotta's scheme.
89. Sextus Empiricus *Adv. math.* 9.19 (DK 68 B 166). For a different view of the relationship between Democritean and Epicurean theology, see Albert Henrichs, "Two Doxographical Notes: Democritus and Prodicus on Religion," esp. 103.

since they produce presentations of living creatures.[90] The huge size of the images, which is sufficient to embrace the world, seems to be linked with the erroneous belief of humankind, as noted by Democritus, that the gods are responsible for the frightening events in the heavens, such as thunder and eclipses.[91] In admitting images that embrace the world, Democritus undermines the contemporary belief that divine forces govern the world by embracing it: these divine forces, Democritus points out, are nothing but phantoms—thoughts produced by atoms arranged as eidola.

The preceding examination of Epicurus' more specialized theories has shown that they are proved by the same basic method of inference employed in the fundamental theories, that of using the phenomena as signs of what is unobserved. There is a difference, however, in that induction—that is, the method of "similarity," as Philodemus calls it—appears to be used much more widely in the specialized doctrines. Epicurus' own extant writings contain few traces of this type of reasoning in the specialized doctrines other than multiple explanations (and no traces in his outline of fundamental doctrines); but Lucretius, who uses induction very sparingly in his arguments for the fundamental theories, uses it extensively in the specialized doctrines. Lucretius, moreover, provides a justification for induction: this is the principle of indifference, and it ensures that inductions have the same deductive validity as proofs by counterevidence.

We have much less information about the early atomists' method of inference. There is enough evidence, however, to show that the early atomists also used induction in their specialized theories and, in general, that they used the phenomena as signs of what is unobserved. The Epicureans seem to differ from the early atomists only in concluding, by a renewed use of the same method, that some of the theories proposed by the early atomists are incorrect.

In elaborating his physical doctrines, Epicurus adds precision and detail to the earlier explanations. At the same time, it is clear that there is a limit to the degree of precision that can be attained. Supposing we take any perceptible type of substance, we may assert that it contains a large number of very rapidly moving atoms, having a variety of shapes; and to some extent we can know what types of shapes are contained in the complex. But it is impossible to know precisely how many atoms or precisely what shapes are in the complex. There is, then, a limit of precision to our knowl-

90. On the life of the eidola, see also above, n. 50.
91. Sextus Empiricus *Adv. math.* 9.24.

edge, which consists in specifying a number of alternative possibilities, all of them equally in agreement with the phenomena. Or, in the case of the eidola, we know a variety of ways in which these are formed; but it may not be possible in any particular instance to know in what particular way the eidolon has been formed. Here, too, we can state a number of possibilities, all of which are known to be ways in which eidola in general are formed, and all of which are in agreement with the phenomena. Or, as Epicurus himself points out, with respect to the infinite worlds it is impossible to know what shape any particular world has; what we know is that any shape at all is in agreement with the phenomena. Thus it is an integral feature of the method of using the phenomena as signs that it encompasses multiple explanations. The next chapter examines multiple explanations further.

# [ 18 ]

# Multiple Explanations

TOWARD the end of the *Letter to Herodotus* and again at the beginning of the *Letter to Pythocles,* Epicurus draws a distinction between single and multiple explanations. There are certain basic causes, Epicurus claims, that need to be known exactly if we are to be happy; for example, we need to know that the universe consists of bodies and void and that the elementary bodies are atomic. These are single explanations; and here what is unobserved "has a single agreement with the phenomena" (μοναχὴν ἔχει τοῖς φαινομένοις συμφωνίαν).[1] But there are other causes, especially of events in the heavens such as the risings and settings of heavenly bodies and eclipses, that do not need to be determined with precision; it is sufficient for our happiness that several explanations be discovered. In these cases, the events "have a multiple [πλεοναχὴν] cause of coming into being and a multiple predication of what exists, in agreement with the perceptions."[2] Here several explanations are in agreement with the phenomena; and it is not known precisely which explanation applies to a particular case.

As indicated earlier, multiple explanations pose a difficult problem for Epicurean methodology. If not all the multiple explanations are true, then it seems that the agreement of a theory with the phenomena is not a sufficient criterion of truth; and hence all inductive inferences seem to admit of being false. The following

1. *Pyth.* 86; and *Her.* 78–79.
2. *Pyth.* 86 (including πλεοναχὴν ἔχει καὶ τῆς γενέσεως αἰτίαν καὶ τῆς οὐσίας ταῖς αἰσθήσεσι σύμφωνον κατηγορίαν); and *Her.* 78–80.

discussion attempts to show that in Epicureanism agreement with the phenomena does serve as a criterion of truth; for although only one explanation can be true with respect to any particular event, all multiple explanations are true with respect to the general state of affairs that they serve to explain.

Epicurus makes a special effort to show that multiple explanations do not fall short of the goal of scientific investigation. He has two lines of defense. One is that the degree of precision achieved by multiple explanations is sufficient for human happiness.[3] The other is that it would be unscientific to prefer one explanation to another when both are equally in agreement with the phenomena; this, he says, would be to "abandon physical inquiry and resort to myth."[4] He sums up this attitude as "madness,"[5] and attributes it to a failure to recognize what is possible for a human being and what is not possible.[6] Lucretius later presents multiple explanations as a stage in scientific progress. To select one explanation from several equally good ones, he says, is not appropriate for the person who would "proceed step by step."[7] It is implied that science proceeds by narrowing ever further the range of possible explanations. Epicurus has often been accused of fashioning his physics to suit his ethical needs. The principle of multiple explanation, however, is in itself a sound scientific one; and the subordination of physical inquiry to ethical concerns is certainly not unique to Epicureanism.

In the *Letter to Herodotus* Epicurus writes this about multiple explanation, as previously quoted in part:

> We must give explanations about the events in the heavens and everything that is nonapparent by comparing in how many ways a similar thing happens in our experience, scorning those who know neither that which is or comes to be in a single way nor that which happens in more than one way; they overlook the presentation from a distance and furthermore do not know in what sort of things tranquillity is found.[8]

3. *Her.* 78–80 and *Pyth.* 85–87.
4. *Pyth.* 87.
5. *Pyth.* 113.
6. *Pyth.* 94; cf. 98.
7. Lucretius 5.532–33.
8. *Her.* 80: ὥστε παραθεωροῦντας ποσαχῶς παρ' ἡμῖν τὸ ὅμοιον γίνεται, αἰτιολογητέον ὑπέρ τε τῶν μετεώρων καὶ παντὸς τοῦ ἀδήλου, καταφρονοῦντας τῶν οὔτε ⟨τὸ⟩ μοναχῶς ἔχον ἢ γινόμενον γνωριζόντων οὔτε τὸ πλεοναχῶς συμβαῖνον τήν ⟨τ'⟩ ἐκ τῶν ἀποστημάτων φαντασίαν παριδόντων, ἔτι τε ἀγνοούντων καὶ ἐν ποίοις οὐκ ἔστιν ἀταρακτῆσαι. This is Usener's text; Usener, followed by Long, emends mss. παραδιδόντων to παριδόντων.

In addition, Epicurus explains in the *Letter to Pythocles* that we must use the phenomena here on earth, "which are viewed as they are," and not the phenomena of the heavens, as signs of what occurs in the heavens; the reason, he notes, is that the phenomena in the heavens can be produced in several ways. The appearance in the heavens, he continues, must nonetheless be kept under observation (τηρητέον) and must be distinguished from the multiple features that are not "counterwitnessed" (ἀντιμαρτυρεῖται) by events in our experience as belonging to it.[9] Epicurus repeatedly justifies multiple explanations by claiming that they are not counterwitnessed by the events in our experience or, equivalently, that they are in agreement with the phenomena.[10]

In these remarks, Epicurus indicates that multiple explanations are obtained by induction, through a comparison of the event to be explained with observed events. He also indicates that all scientific investigation consists in making comparisons between unobserved and observed events and hence that induction is used to obtain single as well as multiple explanations. The question was raised earlier whether Epicurus is here committing himself to the view, later defended by Philodemus, that all scientific conclusions are obtained inductively by establishing that what is unobserved is similar to what is observed. According to his extant writings, Epicurus certainly does not prove his fundamental theories as inductions, but views them as deductions, derived ultimately from observed facts by the principle of counterevidence. It is possible that Epicurus held, like Philodemus, that all of these theories may be reformulated as inductions; but it is consistent with his procedure and his remarks that he proposed the search for similarities as a heuristic device that may result in counterinductive conclusions and that accordingly he recognized both inductive and counterinductive theories, the latter proved by counterevidence.

Epicurus claims that multiple explanations must be admitted whenever there is a distant presentation that has a similarity to several kinds of events observed here on earth. Even though imprecise, the distant presentation must not be neglected; for although it is not sufficiently precise to admit of a single explanation, it admits of multiple explanations. Lucretius explains with the following illustration how multiple explanations apply to distant phenomena:

9. *Pyth.* 87–88.
10. *Pyth.* 88, 92, 93, 95, and 98.

There are also some things for which it is not enough to state a single cause, but [one must state] several, of which one, however, is the case. Just as if you were to see the lifeless corpse of a man lying far away, it would be fitting to state all the causes of death in order that the single cause of this death may be stated. For you would not be able to establish conclusively that he died by the sword or of cold or of illness or perhaps by poison, but we know that there is something of this kind that happened to him. We can say the same thing in many cases.[11]

Lucretius shows that the distant phenomenon that is to be explained is observed only sufficiently clearly to be identified as an instance of a general category, in this case death, without being recognized as a specific type within this general category. Thus all specific explanations of death must be cited if the explanation that applies to this particular death is to be included. Lucretius implies that all of these explanations are true at one time or another; death is viewed as a general event, subdivided into a number of specific types, each corresponding to one of the multiple explanations. Hence all explanations are true, even though only one can be true of any particular instance of death.

Whether all multiple explanations are true, therefore, depends on whether the problem under investigation is viewed as a general feature or as a particular event. Since the scientist, who is presented only with a distant appearance, can view the problem that is to be explained only as a generic feature, all the multiple explanations are applicable to the problem under investigation, and hence all are true. Implicit in this view is the assumption that the problem under investigation is defined by the information that the investigator presently has about the event. Thus it is beside the point to object that, in giving multiple explanations, the scientist is not explaining the particular event that occurs just then and there. For this problem is not formulated by the scientist at all; the event does of course happen at a certain time and place, but

11. Lucretius 6.703–11:

> sunt aliquot quoque res quarum unam dicere causam
> non satis est, verum pluris, unde una tamen sit;
> corpus ut exanimum siquod procul ipse iacere
> conspicias hominis, fit ut omnis dicere causas
> conveniat leti, dicatur ut illius una.
> nam neque eum ferro nec frigore vincere possis
> interiisse neque a morbo neque forte veneno,
> verum aliquid genere esse ex hoc quod contigit ei
> scimus. item in multis hoc rebus dicere habemus.

what is known about the event allows it to be classified only as a generic event. There is a limit to the degree of precision with which the scientist can define a problem; and the answer corresponds to this degree of precision.

Lucretius shows in the following passage how the distinction between a generic event and specific types of events applies to the events in the heavens. After listing a number of alternative explanations of the movements of the stars, Lucretius points out:

> . . . it is difficult to state for certain which of these causes applies to this world; but what can and does happen in the universe in the various worlds created in various ways, this I teach, and I proceed to set out multiple causes of the motion of the stars, as they can be throughout the universe. Of these there is, however, necessarily one cause here also that provides the force of motion to the stars.[12]

The motion of the stars throughout the universe is of various types, each having its own explanation; and although we do not know the specific type exemplified by the stars in our world, we know that one of the explanations applies to the stars in our world, whereas all explanations are realized in the universe at large. Lucretius assumes that a study of the phenomena furnishes a complete set of valid alternative explanations; accordingly, since all possible explanations are known, one of the explanations must apply to this world. In saying that he will show "what can and does happen," Lucretius shows that each explanation does apply to some world; for in Epicureanism what can happen does happen. That an explanation applies to some world, and hence to the general state of affairs that is being explained, is precisely what makes it true.

In the case of multiple explanations, then, no less than in the case of single explanations, each explanation is true as determined by the criterion of "no counterwitnessing." If one objects that an explanation is only possibly true of this particular state of affairs,

12. Lucretius 5.526–32:

nam quid in hoc mundo sit eorum ponere certum
difficile est; sed quid possit fiatque per omne
in variis mundis varia ratione creatis,
id doceo plurisque sequor disponere causas,
motibus astrorum quae possint esse per omne;
e quibus una tamen siet hic quoque causa necessest
quae vegeat motum signis.

the answer is that this is not the state of affairs that is being explained. The only remaining way of saving the traditional view that each alternative explanation is only possibly true is to maintain that the causes of distant phenomena are really things that are "waiting" to be manifest (προσμένοντα) and should be investigated as such; accordingly any explanation that falls short of an actual observation would be only possibly true.[13] As noted before, however, Epicurus himself classifies the causes of distant phenomena in the heavens as things that are nonapparent (ἄδηλα); the reason is that the scientist proceeds on the basis of present evidence, and so treats the events in the heavens, since they have never been observed from nearby, as not admitting of close inspection.

The example of the distant death, which Lucretius uses to illustrate multiple explanations, is somewhat misleading in this respect. In this case it is possible to come closer in such a way as to determine the single cause of death, whereas it is not possible to approach the heavenly bodies. With respect to the dead body too, however, the cause of the event is inferred from observed details as something that is nonapparent; it is by looking at the position of the body, the condition of the skin, and so on, that the doctor infers the unobserved cause of death. Lucretius' example is apposite because it illustrates that if only we could penetrate ever further by our powers of observation into the hidden territory of what is nonapparent, we would be able to construct ever more exact answers about what still remains outside the range of observation. Observation provides sure answers to our questions; but it does not reach far enough. Reason then takes over, using observed facts as evidence of what is hidden from observation; and the more detailed the observations on which it relies, the more detailed its answers. But just as our powers of observation have a limit, so does reason. If only we could penetrate to the ultimate boundaries of existence through observation, there would be no need for reason and we would be able to attain the goal of complete knowledge. As it is, the limitations of our perceptual powers not only prevent us from having a direct acquaintance with much of reality; they also impose a limit on the degree of precision with which we can answer problems about what is nonapparent.

This view of scientific investigation is very different from Plato's or Aristotle's. Plato and Aristotle aimed for absolutely precise principles that would explain the types of events that occur in the

13. See chap. 10 (Epicurus' Theory of Signs in a Hellenistic Context).

physical world. Although Epicurus includes among his scientific theories certain basic principles that do not admit of alternatives and that, according to Epicurus, have absolute precision, and although Epicurus would agree with Plato and Aristotle that individual events do not admit of precise explanation, the aim of Epicurean science is to achieve as complete an explanation of individual events as our observations will permit. Accordingly, Epicurus admits a wide range of precision among scientific theories; and the degree of precision depends exactly on the amount of observational detail that is available for the scientist to study. Contrary to Plato and Aristotle, Epicurus maintains that the aim of science is not to move from the confusion of sensory data to precise general principles but rather to supplement observational detail with nonobservational detail in order to achieve as complete a view of each event as possible.

Both Lucretius and Epicurus cite numerous examples of multiple explanations for the events in the heavens. Epicurus' more concise account in the *Letter to Pythocles* contains numerous references to the phenomena in general as evidence of multiple explanations, but is very sparing in showing how particular phenomena support particular explanations. We have already noted the comparison of the heavenly bodies with fires observed here on earth.[14] In addition, as evidence for the two possibilities that the moon may shine with its own light or else with the light of the sun, Epicurus adduces the fact that "in our experience" (παρ' ἡμῖν) many things shine with their own light and many with borrowed light.[15] This explanation is disappointingly vague, as is the one that the regularity of the rotation of the heavenly bodies is similar to certain phenomena.[16] Last, Epicurus mentions that thunder may be produced by wind being pent up in hollow clouds just as happens "in the case of vessels" in our experience; Epicurus here seems to be alluding to the act of blowing into a vessel with a narrow neck.[17]

In contrast to Epicurus, Lucretius offers lavishly detailed analogies from sense experience in support of many of the multiple explanations that he outlines. In adding these analogies, Lucretius is elaborating on Epicurus' own procedure without making any changes in the method of inference. In one representative section

14. *Pyth.* 91; see chap. 17 (Worlds).
15. *Pyth.* 94–95.
16. *Pyth.* 97.
17. *Pyth.* 100; see also Bailey's note on this passage (*Epicurus*, 302).

of explanation, which also throws light on Epicurus' relationship to the early atomists, Lucretius gives two explanations for the orbits of the heavenly bodies.[18] One is the "sacred opinion" of Democritus that the closer the heavenly body is to the earth, the less it is influenced by the whirl of the outer heaven, with the result that the sun, and even more the moon, fall behind the movement of the rest of the stars.[19] The second explanation is that the sun, moon, and stars may be moved by different winds. Here Lucretius provides an analogy:

> Do you not see that the lower clouds also, as a result of different winds, go in directions that differ from those of the upper clouds? How are those stars any less able to be carried by different currents through the great circles of the ether?[20]

Since there is no reason why the clouds can be driven by different winds and the sun, moon, and stars cannot, it must be inferred that the latter can be driven by different currents and hence are so moved in some world. Here again Lucretius makes explicit the justification for all inductive inferences. As in the case of single explanations, so in multiple explanations the induction holds because there is no reason to suppose that what is observed is any "more" the case than what is unobserved.

Lucretius' text gives the impression that Democritus provided a single explanation of the movements of the sun, moon, and stars, in contrast to Epicurus' multiple explanations. Did Democritus, then, regularly offer single instead of multiple explanations? If so, this would be a significant difference in the method of inference. At first sight, there seems to be confirmation of such a difference. Numerous other single explanations about meteorological and astronomical events are attributed in our sources to Democritus, among them the claim that the moon receives its light from the sun.[21] In addition, Epicurus' and Lucretius' multiple explanations seem to be gleaned in part from a doxographic collection made by

18. Lucretius 5.614–49.
19. Lucretius 5.621–36 (DK 68 A 88); see also DK 68 A 89.
20. Lucretius 5.646–49:

nonne vides etiam diversis nubila ventis
diversas ire in partis inferna supernis?
qui minus illa queant per magnos aetheris orbis
aestibus inter se diversis sidera ferri?

The whole argument occupies 5.637–49 and contains many difficulties of interpretation; see Bailey's detailed commentary in his annotated edition of Lucretius, 1417–20 and 1423.
21. DK 68 A 89a; see also DK 68 A 85–87, 90–93a, 96, 97, 99, 100.

Theophrastus; and in any event they seem to be drawn in large part from ideas proposed by a variety of much earlier thinkers.[22] We also have evidence, however, that Democritus gave multiple explanations. According to Seneca, Democritus explained that earthquakes are sometimes caused by the wind, sometimes by water, and sometimes by both.[23] The fact that Aristotle attributes only the first of Seneca's three explanations to Democritus indicates that in some cases the single explanations attributed to Democritus may have been selected from multiple explanations.[24] It appears, therefore, as one would expect from Democritus' reliance on the phenomena as signs, that Democritus too gave multiple explanations, though probably not as abundantly as Epicurus. Specific evidence of Democritus' use of the phenomena as signs of meteorological events is his comparison of the formation of wind to the gathering of a crowd in the marketplace.[25]

Aristotle not only claims that the method of using the phenomena as signs of what is unobserved results in multiple explanations, but also illustrates this feature with his own use of signs. His *Meteorologica* is conspicuous for the use of analogies to provide both single and multiple explanations.[26] Aristotle offers, for example, two explanations of why heat from the sun reaches the earth. One is that the surrounding fire is scattered by the sun's motion and carried downward; the other is that the sun heats the air with its motion. In support of the latter explanation, Aristotle cites the example of bodies "in our experience" (παρ' ἡμῖν) heating the nearby air when they are hurled with force. He also describes his method of inference as that of "taking what is similar from our experience" (λαμβάνοντας τὸ ὅμοιον ἐκ τῶν παρ' ἡμῖν γιγνομένων);[27] this formulaic expression was reiterated by Epicurus and his followers.

22. Erich Reitzenstein argues in detail for Epicurus' dependence on Theophrastus in *Theophrast bei Epikur und Lukrez*; see esp. 24–40 and the appendix (86–108), which contains a translation of the Theophrastean text along with parallel passages from other authors.

23. DK 68 A 98 (Seneca *Naturales quaestiones* 6.20).

24. Aristotle *Meteorologica* 365b1–6 (DK 68 A 97).

25. DK 68 A 93a (Seneca *Naturales quaestiones* 5.2); see chap. 12 (Aristotle and Earlier).

26. Analogies from sense experience occur at *Meteorologica* 341a17–27, 342a3–12 and 30–33, 344a25–28, 358a4–26, 358b8–16, and 366b14–25. The multiple explanations are at 341a12–31 (on the heat of the sun), 341b1–342a16 (on meteors), and 344a8–b8 (on comets). We may note that in *De generatione animalium*, too, Aristotle proposes the use of multiple explanations; he remarks with special reference to genetic resemblance that it is "not easy to state the cause of all things by citing a single manner of causation" (769b3–4).

27. *Meteorologica* 341a25–26.

It is clear that Aristotle does not share Epicurus' faith in this inductive method. In offering multiple explanations of how comets are formed, he writes: "Concerning things that are nonapparent to perception [τῶν ἀφανῶν τῇ αἰσθήσει] we think that a sufficient demonstration by argument has been given if we refer to what is possible; and from the present phenomena [ἐκ . . . τῶν νῦν φαινομένων] one might suppose that these events [concerning comets] happen approximately in this way."[28] While reflecting Aristotle's doubts, this statement is also an excellent guide to the claims made by the proponents of the method of signs. Dividing all occurrences into the phenomena and what is nonapparent, the proponents claim that scientific demonstration consists in using present observations ("the present phenomena" or, simply "phenomena") as the basis of inference for what is nonapparent. Though agreeing with Aristotle that in cases of multiple explanations each explanation is "possible," they differ from him in maintaining that this possibility is an actuality with respect to the general state of affairs that is being explained; and they differ, too, in upholding the general principle that there is no more certain scientific demonstration than the type of demonstration made by using the phenomena as signs.

It appears, therefore, that the method of multiple explanations was well developed before the time of Aristotle as part of the general method of using the phenomena as signs, and that Epicurus derived both his method of obtaining single explanations and that of obtaining multiple explanations from the early atomists. Both types of explanation follow from the principle that what is unobserved is similar to what is observed unless the phenomena provide a reason why it should be different. Since the phenomena may exhibit not just one, but a number of similarities with what is unobserved, none of which is counterevidenced by the phenomena, multiple explanations are as valid as single explanations.

28. Ibid., 344a5–7: ἐπεὶ δὲ περὶ τῶν ἀφανῶν τῇ αἰσθήσει νομίζομεν ἱκανῶς ἀποδεδεῖχθαι κατὰ τὸν λόγον, ἐὰν εἰς τὸ δυνατὸν ἀναγάγωμεν, ἔκ τε τῶν νῦν φαινομένων ὑπολάβοι τις ἂν ὧδε περὶ τούτων μάλιστα συμβαίνειν.

# PART VI

*Epicurus and
the Early Atomists*

# [ 19 ]

# Summary of Epicurus' Scientific Method

THIS study has attempted to show that Epicurus proposed two rules of investigation: a requirement for initial concepts to demarcate the problem, and a requirement for empirical facts to provide a solution. The initial concepts consist in an awareness of empirical facts; and empirical facts are known directly through perception. The two rules together constitute a single method of inquiry, that of inferring what is unobserved on the basis of what is observed. This method was known in antiquity as the method of using the phenomena as signs (σημεῖα) of what is unobserved.

The observations that serve as the basis of inference are uninterpreted presentations obtained as the direct result of an activity by a perceptual organ. In Epicurus' terminology, the organ of perception makes an "application" (ἐπιβολή) that results in a presentation of some feature of the world. What is presented in this way is in every case a real feature of the world. A perceptual presentation does not admit of being false or deceptive; rather, what it shows must be taken as existing exactly as it appears. Falsehood and error are in every case the result of an interpretation added to a perceptual presentation. Epicurus' followers expressed his doctrine by saying that all presentations, or, equivalently, all perceptions, are "true"; his position, therefore, may be said to be that whatever appears as a direct result of a perceptual act is true, or in brief that the phenomena are true. That perception shows, without exception, a real feature of the world is an initial assumption, laid down by Epicurus as a rule of investigation prior to all investigation. It follows that the organs of perception are the standards, or "criteria" (κριτήρια), by reference to which all beliefs are judged to be true or false.

Part of the difficulty in studying Epicurus' rules of investigation arises from some change in terminology from the time of Epicurus to that of later interpreters. As used so far in this summary, the term "perception" has the wide sense used by the later interpreters. Epicurus himself uses the term in a narrower sense; he distinguishes between "perceptions" (αἰσθήσεις) and "affections" (πάθη, or "feelings"), the former denoting perceptions of things external to our own persons, the latter denoting perceptions of our own conditions; both kinds of perception are viewed by Epicurus as acts of awareness of what is real. Another terminological problem concerns the use of the word "criterion." Epicurus applies this term to the organs of perception, for these show the facts by reference to which all beliefs are judged true or false. Later authors use the term to refer to the acts of perception; this coincides with Epicurus' own use. The later sources also use "criterion" in a wide sense to refer to the initial concepts of investigation; since these consist in a memory of what is perceived, this extension of usage is compatible with Epicurus' own usage. Diogenes Laertius' division of Epicurus' criteria into three kinds, perceptions, presumptions (that is, initial concepts of investigation), and affections, is thus compatible with Epicurus' understanding of criteria and his recognition of precisely two rules of inquiry.

Another difficulty concerning Epicurus' methodology is that the initial assumption that whatever we perceive is real seems to be subverted by the theory that is developed on the basis of this assumption. For the theory shows that the world consists of atoms and void, which are very different from what we perceive. Epicurus attempts to save the initial reliance on the perceptions by arguing that since, as the theory shows, every perception is produced from outside by particles that are real, what is perceived is nonetheless real. This is joined by another defense, which consists in pointing out that the theory would itself collapse if the facts on which it is based were eliminated. It follows that the falsity of the initial assumption would be no less in doubt than its truth and, moreover, that the whole scientific enterprise would collapse. Epicurus attempts to save scientific investigation by insisting from beginning to end that the phenomena must be accepted as real.

By relying on the phenomena as self-evidently real, the scientist seeks to discover through the use of reason what is nonapparent (ἄδηλον). All scientific inferences are verified or falsified by reference to the phenomena: they are true whenever there is "no counterwitnessing" (οὐϰ ἀντιμαρτύρησις), that is, whenever there is no counterevidence by the phenomena; and they are false whenever there is "counterwitnessing" (ἀντιμαρτύρησις), that is, when there is counterevidence by the phenomena. When there is counterwitnessing, a theory has observational consequences that are not confirmed directly by perception; in this case, there is a disagreement with the phenomena. When there is no counterwitnessing, the theory does not have observational consequences that are not confirmed directly by perception; in this case, there is an agreement with the phenomena. The failure to observe an observational consequence is sufficient to disprove a theory; for the scientist relies on a present collection of observations—the phenomena—as the total evidence for a theory.

An important restriction implicit in the notion of agreement is the principle that whatever is unobserved is like what is observed unless there is a reason to suppose a difference. This inductive principle is an application of the principle of indifference, which pervades all of Epicurean science. Accordingly, inductive claims about what is unobserved are true unless the phenomena furnish a specific reason why what is unobserved should be different from what is observed; that is, they are true by the principle of "no counterwitnessing." It follows that any counterinductive theory that is not supported by a specific reason for a difference is false by the principle of counterwitnessing. Although we have no explicit testimonies, the Epicurean position may be stated in this way: supposing that a counterinductive theory of this sort were true, then there would be no reason why the phenomena should not be different than they are, so that they would in fact be different from what they are and so would counterwitness the theory. It is beside the point to object that there might be a reason for a difference although we do not know it or do not yet know it. The scientist relies on presently known observations as the factual basis of inference, deducing from them all other facts.

Many events, especially events in the heavens, can be explained only by multiple explanations, that is, by several different theories. Epicurus and Lucretius defend multiple explanations as inductive inferences, whereby a distant phenomenon is recognized as having several similarities with what is observed nearby. Although only one of the multiple explanations applies to any particular event, all are true; for they are explanations of a general event that is divided into as many types as there are explanations.

In the *Letter to Herodotus,* Epicurus proves the fundamental theories of his physics by showing a disagreement of the contradictory with the phenomena—that is, by counterwitnessing—or by deducing the theory from previous conclusions. Induction is used in addition in the more specialized theories; in Epicurus' extant writings, by far its most important use is to support multiple explanations. The two methods of using the phenomena, the reduction of a hypothesis to an incompatibility with the phenomena and induction, are united in the single method of deducing from the phenomena what is unobserved. In the second and first centuries B.C., some followers of Epicurus, as attested by Philodemus, defended the coherence of Epicurus' method of inquiry by interpreting the method as a whole as an inductive method, arguing that all valid scientific inferences are ultimately inductions. According to them, even conclusions obtained by reduction to an incompatibility with the phenomena are basically inductive inferences. It is possible that Epicurus himself adopted this view; but if so, it did not affect the presentation of his fundamental theories in the *Letter to Herodotus.* Lucretius' use of induction suggests that he knew of the current controversy on induction and was a staunch defender of it, and that he may even have agreed that all of Epicurus' doctrines may be formulated as inductions. In general, however, Lucretius' choice of proofs seems to reflect Epicurus' own preferences: counterwitnessing predominates in Lucretius' presentation of the fundamental theories, and induction becomes important in the more specialized theories.

Epicurus derived his general method of inference, together with almost all of his fundamental theories and some of his specialized theories, from the early atomists. The early atomists proposed to deduce what is unobserved from the phenomena, in opposition to Parmenides' attempt to deduce what there is from a concept of being. The next chapter discusses further the origin of Epicurus' method of inference.

# The Early Atomists

IN the discussion of Epicurus' physical doctrines, it became apparent that Epicurus was indebted to the early atomists not only for his most basic theories but also for the general method of using the phenomena as signs of what is unobserved. It now remains to test this conclusion by examining the extant evidence concerning the early atomists' epistemology. This examination is the more important because it has generally been held that the early atomists took the position that the phenomena as such are not real, and that their view of scientific inference was very different from that of Epicurus.

Let us first consider the early atomists' methodology in general. Democritus is said to have written a treatise titled Κανών, or Κανόνες, in three books.[1] This appears to have treated the general topic of scientific inference, as did Epicurus' book by the same title. Sextus Empiricus mentions that in this treatise Democritus opposed demonstration (ἀπόδειξις), and that he made a contrast between the "dark" (σκοτίη) cognition of the senses and the "genuine" (γνησίη) cognition of the mind.[2] In addition, we have the detailed but suspect testimony, which Sextus attributes to a certain Diotimus, that Democritus recognized three criteria: the phenomena as a standard of what is unobserved, the concept as a standard of investigation, and the affections as a standard of choice and avoidance.[3] As previously discussed, this classification is identical

1. DK 68 B 10b.
2. Sextus Empiricus *Adv. math.* 8.327 (DK 68 B 10b) and 7.138 (DK 68 B 11).
3. Ibid., 7.140 (DK 68 A 111).

with that attributed to Epicurus; and this fact makes it doubtful whether it should be assigned to Democritus. Under the first criterion, Democritus is said to have approved Anaxagoras' dictum that the "phenomena are the sight of what is nonapparent." This particular testimony may well be authentic even though the scheme as a whole is unlikely to be Democritean as it stands. Another report concerning Epicurus' dependence on Democritus is the charge, preserved by Diogenes Laertius, that Epicurus plagiarized his book Κανών from the *Tripod* of Nausiphanes.[4] Nausiphanes is said to have been a Democritean and to have studied with the Skeptic Pyrrho; and Epicurus is said to have studied with Nausiphanes.[5] We have no details about what Epicurus took from Nausiphanes' book.

Although we have no firm evidence that Democritus framed any rule of investigation corresponding to Epicurus' requirement for concepts, we know from Aristotle and Sextus Empiricus that Democritus held that concepts are acquired empirically, so that "man," for example, is explained ostensively, without any definition, as a certain shape and color.[6] This view agrees with Epicurus' own claim that the initial concepts of investigation are memories of perceptual impressions.

For Democritus' view of the validity of the phenomena, we have a wide range of testimonies, including quotations from his own writings, from the time of Aristotle to Sextus Empiricus and later. This evidence looks contradictory and has been reviewed by many scholars in an attempt to resolve the contradictions.[7] To begin with, Aristotle repeatedly attributes to Democritus the view that the phenomena are "true." As has already been noted, Aristotle claims in *On Generation and Destruction* that the atomists thought that "the truth is in the phenomena" (or "in appearing," τἀληθὲς ἐν

4. DL 10.14. Diogenes mentions a certain Ariston as the author of the charge; but it is not clear which Ariston this is (if indeed the name is correctly transmitted). Estelle and Phillip De Lacy conjecture that Nausiphanes' *Tripod* probably dealt with the Empiricists' three standards, personal observation, ἱστορία or inquiry, and inference by similarity (*Philodemus*, rev. ed., 174); but there is no evidence for this. It seems to me at least as likely that Nausiphanes conceived of the "tripod" as resting on the three supports of concepts, perceptions, and affections, as attributed later to Democritus and to Epicurus.

5. DK 75 A 1–7.

6. See chap. 2, n. 37, for Democritus' concept of man. Hirzel suggests that the "germ" of Epicurus' notion of πρόληψις is in Democritus' philosophy (*Untersuchungen*, 118–21).

7. W. K. C. Guthrie presents a very useful survey of the testimonies in his *History of Greek Philosophy*, 2: 454–65. A detailed survey of the secondary literature on the sources is provided by Sassi (*Le teorie della percezione*, 199–203).

τῷ φαίνεσθαι).[8] Aristotle also claims in *On the Soul* that Democritus identified soul and intellect (νοῦς) because he supposed that "what is true is the phenomenon" (τὸ . . . ἀληθὲς εἶναι τὸ φαινόμενον); Aristotle adds that Democritus did not use "intellect" (νοῦς) as a faculty concerning the truth.[9] Last, in the *Metaphysics* Aristotle includes Democritus among thinkers who hold that "what appears in accordance with perception is necessarily true" (τὸ φαινόμενον κατὰ τὴν αἴσθησιν ἐξ ἀνάγκης ἀληθὲς εἶναι); and he explains that they hold this belief because they suppose that perception, which they regard as alteration (ἀλλοίωσις), is understanding (φρόνησις).[10]

By adding the qualification "in accordance with perception" to "phenomenon" in his statement in the *Metaphysics*, Aristotle makes explicit what is implicit in the other two uses of the term. In each case, the phenomenon is something given directly by perception; since perception is a process of physical alteration and a phenomenon is an immediate effect of this process, a phenomenon is free of any interpretation by a cognitive agency supposedly set over the physical process. The physical process of perception is itself a process of understanding, determining by itself that a phenomenon is true. Accordingly, the soul is identical with mind (νοῦς); for the soul, as the agent in the act of perception, judges what is true. In accusing Democritus of identifying soul with mind, Aristotle probably views mind, in accordance with his own theory, as a faculty that obtains by induction the primary truths of scientific investigation. In any case, Aristotle understands Democritus to reject any true inductive insight about the phenomena by taking the phenomena themselves as true. This criticism agrees with Aristotle's report about Democritus' view of concepts; for these concepts consist entirely in an accumulation of individual phenomena.

Just before the remarks in the *Metaphysics*, Aristotle explains that some persons came to the conclusion that the phenomena are true by noting that humans have different perceptions from one another and from other animals, and from themselves at different times, and claiming that there is no way of telling which are true and which are false. According to this view, "it is nonapparent which of these [perceptions] are true or false; for these are no more than those, but equally." He adds that for this reason Democritus maintained that "either nothing is true or it is nonapparent to

8. Aristotle *De generatione et corruptione* 315b9–10; see chap. 15 (The Shape and Size of the Infinite Atoms).
9. *De anima* 404a28–31.
10. *Metaphysics* 1009b12–15.

us."[11] This testimony has been interpreted by some scholars to
show that Democritus did not in fact hold the position that Aristotle assigns to him immediately afterward—that whatever appears in accordance with perception is true—but that in making
this latter judgment Aristotle is forcing his own interpretation on
Democritus along with other thinkers.[12] Democritus' skepticism is,
however, reconcilable with the view that the phenomena are true:
it is possible that Democritus, like Epicurus, made it an initial rule
of investigation that the phenomena are true (in the sense of
showing real features of the world) and that, unlike Epicurus, he
concluded on the basis of the theory developed by means of this
assumption that the phenomena are nothing but subjective impressions, all equally without truth; from this conclusion it follows
that either nothing is true or we cannot discover the truth.

In *On Generation and Destruction* Aristotle also attributes to the
atomists both the view that the truth is in the phenomena and the
view that the phenomena do not have objective existence. As Aristotle points out, Democritus maintained that "color is not; for
coloring is by position [of the atoms]."[13] Here, too, there is no
inconsistency in Aristotle's report, so long as we take the claim
that the truth is in the phenomena as an initial rule of investigation that subsequently leads to the discovery that the phenomena
are not real.

The most important source for Democritus' epistemology after
Aristotle is Sextus Empiricus. His testimony differs strikingly from
that of Aristotle in that he consistently attributes to Democritus
the view that there is *no* truth in sense perception. According to
Sextus, Democritus held that none of the objects of perception
"underlie" as externally real objects, but all are "empty affections";
this view, Sextus points out, is contrary to Epicurus', that all the
objects of perception "underlie" as externally real objects.[14] We are

11. Ibid., 1009b9–12: ποῖα οὖν τούτων ἀληθῆ ἢ ψευδῆ, ἄδηλον· οὐθὲν γὰρ μᾶλλον τάδε ἢ τάδε ἀληθῆ, ἀλλ' ὁμοίως. διὸ Δημόκριτός γέ φησιν ἤτοι οὐθὲν εἶναι
ἀληθὲς ἢ ἡμῖν γ' ἄδηλον. Theophrastus puts this οὐ μᾶλλον claim by saying that, according to Democritus, "no one person attains the truth more than any other" (*De
sensu* 69, DK 68 A 135).

12. See Natorp, *Forschungen,* 173–78, and Ross, *Aristotle's Metaphysics,* 1:275. Alfieri takes Aristotle's testimony as evidence that Democritus attacked the Protagorean theory that whatever appears is true by showing that this theory has the
absurd consequence that "nothing is true or it is nonapparent to us"; Alfieri suggests that Democritus concluded that reason is the sole judge of what is the case
(*Atomos idea,* 1st ed., 127–28). See also n. 32 below.

13. Aristotle *De generatione et corruptione* 316a1–2.

14. Sextus Empiricus *Adv. math.* 8.184 and 355; cf. 8.6 and 7.135. See also
above, chap. 8 (Truth, Falsehood, and Evidence).

fortunate that Sextus supplies abundant quotations from Democritus to support his interpretation, among them the saying: "By convention [νόμῳ] [there is] sweet, by convention bitter, by convention warm, by convention cold, by convention color, but in truth [ἐτεῇ] atoms and void."[15] Further, Sextus notes that although in his book *Confirmations* (Κρατυντήρια) Democritus "promised to assign the power of proof [τὸ κράτος τῆς πίστεως] to the perceptions, he is found nonetheless to convict them, for he says: 'in reality we understand nothing true, but what shifts according to the disposition of the body and of the things that enter and those that resist.'"[16] The senses are here presented as admitting that since they recognize only subjective impressions, they are without understanding; this admission, which is forced from the senses as though they were prosecuted in a court of law, is in conflict, according to Sextus, with Democritus' initial promise to assign to the senses the power of proving claims. Sextus also reports that Democritus, along with Plato, attacked Protagoras' view that "every presentation [φαντασία] is true" on the ground that this results in an overturning (περιτροπή) of this very view; for if every presentation is true, then the presentation that "it is not the case that every presentation is true" is also true.[17]

According to Sextus, Democritus combined the view that there is no truth in sense perception with the view that the truth is discoverable by reason. This interpretation is in conformity with Sextus' threefold division of all thinkers, who believe that something is true, into those who hold that only objects of perception are true, those who hold that only objects of thought (νοητά) are true, and those who hold that both objects of perception and objects of thought are true. Sextus assigns Democritus, along with Plato, to the second category.[18] Sextus adds the explanation that according to Democritus none of the objects of perception "underlie," since the atoms, which make up all things, are devoid of any perceptible property.

In support of his interpretation of Democritus as a rationalist, Sextus notes that in his book Κανόνες Democritus shows that sensory perception is unreliable as a means of judging the truth, whereas mental cognition is reliable, by calling the former "dark" (σκοτίη, connoting "bastard") and the latter "genuine" (γνησίη).[19]

15. Ibid., 7.135 (DK 68 B 9).
16. Ibid., 7.136 (DK 68 B 9).
17. Ibid., 7.389 (DK 68 A 114).
18. Ibid., 8.6 and 8.56.
19. Ibid., 7.139 (DK 68 B 11).

# 342     *Epicurus and the Early Atomists*

Sextus then offers a quotation in which Democritus distinguishes the "dark" type of cognition, identified as sight, hearing, smell, taste, and touch, from the "genuine" cognition, which Democritus asserts to be "distinct" from the other. According to Sextus, Democritus preferred the genuine to the dark cognition and went on to say: "whenever the dark [cognition] can no longer see what is less [ἐπ' ἔλαττον], or hear or smell or taste or perceive by touch, but [there is a passage] to what is finer [ἐπὶ λεπτότερον]. . . ." Unfortunately this quotation is incomplete, so that it is not clear what the place of genuine cognition is in the progression. What is clear is that Democritus sets out a cognitive progression from the gross objects of sense perception to objects that are too fine to be perceived, and that he held that if anything is known, it is known by a faculty distinct from the senses. Sextus interprets the genuine type of cognition as reason (λόγος) and takes this to be Democritus' criterion of truth.

Although Sextus thus presents Democritus as a rationalist, he also suggests that Democritus eliminated the possibility of knowledge altogether. His evidence includes the following three excerpts from Democritus' *On Forms* (Περὶ ἰδεῶν): "man must know by this rule [κανόνι] that he is removed from truth [ἐτεῆς]"; "this argument too shows that in truth [ἐτεῇ] we know nothing about anything, but one's opinion is for each a changing condition [ἐπι-ρυσμίη]"; and "it will be clear that in truth [ἐτεῇ] there is no way of knowing what sort each thing is."[20] Sextus says of the excerpts and of the quotations on the senses, already cited, that "in these Democritus assails just about all apprehension, even though he singles out only the perceptions for attack."[21] In agreement with this interpretation, Sextus conjectures that "perhaps" Democritus eliminated demonstration (ἀπόδειξις), since in his Κανόνες he strongly opposed it.[22]

Sextus himself held that if the senses do not show us what is real, neither can reason show us what is real, since reason depends ultimately on the evidence of the senses. Sextus also maintained that concepts are based ultimately on sensory experience. For Sextus, then, it follows that by denying all validity to sense perception, Plato and Democritus "throw things into confusion and undermine not only the truth about existent things but also our concepts of

20. Ibid., 7.137 (DK 68 B 6, 7 and 8). I accept Hermann Langerbeck's interpretation of ἐπιρυσμίη as "Umformung, Umgestaltung" (ΔΟΞΙΣ ΕΠΙΡΥΣΜΙΗ. *Studien zu Demokrits Ethik und Erkenntnislehre*, 113).
21. Sextus Empiricus *Adv. math.* 7.137.
22. Ibid., 8.327.

them."[23] It is not clear from the information provided by Sextus whether Democritus agreed that if the senses do not show what is real, knowledge is impossible for us. But such a position is at least consistent with Sextus' testimony; and it receives support from Aristotle's report that Democritus inferred the impossibility of human knowledge from the claim that sensory impressions are all equally true.

Sextus' assessment of Democritus covers a range of interpretation that is exemplified by other Hellenistic criticisms. Among Democritus' Epicurean critics, Epicurus' friend and pupil Colotes made the accusation that by repudiating the senses, as shown by the assertion that "color is by convention" (and so on) "but in truth there are atoms and void," Democritus made it impossible for a person even to conceive of himself as living.[24] Plutarch, who reports this criticism, responds that Democritus at least recognized the consequences of his own teaching, whereas the Epicureans proposed the same doctrines but failed to recognize that these result in the elimination of perceptible qualities.[25] A century or two after Plutarch, the Epicurean Diogenes of Oenoanda referred to the same saying of Democritus to accuse him of making both knowledge and life impossible: it follows, he claims, that "it is not only impossible to find the truth but we will not even be able to live."[26]

Colotes' objection to Democritus' view of perception was part of a full-scale attack in which Colotes also accused Democritus of eliminating all distinctions. As Plutarch reports, Colotes accused Democritus of throwing all of life into confusion by asserting of each thing that it is "no more of this sort than of that." Plutarch responds by accusing Colotes of putting a false interpretation on Democritus' saying "δέν is no more than οὐδέν," that is, that "body is no more than void"; this statement means, according to Plutarch, that both body and void are equally real. Plutarch also notes that Democritus attacked Protagoras at length precisely for holding that "nothing is more of this sort than of that"; and he attempts to turn Colotes' charge against the Epicureans by claiming that it applies to Epicurus' own theory of perception.[27]

23. Ibid., 8.56.
24. Plutarch *Adv. Colotem* 1110e.
25. Ibid., 1110f–1111e.
26. Diogenes of Oenoanda fr. 6 col. 2.2–12 Chilton.
27. Plutarch *Adv. Colotem* 1108f–1109a and following. Phillip De Lacy argues that Colotes is here misinterpreting Democritus' view that the atoms are "no more" one shape than another; according to De Lacy, Colotes takes this to imply that all

In this criticism of Democritus, Colotes seems to accuse Democritus not only of making knowledge impossible, but also of eliminating the truth, by allowing that anything can be of any sort. Plutarch defends Democritus by claiming that he did assert that there are atoms and void; Plutarch thus takes Democritus as a rationalist, who holds that through reason we are able to discover the truth.

Cicero states explicitly in the *Academica* that Democritus abolished not only all knowledge but also all truth. In a clear attempt to muster support for skepticism, Cicero includes Democritus in a long list of thinkers whom he claims as skeptical forerunners of the Academics; and he asserts that whereas the Academics do not go so far as to deny that there is truth but deny only that anything can be apprehended, Democritus denied altogether that there is truth.[28] A little earlier in the *Academica*, Cicero attributes to Democritus the less extreme view that nature "has hidden the truth utterly in the depths."[29] This appears to be a version of Democritus' statement, as reported by Diogenes Laertius, that "in truth [ἐτεῇ] we know nothing, for truth is in the depths."[30] Diogenes cites this statement as evidence that Democritus was a forerunner of the Pyrrhonist Skeptics; and, like Cicero, he takes the claim that truth is in the depths to mean that the truth is hidden from humankind. This interpretation is in agreement with Aristotle's testimony in the *Metaphysics*; on the other hand, the extreme claim that Democritus abolished all truth seems to be an inference made by Hellenistic thinkers.

Our final testimony from the Hellenistic period is a quotation from Democritus preserved by Galen. Galen introduces the fragment by asserting that reason (λόγος), which must start with evidence (ἐνάργεια), cannot be trustworthy if it spurns that with which it starts. This is standard Hellenistic doctrine: reason must be able to rely on the evidence presented by the senses if its con-

---

perceptible distinctions would be destroyed, since, in the Epicurean view, an infinity of shapes implies an infinity of perceptible types ("Colotes' First Criticism of Democritus," in *Isonomia*, 74–76). De Lacy suggests further that Democritus' οὐ μᾶλλον "carries no suggestion of scepticism" ("οὐ μᾶλλον and the antecedents of ancient scepticism," 59). I agree that Democritus' use of οὐ μᾶλλον does not imply falsehood or doubt, but it seems to me unlikely that Colotes would infer the destruction of phenomenal distinctions from an infinity of perceptible shapes; nor is Colotes accusing Democritus of destroying perceptible distinctions only, but of destroying all distinctions whatsoever.

28. Cicero *Academica* 2.73.
29. Ibid., 2.32: [natura] . . . in profundo veritatem . . . penitus abstruserit.
30. DL 9.72 (DK 68 B 117).

clusions are to be sound. Galen then adds that Democritus knew this; for when he slandered the phenomena (φαινόμενα) by saying that "by convention is color, by convention sweet, by convention bitter, but in truth atoms and void," he made the senses speak to the mind as follows:

> Miserable mind, who after taking your proofs from us overthrow us: that overthrow is your downfall [πτῶμά τοι τὸ κατάβλημα].[31]

Using a metaphor from wrestling, the senses here accuse the mind of taking from them the truths on which the mind's conclusions are based, and then rejecting the validity of sense perception; this rejection is the downfall of the mind itself, for its conclusions are supported entirely by the evidence of the senses. The senses and the mind are here viewed as antagonists in a legal suit in which each tries to convict the other of not being capable of attaining the truth. The claim "by convention color . . . but in truth atoms and void" must be viewed in the context of this debate. It is a claim made by the mind against the senses, asserting that it knows the truth, whereas the senses do not. The senses reply by maintaining that if they do not recognize the truth, neither does the mind.

Galen's fragment shows that Democritus did in fact assign to the senses the power of proof, as Sextus reports he promised in his *Confirmations*. Sextus writes that Democritus then convicted the senses of not knowing anything for certain. As it turns out, it is the mind that convicts the senses by relying on their evidence. Although the senses are initially promised the power of proof, and in fact have the power of proof, the mind presumes to take it away from them, only to find itself deprived of all of its power at the very moment when it attempts to remove that of the senses. The claim that "in truth" there are atoms and void whereas the phenomena are not real thus turns out to be self-invalidating: if it is true, and the phenomena are not real, then the claim rests on false evidence and is false. Reason, therefore, cannot attain the truth, since it relies on the evidence of the senses. Nor do the senses attain the truth; for as the reasoning mind demonstrates, supposing that there is truth in the phenomena, it follows that the phenomena are nothing but subjective impressions, so that there is no

---

31. Galen *On Medical Experience* 15, p. 114 Walzer (fr. 23b D; DK 68 B 125): τάλαινα φρήν, παρ' ἡμέων λαβοῦσα τὰς πίστεις ἡμέας καταβάλλεις; πτῶμά τοι τὸ κατάβλημα.

346    *Epicurus and the Early Atomists*

truth in the phenomena. The conclusion, as attested by Aristotle, is that either nothing is true or we cannot attain the truth. It is understood that we cannot attain the truth because we have just two methods of cognition, sense perception and reason relying on the evidence of the senses.

In the past, scholars have generally attempted to adjudicate between Aristotle's testimony and that of the later sources by rejecting, as an exaggeration or misinterpretation, Aristotle's claim that Democritus held that the phenomena are real, and by proposing either that Democritus assigned partial validity to the senses or that he recognized only reason as a means of determining the truth.[32] Aristotle's and the later testimonies are, however, much

32. Some representative views are as follows. Gomperz suggests that according to Democritus the senses' evidence does not extend far enough and is not wholly to be rejected, and is moreover capable of self-correction (*Griechische Denker*, 300–01). Similarly, Hirzel argues (against Zeller) that Aristotle shows that Democritus did rely on the senses, but that Aristotle is mistaken in attributing to him the view that they are absolutely reliable (*Untersuchungen*, 110–17). Hirzel is followed by Adolf Brieger ("Demokrits angebliche Leugnung der Sinneswahrheit," esp. 63). Both contend that Democritus and Epicurus have the same view of the reliability of the senses (*Untersuchungen*, 117–34; "Democrits angebliche Leugnung," 57). Kurt von Fritz proposes that Democritus found in the qualities of sense perception an "image" ("Abbild") of the structure of things, even though this image is confused and dark (*Philosophie und Sprachlicher Ausdruck bei Demokritos, Plato und Aristoteles*, 22–23). Luria inclines to a more rationalist interpretation, proposing that the senses must be cleansed of contradiction by the genuine type of cognition, and that all our thoughts must be tested against certain postulates of being ("Zwei Demokrit-Studien," in *Isonomia*, 40–41). Probably the most influential interpretation in this century has been that of Helene Weiss. Weiss argues that sense perception is reliable so long as we go beyond it, and that it is a starting point, as well as a point of return, of cognition ("Democritus' Theory of Cognition," 50). Weiss also suggests that Aristotle attributed to Democritus the view that the objects of sense perception are true for the reason that Democritus did not recognize νοῦς, Aristotle's intuitive faculty, as a source of knowledge, and hence did not recognize immaterial universals as objects of knowledge. According to Weiss, Aristotle viewed the atoms, which are the material causes of perception, as belonging to the domain of perception (see esp. 52–54). Guthrie agrees with Weiss' interpretation (*History of Greek Philosophy*, 2: 456 and 463), as do Francesco Romano ("Esperienza e ragione in Democrito," in *Democrito e l'atomismo antico*, 207–23) and Fritz Jürss (*Zum Erkenntnisproblems bei den frühgriechischen Denkern*, esp. 107–12). Very similarly to Weiss, Langerbeck maintains that Aristotle took Democritus' conception of being as restricted to αἰσθητά for the reason that Democritus did not recognize the Platonic type of οὐσία (ΔΟΞΙΣ ΕΠΙΡΥΣΜΙΗ, 6); and Alfieri proposes that Aristotle's interpretation reflects the fact that he found only matter and not also essence or teleology in Democritus' system (*Atomos idea*, 1st ed., 133 and 126). In my opinion, it is highly unlikely that Aristotle would have obliterated the distinction between what is perceived and what is not perceived, which is commonplace among post-Parmenidean physical thinkers and which Aristotle clearly preserves elsewhere in his discussions of the early thinkers, by subsuming the latter under the former; and Aristotle's interpretation of Democritus as one who eliminated νοῦς seems to me to rest precisely on the claim that Democritus took the immediate objects of

more accurate than has been thought and indeed complement each other. As Aristotle maintains, Democritus did suppose that "the truth is in the phenomena"—that is, that everything appearing directly to the senses is real. But Democritus proposed this as an initial rule of investigation, which is subsequently shown to be invalid. The later authors are right to point out that Democritus denied any truth to the phenomena; for the theory that is developed on the basis of the assumption that the phenomena are real shows that the phenomenon are not real. Aristotle thus focuses on the initial rule, on which all of atomic theory rests, whereas the later authorities focus on the consequences of the theory. This change of emphasis may be explained by the difference between Democritus' position and that of Epicurus later on. Epicurus made the same initial assumption as Democritus, but subsequently refused to give up the assumption. Contrary to Democritus, Epicurus insisted that the theory does not show that the phenomena are not real. Accordingly, Democritus' position came to be viewed as the opposite of Epicurus': Democritus was recognized as one who acknowledged the falsehood of the phenomena whereas Epicurus did not.

Those Hellenistic thinkers who interpreted Democritus as a rationalist rather than a skeptic seem to have been misled by isolated sayings of Democritus, taken out of context. But there is a sense in which they may well be right. Since reason is defeated by its reliance on the senses, the possibility remains that reason may nonetheless attain the truth *if* it functions entirely without any reliance on sense perception. It is very possible that in distinguishing reason as "genuine" cognition from sense perception as "dark" cognition Democritus had in mind the use of reason entirely by itself, without any reference to sense perception. As Democritus' own experiment in the use of reason illustrates, such a use of reason is denied to mankind. In this position Democritus is in agreement with Parmenides, Plato, and others: humankind cannot transcend sensory experience to achieve a pure rational insight into what there is. That is why Democritus concludes that "either nothing is true or it is nonapparent to us"; it is possible that

---

sense perception as true. My interpretation is perhaps closest to that of C. C. W. Taylor in "Pleasure, Knowledge and Sensation in Democritus." Taylor suggests that Democritus took the evidence of the senses unquestioningly as a starting point of investigation, that the theory in turn showed that the senses are weak (since they give conflicting reports), and that the theory is therefore asserted only with the confidence due to the weakness of the evidence (see esp. 20–24). This interpretation seems to me essentially correct, although it does not go far enough.

reason by itself may attain the truth, but we at any rate are excluded from this use of reason.

If Democritus was a rationalist, then, his rationalism, being unattainable by humankind, is empty; and it is not exemplified by Democritus' own scientific investigations. In these investigations Democritus was an empiricist who used reason to reach beyond the phenomena by taking the phenomena as facts.

This conclusion agrees with our earlier analysis of Democritus' physical doctrines as deductions from the phenomena. Democritus opposed Parmenides and at the same time tried to save human experience and human inquiry by attempting to infer all of reality from the phenomena. This was an empirical enterprise, resting on the assumption that the phenomena are real. Parmenidean rationalist assumptions were excluded, and any similarities with Parmenidean claims were obtained by inference from the phenomena. Democritus' bold venture ended in skepticism, but it also resulted in a marvelously detailed system of explanation of the physical world. This system may be regarded as a testimony to the power of human inquiry, including its limitations. For Democritus, it was ultimately a testimony to the futility of human inquiry: there remains only reason divorced from all perception, and from this humankind is wholly cut off.

Epicurus later attempted to make scientific investigation meaningful once again by refusing to take the step that forced Democritus to the dilemma that either there is no truth or it is beyond the reach of humankind. By retaining the initial assumption that the phenomena are real, Epicurus proposed to save the atomic theory and, with it, all of human inquiry.

The testimonies that have been cited show that Democritus concerned himself deeply with the problem of scientific method.[33] Since Democritus clearly did attempt to find the rules or standards by which the truth is measured, he may be said to have been the founder of canonic, the branch of inquiry that Epicurus recog-

33. Langerbeck maintains that no Pre-Socratic had the concepts of appearance and perception; that these originated with Plato; and that Democritus did not treat of any general problem of αἴσθησις or of knowledge at all (ΔΟΞΙΣ ΕΠΙΡΥΣΜΙΗ, esp. 105, 110, and 114). Langerbeck's position has been attacked in detail (by, among others, Alfieri in "Una nuova interpretazione di Protagora e di Democrito"), and his general thesis is clearly untenable. Langerbeck's interpretation has, however, had some influence on subsequent scholarship. Though with judicious caution, Guthrie prefaces his discussion of Democritean epistemology with the claim that "epistemology . . . occupied a much humbler place in the mind of a fifth-century thinker" than later, and that "we must not expect to find it discussed for its own sake" at this period (*History of Greek Philosophy*, 2: 454.). This statement seems to me to conflict with Democritus' own preserved sayings.

nized later as a preliminary to all physical investigation. It is not clear from our testimonies whether Democritus originally formulated the two rules of investigation that Epicurus proposed later, but in effect Democritus adopted these rules by proposing to take the phenomena as signs of what is unobserved. It is very possible that Democritus' reported disagreement with Protagoras consisted in Democritus insisting, like Epicurus later, that what is presented directly by the senses as a phenomenon must be kept distinct from the addition of any opinion. As for the early atomists' method of inference, our earlier discussion indicates that the early atomists, like the Epicureans, used both induction and the reduction of a hypothesis to an incompatibility with the phenomena. Although there is no evidence that the early atomists themselves used the terms "witnessing" and "no witnessing" to designate the criteria of truth and falsehood for perceptible objects, and "no counterwitnessing" and "counterwitnessing" to designate the criteria of truth and falsehood for scientific theories, it follows from the early atomists' view of the phenomena as signs that in effect they used the same criteria as the Epicureans.

After Democritus, others continued to use the phenomena as signs, but attempts were also made to find certainty by other means. Plato and Aristotle offered new theories of scientific explanation that, by admitting certain primary truths that transcend the phenomena, were intended to make scientific conclusions safe from collapsing through the imperfections of the sensory evidence. Plato's opposition to the use of the phenomena as signs accounts for much of the anti-Platonic bias of Epicurus' writings. Aristotle not only opposed, but also was clearly indebted to, the method of using the phenomena as signs, or the method of "signs" simply, as Aristotle called it. Aristotle both criticized the method for not having demonstrative validity and used it at times to give tentative support to his own theories. It is therefore appropriate that Aristotle should close his *Posterior Analytics*, a work devoted to his own method of scientific inquiry, with a parting look at the method of signs. Using the terms δόξα, "opinion," and λογισμός, "calculation," which are key terms in Epicurus' use of signs and which may be said to characterize the method of signs as a whole, Aristotle contrasts these notions with his own notions of ἐπιστήμη, scientific reasoning, and νοῦς, inductive insight. The former, Aristotle charges, are receptive of falsehood, whereas the latter are always true.[34] Aristotle's entire system of scientific demonstration may be

---

34. Aristotle *Posterior Analytics* 100b5–17.

viewed as an attempt to correct the shortcomings of the method of signs while yet preserving an empirical foundation for scientific inquiry.

Epicurus later reaffirmed the method of signs. As a faithful adherent of the method, he used it to correct some of the conclusions obtained earlier by his atomist predecessors by the same method. In this endeavor, Epicurus continued the scientific program of admitting no scientific theories as true except those that follow from the phenomena. At the same time, Epicurus refused to give up the initial assumption that the phenomena are real. Like Democritus, he recognized that the theory itself collapses if the initial assumption is eliminated; unlike Democritus, he retained the initial assumption and preserved the theory.

As a result of the accidents of textual transmission, the method of using the phenomena as signs of what is unobserved has largely been lost from view. This study has aimed to show that this method, which consists in deducing scientific theories from the facts given directly by sensory experience, formed an important empirical tradition of scientific inquiry from the time of Democritus to Epicurus and later, and that ancient atomism is a product of this method of inquiry. The fundamental aim of this method was to base scientific inferences on incontrovertible facts, as ascertained directly by sense perception. Like Sir Isaac Newton much later, Democritus and Epicurus might have claimed *hypotheses non fingo*; for they, too, refused to admit any theory which was not "deduced from the phenomena."[35]

35. Newton writes in the "General Scholion" of his *Principia*: "Hypotheses non fingo. Quidquid enim ex phaenomenis non deducitur, hypothesis vocanda est."

# Glossary of
# Epicurean
# Terms

ἄδηλον   nonapparent; unobservable; what cannot be perceived.

αἴσθησις   perception; an activity of the sense organs (and, by extension, of the mind) resulting in an impression produced directly from outside, without the addition of any interpretation by the mind.

ἀνασκευή   removal; the hypothetical elimination of a phenomenon as a result of the elimination of something nonapparent. The followers of Epicurus used this term to designate the method of counterwitnessing (ἀντιμαρτύρησις).

ἀντιμαρτύρησις   counterwitnessing; counterevidence; the incompatibility of something nonapparent with a phenomenon. The method of counterwitnessing is the method of falsifying a claim about what is nonapparent and hence of verifying its contradictory.

ἀπόδειξις   demonstration; showing by argument (that is, by λογισμός, "calculation") something nonapparent.

δόξα   opinion; belief. Opinions are judgments about the phenomena or about what is unobserved; and there is no more certain type of cognition than true opinion. All scientific theories are opinions.

εἴδωλον   eidolon, image (Latin *simulacrum, imago*); a network of atoms that enters the eyes or the mind. By entering the eyes or the mind in quick succession, the eidola produce vision or thought.

ἐνάργεια   evidence; a presentation obtained directly by the senses or the mind from outside, without any interpretation by the mind. The term is synonymous with φαντασία.

ἐναργής   evident; not requiring demonstration. All immediate objects of perception, and consequently all presumptions, are evident.

ἐπαίσθησις  perception; immediate perception. The term is synonymous with αἴσθησις; the prefix ἐπ– is intended to show that this is an immediate response by the perceptual organ to external influences, without any interpretation by the mind.

ἐπιβολή  application; an act by which the senses or the mind apprehend an object, either (in the case of both senses and the mind) by obtaining a perceptual impression or (in the case of the mind) by making an interpretation that is verified by the phenomena (whether directly by ἐπιμαρτύρησις or indirectly by οὐκ ἀντιμαρτύρησις).

ἐπιλογισμός  calculation; reasoning about the phenomena; an analysis of the phenomena. The prefix ἐπ– signifies that this is a calculation directed at the phenomena.

ἐπιμαρτύρησις  witnessing; direct confirmation by a phenomenon. The method of witnessing is the method of verifying a claim concerning what is expected to be perceived; the claim is verified when there is a presentation (φαντασία) of what was expected.

κατάληψις  apprehension; an assent to a claim that is necessarily true. This is a Stoic term, taken over by the followers of Epicurus to designate a true opinion.

κριτήριον  criterion; instrument of judgment; standard of truth. Epicurus' criteria are the senses and the mind responding directly to stimuli from outside.

λογισμός  calculation; reasoning. Three important types of λογισμός are ἀναλογισμός, analogy, ἐπιλογισμός, an analysis of the phenomena, and συλλογισμός, reasoning used to draw a conclusion.

οὐκ ἀντιμαρτύρησις  no counterwitnessing; the contradictory of "counterwitnessing"; the compatibility (or "agreement," συμφωνία) of something nonapparent with the phenomena. The method of no counterwitnessing is the method of verifying a claim about what is nonapparent.

οὐκ ἐπιμαρτύρησις  no witnessing; the contradictory of "witnessing." The method of no witnessing is the method of falsifying a claim about what is expected to be perceived; the claim is falsified by the absence of the expected presentation.

πάθος  affection; feeling. The two primary affections are pleasure and pain. Along with the perceptions, (αἰσθήσεις), the affections furnish the basic facts of scientific inference.

πρόληψις  presumption; first concept; initial concept; preinvestigative concept. A presumption is empirically acquired, and all investigations are conducted by reference to presumptions.

προσμένον  waiting to appear; expected to appear; expected to be evident. All investigation concerns either προσμένοντα or ἄδηλα; and an opinion concerning something προσμένον is verified by witnessing (ἐπιμαρτύρησις) and falsified by no witnessing (οὐκ ἐπιμαρτύρησις).

σημεῖον   sign; a self-evident fact on which an inference is based. All signs are phenomena; and they signify either what is expected to appear or what is nonapparent.

σημειοῦσθαι   use a sign; infer. The phenomena are used as signs, either to conjecture what will appear or to discover what is nonapparent.

τηρεῖν   observe; keep in one's awareness an object of perception.

φαινόμενον   phenomenon; an object appearing directly to the senses or the mind in an act of perception, without any interpretation by the mind.

φαντασία   presentation; the appearance of an object of perception, without any interpretation by the mind.

# Bibliography

### ANCIENT SOURCES

The following list includes the major texts, commentaries, and translations that have been consulted in addition to the collections listed under "Abbreviations" (p. 15). All the translations in this book are my own.

*Alexander of Aphrodisias*

*De anima liber cum mantissa.* Edited by Ivo Bruns. Vol. 2, pt. 1 of *Commentaria in Aristotelem Graeca: Supplementum Aristotelicum.* Berlin: G. Reimer, 1887.
*In librum de sensu commentarium.* Edited by Paulus Wendland. Vol. 3, pt. 1 of *Commentaria in Aristotelem Graeca.* Berlin: G. Reimer, 1901.

*Aristotle*

*De anima.* Edited by Sir David Ross. With commentary. Oxford: Clarendon Press, 1961.
*Ars rhetorica.* Edited by W. D. Ross. Oxford: Clarendon Press, 1959.
*Categoriae et liber de interpretatione.* Edited by L. Minio-Paluello. Oxford: Clarendon Press, 1949.
*De generatione animalium.* Edited by H. J. Drossaart Lulofs. Oxford: Clarendon Press, 1972.
*On Coming-to-be and Passing-away (De generatione et corruptione).* Edited by H. H. Joachim. With commentary. Oxford: Clarendon Press, 1922.
*Metaphysics.* Edited by W. D. Ross. With commentary. 2 vols. Oxford: Clarendon press, 1924.
*Meteorologica.* Edited by F. H. Fobes. Cambridge: Harvard University Press, 1919.

355

*Parva naturalia.* Edited by Sir David Ross. Oxford: Clarendon Press, 1955.

*Physics.* Edited by W. D. Ross. With commentary. Oxford: Clarendon Press, 1936.

*The Physics.* Translated by Philip H. Wicksteed and Francis M. Cornford. 2 vols. Rev. ed. Loeb Classical Library. London: Heinemann, 1957.

*Prior and Posterior Analytics.* Edited by W. D. Ross. With commentary. Oxford: Clarendon Press, 1949.


### Cicero

*Academica.* In *De natura deorum. Academica,* translated by Horace Rackham. Loeb Classical Library. London: Heinemann, 1933.

*De divinatione libri duo.* Edited by Arthur Stanley Pease. With commentary. University of Illinois Studies in Language and Literature. Vol. 6, nos. 2 and 3 (1920); vol. 8, nos. 2 and 3 (1923). Reprint Darmstadt: Wissenschaftliche Buchgesellschaft, 1963.

*De finibus bonorum et malorum, libri I, II.* Edited by J. S. Reid. Cambridge: Cambridge University Press, 1925.

*De finibus.* Translated by Horace Rackham. 2d ed. Loeb Classical Library. London: Heinemann, 1931.

*De natura deorum.* Edited by A. S. Pease. 2 vols. With commentary. Cambridge: Harvard University Press, 1955, 1958.

*De natura deorum.* Edited by M. van den Bruwaene. 3 vols. Collection Latomus, vols. 107, 154, 175. Brussels, 1970, 1978, 1981.


### Demetrius Lacon

De Falco, Vittorio, ed. *L'epicureo Demetrio Lacone.* Naples: R. Università e R. Accademia di Archeologia, Lettere e Belli Arti, 1923.


### Democritus

Luria, Salomo, ed. *Democritea.* Leningrad: Acad. Nauk, 1970.


### Diogenes Laertius

*Vitae Philosophorum.* Edited by H. S. Long. 2 vols. Oxford: Clarendon Press, 1964.


### Diogenes Oenoandensis

Chilton, C. W., ed. *Diogenes Oenoandensis Fragmenta.* Leipzig: Teubner, 1967.

*Diogenes of Oenoanda: The Fragments.* Translated by C. W. Chilton. With commentary. Oxford: Oxford University Press, 1971.

Smith, Martin Ferguson. "Fragments of Diogenes of Oenoanda Discovered and Rediscovered." *American Journal of Archaeology* 74 (1970): 51–62.

———. "New Fragments of Diogenes of Oenoanda." *American Journal of Archaeology* 75 (1971):357–89.

———. "Two New Fragments of Diogenes of Oenoanda." *Journal of Hellenic Studies* 92 (1972):147–55.

———. *Thirteen New Fragments of Diogenes of Oenoanda.* Österreichische Akademie der Wissenschaften, Philosophisch-historische Klasse, Denkschriften, vol. 117. Vienna, 1974.

## Epicurus

Arrighetti, Graziano, ed. and trans. *Epicuro: Opere.* 2d ed. With commentary. Turin: Einaudi, 1973.

Bailey, Cyril, ed. and trans. *Epicurus: The Extant Remains.* With commentary. Oxford: Clarendon Press, 1926.

Bignone, Ettore, trans. *Epicuro.* With commentary. Bari: Laterza, 1920.

Boer, Emilie, ed. and trans. *Epikur: Brief an Pythokles.* Deutsche Akademie der Wissenschaften zu Berlin, Institut für hellenistisch-römische Philosophie, no. 3. Berlin: Akademie-Verlag, 1954.

Bollack, Jean, ed. *La Pensée du plaisir. Épicure: Textes moraux, commentaires.* Paris: Editions de Minuit, 1975.

Bollack, Jean; Bollack, Mayotte; and Wismann, Heinz, eds. and trans. *La Lettre d'Épicure.* With commentary. Paris: Editions de Minuit, 1971.

Bollack, Jean, and Laks, André, eds. and trans. *Épicure à Pythoclès.* With commentary. Lille: Publications de l'Université de Lille, 1978.

Diano, Carlo, ed. *Epicuri Ethica et Epistulae.* With commentary. 2d ed. Florence: Sansoni, 1974.

von der Muehll, P. ed. *Epicuri Epistulae tres et Ratae Sententiae.* Leipzig: Teubner, 1922.

Usener, Hermannus, ed. *Epicurea.* Leipzig, 1887.

Vogliano, Achilles, ed. *Epicuri et Epicureorum scripta in Herculanensibus papyris servata.* Berlin: Weidmann, 1928.

## Anonymous Epicureans

Schmid, W., ed. *Ethica Epicurea Pap. herc. 1251.* Studia Herculanensia fasc. 1. Leipzig: O. Harrassowitz, 1939.

Scott, Walter, ed. *Fragmenta Herculanensia.* Oxford: Clarendon Press, 1885.

## Galen

Kalbfleisch, Carolus, ed. *Galeni Institutio Logica.* Leipzig: Teubner, 1896.

Kühn, D. Carolus Gottlob, ed. *Claudii Galeni Opera Omnia.* 20 vols. Leipzig: C. Cnobloch, 1821–33.

Marquardt, I.; Mueller, I.; and Helmreich, G., eds. *Claudii Galeni Pergameni Scripta Minora.* 3 vols. Leipzig: Teubner, 1884, 1891, 1893.
Walzer, R., ed. and trans. *Galen: On Medical Experience.* Oxford: University Press, 1944.

*Hermarchus*

Krohn, Carl W. G. *Der Epikureer Hermarchos.* Berlin: Weidmann, 1921.

*Hippocrates*

*Hippocrates and the Fragments of Heracleitus.* Translated by W. H. S. Jones and E. T. Withington. 4 vols. Loeb Classical Library. London: Heinemann, 1923–31.
Littré, Emile, ed. and trans. *Oeuvres complètes d'Hippocrate.* 10 vols. Paris: J. B. Baillière, 1839–61.

*Lucretius*

Bailey, Cyril, ed. *Titi Lucreti Cari De rerum natura.* 3 vols. With translation and commentary. Oxford: Clarendon Press, 1947.
Ernout, Alfred, and Robin, Léon. *Lucrèce: De rerum natura. Commentaire.* 3 vols. Paris: Belles Lettres, 1925–28.
Guissani, Carlo, ed. *T. Lucreti Cari De rerum natura libri sex.* 4 vols. Introductory essays, text, and commentary. Turin: Ermanno Loescher, 1896–98.
Munro, H. A. J., ed. *T. Lucreti Cari De rerum natura libri sex.* 3 vols. Text, commentary, and translation. 4th rev. ed. Cambridge: D. Bell, 1886.

*Philodemus*

De Lacy, Phillip H., and Estelle A. De Lacy, eds. and trans. *Philodemus: On Methods of Inference.* American Philological Association Monograph no. 10. Philadelphia, 1941. 2d rev. ed. Naples: Bibliopolis, 1978.
Diels, Hermann, ed. *Philodemus über die Götter. Erstes Buch,* text and commentary (1915, no. 7); and *Philodemus über die Götter. Drittes Buch,* text (1916 no. 4) and commentary (1916, no. 6). Abhandlungen der Königlich Preussischen Akademie de Wissenschaften, Philosophisch-historische Klasse. Berlin: Akademie-Verlag.
Gomperz, Theodor, ed. *Philodem: Über Frömmigkeit.* Herkulanische Studien 2. Leipzig: Teubner, 1866.
————. *Philodem: Über Induktionsschlüsse.* Herkulanische Studien 1. Leipzig: Teubner, 1865.
Hausrath, Augustus, ed. "Philodemi Περὶ ποιημάτων libri secundi quae

videntur fragmenta." *Jahrbücher für classische Philologie,* suppl. 17 (1890):211–76.

Jensen, Christianus, ed. *Philodemi Περὶ οἰκονομίας qui dicitur libellus.* Leipzig: Teubner, 1906.

———. *Philodemus: Über die Gedichte. Fünftes Buch.* Berlin: Weidmann, 1923.

Kemke, Ioannes, ed. *Philodemi De musica quae exstant.* Leipzig: Teubner, 1884.

Oliveri, Alexander, ed. *Philodemi Περὶ παρρησίας libellus.* Leipzig: Teubner, 1914.

———. *Philodemi Περὶ τοῦ καθ᾿ Ὅμηρον ἀγαθοῦ βασιλέως libellus.* Leipzig: Teubner, 1909.

*The Rhetorica of Philodemus.* Translated by H. M. Hubbell. With commentary. *Transactions of the Connecticut Academy of Arts and Sciences* 23 (1920):243–382.

Sudhaus, Siegfried, ed. *Philodemus: Volumina rhetorica.* 2 vols. and suppl. Leipzig: Teubner, 1892–96.

Wilke, Carolus, ed. *Philodemi De ira liber.* Leipzig: Teubner, 1914.

*Plato*

Burnet, J., ed. *Platonis Opera.* 5 vols. Oxford: Clarendon Press, 1900–7.

Diels, H., and Schubart, W., eds. *Anonymer Kommentar zu Platons Theaetet (Papyrus 9782).* Berlin: Weidmann, 1905.

*Plutarch*

*Moralia.* Vol. 6, pt. 1, rev. ed., edited by C. Huber and H. Drexler; vol. 6, pt. 2, 2d ed., edited by M. Pohlenz and R. Westman. Leipzig: Teubner, 1959.

*Plutarch's Moralia.* Vol. 13, pt. 2 (1033a–1086b), translated by Harold Cherniss; vol. 14 translated by B. Einarson and P. H. De Lacy. Loeb Classical Library. London: Heinemann, 1976, 1967.

*Polystratos*

Indelli, Giovanni, ed. and trans. *Polistrato sul disprezzo irrazionale delle opinioni popolari.* Naples: Bibliopolis, 1978.

Wilke, Carolus, ed. *Polystrati Epicurei Περὶ ἀλόγου καταφρονήσεως libellus.* Leipzig: Teubner, 1905.

*Sextus Empiricus*

*Outlines of Pyrrhonism* (vol. 1); *Against the Logicians* (vol. 2); *Against the Physicists, Against the Ethicists* (vol. 3); *Against the Professors* (vol. 4). Translated by R. G. Bury. 4 vols. Loeb Classical Library. London: Heinemann, 1933–49.

*Sexti Empirici Opera.* Vols. 1–2 edited by H. Mutschmann; vol. 3 edited by J. Mau; vol. 4 (indices) edited by K. Janáček. Leipzig: Teubner, 1912, 1914, 1954, 1962.

*Simplicius*

*In Aristotelis Physicorum libros commentaria.* Edited by H. Diels. Vols. 9–10 of *Commentaria in Aristotelem Graeca.* Berlin: G. Reimer, 1882, 1895.

## MODERN SOURCES

This list includes full references to studies cited in an abbreviated form in the notes, as well as some additional references to works that are of general usefulness.

Alfieri, Vittorio Enzo. "Una nuova interpretazione di Protagora e di Democrito." *Giornale Critico della Filosofia Italiana* 17 (1936):66–78, 264–77.

———. *Atomos idea.* Florence: Le Monnier, 1953. Rev. ed. Galatina: Congedo, 1979.

———. "L'atomo come principio intelligibile." In *Epicurea in memoriam Hectoris Bignone,* 61–68. Genoa: Università di Genova, Facoltà di Lettere, Istituto di Filologia Classica, 1959. Reprinted in *Atomos idea,* rev. ed., 199–204.

Amerio, R. "L'epicureismo e gli dei." *Filosofia* 4 (1953):97–137.

Arrighetti, Graziano. "Sul problema dei tipi divini nell' epicureismo." *Parola del Passato* 10 (1955):404–15.

———. "Sul valore di ΕΠΙΛΟΓΙΖΟΜΑΙ ΕΠΙΛΟΓΙΣΜΟΣ ΕΠΙΛΟΓΙΣΙΣ nel sistema epicureo." *Parola del Passato* 7 (1952):119–44.

Asmis, Elizabeth. "Epicurus' Theory of Free Will." Ph.D. dissertation, Yale University, 1970.

———. Review of *Epicurus: An Introduction,* by J. M. Rist. *Philosophical Review* 83 (1974):413–16.

———. "Lucretius' Explanation of Moving Dream Figures at 4.768–76." *American Journal of Philology* 102 (1981):138–45.

———. "Rhetoric and Reason in Lucretius." *American Journal of Philology* 104 (1983):36–66.

Avotins, Ivars. "Alexander of Aphrodisias on Vision in the Atomists." *Classical Quarterly* 30 (1980):429–54.

Bailey, Cyril. *The Greek Atomists and Epicurus.* Oxford: Oxford University Press, 1928.

Baldes, Richard W. "Democritus on Visual Perception: Two Theories or One?" *Phronesis* 20 (1975):93–105.

Barigazzi, Adelmo. "Cinetica degli ΕΙΔΩΛΑ nel ΠΕΡΙ ΦΥΣΕΩΣ di Epicuro." *Parola del Passato* 13 (1958):249–76.

———. "Il concetto del tempo nella fisica atomistica." In *Epicurea in memoriam Hectoris Bignone*, 29–59. Genoa: Università di Genova, Facoltà di Lettere, Istituto di Filologia Classica, 1959.

Barnes, Jonathan. *The Presocratic Philosophers*. Vols. 1 and 2. London: Routledge & Kegan Paul, 1979.

———. "Proof Destroyed." In *Doubt and Dogmatism*, ed. Malcolm Schofield, Myles Burnyeat, and Jonathan Barnes, 161–81. Oxford: Clarendon Press, 1980.

Beare, John I. *Greek Theories of Elementary Cognition from Alcmaeon to Aristotle*. Oxford: Clarendon Press, 1906.

Berti, Enrico. "La critica di Aristotele alla teoria atomistica del vuoto." In *Democrito e l'atomismo antico*, ed. Francesco Romano, 135–59. Catania: Università di Catania, 1980.

Bicknell, Peter J. "The Seat of the Mind in Democritus." *Eranos* 66 (1968): 10–21.

Bignone, Ettore. *L'Aristotele perduto e la formazione filosofica di Epicuro*. 2 vols. Florence: Nuova Italia, 1936. 2d enl. ed. 1973.

Bourgey, Louis. "La doctrine épicurienne sur le rôle de la sensation dans la connaissance et la tradition grecque." In Association Guillaume Budé, *Actes du VIII^e Congrès, Paris, 5–10 avril 1968*, 252–58. Paris: Belles Lettres, 1969.

Brieger, Adolf. "Das atomistische System durch Correctur des Anaxagoreischen entstanden." *Hermes* 36 (1901):161–86.

———. "Demokrits angebliche Leugnung der Sinneswahrheit." *Hermes* 37 (1902):56–83.

Brunschwig, Jacques. "Proof Defined." In *Doubt and Dogmatism*, ed. Malcolm Schofield, Myles Burnyeat, and Jonathan Barnes, 125–60. Oxford: Clarendon Press, 1980.

Cherniss, Harold. *Aristotle's Criticism of Presocratic Philosophy*. Baltimore: Johns Hopkins Press, 1935.

Clay, Diskin. "An Epicurean Interpretation of Dreams." *American Journal of Philology* 101 (1980):342–65.

———. "Epicurus' Last Will and Testament." *Archiv für Geschichte der Philosophie* 55 (1973):252–80.

Cornford, Francis M. *Principium Sapientiae: The Origins of Greek Philosophical Thought*. Cambridge: Cambridge University Press, 1952.

Couissin, Pierre. "L'Origine et l'évolution de l'ΕΠΟΧΗ." *Revue des études grecques* 42 (1929):373–97.

Crönert, Wilhelm. *Kolotes und Menedemos*. Leipzig: Avenarius, 1906.

D'Andrea, A. "Nota ai §§ 61 e 62 dell' 'Epistola a Erodoto' di Epicuro." *Rivista di Filologia e di Istruzione Classica*, 64 (1936):126–33.

Deichgräber, Karl. *Die griechische Empirikerschule*. 1930. Reprint Berlin and Zurich: Weidmann, 1965.

De Lacy, Estelle A. "Meaning and Methodology in Hellenistic Philosophy." *Philosophical Review* 47 (1938):390–409.

De Lacy, Phillip. "The Epicurean Analysis of Language." *American Journal of Philology* 60 (1939):85–92.

――――. "Lucretius and the History of Epicureanism." *Transactions of the American Philological Association* 79 (1948):12–23.

――――. "οὐ μᾶλλον and the Antecedents of Ancient Scepticism." *Phronesis* 3 (1958):59–71.

――――. "Epicurean ΕΠΙΛΟΓΙΣΜΟΣ." *American Journal of Philology* 79 (1958):179–83.

――――. "Colotes' First Criticism of Democritus." In *Isonomia*, ed. Jürgen Mau and E. G. Schmidt, 67–77. Berlin: Akademie-Verlag, 1964.

De Ley, Herman. "Aristotle, *De gen. et corr.* A8, 324b35–325b11: A Leucippean Fragment?" *Mnemosyne*, 4th ser., 25 (1972):56–62.

Detel, Wolfgang. "Αἴσθησις und Λογισμός: Zwei Probleme der epikureischen Methodologie." *Archiv für Geschichte der Philosophie* 57 (1975): 21–35.

DeWitt, Norman Wentworth. "Epicurus, Περὶ Φαντασίας." *Transactions of the American Philological Association* 70 (1939):414–27.

――――. "The Gods of Epicurus and the Canon." *Transactions of the Royal Society of Canada* 36 (1942):33–49.

――――. "Epicurus: All Sensations Are True." *Transactions of the American Philological Association* 74 (1943):19–32.

――――. *Epicurus and His Philosophy*. Minneapolis: University of Minnesota Press, 1954.

Diano, Carlo. "Questioni epicuree." *Rendiconti, Reale Accademia Nazionale dei Lincei*. Classe di Scienze morali, storiche, e filologiche, 6th ser., 12 (1936):819–95.

――――. "La psicologia d'Epicuro e la teoria delle passioni." Pts. 1–4. *Giornale Critico della Filosofia Italiana* 20 (1939):105–45; 21 (1940): 151–65; 22 (1941):5–34; 23 (1942):5–49 and 121–50.

――――. "Questioni epicuree." *Giornale Critico della Filosofia Italiana* 28 (1949):205–24.

――――. *Scritti epicurei*. Florence: Olschki, 1974.

Diller, Hans. "ΟΨΙΣ ΑΔΗΛΩΝ ΤΑ ΦΑΙΝΟΜΕΝΑ." *Hermes* 67 (1932): 14–42.

Drabkin, Israel E. "Notes on Epicurean Kinetics." *Transactions of the American Philological Association* 69 (1938):364–74.

Frassinetti, Paolo. "Cicerone e gli dei di Epicuro." *Rivista di Filologia e di Istruzione Classica* 82 (1954):113–32.

Freymuth, Günther. *Zur Lehre von den Götterbildern in der epikureischen Philosophie*. Deutsche Akademie der Wissenschaften zu Berlin, Institut für hellenistisch-römische Philosophie, no. 2. Berlin: Akademie-Verlag, 1953.

――――. "Methodisches zur epikureischen Götterlehre." *Philologus* 99 (1955): 234–44.

Fritz, Kurt von. *Philosophie und Sprachlicher Ausdruck bei Demokritos, Plato und Aristoteles.* New York: G. E. Stechert, 1938. Reprint Darmstadt: Wissenschaftliche Buchgesellschaft, 1963.

———. Review of *Epicuri et Epicureorum scripta in Herculanensibus papyris servata,* ed. Achilles Vogliano, *Gnomon* 8 (1932):65–84.

Furley, David J. "Lucretius and the Stoics." *Bulletin of the Institute of Classical Studies, University of London* 13 (1966):13–33.

———. *Two Studies in the Greek Atomists.* Princeton: Princeton University Press, 1967.

———. "Aristotle and the Atomists on Infinity." In *Naturphilosophie bei Aristoteles und Theophrast,* ed. Ingemar Düring, 85–96. Heidelberg: Stiehm, 1969.

———. "Knowledge of Atoms and Void in Epicureanism." In *Essays in Ancient Greek Philosophy,* ed. J. P. Anton and G. L. Kustas, 607–19. Albany: State University of New York Press, 1971.

———. "Aristotle and the Atomists on Motion in a Void." In *Motion and Time, Space and Matter: Interrelations in the History of Philosophy and Science,* ed. Peter K. Machamer and Robert G. Turnbull, 83–100. Columbus: Ohio State University Press, 1976.

Gigante, Marcello. "Filodemo *De morte* IV 37–39. *Pap. Herc.* 1050." *Parola del Passato* 10 (1955):357–89.

Glidden, D. K. "The Epicurean Theory of Knowledge." Ph.D. dissertation, Princeton University, 1971.

———. "Epicurus on Self-Perception." *American Philosophical Quarterly* 16 (1979):297–306.

———. "*Sensus* and Sense Perception in the *De Rerum Natura.*" *California Studies in Classical Antiquity* 12 (1981):155–81.

Goedeckemeyer, Albert. *Epikurs Verhältnis zu Demokrit in der Naturphilosophie.* Strassburg: Karl J. Trübner, 1897.

Goldschmidt, Victor. "Remarques sur l'origine épicurienne de la prénotion." In *Les Stoïciens et leur logique,* 155–69. Actes du Colloque de Chantilly, September 18–22, 1976. Paris: J. Vrin, 1978.

Gomperz, Theodor. *Griechische Denker.* vol. 1. 4th rev. ed. Berlin and Leipzig: Walter de Gruyter, 1922. Vol. 1 of 1st ed. translated by Laurie Magnus as *Greek Thinkers.* New York: Scribner, 1901.

Graeser, Andreas. "Demokrit und die skeptische Formel." *Hermes* 98 (1970):300–317.

Guthrie, W. K. C. *A History of Greek Philosophy,* vol. 2: *The Presocratic Tradition from Parmenides to Democritus.* Cambridge: Cambridge University Press, 1965.

Heidel, William Arthur. *The Heroic Age of Science.* Baltimore: Carnegie Institution of Washington, 1933.

Heintz, Werner. *Studien zu Sextus Empiricus.* Schriften der Königsberger Gelehrten Gesellschaft, vol. 2. Halle (Saale): Max Niemeyer, 1932.

Henrichs, Albert. "Two Doxographical Notes: Democritus and Prodicus on Religion." *Harvard Studies in Classical Philology* 79 (1975): 93–123.

Hirzel, Rudolf. *Untersuchungen zu Cicero's philosophischen Schriften.* Vol. 1, *De natura deorum.* Leipzig: S. Hirzel, 1877.

Inwood, Brad. "The Origin of Epicurus' Concept of Void." *Classical Philology* 76 (1981):273–85.

Jensen, Ingeborg Hammer. "Demokrit und Platon." *Archiv für Geschichte der Philosophie* 23 (1910):92–105, 211–29.

Jürss, Fritz. "Epikur und das Problem des Begriffes (Prolepse)." *Philologus* 121 (1977):211–25.

―――. *Zum Erkenntisproblems bei den frühgriechischen Denkern.* Berlin: Akademie-Verlag, 1976.

Kerferd, G. B. "Epicurus' Doctrine of the Soul." *Phronesis* 16 (1971):80–96.

Kleve, Knut. "Wie kann man an das Nicht-Existierende denken?" *Symbolae Osloenses* 37 (1961):45–57.

―――. "Zur epikureischen Terminologie." *Symbolae Osloenses* 38 (1963):25–31.

―――. *Gnosis Theon.* Symbolae Osloenses Fasc. Suppl. 19. Oslo: Universitetsforlaget, 1963.

―――. "Empiricism and Theology in Epicureanism." *Symbolae Osloenses* 52 (1977):39–51.

―――. "The Philosophical Polemics in Lucretius: A Study in the History of Epicurean Criticism." In *Fondation Hardt Entretiens: Lucrèce,* 24: 39–71. Geneva, 1978.

―――. "On the Beauty of God. A Discussion between Epicureans, Stoics, and Sceptics." *Symbolae Osloenses* 53 (1978):69–83.

Kneale, William, and Kneale, Martha. *The Development of Logic.* Oxford: Clarendon Press, 1962.

Konstan, David. "Epicurus on 'Up' and 'Down' (*Letter to Herodotus* § 60)." *Phronesis* 17 (1972):269–78.

Kullmann, Wolfgang. "Zu den historischen Voraussetzungen der Beweismethoden des Lukrez." *Rheinisches Museum* 123 (1980):98–125.

Lachelier, J. "Les Dieux d'Epicure." *Revue de Philologie* n.s. 1 (1877):264–66.

Langerbeck, Hermann. ΔΟΞΙΣ ΕΠΙΡΥΣΜΙΗ: *Studien zu Demokrits Ethik und Erkenntnislehre.* Neue Philologische Untersuchungen no. 10. Berlin: Weidmann, 1935.

Lee, Edward N. "The Sense of an Object: Epicurus on Seeing and Hearing." In *Studies in Perception,* ed. Peter K. Machamer and Robert G. Turnbull, 27–59. Columbus: Ohio State University Press, 1978.

Lemke, Dietrich. *Die Theologie Epikurs: Versuch einer Rekonstruktion.* Munich: C. H. Beck, 1973 [= *Zetemata* 57].

Liebich, Werner. "Ein Philodem-Zeugnis bei Ambrosius." *Philologus* 98 (1954):116–31.

Lloyd, G. E. R. *Polarity and Analogy.* Cambridge: Cambridge University Press, 1971.

————. *Magic, Reason, and Experience.* Cambridge: Cambridge University Press, 1979.

Long, A. A. "*Aisthesis, Prolepsis,* and Linguistic Theory in Epicurus." *Bulletin of the Institute of Classical Studies, University of London* 18 (1971): 114–33.

————, ed. *Problems in Stoicism.* London: Athlone Press, 1971.

————. "Sextus Empiricus on the Criterion of Truth." *Bulletin of the Institute of Classical Studies, University of London* 25 (1978):35–49.

Luria, Salomo. "Die Infinitesimaltheorie der antiken Atomisten." *Quellen und Studien zur Geschichte der Mathematik, Astronomie, und Physik,* pt. B, vol. 2 (1933):106–85.

————. "Zwei Demokrit-Studien." In *Isonomia,* ed. Jürgen Mau and E. G. Schmidt, 37–54. Berlin: Akademie-Verlag, 1964.

Manuwald, Anke. *Die Prolepsislehre Epikurs.* Bonn: R. Habelt, 1972.

Mates, Benson. *Stoic Logic.* Berkeley: University of California Press, 1953.

Mau, Jürgen. *Studien zur erkenntnistheoretischen Grundlage der Atomlehre im Altertum.* Wissenschaftliche Zeitschrift der Humboldt-Universität zu Berlin, vol. 2; Gesellschafts- und sprachwissenschaftliche Reihe, no. 3. Berlin, 1952–53.

————. "Raum und Bewegung: Zu Epikurs Brief an Herodot § 60." *Hermes* 82 (1954):13–24.

————. *Zum Problem des Infinitesimalen bei den antiken Atomisten.* Deutsche Akademie der Wissenschaften zu Berlin, Institut für hellenistisch-römische Philosophie, no. 4. Berlin: Akademie-Verlag, 1954.

————. "Über die Zuweisung zweier Epikur-Fragmente." *Philologus* 99 (1955):93–111.

Merbach, Fridericus. *De Epicuri Canonica.* Inaugural dissertation, Leipzig, 1909.

Merlan, Philip. "Zwei Fragen der epikureischen Theologie." *Hermes* 68 (1933):196–217.

————. *Studies in Epicurus and Aristotle.* Wiesbaden: O. Harrassowitz, 1960.

Mondolfo, R. *L'infinito nel pensiero dell' antichità classica.* Florence: Nuova Italia, 1956.

Montano, A. "Il metodo induttivo in Democrito?" In *Democrito e l'atomismo antico,* ed. Francesco Romano, 263–92. Catania: Università di Catania, 1980.

Moreschini, Claudio. "Due fonti sulla teologia epicurea." *Parola del Passato* 16 (1961):342–72.

Mugler, Charles. "Sur quelques particularités de l'atomisme ancien." *Revue de Philologie* 27 (1953):141–74.

————. "L'Isonomie des atomistes." *Revue de Philologie* 30 (1956):231–50.

————. "Les Théories de la vie et de la conscience chez Démocrite." *Revue de Philologie* 33 (1959):7–38.

————. "L'Invisibilité des atomes." *Revue des Etudes Grecques* 76 (1963): 397–403.

Natorp, Paul. *Forschungen zur Geschichte des Erkenntnissproblems im Alterthum.* Berlin: Wilhelm Hertz, 1884.

O'Brien, D. "Two Conceptions of Change and Identity." *Journal of Hellenic Studies* 97 (1977):64–74.

————. *Democritus: Weight and Size,* vol. 1 of *Theories of Weight in the Ancient World.* Philosophia Antiqua, vol. 27. Paris and Leiden: Brill, 1981.

Pesce, Domenico. *Saggio su Epicuro.* Rome and Bari: Laterza, 1974.

Pfligersdorffer, G. "Cicero über Epikurs Lehre vom Wesen der Götter (nat. deor. 1, 49)." *Wiener Studien* 70 (1957):235–53.

Philippson, Robert. *De Philodemi libro qui est* περὶ σημείων καὶ περὶ σημειώσεων *et Epicureorum doctrina logica.* Ph.D. dissertation, Berlin, 1881.

————. "Zur Wiederherstellung von Philodems sog. Schrift ΠΕΡΙ ΣΗΜΕΙΩΝ ΚΑΙ ΣΗΜΕΙΩΣΕΩΝ." *Rheinisches Museum* 64 (1909):1–38.

————. "Zu Ciceros erstem Buche *De finibus.*" *Rheinisches Museum* 66 (1911):231–36.

————. "Zur Epikureischen Götterlehre." *Hermes* 51 (1916): 568–608.

————. "Nachträgliches zur Epikureischen Götterlehre." *Hermes* 53 (1918):358–95.

————. "Neues über Epikur und seine Schule." Pts. 1 and 2. *Gesellschaft der Wissenschaften zu Göttingen, Nachrichten, Philologisch-Historische Klasse* 1929, 127–49; 1930, 1–32.

————. Review of *The Greek Atomists and Epicurus,* by Cyril Bailey. *Gnomon* 6 (1930):460–73.

————. "Zu Epikur." *Philologische Wochenschrift* 51 (1931):61– 64.

————. "Epikurs Buch 28 Περὶ φύσεως." *Philologische Wochenschrift* 52 (1932):1458–61.

————. "Die Götterlehre der Epikureer." *Rheinisches Museum* 83 (1934): 171–75.

————. "Die Quelle der Epikureischen Götterlehre in Ciceros erstem Buche *De natura deorum.*" *Symbolae Osloenses* 19 (1939):15–40.

————. "Des Akademikers Kritik der Epikureischen Theologie im ersten Buche der Tuskulanen [read "*De natura deorum*"] Ciceros." *Symbolae Osloenses* 20 (1940):21–44.

Puglia, Enzo. "Nuove letture nei PHerc. 1012 e 1786 (Demetrii Laconis opera incerta)." *Cronache Ercolanesi* 10 (1980):25–53.

Regenbogen, Otto. "Eine Forschungsmethode antiker Naturwissenschaft." *Quellen und Studien zur Geschichte der Mathematik, Astronomie, und Physik,* pt. B, vol. 1 (1930):131–82.

Reitzenstein, Erich. *Theophrast bei Epikur und Lucrez.* Heidelberg: Carl Winter, 1924.

Rist, J. M. *Epicurus: An Introduction.* Cambridge: Cambridge University Press, 1972.

Robin, Léon. "L'Atomisme ancien." *Revue de Synthèse* 6 (1933): 205–16.

Romano, Francesco. "Esperienza e ragione in Democrito." In *Democrito e l'atomismo antico,* ed. F. Romano, 207–23. Catania: Università di Catania, 1980.

Romeo, Costantina. "Demetrio Lacone sulla grandezza del sole (PHerc. 1013)." *Cronache Ercolanesi* 9 (1979):11–35.

Sandbach, F. H. "ΕΝΝΟΙΑ and ΠΡΟΛΗΨΙΣ in the Stoic Theory of Knowledge." *Classical Quarterly* 24 (1930):44–51. Reprinted with revisions in *Problems in Stoicism*, ed. A. A. Long, 22–37. London: Athlone Press, 1971.

Sassi, Maria Michela. *Le teorie della percezione in Democrito*. Florence, Nuova Italia, 1978.

Schmekel, A. *Die Philosophie der mittleren Stoa*. Berlin: Weidmann, 1892.

Schmid, Wolfgang. *Epikurs Kritik der Platonischen Elementenlehre*. Leipzig: O. Harrassowitz, 1936.

——. "Götter und Menschen in der Theologie Epikurs." *Rheinisches Museum* 94 (1951):97–156.

Schwenke, Paul. "Zu Cicero *De natura deorum*." *Jahrbücher für classische Philologie* 28 (1882):613–33.

Scott, Walter. "The Physical Constitution of the Epicurean Gods." *Journal of Philosophy* 12 (1883):212–47.

Sedley, David. "Epicurus, *On Nature* Book XXVIII." *Cronache Ercolanesi* 3 (1973):5–83.

——. "The Structure of Epicurus' *On Nature*." *Cronache Ercolanesi* 4 (1974):89–92.

——. "Epicurus and the Mathematicians of Cyzicus." *Cronache Ercolanesi* 6 (1976):23–54.

——. "Two Conceptions of Vacuum." *Phronesis* 27 (1982):175–93.

——. "On Signs." In *Science and Speculation*, ed. Jonathan Barnes, Jacques Brunschwig, Myles Burnyeat, and Malcolm Schofield, 239–72. Cambridge: Cambridge University Press, 1982.

Senn, G. "Über Herkunft und Stil der Beschreibungen von Experimenten im Corpus Hippocraticum." *Sudhoffs Archiv für Geschichte der Medizin* 22 (1929):217–89.

Solmsen, Friedrich. "Epicurus and Cosmological Heresies." *American Journal of Philology* 72 (1951):1–23.

——. "Epicurus on the Growth and Decline of the Cosmos." *American Journal of Philology* 74 (1953):34–51.

——. "αἴσθησις in Aristotelian and Epicurean Thought." *Mededelingen der Koninklijke Nederlandse Akademie van Wetenschappen, Afd. Letterkunde* 24, no. 8 (1961):241–62.

——. "Epicurus on Void, Matter, and Genesis." *Phronesis* 22 (1977): 263–81.

Staden, Heinrich von. "Experiment and Experience in Hellenistic Medicine." *Bulletin of the Institute of Classical Studies, University of London* 22 (1975):178–99.

Stocks, J. L. "Epicurean Induction." *Mind* 34 (1925):185–203.

*Les Stoïciens et leur logique*. Actes du Colloque de Chantilly, September 18–22, 1976. Paris: J. Vrin, 1978.

Stokes, Michael C. *One and Many in Presocratic Philosophy*. Cambridge: Harvard University Press, 1971.

Stough, Charlotte L. *Greek Skepticism*. Berkeley: University of California Press, 1969.

Stratton, George Malcolm. *Theophrastus and the Greek Physiological Psychology before Aristotle*. London: George Allen & Unwin, 1917; New York: Macmillan, 1917.

Striker, Gisela. Κριτήριον τῆς ἀληθείας. Nachrichten der Akademie der Wissenschaften in Göttingen, Philologisch-Historische Klasse, no. 2. Göttingen: Vandenhoeck & Ruprecht, 1974.

―――. "Epicurus on the Truth of Sense Impressions." *Archiv für Geschichte der Philosophie* 59 (1977):125–42.

Taylor, C. C. W. "Pleasure, Knowledge, and Sensation in Democritus." *Phronesis* 1967 (12):6–27.

―――. "'All Perceptions Are True.'" In *Doubt and Dogmatism*, ed. Malcolm Schofield, Myles Burnyeat, and Jonathan Barnes, 105–24. Oxford: Clarendon Press, 1980.

Tohte, Theodor. *Epikurs Kriterien der Wahrheit*. Clausthal: Pieper, 1874.

Usener, Hermannus. *Glossarium Epicureum*, ed. M. Gigante and W. Schmid. Rome: Ateneo & Bizzarri, 1977.

Vlastos, Gregory. Review of *Principium Sapientiae*, by F. M. Cornford. *Gnomon* 27 (1955):65–76.

―――."Zeno of Sidon as a Critic of Euclid." In *The Classical Tradition: Literary and Historical Studies in Honor of Harry Caplan*, ed. L. Wallach, 148–59. Ithaca: Cornell University Press, 1966.

Wasserstein, A. "Epicurean Science." *Hermes* 106 (1978):484–94.

Weiss, Helene. "Democritus' Theory of Cognition." *Classical Quarterly* 32 (1938):47–56.

West, David. "Lucretius' Methods of Argument." *Classical Quarterly* 69 (1975):94–116.

Westman, Rolf. *Plutarch gegen Kolotes*. Acta Filosophica Fennica 7. Helsinki, 1955.

Zeller, Eduard. *Die Philosophie der Griechen*. 3 vols. 5th ed. Leipzig: O. R. Reisland, 1892–1923.

# General Index

369

# Index of Passages Cited

375

# Index of Selected
# Greek Terms

384

*Library of Congress Cataloging in Publication Data*

ASMIS, ELIZABETH.
   Epicurus' scientific method.

   (Cornell studies in classical philology; v. 42)
   Bibliography: p.
   Includes index.
   1. Epicurus—Science.   2. Science—Methodology—History.
I. Title.   II. Series.
B573.A84   1984      183      83-45133
ISBN 0-8014-1465-2   (alk. paper)